Un/knowing Bodies

A selection of previous *Sociological Review* Monographs

*Available from John Wiley & Sons, Distribution Centre, 1 Oldlands Way, Bognor Regis, West Sussex, PO22 9SA, UK

Most earlier monographs are still available from: Caroline Baggaley, The Sociological Review, Keele University, Keele, Staffs ST5 5BG, UK; e-mail srb01@keele.ac.uk

The Sociological Review Monographs

Since 1958 *The Sociological Review* has established a tradition of publishing Monographs on issues of general sociological interest. The Monograph is an edited book length collection of research papers each of which is refereed, published and distributed in association with Blackwell Publishing. We are keen to receive innovative collections of work in sociology and related disciplines with a particular emphasis on exploring empirical materials and theoretical frameworks which are currently underdeveloped. If you wish to discuss ideas for a Monograph then please contact the Monographs Editor, Chris Shilling, at *The Sociological Review*, School of Social Policy, Sociology and Social Reseach, Cornwallis North East, Canterbury, Kent, CT2 7NF, UK. Email c.shilling@kent.ac.uk

Un/knowing Bodies

Edited by Joanna Elizabeth Latimer and Michael W. J. Schillmeier

Blackwell Publishing Ltd/The Sociological Review

BLACKWELL PUBLISHING
350 Main Street, Malden, MA 02148–5020, USA
9600 Garsington Road, Oxford OX4 2DQ, UK
550 Swanston Street, Carlton, Victoria 3053, Australia

First published 2009 by Blackwell Publishing Ltd

Library of Congress Cataloging-in-Publication Data

Un/knowing bodies / edited by Joanna Elizabeth Latimer and Michael W.J. Schillmeier.
    p.   cm. – (Sociological review monograph series)
    Includes bibliogrpahical references and index.
    ISBN 978-1-4051-9083-1
1. Human body.   I. Latimer, Joanna.   II. Schillmeier, Michael W.J.
    HM636.U55 2008
    306.4–dc22

                                                                              2009008820

A catalogue record for this title is available from the British Library

Set in 10/12 Times NR MT

by SNP Best-Set Typesetter Ltd., Hong Kong

Printed and bound in the United Kingdom

by Page Brothers, Norwich

For further information on Blackwell Publishing, visit our website:
http://www.blackwellpublishing.com

Content

Introduction: body, knowledge, worlds

Joanna Latimer

> The body is our general medium for having a world. Sometimes it is restricted to the actions necessary for the conservation of life, and accordingly it posits around us a biological world; at other times, elaborating upon these primary actions and moving from their literal to a figurative meaning, it manifests through them a core of new significance: this is true of motor habits [sic] such as dancing. Sometimes, finally, the meaning aimed at cannot be achieved by the body's natural means; it must then build itself an instrument, and it projects thereby around itself a cultural world. (Merleau-Ponty, 1974: 146)

The aim of this research monograph is to open up assumptions that pivot the lived body as 'knowing'. The shift in attention towards the lived body has been a welcome turn away from earlier perspectives within the social and medical sciences that treated the body mainly as an *object* of knowledge. It appears prudent, however, to remain alive to the pitfalls involved in placing the body centre-stage, particularly over a tendency to treat the body discursively as the *subject* of knowledge and understanding.

What is at stake in the chapters that follow is precisely how bodies are incorporated *as* knowing. Many of these also stress how bodies, at times, seem to become unknowing. In opening up this issue to question a first aim is to unsettle the current emphasis on treating bodies as 'subjects'. Csordas (1990), for instance, claims:

> The body is not an object to be studied in relation to culture, but is to be considered as the subject of culture, or in other words as the existential ground of culture. (p. 5)

Productive as Csordas's emphasis has proved, especially on the importance of founding culture existentially, there are surely limits as to how far this perspective should be taken.

All too easily, pictures of the knowing body exaggerate any involvement of bodily 'subjects' in the creation and reproduction of culture. Insofar as culture is defined as much through the diversity of technologies in use as by any sedimentation of its social practices, bodies come into play in different ways. In certain circumstances, for instance, bodies may be prone to attenuation and circumvention rather than engagement and involvement. Most obviously this is the case in the rigorous application of mathematical logics, which have their counterpart in the form of material automation as well as computation. Consequently the lived body is far from being the only medium of communication or action in a universe full of non-human intermediaries.

Variations in body formation thus create key differences in both the degree and kind of involvement to which bodies are made subject. The point here is not just to recognize asymmetries in power and influence. It is to open up to debate the very relations between body and world. Specifically, at the same time as noting how bodies are inscribed into their worlds by virtue of a variety of processes of discipline and accountability, it is necessary also to enquire more carefully into what *worlds* are elicited in the process. This is to say that, rather than take the social universe for granted, the interest is with the kind of limits and assumptions that would fix, albeit partially and temporarily, the nature of 'world'. Thus, there is a need to recognize that differently performed bodies perform different worlds and vice-versa.

In what follows I begin by saying more about why there is a need to step back from the centring of the body and re-question what is at stake, particularly in terms of the way issues of quality and scale affect the 'world-forming' reflexivity of body-world relations. I go on to outline four theoretical traditions that are important as a platform here for reading the chapters that follow: *embodiment*, in which the body is imagined largely as 'world-reflecting'; the notion of *group* and the concomitant idea of bodies being 'world-making' in their everyday interaction; *assemblages*, the re-conceptualizing of bodies in terms of complex forms of relationality, wherein the powers accorded to flesh (and subjects) to engage in 'world-building' are decentered and kept symmetrical to other material forms; and *relational extension*, in which the 'world-shifting' bodies undergo is re-theorized in terms of relations as these are elicited and extended from moment to moment. Finally, I give a brief introduction to each of the chapters that make up the body of the book.

Bringing body out

Much interest, as is discussed below, has focussed around the creation of a sociology of the body. Yet bodies are also now recognized as far more involved in 'world-forming' than was previously recognized (Turner, 2007). Consequently there is an unresolved tension between scholars who seek better stories of the body, narratives that grasp how the flesh and blood is brought under control and tamed, and those for whom the issue is more one of understanding the reflexivity of world and body relations.

Welcoming the emergence of a sociology of the body is not of course to imply any particular hegemony among the studies involved. Yes, there is today a better grasp of how bodies fit in with cultural and economic mores. Yes, there is now a great deal of research about how body practices are socially constructed along the fault lines of gender, class, age and ethnicity. So more and more is known about the body and how it is inscribed into the production and reproduction of social and institutional practices. Yet, for many, the body has become rather the site of contested political and ethical debate. Ideas and assumptions about the body, its limits and its proclivities, quickly divide commentators.

The time seems ripe to step back from this centring of the body and re-question what is at stake. Finding ways to explore the body as the existential ground of culture, however, is not as simple as it sounds:

> You think you are on to the body yet it becomes apparent that what you are describing is symbolic systems, the structures and effects of class, race, or gender, practices of sport, or organizational principles of sociality. Recently, some feminist critics of science have chastised those of us who 'do' theories of embodiment as merely studying 'culture' or 'semiotics'. It is a harsh and overly generalized critique. And truth be told, it's not that novel. Years ago, the reaction to discussions of body and discourse was that it missed 'the flesh and blood' of bodies. (Probyn, 2004: 215)

Making the body the focus of research does not solve the problem, because questions arise as to which body is fore-grounded. As Douglas (1996) and Synnott (1993), amongst others, have illuminated, there is always more than one body.

In addition to the large amount of research and thought that has gone into bringing the lived body 'back in' (Frank, 1990) as the medium of experience and subjectivity, there has been a focus on the relation between the body and the reproduction of culture. This work brings together understandings of the materiality of the body with ideas of being bodied as the grounds of social order (see Douglas, 1996; Foucault, 1977; Goffman, 1959, 1963, 1966; Mauss, 1973 [1936]). For example, research on body 'pedagogics' (Shilling, 2007) has focused on how subjects are disciplined and changed by training the body in, for example, ballet or martial arts (eg Delamont and Stephens, 2008). This work has helped to illuminate how knowledge is embodied as the effects of processes of inscription. These processes, and the embodied knowledge they instill, are shown to be central to acculturation and socialization, and to the production and reproduction of particular forms of social order. In this view then it seems that the body is always at the *disposal* (Munro, 2001) of social and cultural orders.

Going beyond the body as a site of inscription, there is a contemporary concern for exploring ways to examine the significance of the materiality of bodies for social science more radically. This is not just to note with Nettleton and Watson (1998: 12) how evident the body is in everyday life; it is to recognize that alongside the rise of social science writing on the body goes attention to bodily 'affect'.

Specifically, an emphasis on the knowing body already puts the material body squarely at the centre of culture and social action. But what needs further development are ways to go beyond thinking of the knowing body merely as a set of effects. For example, how can we incorporate understandings of bodily knowing as more than inscription? How can we pay attention to how the body seems at times to have life of its own: it seems to know how to breathe, process food, reproduce parts of itself and others?

Elaine Scarry's (1985) work, amongst others, offers one way to think about how the body has a life of its own, and that this propensity of the body becomes visible particularly as the basis of torture: torture turns the body into the enemy of the person being tortured. Of course, it is not only torture that does this. Illness and disability can make visible how bodies have lives of their own: arteries fur up, blood clots, bones disintegrate, tumors grow, viruses and bacteria colonize, genes mutate. At times, then, it seems that bodies (or their parts) can get it wrong. And bodies, to put it simply, despite our best efforts, seem to get out of line: they do not just hurt, scream, giggle, leak, cramp, faint, get numb, they also at times seem to conceal, rebel, falsify and distort. That is, bodies can seem to be or become *unknowing*.

In contrast, following Deleuze and Guattari, Probyn (1996) has illuminated how there are other ways that bodies get out of line, in ways that actually seem to imply how bodies can know better. Specifically, bodies can be implicated in forms of resistance because of how they transport along '*lines of flight*' (Deleuze and Guatarri, 2004):

> If I grew up with pony-club stories about perfect little girls on their well-behaved mounts, the actuality was rather different. And if my mother dreamed of the upper-class hunts of the South of England, in our context riding was a rough passion, one that was addictive for speed. The motion, the feeling of and desire for being at the very edge of control: a wild running together of horse and girl (Probyn, 1996: 39).

Through the specificities of her escapades with ponies, the figure of Probyn comes into view as a kind of relational extension that offers a break from belonging to the usual categories of horsey girls: she is female, sure, but once attached to the horse she is also a wild girl, addicted to a desire for a rough passion. Thus the *how* of affectual embodiment can constitute a line of flight from dominant social orderings, in this case particular gendered relations of power.

So how does recognizing, indeed even foregrounding the body as organic, animate, vital, processual, generating and degenerating, affect how we incorporate understandings of the body, and being (un)bodied, into social science? These are some of the issues and questions addressed by the contributions in the current volume. In the next section I situate various positions which have been taken up across social theory, social philosophy and anthropology, and emphasize how bodies are being re-membered, not just as objects or subjects to be known, but as themselves knowing. I then go on to briefly outline how the chapters in this collection contribute to these debates.

Body/world relations

The return to the body in sociology and anthropology is marked by a focus on materiality. For many this has proved to be a chance to centre inwards on the importance of our being flesh. This is not the only way to go, however, and, critically, others have focussed outwardly on *world* as constituted in relation to the materials that encompass the body:

> The world is ... the natural setting of, and field for, all my thoughts and all my explicit perceptions. Truth does not 'inhabit' only 'the inner man', or more accurately, there is no inner man, man is in the world, and only in the world does he know himself. (Merleau-Ponty, 1974)

This granted, a range of assumptions come into play about the social universe being constructed and, in this respect, different directions can be taken as to the nature of body-world relations. As mentioned earlier, four major perspectives can be distinguished, each of which draws out the afore-mentioned disposition for humankind to be 'world-forming'. These are now compared in turn under the four headings of embodiment, group, assemblages and relational extension.

1. Talk of embodiment and embodied practices tends towards inscribing bodies as 'world-reflecting'. Bodies are seen as moulded into shape through a combination of culture and social practices, offering little scope for changes in narrative, other than locally derived effects. Here the body is largely imagined as individuated and as the creature of habit, a perspective inherited from sociological emphases on routines and repetition. For example, reflecting writings of Enlightenment philosophers such as David Hume, Weber relegates day-to-day conduct in society to that of the sub-rational:

> For it is very often a matter of almost automatic reaction to habitual stimuli which guide behaviour in a course which has been repeatedly followed. The great bulk of all everyday action to which people have become habitually accustomed approaches this type (Weber, 1947/1922: 116).

This tendency to treat the body as a kind of Platonic wax implies that when change does come about, bodies and their performances tend to mirror structural change. For example, emerging in the form of late 20th century capitalism, consumer choice arguably displaces ascetic denial as the supplement to hard work in the sphere of production (Featherstone, 1982).

This emphasis on 'docility' persists in Foucault's work, which has been instrumental in focusing attention on technologies of power whereby the flesh is pressed into service, first through techniques of dressage and then through the disciplining effects of discourse. In surfacing a distinct set of rationalities to the state control of bodies, Foucault (1979) thus gives the body a more political charge than is evident, for instance, in Marcel Mauss' close attention to body pedagogics and body techniques (cf Crossley, 2007).

Consequently, as a set of unquestioned assumptions and as an instrument of training, discipline and control, the body has become a focal point for studies in ethnicity, gender, sexuality, age and disability. However, while for the most part it is assumed that the disciplined body has to articulate with the world as it finds it, more radical approaches have attended to resistances in the body engendered by technologies of power (see for example, Davies, 1997; Grosz, 1995; Harding, 1993; Haraway, 1991; Ong, 1987). As stated above with reference to Probyn's work, affectual bodies can also trouble dominant forms of social order.

Recent studies explore topics that have brought the body into areas where its spatial presence is insistently obvious. In terms of body image (eg Weiss, 1999; Weiss and Haber, 1999), and what can be 'written on the body', for instance, many sociologists appear dazzled by the 'spectacular', especially with body modification practices such as piercing and tattoos (Lloyd, 2004) or enhancement (eg Moglen and Chen, 2006). Others have taken a very different tack. Shilling (2003) especially has theorized the body more as a 'project', a perspective that has potential to draw together a range of diverse views not discussed so far that include therapy and body ecology as well as control and technology. As he wisely notes in his discussion on what he calls the 'mindful body' (see also Scheper-Hughes and Lock, 1987), the sheer quantity and range of work that has gathered to challenge the assumption that 'society operates on us intellectually and consensually rather than directly upon our bodies' (O'Neill, 1985: 48) has the effect of making the body recede and slide from view, 'while undergoing a series of metamorphoses that render it unrecognizable from one incarnation to the next' (Shilling, 2007: 10).

2. Attention shifted to the notion of group during the middle part of the last century, with subsequent work on inter-active bodies as 'world-making' owing much to the work of Goffman (1959, 1963, 1966) and Garfinkel (1967). This full-blooded reinsertion of the 'everyday' into sociology brought into prominence the extent to which bodies are *read* interactively, rather than merely sedimented together by habit. Whereas Goffman (1955, 1963, 1959) emphasizes such readings in terms of 'face' and 'facework', Garfinkel assumes 'knowledge-ability' is distributed among members. Critically, in terms of understanding the group, the consumption and reproduction of this knowledgeability involves sanctioning each other continuously in ways that create what Garfinkel sees as a 'moral universe'. Members thus actively concern themselves with acting as a body but, insofar as they deploy methods in the form of 'going along with things to see where they lead' (Garfinkel, 1967), they need never be so habituated as to become 'judgemental dopes'.

It is difficult to place here another direction, of which the most relevant for sociology may be Bourdieu. Bourdieu (1984) develops Mauss' (1973 [1936]) theory of body technique, 'habitus' and 'hexis':

> The habits of the body 'do not just vary with individuals and their imitations, they vary especially between societies, educations, proprieties and fashions, prestiges. In them we should see the techniques and work of collective and individual practical reason rather than . . . merely the soul and its repetitive facilities'. (Mauss, 2005: 75)

Bourdieu extends Mauss' work to make visible how the ways that bodies are skilled socially and culturally have to be taken into account in any understanding of social and cultural ordering:

Nor do these [bodily] practices become habitual simply as a result of explicit rules – rather dispositions can be collectively orchestrated – a group's structuring principles are made body by the hidden persuasion of a hidden pedagogy which can instill a whole cosmology, through injunctions as insignificant as 'sit up straight' or 'don't hold your knife in your left hand' . . . arms and legs are full of numb imperatives (Bourdieu, 1984, 69).

In this way Bourdieu's emphasis overlaps with research in sociology that takes body pedagogics as the grounds of social ordering as its focus (eg Aalten, 1997; Foster, 1996; Shilling, 2007). Inasmuch as bodies are inscribed to produce and reproduce the social forms that underpin particular structural arrangements, such as class and gender relations, or cultural preoccupations, such as particular notions of femininity or responsibility, Bourdieu paints a picture of habitus as world-reflecting rather than world-forming. And, critically, there is a whole world to reflect.

By contrast, and in their different ways, Goffman and Garfinkel each highlight considerable elasticity in the forming of worlds, precisely by focussing on the kinds of action Weber sought to by-pass. For example in his focus on affect, such as shame in the form of embarrassment, Goffman (1959; cf Kuzmics, 1991) attends to aspects of conduct Weber sought to dismiss as 'purely affectual'. It is especially in his studies on interaction rituals that Goffman re-incorporates the everyday presentation of emotion into the kind of 'meaningful social action' Weber would recognize (cf Craib, 1997: 46). In re-interpreting everyday social practices as ways members have of accounting to each other, Garfinkel also surely enlarges Weber's conception of action as being orientated to 'ultimate values' (cf Craib, 1997: 47)? Insofar as different groups engage in exhibiting commonalities in their identity, for instance by making 'occasions' for coming together, it becomes rational for members to make actions 'visible and accountable' (Garfinkel, 1967: 1) to each other (see also Kessler and McKenna, 1978).

3. A different line of thinking decentres locations of flesh by reconceptualizing bodies in terms of 'assemblages' (Deleuze and Guattari, 1983; Cooper, 1998). Indeed, Latour (1987) and Callon (1986) tend to dispense with embodied persons and, instead, distribute agency and knowledge across a *heterogeneity* of materials. The complex forms of relationality that come into being are often called actor-networks. Here the powers accorded to flesh to engage in 'world-building' are kept symmetrical to other material forms. In Latour's view, 'one is not obliged to define an essence, a substance (what the body is by nature), but rather *an interface that becomes more and more describable when it learns to be affected by many more elements'* (Latour, 2001: 2, original emphasis).

What makes this view important sociologically is that the emphasis on 'world-building' develops the conflict tradition on power (cf Giddens, 1968), rather than relying on consensual models. It is possible, however, to take this line of enquiry further so that, rather than see the universe in terms of schisms between contesting communities over resources and territory, conflict runs deep into the very nature of worlds that are being built. So deep indeed, that interpretation and perspective lie at the heart of any division. That there is always the potential for novelty and any stability in interpretation (which is one way of understanding what is meant by the term translation) implies power.

In terms of knowledge, therefore, actor-network theorists do not grant themselves any more wisdom or far-sightedness than anybody else. Rather, they promote a 'myopic' view (see Latour, 2005; Schillmeier, 2007b, 2008a & b). Insofar as knowledge is distributed, information asymmetries exist; but any relative advantage here is contingent and most likely ephemeral. Yet it would be a mistake to think of the human body as lacking influence altogether, even when it remains in the corporeal background. In terms that reflect Heidegger's notion of thrownness, Latour (2001: 2) suggests 'The body is thus . . . the dynamic trajectory by which we learn to register and become sensitive to what the world is made of'.

4. Within the ideas of relational extension, bodies can be re-theorized in terms of *relations* as these are elicited from moment to moment (Latimer, 2001, 2004, 2007; Latimer and Munro, 2006; Munro, 1996a; Strathern, 1991; 2007). Here in a process of 'world-shifting', affiliations and attachments are secured and re-secured through an exchange of prosthetic materials. Such 'switches' in the world thus require a constant 're-attachment' in terms of affiliations and belongings. In this double movement, bodies can be understood to be always shifting first from one form of extension, and therefore relationality, to another, and second, with this, from one set of 'belongings' to another. Yet these bodies are knowing only in a strictly limited sense; what counts as 'knowledge' changes with each switch of world and is as much the result of arrival, rather than something that can be known beforehand. As much as materials are in play within these processes of attachment and detachment, it is the 'worlds' of participants that are most liable to alter and shift in line with relations (Strathern, 2007).

Munro (1996a) in particular has stressed the kind of locution in which there is no single self, identity or core from which social persons emerge or to which they return. Avoiding the temptation to reify relations into a series of 'wholes', in which self moves along a series of relations, from enjoying one set of relations to another, Munro (1999) sees the performed body as always, if temporarily, *emplaced*; its attachment and detachment to the myriad of locally available technologies helping give different parts of body presence or absence. As Munro (1996a: 264) explains about relations: 'We are always in extension. *Indeed, extension is all that we are ever "in"* '. There is here another aspect to ideas of extension and figuration that bears upon Strathern's (1991) partial connections and Munro's refusal to reduce 'relations' to the Western concepts of a division between body and 'things'. Attachments, including prosthetics like that of a wooden leg, or an account such as that of 'I have come to help', always *take place*, if they 'take place' at all, in an exchange of perspectives (Strathern, 1991, 1992; see also Latimer, 2007; Munro, 2005; Schillmeier, 2007).

Although there is overlap here with the assemblages of actor-network theory, there is less insistence on symmetry between different forms of materials. Within the strictures of 'partial connections' (Strathern, 1991) what is being resisted is not the fact of embodiment so much as the more holistic locations for body, such as self, kin, group or society (see also Strathern, 2007). Helpful as such perspectives are in countering over-simplistic 'centrings' of the body, it seems too precipitate to dispose of more common notions of flesh and blood altogether. Where there is overlap, then, with Latour is not so much over his substitution of 'interfaces' for flesh and blood, as with his recognition that 'to have a body is to learn to be affected'.

The related issues that arise here over presence and absence are not to be underestimated. As several of the chapters that follow indicate, the materiality of bodies may be better understood in terms of their intermittency than their more permanent features. Indeed, if the body is to be understood today as 'project', in line with Shilling, then surely part of that wider project is also to be better able to note its appearances and absences? As Goffman (1959, 1963, 1966) has so deftly depicted, persons learn, wittingly or unwittingly, to make bodily affect 'visible' in their presentation of self in everyday life. Hopefully this direction will help us depart from accounts that both dwell on the spatiality of the body and ignore its inconvenient and surprising irruptions.

The book

Un/Knowing Bodies[1] is a collection of papers developed from a research meeting held in Cardiff in 2007. The colloquium was aimed at debate around ways of re-theorizing bodies as known, knowing and unknowing. In particular, the organizers wanted to move beyond pursuing an agenda that centralized the body as a set of effects: the body as an effect of, for example, modes of governing or individual identity-work. Whilst wanting to preserve existential perspectives, we also wanted to move beyond Merleau-Ponty's emphasis on the body merely as a *medium* for having a world. That is we wanted to recognize the body as more than just a means or a conduit. We also wanted to help illuminate how there is more than one world just as there is more than one body. It is not that any of these aspects of being bodied are unimportant: we recognized that as at the same time as the body appears to be both a mental and physical effect, how it is either of these things is *entangled* in all kinds of ways. This said, we wanted to move understanding beyond the body as either a discursive effect or as a means to consciousness. Instead we hope to have foregrounded the substantive, living body as conditioned possibilities for both *being* in the world and for *shifting* worlds.

We thus invited exploration of ways for taking the phenomenology of the material, substantive, living body seriously for social science. While questioning the contemporary emphasis on discourse, and theories that leave the body as a mere effect, we did not wish, nonetheless, to return to an ontology that positions the body only as physical presence, as mere flesh and blood. And, like others before us, we wanted contributors also to explore the practical consequences of foregrounding bodies as knowing and known. By practices we mean ways of doing social science, including the practical work of social theory and of researching the social, as well as ways of doing medicine and care.

A major outcome of the conference, as I recapitulate here, has been for us to distinguish more carefully between four different perspectives on the 'world-forming' theme of bodies. First, embodiment. Much work here focuses on the body as 'world-reflecting'. Issues centre on the creation and reproduction of the *knowing body*. Specifically, questions arise as to how our fleshy substance articulates with narrative, especially those of patriarchy, capitalism, governmentality and democratic choice. Second, group. Here the concern figures around the *interaction* necessary to be involved in 'world-making'. Knowledgeability is distributed among members and is seen as consumed and reproduced in ways that involves members continuously sanctioning each other. Third, assemblages. This is where the powers accorded to flesh to engage in 'world-building' are kept symmetrical to other material forms. For instance in discussions about actor-networks, agency and knowledge are distributed across a heterogeneity of materials as these juxtapose and combine into human and non-human forms also known as *agencements*. Fourth, relational extension, whereby affiliations and attachments are secured and re-secured in a process of 'world-shifting'. Here *relations* are elicited and extended from moment to moment through an exchange of prosthetic materials, rather than known beforehand.

As editors we have drawn on the four directions described above to organize the book. In so doing we want to stress that these are analytical distinctions only, and many of the chapters do not fit neatly into any one category. For example, certain themes are explored across many of the chapters, including affect, chiasms, relationality, as well as presence/absence. In addition, some chapters take group and belonging as fundamental to social life while others make the way they are reworking ideas about the body more explicit in relation to group and belonging. But, importantly, each helps to illuminate different body-world relations.

Opening up the body

The first chapter of this section takes on board the dominant discourses in medicine that privilege scientific constructions of sick or diseased bodies as simply unknowing, whether biologically or socially. Reexamining the work of Karl Jaspers and Georges Canguilhem, Monica Greco outlines the implications of a 'vitalist' approach to bodily events:

> . . . vitalism should be understood as an imperative and as an ethical system, rather than a method or theory. Vitalists affirm the originality of life, and this is an attitude before being a doctrine: if the concepts of classical science cannot quite account for vital phenomena – be these epigenesis, the placebo effect, or the flight of a bird – vitalists refuse to have the latter explained away . . . When faced with the uncomfortable

choice of whether to place their trust in knowledge or in life, whether to deny one or the other, vitalists side with life. (this volume, page 27).

As a form of thought that explicitly addresses the relations between knowledge and life, vitalism problematizes the assumption that the negative cultural value expressed in disease/illness should be regarded as a form of 'unknowing' (and/or of 'knowing wrongly').

Greco suggests how this seemingly abstract and counter-intuitive proposition is entirely compatible with a number of recent developments in medical discourse and practice, notably in the field of narrative or humanist medicine. She suggests that what her analysis enables us to see more clearly is that a paradigm shift to a more humanist medicine remains meaningless except in the context of a wider set of questions, questions that challenge dominant relations between culture, the body, knowledge and science. What is at stake, she suggests, is the question of how medicine might best serve the perfectibility of human beings, or what Whitehead calls the 'art of life', where life is more than just an objectively assessed function of the body.

The next chapter opens up forms of perspective that create and reproduce knowing and unknowing bodies. In exploring the self-portraits of the Mexican-born painter Frida Kahlo, Joanna Latimer offers a different vision of personhood to that which links the body to the figure of the individual. This is important, she argues, because the figure of the individual underpins dominant forms of Euro-American social organization and social theory. Latimer shows how Kahlo's methods of assemblage and juxtaposition shape her representations of 'Frida' in different and complex ways, unsettling the relations between bodies, their form and functions, and ideas about origins, persons and selves. In thinking through the complexities of her 'thrownness' (Heidegger, 1962), Kahlo's painting not only re-works the multiplicity of ideas and diverse sets of consciousness she inherited, but brings into question the very idea of representation.

For Latimer, personhood is irreducible and relational. Drawing on the work of the social anthropologist Marilyn Strathern, Latimer challenges contemporary emphases on multiplicity and hybridity. Such pluralist ideas, she suggests, merely complicate the figure of the individual rather than get beyond the dominance of humanism. So, against settling for the dominant figure of the complex-if-hybrid individual, Latimer emphasizes how Kahlo keeps apart the heterogeneous parts that make up each version of 'Frida'. Showing how Kahlo's work offers us alternative ways of knowing bodies, Latimer brings to life a vision of dividuality rather than individuality.

The last chapter in this section critiques objectivist or behavioural approaches. Hugo Letiche argues for a radically different approach to care work that incorporates a notion that 'in care, body (materiality) and self (consciousness) *fold in double envelopment*, crossing into one another' (this volume, page 64). Drawing on Merleau-Ponty's later work, he interrogates the theory of the body that assumes that researcher and researched are part of the same flesh of the world and can be understood in radical conjunction and not in duality. Through presentation of two different analyses of a video-taped interview with Hendriënne, Letiche performs the difference between a phenomenological approach to embodiment characteristic of life-world research and an approach to embodiment that, he proposes, is more appropriate to care work. Hendriënne is a woman who is 'known' from a medical perspective to have some form of brain damage following a stroke. The question arises as to whether the person being interacted with is really Hendriënne; or whether it is Hendriënne's now 'unknowing' body that puts Hendriënne out of line.

A first analysis by Letiche focuses on how Hendriënne cannot 'do the social'. Hendriënne evidently has partially lost her ability to participate in the standard, socially necessary, constitutive dialogue. Her brain damage impairs her ability to successfully 'do' speaking and listening, looking and defining, declaring and doing. In this view of embodiment, Hendriënne's body impedes her successful ability to do and be social. She comes to be defined as a lack – 'the lack of successful social construction and languaged intentionality'. In his second analysis, instead of accounting for (and disposing) of Hendriënne as someone whose body means they can no longer get into line, Letiche takes seriously how Hendriënne is being in the world and how he is (not) touched by Hendriënne:

> . . . she is constantly creating relationships by denying them. She relates to her surroundings via the denial of belonging. She is present to others as a refusal to join, merge, identify, or fit in. She touches us who watch the CD in her stubbornness, inflexible attitude and denial of some deeper hurt. . . . She *is* visible and invisible. (this volume, page 75)

Letiche thus explores a way to understand Hendriënne as an 'alternative folding into relationships' and argues for the critical importance for care work in taking account of how persons such as Hendriënne are being in the world. The question that is being pressed to the limit is that of knowing just who Hendriënne is and when she occupies a different world.

Moving worlds

In raising the topic of 'the body in time' Rolland Munro and Olga Belova argue against dispensing with notions of narrative altogether. Noting a relative *absence* of body within everyday life, they trace the experience of durée and duration to the matter of the body getting 'in line' with one narrative or another. Contrastingly, they pick up on those moments in which bodies 're-appear' as moments in which narrative fails. Bringing together an examination of the phenomenology of Merleau-Ponty and Heidegger with attention to the grounded work of members in everyday life, Munro and Belova review theories of embodiment that over-emphasize the body as presence and stress, as more likely, its more usual absence from the durée of everyday life. Their question then is more concerned with how – and at what moments – the body comes into play.

Unlike the body implied by theorists such as Bourdieu, the *body in time* is not just inscribed to know how and when to go long and get along. While recognizing that social actors are almost never out of narrative, Munro and Belova argue instead that there is always more than one narrative or 'world' to be in. Indeed, they suggest that the onus in contemporary life is precisely on individuals 'knowing' when to switch from one world to another. And it is here, in this *unknowing*, that body can become intermittently present. This is because the body is more or less busy trying to get 'in line' with narrative. So that when someone becomes 'out of place', even momentarily, the body registers its being out of line. This is to suggest that bodies, typically if tentatively, dispose of themselves by 'getting in line' with one story or another. Only by finding another narrative with which to construct and reproduce its 'world' can the body thus become absent again.

A further contribution of the paper is to identify the possibility that 'affect', the sense of being turned over rather than just turned around, might seldom be exhibited as such. As Munro and Belova illustrate, body becomes present, if momentarily, as a register of 'affect'. In depicting how body is 'turned over' prior to shifting its readings of the world, they go on to point out the likelihood of narratives being recovered almost instantaneously. So that, in turn, affect is 'disposed' of by a continual, if imperceptible, switching of identities and accounts. Imperceptible switches in 'world', whereby bodies and narratives keep themselves aligned and so try to continue to run together 'in time'. Consequently, the moments in which bodies are 'thrown' back into perception as *unknowing* are likely to be few and far between.

In examining the complexities and difficulties of working with experiences of violence amongst Bahá'í migrants from Iran, Megan Warin and Simone Dennis turn towards relationships of knowing between the anthropologist and their participants. Rather than elicit 'refugee narratives', the authors argue that stories of suffering and trauma are tightly bound up in 'bodies of knowledge', in both the performance of embodied memories of persecution, and the intimate knowledge that Islamic authorities collected about these women and their families. Warin and Dennis pose a series of questions that problematize working with violence. They argue that ethnographic techniques of inquiry (such as recording family relationships, tracing movements and enquiring about practices of faith) can actually reproduce past experiences of intense surveillance and threat. Others working in this field resort to psychological, psychiatric or indeed anthropological understandings of 'opening up', in which narratives become spectacular and sentimental stories of suffering. These therapeutic narratives rely on story-telling, thus obscuring the ways in which trauma is remembered, forgotten and re-remembered in everyday life.

Following Kalpana Ram, Warin and Dennis argue that to carry history in one's body does not necessarily mean that one has intellectual access to this kind of social history (Ram, 2005: 127). Bodily knowledge is not discursively constructed or represented, but is actively engaged with through tacit knowledge, or what Casey (2000 [1987]) refers to as habitual bodily memory. For these women (who had learnt to mute emotion), Warin and Dennis are interested in their body's capacity to conceal, reveal and restrict meaning, and the constant working and reworking of bodily meaning through the aesthetics of everyday practice. This is a specific phenomenological 'labour of investigation' that restores a sense of the past, not as history, but as vitally present in the bodies of actors in the present (Ram, 2000). The intertwined theoretical and method-ological approach taken in this chapter examines the ways in which traumatic memories are enfolded and transformed into mundane and creative practices of ordinary life, thus diverting from understandings of memory and embodiment that rest on social constructivism.

Drawing upon an ethnography of intensive care medicine, Paul White traces how the body is (un)concealed through attachment to the heterogeneous cul-tural materials that surround the anaesthetised and non-anaesthetised patient. While these attachments enable a reading of the critically ill body, including of the patient as person, by intensive care staff, White shows how the tacit under-standings and processes of mundane social life, such as interacting or breathing, are inverted: that is, interaction is concealed through anaesthesia whilst breath-ing is made visible through technological displays.

White describes how bodies are made legible in relation to organizational and medical technologies including being inscribed into notes and charts, which in turn is reproduced as a means through which the body is read. Drawing on Strathern and Munro, White's line of inquiry takes as its starting point that culture is bodied forth through relations of extension to cultural materials. As a consequence, the means through which the critically ill perform the social, and which are read by staff to emplace them, is in relation to the incorporation of cultural materials. White argues that the means through which bodies can be understood in relation to the availability of cultural materials within intensive care, acts as a trope for how social theory itself acts as a cultural material through which the body can be understood as an epistemological gestalt. White's aim here is to make visible some of the tacit assumptions concerning how the body can be read in relation to an array of cultural materials and how the fabric of relations that is extended to constitute perceptions of the body. In particular, White emphasizes the power such cultural materials have in demanding atten-tion to perceive and act upon both the body and the other in social life. Bodying forth particular cultural materials, from a plethora that are available, partially reproduces people's relations to the world and the ways social actors conduct themselves within it.

Bodies and technology

In his chapter, Michael Schillmeier explores his experience of 'being touched' by Mrs. M in an ethnographic film. Mrs. M is a woman who is 'known' medi-cally as having dementia, and who is in a residential care home, she is thus being constituted as a 'body-at-risk', to use a phrase of Lopez and Domenech (this volume). The chapter offers a poignant reflection upon the fading, the mixing up and the loss of remembrances and how people experience living in a long-term residential care facility.

Drawing together ideas from actor-network theory and Martin Heidegger, Schillmeier explores how dementia illustrates so succinctly the problem of bodies being indecisively known and knowing, or unknown and unknowing. Such a move allows Schillmeier to link central 'non-materialist' concepts like 'Angst' or 'conscience' with an actor-network approach. Along Heidegger's work Schillmeier relates concepts of non-knowledge like feelings, moods, affections – *Befindlichkeiten* [attunements] – with an analysis of knowledge production, its disruptions and alterations of common modes of ordering – as in the case of dementia. He shows how, with pre- or senile dementia, the question of what is known and not-known remains within the twilight of not-knowing what is known and not-known by the people involved. He suggests that dementia precisely performs what it is to be knowing and not-knowing, indeed that it sews knowing and not-knowing into the uncanniness of what is usually meant when we (are always being made to) divide between knowing and unknowing as itself a cultural effect. In this way Schillmeier shows how the pragmatics of remembering and its failures bring to the fore the ethos of inclusive differences by which the sociality of humans cannot be thought of without the caring for the other, non-human and non-social alike. It follows from this, Schillmeier argues, that we cannot describe dementia merely as a biological or mental condition or as a pure social construction. Rather, the social itself becomes an event of dementia that mediates the physiological and the psychological, the human and the non-human, the social and the individual. These networks re-assemble the social orderings of our everyday life in rather uncertain and often undecidable ways that cannot be fully grasped by modernist, exclusivist perspectives.

Bernd Kraeftner and Judith Kroell explore their engagement in a neuro-rehabilitative care setting where quadriplegic persons who are physically dependent, medically vulnerable and cognitively impaired spend years of their lives. The people cared for in this setting are usually described as in a 'persistent vegetative state', that is as absent presences or present absences. This description rests on the premise that, because of severe brain damage and cognitive impairment, these people cannot interact in any of the usual ways. In this experimental unit, however, there are other ways of knowing these people as body-persons. The authors offer their account of events and of their involvement as members of the interdisciplinary group of scientists and artists. They show how new scientific and artistic methods for exploring the predicament and care of these body-persons can allow the displacement of issues, questions and positions, and the creation of renewed and surprising arrangements, co-operations and agreements between the actors involved. Specifically, Kraeftner and Kroell explore how they and the medical and nursing practitioners perform very different ways of thinking or knowing these body-persons – different both from each other and from mainstream renderings of these people. And it is the particularities of the tensions between how these different or multiple ways of knowing bodies cross and recross that the authors examine. What emerges are ways of doing and relating to body-persons, particularly in terms of how to recover them into presence, that offer alternative understandings of being. In part this means changing the very notion of what being present is being made to mean, that is, there are ways to interact with these body-persons that both affirms and enhances their presence as at the same time as it translates the ontology and materiality of those caring for them. In part it means paying attention to these body-persons, and exercising them and the people interacting with them, in new ways. These ways of interacting involve two clinical technologies or procedures: 'whole-body-washing' and the SMART-assessment-technique. These procedures are juxtaposed in what the authors refer to as an 'experiment' in the real world of multiple medical and nursing diagnostic and treatment practices. This experiment was originally initiated to improve the 'knowing' concerning these bodies/persons, as well as therapy to help recover them to greater presence. What the authors suggest, however, is a dynamics of unknowing that plays an important role when carers intend to become, together with their patients, talented bodies themselves.

Daniel Lopez and Miquel Domenech are also concerned with modes of ordering and technologies of care, but ones that depend upon the institution of autonomous yet docile body-persons. They focus on an ethnography of Telecare practices, a technology that has arisen from the progressive deinstitutionalization of care work for older people and the widespread introduction of community care. They show how Telecare practices supposedly make it possible to care at a distance by attending to different people at risk. Telecare organizes personal and institutional as well as formal and informal resources remotely. Lopez and Domenech show however that Telecare relies on the people being cared for constituting themselves as at risk and on them attaching themselves to the proper technologies in the proper way. The proper way is both to wear a pendant at all times, with which users can call emergency services in times of trouble, and to 'ring' in at particular times as a way of reporting that there is no trouble. Failure to 'ring in' means the emergency services will be automatically alerted. Of course users wear the pendant selectively! One user, for example, hangs her pendant from the crucifix above her bed, but wears it when she thinks of herself as at risk, such as when she climbs a ladder to do her decorating. Of course things turn out to be much more complex: on the one hand, the device relies on users being enacted as fragile, inconsistent and unreliable bodies – that always threaten to fail or to cause problems – and, on the other hand, as vigorous, potent and resistant selves, capable of autonomous living. The authors conclude that two forms of autonomy are expressed in the use/non-use of the telecare device. Specifically, the requirement of wearing and using the pendant can be thought of as a process in which the self-management of a body-at-risk opens up a new kind of 'safer' autonomy, one that necessarily asks for the cancellation of a life based on the practice of a vigorous body. The second conclusion concerns the feeling of being safe, which is deeply linked with autonomy: specifically that security is achieved through a systemic and constant supervision. In these ways Lopez and Domenech help to illuminate how using the pendant concerns the issue of adjustment between two processes of embodiment of autonomy, which turns on adjustment between two forms of being safe, two forms of living with and facing ordinary dangers.

Absences and presences

Brown et al challenge the inadequacy of discursive approaches, particularly for the absence of body and relationality, and situate their work as a return to experimentation but with a phenomenological twist. Specifically, by incorporating ideas of affect, group and embodiment, they extend the possibilities of experimentation. They begin by describing their collective research experiments devised to explore the potential of various methodologies for surfacing embodied experience, including memory work on dizziness and a collective visit to the luminarium, an art installation in Nottingham designed by *Architects of Air*. Their aim with these experiments was to:

> focus on the role of the body in the formation of a sense of self and identity because it works with descriptions of scenes or events that are rich in circumstantial detail. The method is designed to access how a situation was *experienced* rather than how it was explained or accounted for by its participants. Such a focus on 'being in' a situation (as opposed to 'thinking about' it) implicates both body and mind. It provides a way of studying what is sometimes referred to as *embodied subjectivity* (Willig, 2001: 133, emphasis in original) (This volume, page 203)

Brown et al go on to explore these experiments in terms of what they can be taken to mean and conclude that the 'process of engaging in the task itself was not incidental to its perceived success or failure. The way that group members physically share the space with and orient towards one another fed through into the memories and the subsequent process of memory work analysis.' (This volume, page 208) They then shift the significance of experiments for studying embodied subjectivity by way of William James and Dewey. Specifically they show how if embodied subjectivity is to be taken into account into social psychological research then it can be found in the interplay, or chiasm, between the setting up of an experiment, the specific material and interactional conditions of the experiment, and the elaboration and reworking of these conditions. Their chapter ends by suggesting that what they are seeking is not '"in" the body, any more than "self" is in the mind or the brain. It is in the way that embodiment acts as a connective, a way of making and breaking relations within action-complexes.' (Page 214, this volume)

In her chapter, Fiona O'Neill also challenges the centrality of discourses that locate the body as an object. She asks how might the body *know*? And why is it important to medicine to incorporate bodily knowing? Specifically, O'Neill works the chiasm between the materiality of the body and consciousness to reassert bodily knowing as critical to understanding states of health, illness, and well-being. Moving from psychoanalytic and phenomenological definitions of the uncanny, the chapter draws upon Wittgenstein to explore the significance of *ur-trust* (Urvertrauen) as bodily un/canniness for the un/knowing body. Examining her own experience of mastectomy as well as her research with patients in different clinical settings who have to incorporate prostheses such as deaf-aids as well as other medical technologies, O'Neill illustrates examples of bodily un/canniness; including proprioception, somatic memory and the immunological self. O'Neill shows how there is something distinctly uncanny about the canniness of bodily being that becomes especially apparent when bodies interact with and are supported by medical technologies. Normally, she suggests, bodily uncanny canniness is withdrawn from perception; in being a body people are usually unaware of having a body. Yet, she suggests, the body is uncanny in the way that it is almost 'supernatural' in its day to day functions, appearing to "know how" to respond to a host of random situations. She argues, the body's canniness of "knowing how", this knack, or sixth sense, is very much a skilled embodied knowing which problematises and extends rational understanding. While acknowledging that evidence based medicine and evidence based ethics have detracted from the significance of 'bodily knowing' for both the patient and practitioner, O'Neill ends suggesting that her work makes a case for acknowledging the validity and significance of the un/canny and *ur*-trust in 'bodily knowing' for both clinical and ethical practice in medicine.

Drawing on her extraordinary ethnography of nurses and severely injured men in a burns unit, Trudy Rudge discusses some of the dilemmas faced when thinking about bodies and health care practices. In particular Rudge shows how the ways in which people with burns are 'known' and cared for means that they risk becoming unknown in crucial ways. Specifically she presents an ironic, paradoxical effect: how nurses embodied practices that enact the disembodying of patients through reconstructing their skin, and its covering, as the object(ive) of care. Skin is detached from the person it covers to become a thing in its own right. Rudge investigates and makes explicit what is at stake when an ethics of care becomes disembodied. Specifically, she states, that 'if embodiment and emotional containment are objectified, then both the intellectual and affective capacities of caring are denied'. She ends by identifying an ethics of care that rescues embodiment through 'encouraging its intransigence, positioning nurses with patients in an in-between liminal location where mutual and singular responsibilities are acknowledged'.

The last chapter of the volume returns to the perennial puzzle of existence by analyzing the experience of embodied loss. Floris Tomasini explores different facets of ambivalent feeling and knowing a body through two very different experiences of loss. In doing so, he posits a connecting and unifying theme of 'existential absence' (the idea of presence in absence) in two quite separate case studies. The first case study is about phantom limb sensation in the rehabilitation experience of amputees in a hospital clinic. The second case study explores the experience of parents of dead children who perceived their children to have been harmed in the wake of the Alder Hey scandal in the later 1990's, where their dead children's organs and organ systems were stripped without their knowledge or proper consent.

In the first case study, Tomasini, inspired by Merleau-Ponty, depicts phantom limb as presence in absence. Being ontologically and epistemologically ambivalent, the phantom limb is a *felt* presence in a *seen* absence that is subjectively experienced as quasi real and uncanny. The fundamental ambivalence of this experience makes it something that can be seen as both harmful *and* beneficial in rehabilitation, depending on the psycho-emotional state of the amputee. In the second case study, Tomasini explores how presence in absence makes it possible to conceive of how to contradict the commonly held belief that it is nonsensical to be able to harm the dead. Inspired by Sartre and Riceour, Tomasini argues that parents' expectations around their dead loved ones were harmed at Alder Hey, since grieving the recently dead involves investing the dead with a residual (ambivalent) subjectivity, where the integrity of the dead body is still symbolically inscribed with parental relationships to it. Since dead bodies were violated post-mortem at Alder Hey, harm was done to the continuing bond that continues to exist between the living and their recently dead. However, the fundamental ambivalence of embodied harm depends on how survivors of dead loved ones are treated; post-mortem harm needn't be inevitable if, for example, parents' give their consent and donate their dead children's organs altruistically to preserve the integrity of others who need a transplant.

In conclusion, each chapter recognizes that bodies are elusive and allusive. They are hard to define. Additionally, what varies greatly are the conditions of possibility in which bodies are thought and narrated. Indeed in several of the chapters it is particularly the chiasm between consciousness and the materiality of the body that each author is interested in exploring. Thus the pages that follow are peopled by figures who are 'known' to have bodies that have been breached, by, for example, dementia, burns, persistent vegetative state, deafness, mastectomy, old age, amputation, death. Here the authors do not simply set out to tell stories about what it is to experience such breaches. Rather, as authors, they set out to explore and experiment with ways of thinking about how these conditions connect: how the body is thought on the one hand – what the body is made to mean, how it is known – and about the materiality of the body on the other, as being itself living, 'knowing' and implicated in world-forming. By troubling and unsettling dominant Euro-American ways of thinking the body, they offer perspectives that can help rethink the relation between the interaction of knowing bodies and the materiality of their body-worlds.

Note

1 The colloquium Knowing/Unknowing Bodies was held in the School of Social Sciences, Cardiff University, September 4–5th, 2007. It was jointly organized by Joanna Latimer, Rolland Munro and Michael Schillmeier. The organizers are grateful to the Foundation for the Sociology of Health Illness for their generous support.

References

Aalten, A., (1997), Performing the Body, Creating Culture, European Journal of Women's Studies; 4: 197–215.
Bourdieu, P., (1984), *The Logic of Practice*, Oxford: Blackwell.
Callon, M., (1986), Some elements for a sociology of translation: domestication of the scallops and the fishermen of St-Brieuc Bay, in J. Law (ed.), *Power, Action and Belief: a New Sociology of Knowledge?* Sociological Review Monograph, London: Routledge & Kegan Paul: 197–221.
Casey, E.S., (2000 [1987]), *Remembering A Phenomenological Study*, 2nd edition, Bloomington and Indianapolis: Indiana University Press.
Casey, C., (2000), Sociology sensing the body: revitalising a dissociative discourse. In J. Hassard, R. Holliday and H. Willmott (eds), *Body and Organization*, London: Sage: 52–70.
Cooper, R., (1998), Assemblage notes. In: R. Chia (ed.), *Organized Worlds: Explorations in Technology and Organization with Robert Cooper*, London: Routledge.
Cordas, T.J., (1990), Embodiment as paradigm for anthropology, *Ethos*, 18(1): 5–47.
Craib, I., (1997) *Classical Social Theory*, Oxford: Oxford University Press.
Crossley, N., (2007), Researching embodiment by way of 'body techniques'. In C. Shilling (ed.), *Embodying Sociology*, Sociological Review Monograph, pp. 80–94. Oxford: Blackwell.
Davies, K., (1997), *Embodied Practices. Feminist Perspectives on the Body*, London: Sage.
Delamont, S. and Stephens, N., (2008), Up on the Roof: The Embodied Habitus of Diasporic Capoeira: *Cultural Sociology*, 2(1): 57–74.
Deleuze, G. and Guattari, F., (1983), Rhizome. In *On the line*, New York: Semiotext(e).
Deleuze, G. and Guattari, F., (2004 [1980]), *Thousand Plateaus: Capitalism and Schizophrenia*, Contributor Brian Massumi, London: Continuum International Publishing Group.
Douglas, M., (1996 [1970]), *Natural Symbols: Explorations in Cosmology*, London: Routledge.
Featherstone, M., (1982), The Body in Consumer Culture, *Theory, Culture & Society*, 1(2): 18–33.
Foster, S., (ed.), (1996), *Corporealities: Body, Knowledge, Culture and Power*, London: Routledge.
Foucault, M., (1977), *Discipline and Punish*, translated by A. Sheridan. London: Allen Lane.
Frank, A.W., (1990), Bringing bodies back in: a decade review, *Theory, Culture & Society*, 7: 131–162.
Giddens, A., (1968), 'Power' in the recent writings of Talcott Parsons, *Sociology*, 2(2): 257–272.
Goffman, E., (1955), On Face-Work: An Analysis of Ritual Elements in Social Interaction, *Psychiatry: Journal of Interpersonal Relations* 18:3: 213–231 [rpt. in: *Interaction Ritual*, pp. 5–46]
Goffman, E., (1959), *The Presentation of Self in Everyday Life*, Harmondsworth: Penguin.
Goffman, E., (1963), *Interaction Ritual*, New York: Anchor Books.
Goffman, E., (1966 [1963]), *Behaviour in Public Places*, New York: The Free Press.
Garfinkel, H., (1967), *Studies in Ethnomethodology*, Englewood Cliffs, N.Y.: Prentice Hall.
Grosz, E., (1995), *Space, Time, and Perversion: Essays on the Politics of Bodies*, London: Routledge.
Haraway, D.J., (1991), *Simians, Cyborgs, and Women: The Reinvention of Nature*, New York: Routledge.
Harding, S.G., (1993), *The 'Racial' Economy of Science: Toward a Democratic Future*, Bloomington: Indiana University Press.
Heidegger, M., (1962), *Being and Time*, trans. J. McQuarrie and E. Robinson, London: SCM Press.
Kessler, S.J. and McKenna, W., (1978), *Gender. An Ethnomethodological Approach*, New York: Wiley.
Kuzmics, H., (1991), Embarrassment and Civilization: On Some Similarities and Differences in the Work of Goffman and Elias, *Theory, Culture & Society*, Vol. 8, No. 2: 1–30.

Latimer, J., (2001), All-consuming passions: materials and subjectivity in the age of enhancement. In N. Lee and R. Munro (eds), *The Consumption of Mass*, Sociological Review Monograph: 158–173. Oxford: Blackwell.

Latimer, J., (2004), Commanding materials: re-accomplishing authority in the context of multi-disciplinary work, *Sociology*, 38(4): 757–775.

Latimer, J., (2007), Diagnosis, Dysmorphology and the Family: Knowledge, motility, choice. *Medical Anthropology*, 26: 53–94.

Latimer, J. and Munro, R., (2006), Driving the Social. In: *Against Automobility*, S. Bohm, C. Jones and M. Pattison (eds), Sociological Review Monograph: 32–55, Oxford: Blackwell.

Latour, B., (1987), *Science in Action*, Milton Keynes: Open University Press.

Latour, B., (2005), *Reassembling the Social: an introduction to actor-network-theory*, Oxford: Clarendon.

Leder, D., (1990), *The Absent Body*, Chicago: University of Chicago.

Lloyd, M., (2004), Life in the slow lane: Rethinking spectacular body modification *Continuum: Journal of Media & Cultural Studies*, 18(4): 555–564.

Mauss, M., (1973 [1936]), Techniques of the body, *Economy and Society*, 2: 70–88.

Mazis, G.A., (1993), *Emotion and Embodiment: Fragile Ontology*, New York: Peter Lang.

Merleau-Ponty, M., (1974 [1945]), *Phenomenology of Perception*, London: Routledge & Kegan Paul.

Moglen, H. and Chen, N., (eds), (2006), *Bodies in the Making: Transitions and Transgressions*, Santa Cruz, CA: New Pacific Press.

Munro, R., (1996a), A Consumption View of Self: extension, exchange and identity. In S. Edgell, K. Hetherington and A. Warde (eds), *Consumption Matters: the production and experience of consumption*. Sociological Review Monograph: 248–273, Oxford: Blackwell.

Munro, R., (1996b), Disposal of the Meal, in D. Marshall (ed.) 1995, *Food Choice and the Food Consumer*, pp. 313–325. Glasgow: Blackie.

Munro, R., (1999), The Cultural Performance of Control, *Organization Studies*, Vol. 20, No. 4: 619–639.

Munro, R., (2001), Disposal of the Body: upending postmodernism. *ephemera: critical dialogues on organization*, Vol. 1, No. 2: 108–130.

Munro, R., (2004), Punctualising Identity: time and the demanding relation, *Sociology*, Vol. 38, No. 2: 293–311.

Munro, R., (2005), Partial Organisation: Marilyn Strathern and the elicitation of relations. In C. Jones and R. Munro (eds), *Contemporary Organization Theory*, Sociological Review Monograph: 245–266. Oxford: Blackwell.

Nettleton, S. and Watson, J., (eds), (1998), *The Body in Everyday Life*, London and New York: Routledge

O'Neill, J., (1985), *Five Bodies – The Human Shape of Modern Society*, Ithaca: Cornell University Press.

Ong, A., (1987), *Spirits of Resistance and Capitalist Discipline: Factory Women in Malaysia*, SUNY Press.

Probyn, E., (2004), Eating for a Living: a rhizoethnology of bodies. In H. Thomas and J. Ahmed (eds), *Cultural Bodies: Ethnography and Theory*: 215–240, Oxford: Blackwell.

Probyn, E., (1996), *Outside Belongings: Disciplines, Nations and the Place of Sex*. London: Routledge.

Ram, K., (2000), Dancing the past into life. The Rasa, Nritta and Raga of immigrant existence. *The Australian Journal of Anthropology*, Special issue: 261–74.

Ram, K., (2005), Phantom Limbs; South Indian dance and immigrant reifications of the female body, *Journal of Intercultural Studies*, 26(1–2): 121–137.

Scarry, E., (1985), *The body in pain: the making and unmaking of the world*, Oxford: Oxford University Press.

Schillmeier, M., (2008a), Time-Spaces of Becoming In/dependent and Dis/abled, *Time & Society* 2: 215–231.

Schillmeier, M., (2008b), (Visual) Disability. From Exclusive Perspectives to Inclusive Differences, *Disabilty & Society*, 23(6): 611–623.

Schillmeier, M., (2007a), Dis/abling Practices. Rethinking Disability, *Human Affairs*, 17(2): 195–208.

Schillmeier, M., (2007b), Dis/abling Spaces of Calculation – Blindness and Money In Everyday Life, Environment and Planning D: *Society & Space*, 25(4): 594–609.

Shilling, C., (2003 [1993]), *The Body and Social Theory*, 2nd edition, London: Sage.

Shilling, C., (2007), Introduction: Sociology and the body: classical traditions and new agendas. In C. Shilling (ed.), *Embodying Sociology*, Sociological Review Monograph: 2–18, Oxford: Blackwell.

Silverman, H.J., (1981), Merleau-Ponty and the interrogation of language, in J. Sallis (ed.), *Merleau-Ponty, Perception, Structure, Language: A Collection of Essays*: 122–141, Atlantic Highlands, N.J.: Humanities Press.

Strathern, M., (1991), *Partial Connections*, Savage, Maryland: Rowman & Littlefield.

Strathern, M., (1992), *After Nature: English Kinship in the Late Twentieth Century*, Cambridge: Cambridge University Press.

Strathern, M., (2007), Using Bodies to Communicate. Paper presented at '*Social Bodies*', Department of Social Anthropology, University of Cambridge, 2007. http://66.102.9.104/search?q=cache:9_De_YUsllYJ:www.socanth.cam.ac.uk/pdf/SOCIALBODIESfullprogramme.pdf+Using+Bodies+to+Communicate+Strathern&hl=en&ct=clnk&cd=1&gl=uk

Synott, A., (1993), *The Body Social: Symbolism, Self, and Society*, London: Routledge.

Turner, B., (2007), Culture, technologies and bodies: the technological Utopia of living forever, in C. Shilling (ed.), *Embodying Sociology*, Sociological Review Monograph: 19–36, Oxford: Blackwell.

Weber, M., (1947/1922), *The Theory of Social and Economic Organisation*, New York: Oxford University Press.

Weick, K., (1995), *Sensemaking in Organizations*, London: Sage.

Weiss, G., (1999), *Body Images. Embodiment as Intercorporeality*, London/New York: Routledge.

Weiss, G. and Haber, H.F., (1999), *Perspectives on Embodiment. The Intersections of Nature and Culture*, London/New York: Routledge.

Willig, C., (2001), *Introducing Qualitative Research in Psychology*, Buckingham: Open University Press.

Section 1
Opening up the Body

On the art of life: a vitalist reading of medical humanities[1]

Monica Greco

In her most recent book on the practice of narrative medicine, Rita Charon tells the story of when, as a young intern, she took care of a gravely ill elderly man. The gentleman was

> irretrievably sick, bed-bound for months, with a large infected craterlike skin wound on his lower back. He had a serious infection in the blood, and his kidneys were failing. Multiple strokes had left him comatose for many months in the nursing home. And yet his wife sat at his bed all day, every day. . . . She would ask me, every day, 'Is he going to be all right?' And I would page the plastic surgeon to come attend to my patient's wound. Eventually I learned to debride the wound myself, for plastics would not come. The surgeons could do nothing to save the patient's life. I did not know he was beyond saving. I was alone with his wife . . . , her life that was coming apart, and I couldn't get plastics to come. We were in it together, we three – this gravely ill man trying so hard to die, his wife bereft by his loss and unable to fathom her life without him, and me, the intern, who wanted like crazy to save him. (2006: 33)

Charon's words are strongly evocative of the sense of anguish, isolation and powerlessness she experienced on that occasion, which is not an uncommon occurrence in the practice of medicine. Yet the message she carves from that story is one of hope. Further, she writes: 'We had little clinically to offer this man. I did not know, then, that there is no limit to what one can give as a doctor' (2006: 34).

We can read this story, and its significance, in (at least) two registers: one is the immediately practical register proposed by Charon herself. She goes on to explain how, in retrospect, she can see that her training as a physician had entirely failed to provide her with skills designed to manage suffering – skills of empathy, reflection, and communication that would have led her to understand and approach the needs of her patient and his family in a very different way. Skills, she adds, crucially, that might have helped her to confront her own fear and non-acceptance of death. But the story is significant also on another register, which speaks directly to the themes of knowing and unknowing (bodies), and of the entanglement between knowledge and affect. Charon 'did not know' the patient was 'beyond saving', and this knowledge shaped her continued investment in the possibility of saving him – or, to be more exact, her investment in a particular understanding of what it might mean to 'save' him. As for the plastic surgeons who 'would not come', we can only reasonably speculate that their knowing that they could 'do nothing' may have played a part in their lack of immediate response. And what of the idea that 'there is no limit' to what one can give as a doctor? In this context, 'there is no limit' points simultaneously to knowing *and* not knowing: knowing that you *can* give, without knowing the positive content of the aim of that giving. 'There is no limit' here signals an acknowledgment, and an opening towards, indeterminacy: and it is a powerful statement as to the importance of this attitude in a clinical context.

Here is a second story. A few years ago I had a conversation with Dr. Deborah Kirklin, who was then the director of the UCL Centre for Medical Humanities, about her practice of teaching humanities subjects to medical students. She told me that, in essence, the purpose of this teaching was to restore to these doctors-in-the-making a renewed acquaintance with – and respect for – some of the human qualities that they had come to lose sight of as they progressed through their medical training. She mentioned, for example, the ability to identify with the patient, and to see their illness from an experiential perspective; or the ability to imagine the complex life-context that gives a personal, unique meaning to every medical event. These are qualities, she stressed, that each of these students had possessed, as part of their own experience of life, before they started their training. They are qualities, in other words, that they had possessed before they became *subjects that (presume to) know*. Kirklin did not explicitly say something that I will suggest here, namely that the education she provided would not simply restore imaginative qualities to her students, but also re-produce the sense of *not knowing* that is involved in life as we experience it. And, given the educational context, it would restore a sense of *value* (or respect) for the possibilities implicit in what we cannot *know*, but can only imagine, invent, or interact with.

I have chosen these examples to introduce my chapter because they are contemporary representatives of the recent opening of medicine towards education in the humanities. And I have used them to suggest that what is involved in this opening, what is at stake in this opening, is something more than the developing of skills of empathy, reflection, and communication, however valuable these may be. What is involved, I propose, is a form of 'vitalism' – in the non-derogatory sense given to this word by Georges Canguilhem, who described it as 'an imperative rather than a method, and more of an ethical system, perhaps, than a theory' (1994: 288). This framing in terms of vitalism, I propose, makes it possible to consider the work and ideas of contemporary practitioners like Charon and Kirklin in the context of a much broader historico-scientific problematic. And it allows us to connect it with a wider set of implications.

How, then, are we to understand 'vitalism', and with what implications for the practice of medicine? I have already indicated that I am using 'vitalism' here in the sense proposed by Canguilhem, a sense which must be carefully distinguished from what Canguilhem himself called 'classical' forms of vitalism. Classical vitalism, and I am quoting here the Merriam-Webster definition, is the 'doctrine that the functions of a living organism are due to a vital principle distinct from physicochemical forces', or alternatively the doctrine 'that the processes of life are not explicable by the laws of physics and chemistry alone and that life is in some part self-determining'. Canguilhem contradicts these definitions head-on when he states that vitalism should be understood as an imperative and as an ethical system, rather than a method or theory. Vitalists affirm the originality of life, and this is an attitude before being a doctrine: if the concepts of classical science cannot quite account for vital phenomena – be these epigenesis, the placebo effect, or the flight of a bird – vitalists refuse to have the latter explained away. They refuse to believe that the special characteristics we associate with living things are but secondary qualities, illusions to be explained by reference to an underlying, more basic and scientifically more familiar reality. When faced with the uncomfortable choice of whether to place their trust in knowledge or in life, whether to deny one or the other, vitalists side with life. Bergson articulated this attitude very clearly when he wrote, in *Creative Evolution*, that 'the "vital principle" might indeed not explain much, but it is at least a sort of label affixed to our ignorance, so as to remind us of this occasionally, while mechanism invites us to ignore that ignorance' (Bergson, 1911: 42; see also Greco, 2005).

Vitalists, then, affirm the originality of life. And approaching vitalism primarily as an *attitude* changes what we might understand by this 'originality'. Life is not 'original' in the sense that it constitutes an exception to the laws of nature; it is original in the sense that it is the origin, it has logical priority, it is the condition of possibility for knowledge. Science is a manifestation of the activity of the living. And a science of life specifically cannot be indifferent to the fact that knowledge stems from life, and that life is larger than knowledge: this is the ethical imperative that, for Canguilhem, is implicit in vitalism. Abstract though this may sound, it has some specific implications for how we might think about bodies in the context of medicine. And these implications resonate with the work of practitioners like Charon and Kirklin, but also point to something further.

Medical vitalism: health as normativity

In the context of medicine, the logical priority of 'life' leads Canguilhem to insist that the difference between health and illness does not correspond in any simple way to the difference between the normal and the pathological. Being healthy involves being *normative*, rather than being *normal*. A healthy organism is a normative organism, in the sense of one (more) able to live according to its own norms of life. It has a greater margin of freedom with respect to the conditions, or norms, defined by its environment. Canguilhem illustrates this point through the example of a children's nanny,

> who perfectly discharges the duties of her post, [and] is aware of her hypotension only through the neurovegetative disturbances she experiences when she is taken on vaca-

tion in the mountains. Of course, no one is obliged to live at high altitudes. But one is superior if one can do it, for this can become inevitable at any time. A norm of life is superior to another norm when it includes what the latter permits, and what it forbids. (1989: 182)

This is why

[b]ehind all apparent normality, one must look to see if it is capable of tolerating infractions of the norm, of overcoming contradictions, of dealing with conflicts. Any normality open to possible future correction is authentic normativity, or health. Any normality limited to maintaining itself, hostile to any variations in the themes that express it, and incapable of adapting to new situations is a normality devoid of normative intention. When confronted with any apparently normal situation, it is therefore important to ask whether the norms that it embodies are creative norms, norms with a forward thrust, or, on the contrary, conservative norms, norms whose thrust is toward the past. (1994: 351–2)

Health as organic normativity refers to an indeterminate *surplus of vital possibilities* available to an organism; a surplus with respect to those that are actualized in response to any given situation. And here we must resist the crude but common intellectual reflex to conflate the terms 'organic' and 'physical'. The salient point about living organisms is not that they are physical bodies (though they are that too), but that they are enduring individuals capable of original responses to challenges from their environment. There is thus a double aspect to the activity of an organism: one relative to *endurance* in the sense of the ongoing achievement of coherence or self-preservation; another, relative to *creativity* in the sense of the capacity to change, to invent new responses:

Self-preservation is not the most general characteristic of life; it is, rather, a characteristic of a reduced, diminished life. A healthy person is a person capable of confronting risks. Health is creative – call it normative – in that it is capable of surviving catastrophe and establishing a new order. (1994: 355).

This emphasis on normativity is important, on one level, because it points to the dimension of 'health' that is in excess of any evidence of biophysical or psychosocial adaptedness or normality: this margin of excess is indeed crucial to Canguilhem's definition of health as a concept. In practice, however, it is not unusual for the concepts of health and of normality to be used synonymously. This is often the case in everyday language, and it is valid for 'health' as a collective ideal based on criteria derived from epidemiology: we speak of normal values in a set of blood test results, or normal capacities as measured in relation to a given set of tasks, and we associate these with the health of those functions. These norms of health are generated in a social practice of knowledge and as such they are *social* norms. Canguilhem insists we must distinguish them from norms that are *organic* (or *vital*, in his vocabulary), which are always relative to an individual. There is, of course, an intimate relationship, at least in the case of human beings, between social and organic norms.[2] On account of this intimate relationship, it may appear redundant or misleading to propose a distinction between the social and the vital. It is nevertheless important to make the distinction, as a reminder that organic possibilities (and their significance as values) should not be identified, or reductively confused, with those that are intelligible to us in the form of scientific abstractions: 'Physiology is the science of the functions and ways of life, but it is life which suggests to the physiologist the ways to explore, for which he codifies the laws. Physiology cannot impose on life just those ways whose mechanism is intelligible to it' (Canguilhem, 1989: 100).

Ultimately what we get from Canguilhem, and from the form of vitalism to which he subscribes, is the Spinozian notion that *we don't know what bodies can do*. Possibility and potentiality are always greater than those accounted for by the abstractions of knowledge: life, in other words, 'often falls short of its possibilities, but when necessary can surpass expectations' (1989: 198). In concrete practice, we are recurrently reminded of this by phenomena such as spontaneous remissions, or by the placebo effect: instances where health is produced, where bodies act, as if in defiance of what we know about them. More often, of course, we are reminded of this by the ultimate uncertainty of medical prognosis; or by those 'medically unexplained symptoms' that account for a significant proportion of consultations in both primary and secondary care (Reid *et al.*, 2001; Verhaak *et al.*, 2006). What follows from the notion that *we don't know what bodies can do* is that when medicine entrusts itself to biomedical knowledge at the expense of paying attention to the broader context of life, it does so at its peril. And the perils are multiple. On the one hand, we have the blunders occasioned by medical hubris (Genuis, 2006), but this is only one half of the story. The other half of the story involves the very opposite of hubris, namely the misplaced assumption, on so many occasions, that little or nothing can be done – when in fact, to say it with Charon, 'there is no limit to what one can give as a doctor'. I shall come back to this point below.

For Canguilhem, the consequence of acknowledging the normative character of life and health was to stress the primary importance of the *clinic* to the practice of medicine – as opposed to the laboratory, for example. The clinical encounter lies at the origin of medical knowledge, and as such it is originally relevant. It is the place where doctors encounter their patients and the life they bring with them, in all its complexity, uncertainty and indeterminacy. The clinic is also where doctors encounter the practical value and personal meaning of a medical event, not as something given and fixed but as something that, at least in part, is (still) open to dialogical construction.

The importance of the clinic is also underlined by Annemarie Mol in her ethnography of atherosclerosis, *The Body Multiple* (2002). Her line of argument is very different from Canguilhem's, but it lends further support to the same conclusion. As a somewhat understated punchline in the last chapter of the book, Mol proposes that her analysis 'lends support to clinical medicine' and specifically 'sides with those voices that seek to improve the clinic *on its own terms*' (2002: 183, 184 my emphasis). The reason for this emphasis on the clinic's *own terms* is that current efforts to improve medicine, including clinical practice, are based on enacting a 'so-called scientific rationale' (evident, for example, in the quantitative tradition of clinical trials) – a rationale whose purpose is to stabilize and singularize what we understand as the reality of health and disease. Unlike the clinic, that 'lives with adaptable subjective evaluation' and practically manages the uncertainty that comes with it, a so-called scientific rationale works with an ideal of reality from which doubt and contradiction can be eliminated. But doubt and contradiction, as Mol's ethnography so clearly demonstrates, do not stem from inaccurate or insufficient knowledge. They stem from the fact that reality itself is complex, such that multiple enactments of, say, atherosclerosis, can coexist in relations that practically involve mutual exclusion *and* inclusion, contrast *and* interdependence, and so on. If uncertainty as to the best course of action is irreducible, *one* task of politics, Mol argues, is to safeguard and support those sites, practices and spaces where doubt and uncertainty are articulated and debated *as such* – that is, not with the anticipation that better knowledge (or consensus on a single underlying 'reality', eg of atherosclerosis) will be able to resolve them. The clinic is one such space.[3]

Mol describes her argument as favouring a 'politics of *what*' in contrast to a 'politics of *who*'. As her wording suggests, the emphasis is not on empowering different constituencies of *people* in voicing their opinions and making choices. The emphasis is rather on dignifying different *realities* with being taken seriously for the purpose of debating what it might be possible to do. Mol however stops short of specifying what these realities may be, or what it may mean to improve the clinic *on its own terms*: 'Which terms?' she writes, 'How to *do* the clinical good better? These are further questions I leave open here' (2002: 184). I propose that a practical answer to these questions is to be found precisely in the work of practitioners, like Rita Charon and Deborah Kirklin among many others, who have turned to the humanities with the aim of enabling doctors to address better the complexity of each medical situation, particularly with regard to its more intangible, personal and communicative aspects. In order to grasp the significance of such work, however, we must look a little further. Mol's ethnographic approach leads her to focus on realities as practically enacted, rather than on the abstractions that sustain those enactments. A theoretical focus on vitalism, such as Canguilhem's, works the other way around: it offers a set of abstractions, different from those of medical positivism, that invite us to *imagine* what realities we might take seriously, if a vitalist rather than a positivist attitude were assumed as the norm. In order to explore what the character of these realities might be, it is worth coming back to some further implications of the concept of health as normativity.

The art of life versus the art of persistence

The concept of health as normativity, I propose, has notable affinities with what Alfred North Whitehead called the *art of life*. In the same way that Canguilhem contrasts health with the capacity for self-preservation, so Whitehead contrasts the art of life with the art of persistence: '. . . life itself is comparatively deficient in survival value. The art of persistence is to be dead. Only inorganic things persist for great lengths of time' (1958: 4). The value that finds specific and emphatic expression in living beings is thus not endurance (or persistence) but rather *originality*: that is, a particular relationship to novelty. Unlike the beings described by the sciences of physics and chemistry, living beings are 'structured in such a way that novelty may matter, may induce an enduring . . . modification.' (Stengers, 2006: 14). Living beings are defined as such not by 'life' as an essential quality, but by their ability meaningfully to capture novelty, out of the stream of process in which all things participate, into the creation of a new order. Canguilhem, let us recall, described health in terms of a 'forward thrust'; Whitehead offers a definition of the art of life that literally *reads* like a forward thrust: the art of life is 'a three-fold urge: (i) to live, (ii) to live well, (iii) to live better' (1958: 8). The art of life is exhibited, to some extent, in all higher life forms; but, as we shall see, it reaches unprecedented dimensions in the life of human beings.[4]

In reading Whitehead, as in reading Canguilhem, we are once again confronted with the difference between (conservative) adaptation and creativity, a difference which involves an inverse relation to the environment. Living beings are normative not to the extent that they adapt to the environment, but rather to the extent that they are able creatively to *adapt it* to their own purposes and interests. The creative appropriation of the environment is the most prominent fact in the existence of mankind, writes Whitehead, and it reflects the greater importance that the functioning associated with the capture of novelty has assumed for this particular species of higher animal (Whitehead, 1968). Animal life 'can face conventional novelties with conventional devices', in the sense that it captures and canalizes novel possibilities that are actually available, and as they are encountered, in the environment (1968: 25). Human beings, by contrast, are specifically characterized by the capacity to entertain abstract possibilities, that is 'possibilities for ideal realization in abstraction from any sheer physical realization' (1968: 167). Whitehead also describes this as the capacity to imagine *alternatives*, whereby 'outrageous novelty is introduced, sometimes beatified, sometimes damned, and sometimes literally patented or protected by copyright' (1968: 26)! It is worth noting, at this point, the double sense in which such possibilities may be 'ideal'. On the one hand, this simply means that they are realized only 'in abstraction'. On the other hand, however, 'the entertainment of the alternative . . . emphasizes the sense of importance' (1968: 26), a sense which finds expression in the pursuit of *ideals* – moral, religious, aesthetic, scientific, and so on.

What realities, then, might this mode of approach propose that we take *seriously*, for the purpose of considering 'how to do the clinical good better'? If health as normativity refers to a higher, ideal order of individual existence, what possibilities are important in relation to the health of human beings? Contrary to what some might imagine, what follows from adopting a vitalist attitude is not a disqualification of the relevance of biophysical events. The possibility of endurance depends, indeed, on such events, and it would be not only counter-intuitive but foolish to deny this. What follows, rather, is a questioning of the near-automatic primacy accorded to the value of endurance – and to biophysical concerns, as a consequence – as this is reflected in the organization of medical practice, and in the dominance of biomedicine as a practice. Once again: the point is not to deny that endurance is a value, and certainly an important one too, but rather to challenge the power that is currently bestowed on this value to trump virtually all others.

In academic discussions, a classic and hostile dismissal of those who propound social constructionism is to say: 'Tell me that point again, when you are about to jump without a parachute from an airplane flying at 10,000 feet'. Something not dissimilar from this occurs whenever, for example, the practice of alternative medicine is dismissed for disregarding biophysical matters of fact.[5] The important difference between these two examples stems from the contexts in which they typically occur. The dismissal in the first example tends to follow the denial that anything should have the status of a matter of fact – whereas, no matter how constructed such facts may be, it is foolish to jump from such an altitude without a parachute, if your primary concern is to remain alive. In the second example, however, what is at stake is not the denial of a matter of fact. What is at stake rather is the attribution of relevance to a different set of abstractions, in the name of the value of health (and not of life per se). Such an attribution may involve the *disregard* of biophysical matters of fact, rather than their denial. The question is whether such a disregard may be justified, in the context of medicine. Without suggesting that there is any simple answer to this question, I propose we may begin to consider it by listening to another story, a story that points to the multiple dimensions of health as normativity in a human context.

Carlos, or: 'Thank you for saving my life'

Carlos was a terminally ill cancer patient in the care, among other specialists, of psychiatrist and existential psychotherapist Irvin Yalom. 'When I visited him in the hospital', writes Yalom, 'he was so weak he could barely move, but he raised his hand, squeezed my hand, and whispered, "Thank you. Thank you for saving my life"'. (Yalom, 1991: 86).[6] In this example, if we are to take Carlos' words seriously, the fact that the patient ultimately died should not obscure the value of a therapy that restored to him a measure of normativity, a measure of 'forward thrust'. But what does normativity mean, here? And how might this type of normativity be relevant to the practice of medicine? On one level, in a literal and minimal sense, the normativity achieved in this case refers to Carlos' ability to define *for himself* the meaning of being 'saved'. In the face of a barrage of therapeutic efforts aimed at restoring him to a previous cancer-free existence, Carlos, with Yalom's help, became able to think (and feel) 'outside the box'. He managed to find, to create, a new and original order of existence.

In a social and political context where health and illness are explicitly contested concepts, it is no longer possible to dismiss Carlos' experience of being 'saved' as irrelevant to the medical task, in so far as it is subjective and thereby 'only' his own view. Carlos died, and yet he was saved: a fitting example of the contrast between the art of persistence, and the art of life. He was saved not in a universal sense, for the meanings of 'saved' remain multiple; nor in an absolute sense, in the same way as health is never absolute: yet in a sense that warrants Carlos' choice of this very term in relation to his life. In light of our previous discussion, we can see that this choice of terms is by no means accidental. Being 'saved' points to the relative importance of the changes that occurred in the short few months before the end of Carlos' life: short few months in the course of which he lived better, with a greater sense of agency and purposefulness, than during the many years when he was free of disease and thus supposedly 'healthier'. The art of life, we might also say, includes the art of dying well and dying better.

Carlos' choice of terms also warrants regarding Yalom's therapeutic effort as justified. Yalom describes how, after accepting Carlos into therapy, he remained unsure about what therapeutic goals might be 'realistic and appropriate' in his case. 'Realistic and appropriate' would point to modest goals of offering 'sheer presence and support', rather than more ambitious treatment aimed at personal growth and transformation: '*What sense does it make to talk about "ambitious" treatment with someone whose anticipated life span may be, at best, a matter of months? Does anyone, do I, want to invest time and energy in a project of such evanescence?*' (Yalom, 1991: 73). Yet, to Yalom's surprise, Carlos made excellent use of therapy, which completely transformed his legacy to those around him: to his children, to fellow cancer patients in the self-help group he organized, and to Yalom himself among others. The difference between 'realistic and appropriate' treatment goals – goals that would take their cue from 'reality' as defined by the biomedical prognosis – and the 'ambitious' therapy Yalom ultimately strived for, recalls a difference we have already encountered in the story told by Rita Charon. It is the contrast between the notion that the surgeons could 'do nothing', and the notion that 'there is no limit to what one can give as a doctor'. Carlos died, and yet he was saved: the emphasis on health as normativity invites us to regard this as an interesting contrast that speaks of the complexity of human beings, rather than a contradiction to be overcome, eliminated, or explained away as 'only' his own view.

In this example, being 'saved' points to purposefulness itself – which, in a human context, refers to the quality of life as a function of its personal and communicative aspects – as a most relevant dimension of normativity that can be lost and found again, or not. On one level this tells us nothing new, particularly in relation to situations of terminal illness, where the value of prolonging biological existence for its own sake is often a matter for explicit debate. On another level, however, acknowledging purposefulness (or meaning) as a relevant dimension of normative vitality begs the question of what role a loss of meaning may play within vital processes *before* a (biologically) terminal situation. If it is possible to be 'saved' from a loss of meaning, then it is possible to be 'doomed' in a similar sense. Specifying how such doom might feed into any

one biopathological process is a task fraught with special methodological difficulties, which may account (though only partly) for why the proposition remains
marginal to the medical enterprise. This, however, is not a reason to refrain
from speculating: had the problematization of Carlos' health, and hence the
'saving' agenda, followed a different order of priorities, his ultimate predicament might have been different, and he might have survived his cancer (though,
no doubt, eventually found another way to die). As a psychotherapist, Yalom
reports the frequent regret, among terminally ill patients, that they discovered
the value and power of personal transformation only very late in the course of
their disease.

Salvation and the art of medicine: suggestions from an historical excursus

In her foreword to what may be described as the first textbook of narrative
medicine, Rita Charon makes the following, revealing remark: 'The design of
the book is coy, its early sedate presentation of self as a scholarly account of
work from many intellectual disciplines acting as a cover for a subversive invitation to radical change' (Charon in Engel *et al.*, 2008: ix). The interest of this
remark lies in its pointing simultaneously in two directions. On the one hand,
it suggests the possibility of radical change; on the other, it suggests the need
to present this possibility 'under cover'. The latter may be interpreted in terms
of what Isabelle Stengers describes as the *Leibnizian constraint*: namely, the aim
to state the truth in ways that will not 'collide with established sentiments' (2000:
15). This self-imposed constraint, which may be described as a diplomatic effort,
is certainly evident in much of the literature on the value for medicine of engaging with the humanities. The effort can give rise to a number of distortions. It
is not unusual, for example, to present interdisciplinarity as offering different
'perspectives' on the reality of the medical problem, as in this extract from
Martyn Evans and Ilora Finlay's introduction to a collection entitled *Medical
Humanities*:

> Many disciplines, including scientific medicine . . . constitute our many-sided prism
> for looking at medicine as a practice. Of course different disciplines speak somewhat
> different languages from each other, with different interests and concerns . . . They
> will tend to *see* different things in the objects they study . . . The point is that we need
> not choose among these. They are all relevant and important . . . (Evans and Finlay,
> 2001: 2)

We might call this a 'pluralistic' model, a model that enables a certain critique
of the dominance of scientism in medicine, whilst reserving a role for scientific
medicine *as we know it* alongside other disciplines. It is difficult to imagine how
such a happy coexistence might be achieved, however, except in the predictable
sense whereby the 'soft' disciplines (and their soft concerns) remain subordinate
to – trumped by – the relevance ascribed to 'hard' facts. A more radical sugges-

tion, indeed voiced gracefully by Engel *et al.* in the first chapter of their text-book, is that such different perspectives simply do not fit together. And that we need to recognize the inadequacy of the scientific model that remains operant in medical practice, despite having long been discredited among natural scientists themselves. Only then, supposedly, will the full medical potential of an engagement with the humanities really come into its own (Engel *et al.*, 2008). While this suggestion appears radical on a theoretical level, I propose that it can itself be regarded as a 'cover' for the truly subversive implications that might follow from the recognition of such an inadequacy. Why a 'cover'? Where is the compromise? After all, the call for change is still being made in the name of (a better) *science* – whose value as an authorizing discourse is thereby not challenged, but newly confirmed.

Calls for a 'new [medical] cosmology' (Greaves, 2004, 1996), or a 'successor paradigm' (Foss, 2002), or a 'new medical model' (Engel, 1977) are relatively abundant, but they are also invariably relatively marginal, at least in their effects. In a way, this is not surprising. To the extent that it makes sense to speak of a hegemonic biomedical model, its very hegemony would explain why theoretical disagreements may exist, but cease to be of much interest when they extend to the underpinnings of the model itself. As a strategy of ideological challenge, in other words, any talk of paradigm change would seem to be spec-tacularly self-defeating. This is what we glean from a classically sociological analysis of the dynamics of dissent within a given language community, such as those offered by Wolpe with specific reference to the medical profession (Wolpe, 1990, 1994). What we need to interrogate is the character of this hege-mony itself: namely, what values and interests an outdated scientific model may serve to protect and promote, such that it should prove to be so enduring. To say it in a different way, and in the spirit of a vitalist attitude, we need to relin-quish a myopic focus on a problematic of knowledge in order to embrace a wider horizon of experience.

I propose to do this by considering the issues discussed so far in this paper from the vantage point of a longer historical perspective. After all, the call for a transformation and renewal of medical rationality is hardly new. The turn to the humanities in medicine can indeed be regarded as the contemporary version of a number of themes that recur again and again in the self-representation of modern medicine. One of these is the idea that there is an irreducible element of 'art' in the proper practice of medicine, which must be rescued from the increasing dominance of science. A different but related theme is the idea that the 'science' in medicine is not adequate to the nature of its subject-matter, and thus needs itself to be reformed and transformed – in a variety of possible interpretations of this task. To begin with, I would thus like to set what is being prospected under the label of medical humanities (and narrative medicine) in a line of continuity with other forms of what might be called the 'return of the repressed' in the history of modern scientific medicine.[7] This return is reminis-cent of what Canguilhem referred to as the 'vitality of vitalism' in the history of the life sciences: namely, the fact that vitalist thinking has recurred, despite all epistemological imperatives to refute it, in such a way that we are obliged to acknowledge its value as a symptom of the limitations of a positivist approach to living beings (Canguilhem, 1975; see also Greco, 2005). In a similar way, the themes that recur in the recent history of medicine are symptoms – of a range of possibilities that are relevant to health but that remain repressed, excluded from serious consideration, in the mainstream practice of medicine. If this problematic is not new, then the benefit of a longer term perspective lies in providing access to different ways in which it has been previously articulated. Historical circumstances nuance the possibilities of the sayable: and comparison can be instructive. In particular, for the purpose of contextualizing this discussion, I propose to focus on the work of the German neurologist and medical philosopher Viktor Von Weizsäcker, and on the response to some of his propositions by the psychiatrist and philosopher Karl Jaspers.[8]

A subversive invitation to radical change: Viktor von Weizsäcker

Unlike Canguilhem, who was a medically trained philosopher and historian, Weizsäcker was a practising neurologist and neuroscientist who also wrote and taught as a philosopher. He remains best known as a pioneer or even 'founder' of psychosomatic medicine in Germany; he died in 1957.[9] There are many affinities between Weizsäcker's thought and the attitude I have characterized as 'vitalist' throughout this paper. Like Canguilhem, Weizsäcker cannot be regarded as a classical vitalist. In fact, a key point of departure for his thinking was the fact that there are no empirical criteria that might allow us to distinguish what is alive from what is not: 'it is clear', he wrote, 'that the boundaries between the living and the inanimate are not verifiable either in time or in space, in a dynamic or in a causal sense' (1986 [1949]: 452). A mechanist would take this to mean that living phenomena only *appear* different from the inanimate world described by classical physics and chemistry; and that, in time, technical progress will allow us to resolve the dilemma objectively. Weizsäcker, on the contrary, took the uncertainty relative to the definition of life to be symptomatic of the nature of life itself, and indeed of reality in general. He pointed to the work of physicists like Planck, Einstein and Heisenberg, and to concepts like the *uncertainty principle* and the *observer effect* to underline how, in abandoning the claim to objective representation, sciences like physics are moving in the direction of biology, not vice-versa (1987 [1946]). Developments in these sciences make it absolutely clear that science as such 'constitutes a very specific human attitude among many others', certainly not a form of enlightenment worthy of special veneration (ibid. [1949]: 453). What Weizsäcker asserts here, like Canguilhem, is the normative priority of life over knowledge. More specifically, Weizsäcker claimed that there is a constitutive tension between life and knowledge because, as a form of becoming, life is *antilogical*. To say it in his own words, life is

> a significant contradiction . . . whereby something neither is nor is not, but rather, more precisely, loses a being and simultaneously receives one. . . . An antilogical state

of affairs is . . . such that both an assertion and its negation are true . . . If, for instance, I say 'I am becoming', and at the same time I say 'little by little I am dying', both things are true . . . *The living is always something permanent that changes – like the human being.*' (1987 [1946]: 50).

Through a series of neurophysiological experiments on the relation between perception and movement, Weizsäcker sought to demonstrate that there is a subjective and unconscious dimension to every biological fact. On this basis, he argued that medicine should be 'anthropological', in the sense that it should proceed not only from an interrogation of what is given as observable, but also by asking (of any medical phenomenon) the sort of questions that can only be asked of a subject: questions relating to meaning, intention, or 'motive and end' (*Motiv und Ziel*). (Weizsäcker, 1986 [1949]).[10] These are questions that address life in its process of becoming, and that point to the ambiguities and indeterminacy that life, thus understood, implies (Weizsäcker, 1987 [1946]; 2005 [1956]). In the German language, modal verbs – *dürfen, müssen, sollen, können, wollen* – reveal this fundamental ambiguity and indeterminacy. They are terms that indicate existence 'not so much as it is given, but as it is *undergone* [*erlitten*]', and that point to a reality of possibilities beyond the actual, beyond what is objectively the case: if I say 'I want', the implication is that what I want is not already there; if I say 'I can', I similarly imply that what I can do may not come to pass (Weizsäcker, 1987 [1946]: 48).[11] For Weizsäcker, attending to disease as something proper to what is alive implied interrogating its meaning as an instance of something that (a particular) life *may, must, should, can,* or *wants* to undergo. Weizsäcker referred to this move as the 'introduction of the subject within medicine' (*Einführung des Subjektes in die Medizin*).

Weizsäcker's ideal of an anthropological medicine thus envisaged a practice where the event of (somatic) disease would cease to be considered an 'objective' matter of fact, in the sense of a fact evident primarily in or as an object. Now, here is a radical proposal. Weizsäcker saw and accepted that the suspension of objectivity as a criterion of primary relevance for medical practice implied profound practical consequences. For a start, medicine's ability to retain its legitimacy through a claim to scientificity would be put in question. Equally problematized would be the 'forensic' functions that, thanks to its science-based legitimacy, medicine routinely fulfils in the context, for example, of allocating the distribution of resources, or mediating the relation between workers and their employers.[12] In a clinical context, the suspension of objectivity would involve the displacement of a focus on disease (as we know it) as the problem to be resolved. Weizsäcker proposed instead that disease itself should be treated as an instance of value and interrogated in terms of what it achieves and why it matters, as a function of the relations between a person and his or her environment. The radical suggestion here is of a medicine whose practice does not aim directly at the absence of disease or even the avoidance of death: a medicine, we might say, whose effectiveness would be evident in terms of what might properly be called 'quality of life' (although this expression now refers to a construct that purports to measure such a value objectively, and that is certainly not what Weizsäcker had in mind). The introduction of the subject within medicine would thus imply the inclusion of the private life of the patient, in its most subjectively meaningful aspects, into the medical domain – raising issues as to where to set the 'boundary of discretion between doctor and patient and, even more difficult, that between both [doctor and patient] and the institution (eg the insurance) in whose interest, and at whose cost, the treatment follows' (Weizsäcker, 1987 [1935]: 284). Such propositions, as Weizsäcker explicitly suggested, have a revolutionary character:

> What has clinical psychosomatic medicine accomplished up to now? Whoever frames the question in these terms, and by 'accomplishment' refers to nothing but practical utilization within a modern industrial nation, would have to answer more or less as follows: for the majority of internal conditions it has accomplished nothing at all, for some of them very little, and even here only in isolated cases; only for such cases it would be legitimate to speak of competitiveness with respect to modern biochemical treatments. I would also make a similar judgment if I felt subjected to the business ideal of the entrepreneurial state. . . . I believe then that we must make a clarification. The evaluation of theoretical and practical *successes* ultimately depends on the following alternative: whether medicine and doctors subscribe to the value judgment proper to the entrepreneurial state, or whether they locate the value of human life elsewhere, namely in human perfectibility. (1986 [1949]: 457–8)

The proposition here is that medicine cannot hope to change in isolation from a whole host of other social arrangements, which it currently helps to sustain.

Weizsäcker's hope for a psychosomatic medicine that would also be 'anthropological' may be described perhaps as naïve, and this might be a basis on which it could be dismissed. But to dismiss it on this basis would already signify an ability to follow his imaginative adventure into the possibility of a different world, of which a different medicine would be but one aspect, one symptom. Most critics, commentators, and also advocates and practitioners of other versions of psychosomatics (or, more recently, biopsychosocial medicine), did not and do not go that far. This sets them and their vision apart from Weizsäcker's, in so far as they contemplate the notion of a 'new medical model' from the perspective of 'all else remaining equal'. In pointing this out, my intention is not to judge these critics, commentators and practitioners for choosing not to let go of an objective understanding of disease. What I wish to highlight is something different, namely that in the vast majority of examples this 'letting go' simply does not figure as a possibility for thought, let alone for practice.

On the value of objectification: Karl Jaspers

Someone who did follow Weizsäcker's propositions to their logical conclusions, and who was a direct interlocutor of Weizsäcker's on this matter, is the psychiatrist and philosopher Karl Jaspers. In 1946, Jaspers was called to arbitrate between Weizsäcker and Kurt Schneider on the question of whether an institute for psychotherapy should be established within the medical faculty of the University of Heidelberg. The proposed institute was the brainchild of Alexander Mitscherlich, whom Weizsäcker mentored and supported. It had been explicitly conceived 'not to promote psychotherapy in the narrow sense as a method for minor or "neurotic" psychological disorders, but to produce a fundamental revision of the theoretical and methodological repertoire of medicine in general' (Roelcke, 2004: 481).[13] After due consideration, Jaspers voted against the proposal. In an article published seven years later, he explicitly warned against the 'introduction of the subject' as a dangerous slogan which, he maintained, promoted a representation of human perfectibility identified with health. Jaspers defended 'objectification' in the context of medicine, on the grounds that objectification is a precondition for any knowledge capable of finalized intervention. While it is true that human beings in their *Gestalt* are not amenable to being objectified, he continued, for exactly this reason it is wrong to propose to make their humanity the object of a new (medical) science (Jaspers, 1986).

In the same text, Jaspers admitted that there are certain conditions that present an insoluble problem, namely those in which patients themselves favour disease through their own actions or where, in a sense, patients are themselves the disease. Psychiatrists would be most familiar with these situations, since in their field they constitute the norm rather than the exception. This is where, claimed Jaspers, the medical perspective founded on scientific objectification appears no longer viable. However – and here Jaspers argues in a manner diametrically opposed to Weizsäcker's – the relevant point from a medical point of view is *not* that these conditions have a comprehensible meaning or content, but rather that these relations of meaning have their correlate in bodily mechanisms. If we can act on those mechanisms, said Jaspers, their psychological consequences would also disappear. Through understanding, on the contrary, we cannot establish with these mechanisms a relationship capable of ensuing in effective, finalized intervention. To the extent that medical knowledge aspires to the capacity for intervention towards definite goals, these relations of meaning should remain outside the province of medicine itself. The alternative would be to understand 'human perfectibility' itself in terms of a definite set of goals specifiable through research, and this Jaspers rightly regarded as a frightening possibility – for, he claimed, where scientific research (and thus objectification) extends there can be no liberty.

So far I have deliberately abstracted this debate from the historical context in relation to which the relative merits of each position are often discussed. Both Weizsäcker and Jaspers were writing in the more or less immediate aftermath of the Nürenberg medical trials, the first account of which appeared in 1947 and was co-authored by Mitscherlich (who was mentored by Weizsäcker and informed by the latter's approach). That book, published in English two years later under the title *Doctors of Infamy*, squarely attributed the conditions of possibility for the atrocities of Nazi medicine to its narrow focus on natural science and its objectifying methods. The proposal for the institute at Heidelberg had followed a very similar line of argument. More generally, the aftermath of World War II in Germany was such that a rhetoric addressing the need to establish a new order, as a radical departure from the past, found fertile terrain. The explicit denunciation of the role of science in medicine, and the radical nature of the reforms proposed, can be read as an instance of this wider climate – a climate of opportunities which are not available in the same way today. Calling this a 'climate of opportunities' should not be read in the sense that the relevance of science to medicine can and should be dismissed. Its point is to highlight a specific aspect of the very different conditions that shape the articulation of an invitation to 'radical change' today. The radical character of the proposals explicitly articulated in 1946, in other words, matches a radical instability at a social and political level which, despite its many negative features, can also be regarded as a rare opening to innovation.

It has been argued that the spectre of 'objectivity run amok', personified in the figure of Nazi doctors, has since provided a cultural reservoir of images of 'bloodless, merciless instrumentalism [that] are always available . . . as the final court of appeal when arguments about the dangers of "objectification" are made' (Harrington, 1997: 185). Against this background, Jaspers' critique of Weizsäcker's approach reads as an early reminder of the medical value of objectivity which, in Jasper's interpretation, is after all a direct function of the limits it imposes on medicine. But this is not all. The critique reads also as a strong corrective to the notion that a 'soft' medicine premised on the refusal to reduce human beings to their bodily mechanisms would necessarily result in the realization of inherently humane possibilities. Indeed, as historians like Harrington have amply documented, Nazi biomedicine had been strongly characterized by a 'holism' critical of mechanistic science, although this orientation became increasingly less relevant to policy in the context of the war. As Harrington puts it, '[h]olism "lost" the struggle to speak for Nazi medicine and biology, but not for lack of trying' (1997: 193). In the context of Nazi eugenicist thought, there are plentiful examples illustrating that holism is equally liable to the possibility of 'running amok', and of doing so precisely through a reification – a misplaced concretization – of the notion of 'human perfectibility'. To my knowledge, Weizsäcker never saw himself as speaking for Nazi medicine and biology, nor did he ever assign a specific content to the notion of human perfectibility. On the contrary, his characterization of the human as partaking in what he called an 'antilogical' (or also 'pathic') mode of being refers any concrete human quality to a possibility of otherness, with respect to itself, with which it has a fundamental, constitutive relation.[14]

This, I believe, Jaspers understood. And this is evident in his emphasis on a different framing of the inadequacy of Weizsäcker's ambition for medicine. The risk implicit in the reification of an ideal of human perfectibility was one that had produced a horrific experience in the all too recent German past, which was apparent to Jaspers as it must have been to Weizsäcker. Jaspers' text dwells less on the problem of reification than it does on a more radical and remote proposition, namely that medicine *relinquish its aspiration to a capacity for intervention towards definite goals*. The adoption of 'human perfectibility' as an indeterminate ideal of health, he argued, makes the concept of health akin to that of spiritual salvation. And in the revolutionary promise of health-as-salvation, there is an inversion of the relationship between means and ends: health itself becomes a supreme value, rather than the means to attain a supreme value. Yet, surely, human beings should need health in order to attain their goals in life, rather than live in order to attain health. Jaspers feared that this inversion would eventually paralyse all possibilities for action. Accordingly, he insisted that the task of drawing a clear and deliberate distinction between medical healing and the salvation of the soul was 'today again' no less important than the demarcation between medical knowledge and quackery. And what would guarantee this distinction was medicine's self-limitation to the search for objective causal mechanisms and objectively founded treatments (Jaspers, 1986).

We know that, in the sixty or so years that separate us from Jaspers' passionate plea, medicine has done nothing if not pursued the search for mechanisms to infinitesimal proportions, and with results that certainly matched if not exceeded Jaspers' hopes. This is particularly true in his own field of psychiatry, where at the time of his writing any talk of 'mechanisms' remained purely speculative. We also know, however, that the ongoing success of this ambition has not stopped humans 'confusing' the relationship between means and ends when it comes to health and salvation. Few would argue now that, thanks to medical development informed by the value of objectivity, people in Western societies have become any less preoccupied with their health, quite the contrary.[15] And, while it is fair to say that many factors beyond medicine have contributed to this state of affairs, it is also the case that the momentum of technical innovation for the production of 'interventions towards definite goals' generates its own specific dynamics to this effect.[16] One might read in this another irony of history, one that would expose Jaspers' naivety as being at least equal to that of Weizsäcker.

In sum, then, what this historical excursus enables us to see more clearly is that a paradigm shift, no matter how justified in a scientific sense, remains meaningless except in the context of a wider set of questions. The circumstances of the exchange between Weizsäcker and Jaspers enabled these questions to emerge into sharp focus, in their most essential terms. The exchange helps us reframe what is at stake in the proposition that medicine is an art, no matter how well-informed by science it may be. What is at stake is not the importance of skills of empathy, reflection, and communication – an importance that very few would deny. More fundamentally, what is at stake is the question of *how medicine might best serve the perfectibility of human beings, or what Whitehead calls the 'art of life'*. This means interrogating the multiple social functions medicine is called to perform, and the relations (eg of mutual compatibility or incompatibility) that obtain between them. If we agree with Jaspers that the function of medicine is not to promote or facilitate a form of spiritual salvation, then we also need to ask why biophysical health is now, more than ever, pursued precisely as just such a salvational ideal. Or we may not agree with Jaspers, in which case the question is whether the relative importance attributed to biophysical events should be reconsidered. The art of medicine may lie precisely in not fudging the question by the typical move of seeking a 'middle ground' between these two positions, but in participating honestly in a debate that might put the extent of medicine's own power and authority in question.

In conclusion

I proposed, at the beginning of this chapter, that vitalism could provide a lens through which we might read the recent opening of medicine to the humanities, in such a way as to contextualize this development and to link it with a wider set of implications. The outcome of these reflections is by no means in contradiction with the work of practitioners like Rita Charon. Rather it lends greater emphasis to some specific aspects of such work, and invites greater boldness in their articulation, on the part of more people. Charon herself is quite emphatic about the fact that, as a society, and as the saying goes, *we need to talk*. She is equally clear that this is a matter 'not [of] scientific and rational debates, [but of] grave and daring conversations about meaning, values, and courage' (Charon, 2001: 1900). Advocating such conversations is a sophisticated expression of the art of life. Such a process of (self-)questioning may well result in displacing some of the extravagant hopes and promises associated with biomedicine. But equally, it restores a sense of wonder at medical thinking as an expression of the human adventure.

Notes

1 I gratefully acknowledge Paul Stenner for many invaluable discussions on the themes of this paper, and Joanna Latimer and Michael Schillmeier for their helpful editorial comments and suggestions.
2 On organic norms in humans see Canguilhem (1989: 165–172 and 257–273).
3 On processes of objectification and on the mobilization of doubt and uncertainty in the clinical context see also the studies by Joanna Latimer (1999; 2007).
4 My thanks to Paul Stenner for drawing my attention to this quotation in Whitehead's *Function of Reason* (1958). See Stenner (2008) for an exegesis of Whitehead in the context of critical psychology.
5 As distinct from claiming the status of a scientific practice on the basis of preposterous facts, which some practitioners do.
6 In the following discussion I rely on Yalom's reporting of Carlos' words, which may be regarded by some as problematic on account of the obvious difference in their speaking positions (as expert/doctor versus lay/patient, respectively). It is worth noting here that Irving Yalom, who is well-known as the author of several textbooks in psychiatry and as a novelist, is not especially associated with the movement I refer to as 'medical humanities' and/or 'narrative medicine'. His collections of non-fictional 'tales of psychotherapy' are not specifically addressed to audiences in these fields, nor designed to promote the same message to a wider medical audience.
7 It is only surprisingly recently that historians have turned their attention to these themes and their recurrence in the history of twentieth-century medicine. They have done so under the label of *medical holism*, an 'elusive but indispensable' term, in fact hardly ever used

by the practitioners they studied (Rosenberg, 1998: 335, in the volume edited by Lawrence and Weisz).

8 Aside from brief engagements on the part of a handful of historians of science – most notably Anne Harrington in *Re-enchanted Science. Holism in German Culture from Wilhelm II to Hitler* (1999) – Weizsäcker's work remains virtually unknown to the community of English-speaking scholars and physicians. In Germany and Switzerland, on the other hand, his intellectual legacy has been debated with renewed impetus among scholars and practitioners from a variety of disciplines, particularly since the foundation of the Viktor Von Weizsäcker Gesellschaft in 1994. Suhrkamp Verlag published the tenth and final volume of his *Gesammelte Schriften* in 2005.

9 It should be noted that, despite the existence of respected research journals bearing the term in their title (eg *Psychotherapy and Psychosomatics, Journal of Psychosomatic Research, Psychosomatic Medicine*), the adjective 'psychosomatic' is often used in a derogatory and dismissive sense (to imply 'false' illness), among professionals and the lay public alike. It should also be noted, however, that the character and extent of these negative connotations has varied historically, and still varies greatly according to cultural context. In the German-speaking context, unlike in Britain, departments of psychosomatic medicine are integrated within the mainstream medical establishment (see Roelcke, 2004, for a historical account of the institutional relationship between psychiatry, psychotherapy and mainstream medicine in pre- and post-WWII Germany). Although Weizsäcker wrote extensively on the subject of psychosomatics, the designation of him as a 'founder' of German psychosomatic medicine is misleading, since what followed historically in terms of research and practice in psychomatics bears little relationship to what he advocated. If the designation is often made, it is on account of his mentoring of Alexander Mitscherlich, who went on to found and direct the Department of Psychosomatic Medicine at the University of Heidelberg.

10 In his preface to the fourth edition of *Der Gestaltkreis* – the text where these experiments are discussed – Weizsäcker writes that his conception of medical and pathological research involves 'a transformation of the concept of science. Namely, science here does not refer simply to 'objective knowledge', it refers rather to a *fair [redliche] mode of relationship between subjects and objects*. Thus the encounter, the relation, is here at the core of the concept of science' (1997 [1950]: 96).

11 German modal verbs – auxiliary verbs that indicate modality or mood – translate into English as *may, must, should, can* and *want*.

12 These 'forensic' functions had become especially salient in the context of Germany between the two world wars. The experience of war neuroses was an important factor in propelling interest in psychological factors of disease causation and symptom formation. See Lerner (2003) and Roelcke (2004). Weizsäcker wrote extensively on the subject, see volume 8 (1986) of his *Gesammelte Schriften*. See Hagner (2006) for a discussion of this aspect of his work.

13 Roelcke provides a detailed account of the circumstances surrounding the eventual establishment of the department of psychosomatic medicine at the University of Heidelberg, which he presents as 'paradigmatic for the contemporary concerns, debates, and professional strategies' (478).

14 On this see not only the writings that comprise the volume *Der Gestaltkreis* (1997 [1950]), but also his *Anonyma* (1987 [1946]) and his *Pathosophie* (2005 [1956]). It should be noted here that there is an ongoing debate on the relationship between Weizsäcker's propositions – particularly with regard to 'social medicine' – and Nazi health policy. Critics, on the one hand, have claimed that there are definite 'affinities' between the two; others have suggested that this impression is the effect of the use of 'opportunistic' arguments on Weizsäcker's part. For a discussion see Hagner (2006).

15 Recent commentators on this include Zygmunt Bauman (1992a, 1992b, 1995) and, from within medicine, Michael Fitzpatrick (2001).

16 On this see Osborne (1997) on why health policy 'has to fail' and Greco (2004) for a discussion.

References

Bauman, Z., (1992a), *Intimations of Postmodernity*, London and New York: Routledge.
Bauman, Z., (1992b), *Mortality, Immortality, and Other Life Strategies*, Cambridge: Polity.
Bauman, Z., (1995), *Life in Fragments: Essays in Postmodern Morality*, Cambridge, MA: Basil Blackwell.
Bergson, H., (1911), *Creative Evolution*, Lanham, MD: University Press of America.
Canguilhem, G., (1975), *La connaissance de la vie*, Paris: Vrin.
Canguilhem, G., (1989), *The Normal and the Pathological*, New York: Zone Books.
Canguilhem, G., (1994), *A Vital Rationalist – Selected Writings*, New York: Zone Books.
Charon, R., (2001), Narrative medicine: A model for empathy, reflection, profession, and trust, *JAMA*, 286 (15): 1897–1902.
Charon, R., (2006), *Narrative Medicine: Honoring the Stories of Illness*, Oxford and New York: Oxford University Press.
Engel, G.L., (1977), The need for a new medical model: A challenge for biomedicine, *Science*. 196: 129–136.
Engel, J.D., Zarconi, J., Pethtel, L.L. and Missini, S.A., (eds), (2008), *Narrative in Health Care: Healing Patients, Practitioners, Profession, and Community*, Oxford and New York: Radcliffe Publishing.
Evans, M. and Finlay, I.G., (2001), Introduction, in M. Evans and I.G. Finlay (eds), *Medical Humanities*, London: BMJ Books.
Fitzpatrick, M., (2001), *The Tyranny of Health: Doctors and the Regulation of Lifestyle*, London: Routledge.
Foss, L., (2002), *The End of Modern Medicine: Biomedical Science Under a Microscope*, Albany: State University of New York Press.
Genuis, S.J., (2006), Diagnosis: contemporary medical hubris; Rx: a tincture of humility, *Journal of Evaluation in Clinical Practice*, 12 (1): 24–30.
Greaves, D., (1996), *Mystery in Western Medicine*, Aldershot: Avebury.
Greaves, D., (2004), *The Healing Tradition: Reviving the Soul of Western Medicine*, Oxford and New York: Radcliffe Publishing.
Greco, M., (2004), The politics of indeterminacy and the right to health, *Theory, Culture and Society*, 21 (6): 1–22.
Greco, M., (2005), On the vitality of vitalism, *Theory, Culture and Society*, 22 (1): 15–27.
Hagner, M., (2006), Naturphilosophie, Sinnesphysiologie, Allgemeine Medizin. Wendungen der Psychosomatik bei Viktor Von Weizsäcker, in M. Hagner and M.D. Laubichler (eds), *Der Hochsitz des Wissens: Das Allgemeine als wissenschaftlicher Wert*, Zurich and Berlin: diaphanes.
Harrington, A., (1997), Unmasking suffering's masks: Reflections on old and new memories of Nazi medicine. In A. Kleinman, V. Das and M. Lock (eds), *Social Suffering*, Berkeley, CA: University of California Press.
Harrington, A., (1999), *Reenchanted Science. Holism in German Culture from Wilhelm II to Hitler*, Princeton, NJ: Princeton University Press.
Jaspers, K., (1986), *Der Arzt im technischen*, Munich: Piper Verlag.
Lerner, P., (2003), *Hysterical Men: War, Psychiatry, and the Politics of Trauma in Germany, 1890–1930*, Ithaca and London: Cornell University Press.
Latimer, J., (1999), The dark at the bottom of the stair: Participation and performance of older people in hospital, *Medical Anthropology Quarterly*, 13 (2): 186–213.
Latimer, J., (2007), Diagnosis, dysmorphology and the family: knowledge, motility, choice, *Medical Anthropology*, 26 (2): 97–138.
Mol, A., (2002), *The Body Multiple: Ontology in Medical Practice*, Durham and London: Duke University Press.
Osborne, T., (1997), Of health and statecraft, in A. Petersen and R. Bunton (eds), *Foucault, Health and Medicine*, London: Routledge.

Reid, S., Wessely, S., Crayford, T. and Hotopf, M., (2001), Medically unexplained symptoms in frequent attenders of secondary health care: Retrospective cohort study, *BMJ*, 322: 1–4.

Roelcke, V., (2004), Psychotherapy between medicine, psychoanalysis and politics: Concepts, practices and institutions in Germany, c. 1945–1992, *Medical History*, 48: 473–492.

Rosenberg, C.E., (1998), Holism in twentieth-century medicine, in C. Lawrence and G. Weisz (eds), *Greater Than the Parts: Holism in Biomedicine, 1920–1950*, New York and Oxford: Oxford University Press.

Stengers, I., (2000), *The Invention of Modern Science*, Minneapolis and London: University of Minnesota Press.

Stengers, I., (2006), Whitehead and science: From philosophy of nature to speculative cosmology. http://www.mcgill.ca/files/hpsc/Whitmontreal.pdf (accessed on 27 June 2008).

Stenner, P., (2008), A. N. Whitehead and subjectivity, *Subjectivity*, 22: 90–109.

Verhaak, P.F.M., Meijer, S.A., Visser, A.P. and Wolters, G., (2006), Persistent presentation of medically unexplained symptoms in general practice, *Family Practice*, 23: 414–420.

Weizsäcker, V. von, (1986 [1949]), Psychosomatische Medizin, in *Gesammelte Schriften*, Vol. 6. Frankfurt: Suhrkamp Verlag.

Weizsäcker, V. von, (1987 [1935]), Ärztliche Fragen. Vorlesungen über Allgemeine Therapie, in *Gesammelte Schriften*, Vol. 5. Frankfurt: Suhrkamp Verlag.

Weizsäcker, V. von, (1987 [1946]), Anonyma, in Gesammelte Schriften, vol. 7. Frankfurt: Suhrkamp Verlag.

Weizsäcker, V. von, (1987 [1946]), Der Begriff des Lebens. Über das Erforschliche und das Unerforschliche, in *Gesammelte Schriften*, Vol. 7. Frankfurt: Suhrkamp Verlag.

Weizsäcker, V. von, (1997 [1950]), Der Gestaltkreis. Theorie der Einheit von Wahrnehmen und Bewegen, in *Gesammelte Schriften*, Vol. 4. Frankfurt: Suhrkamp Verlag.

Weizsäcker, V. von, (2005 [1956]), Pathosophie, in *Gesammelte Schriften*, Vol. 10. Frankfurt: Suhrkamp Verlag.

Whitehead, A.N., (1958), *The Function of Reason*, Boston: Beacon Press.

Whitehead, A.N., (1968), *Modes of Thought*, New York: The Free Press.

Wolpe, P.R., (1990), The holistic heresy: strategies of ideological challenge in the medical profession, *Social Science and Medicine*, 31 (8): 913–923.

Wolpe, P.R., (1994), The dynamics of heresy in a profession, *Social Science and Medicine*, 39 (9): 1133–1148.

Yalom, I., (1991), *Love's Executioner and Other Tales of Psychotherapy*, London: Penguin Books.

Unsettling bodies: Frida Kahlo's portraits and in/dividuality[1]

Joanna Latimer

They thought I was a surrealist, but I wasn't. I never painted dreams. I painted my own reality. (Frida Kahlo cited in Kettenman, 2002: 48)

Introduction

In this chapter I examine the self-portraits of Frida Kahlo to explore ideas about the significance of the body for understanding notions of self and reality. Kahlo states that her paintings are both of her self and of her own reality: her paintings thus invite examination of how Kahlo portraits self, and how she depicts 'reality'.

Portraits are material, mobile, semiotic objects that are produced in a specific cultural and social time-space location. At one level Kahlo's portraits work as the art of depicting specific persons as *themselves*. For example, in her early portraits such as *Self Portrait in a Velvet Dress* (1926: http://www.fridakahlofans.com/c0020.html) Kahlo experiments with Renaissance traditions of portraiture, adopted by portrait painters in Mexican art (Kettenman, 2002). Here Kahlo's portraits capture and enhance the essence of the personality of the individual as well as depict a realistic physical resemblance. In this way her portraits play upon the idea of the relation between the physical appearance of the body, the uniqueness of the individual and the distinctiveness of how they look from others. But Kahlo's paintings do much more than this. At the same time as her paintings portray Frida in all her vivid distinctiveness; Kahlo also unsettles the relations between bodies, their form and functions, and ideas about persons and selves: put simply, they change how people think.

In their write-up of Kahlo for an exhibition of her work, the Tate Modern state:

That for all her apparent naivety, [Kahlo's] works frequently reveal an incendiary subtext, whether they are questioning power relationships between developed and developing nations, testing the role of women in a patriarchal society, or attempting to reconcile the global histories and religions of East and West. (Tate Modern, 2005)

Specifically, as the film *Frida* (Handprint Entertainment, 2002) depicts, Kahlo was far from naïve; she was an intellectual and a revolutionary who read Nietzsche, Schopenhauer, Hegel and Marx, amongst others, in her youth. Far from the naïve style she adopts reflecting an underdeveloped and unsophisticated set of understandings about the world, Kahlo's painting thinks through her 'thrownness' (Heidegger, 1962),[2] questioning the ideas and consciousness she has inherited. Indeed the point of departure for this chapter is to explore the ideas that these works trouble, 'the incendiary sub-text', and the vision that her paintings offer. Specifically, at the same time as Kahlo makes her fractured and disabled body, maimed by polio and an accident in her youth, the subject of her paintings, her work sufficiently deconstructs dominant ideas of body-self to upset the perspective that produces the figure of the individual. Kahlo offers us a different vision of personhood, a vision of irreducibility and relationality, as an extension of what I want to call, following Strathern, dividual being.

Frida

In naming her pictures *self-portraits*, Kahlo shifts the very notion of what self is. Kahlo creates a figure of her own body, and the figure of Frida, through the repetition of distinctive features. The famous monobrow, the moustache, the dark eyes in a face whose expression is a scrutinizing look that seems to penetrate whoever is looking at her, including Kahlo her creator, with a fierce, sometimes painful, sometimes challenging, courage and candor.

There is thus an iconography that makes Frida recognizable as a distinctive person, a 'somebody'. But while Kahlo's portraits depict images of particular people as themselves – Frida, her family, friends, pets – the method of portraiture is not one in which the figure of Frida simply settles into a solid figure of an individual. Rather the particularities of Kahlo's methods bring into view all that is usually hidden. The methods can best be described as moving away from traditional methods of portraiture, to those of assemblage and juxtaposition. By assemblage I am not referring to the surrealists' method of making three-dimensional objects from the assembling together of diverse and heterogeneous materials, such as the sculptures of Marcel Duchamp.[3] Rather, following Deleuze and Parnet (1987),[4] assemblage in Kahlo is a method of painting that brings together, and yet keeps apart, figures and symbols to portray the relations that go to make her up.

For example, the picture *My Grandparents, My Parents and I* (Figure 1) does not depict a picture of 'Frida Kahlo', the distinctive individual; rather it brings into view what is usually made absent in portraits: how Frida is a creation.[5] Here Kahlo mimics the form of a family tree, but with miniature portraits of those people who have gone before, instead of names or symbols. The figures of Frida's grandparents, suspended in the sky, are painted in formal dress to portray the multiplicities that make up the class she inherits, as well as the complexity of her ethnicity, as a descendent of German Jewish and Mexican Catholic origins. In the face of her Mexican grandmother (the top right of the painting) we can glimpse the features of the Frida to come. A red ribbon reminiscent of an umbilical cord and a rivulet of blood flows from the figures of her grandparents. A naked child who stands giant-like in the courtyard of Frida's home holds a loop of the ribbon of blood/umbilical cord; the figures of her parents are enfolded in its curves. The loop of ribbon that she holds in her right hand connects the child back to her mother and reflects, in reverse, the arm of her mother that enjoins her husband as Kahlo's father. The child stands in front of her father, who prefigures her, and who she refigures (it was her father who was the photographer and amateur artist, and who encouraged Kahlo to paint.) Her parents are in their wedding clothes, and from Frida's mother flows the mirror image umbilicus into the navel of a tiny fetus, which is suspended outside her mother's belly.[6] As we move down the generations we move from busts, to half bodies to the whole bodies of the child and the fetus. Below, and to the left of the fetus, there is the image of an egg and sperm, at the moment of conception, possibly depicting Frida as she is being created.

What Kahlo paints then is a cosmology that borrows from ideas of kinship, and in which what has gone before, portrayed as a flow of substance (in this

Figure 1: *My Grandparents, My Parents and I (1936) Frida Kahlo. Digital Image © 2008, The Museum of Modern Art, New York/SCALA, Florence.*

case, blood), connects persons and helps to make them up. The 'family tree' is obviated in favor of this flow of blood/substance. It also makes visible the multiplicity and plurality of Frida's inheritance, in terms of gender, class and ethnicity. But these flows of substance/blood do not settle into one unique person, the usual image of Western kinship. The usual image of kinship performs *the* trope that informs and underpins modernist ideas of multiplicity and plurality, and that helps constitute the notion of the individual:

> ... one whole was only a part of another. This was evinced in the biology of procreation and death. A child was endowed with material from both parents, literally formed from parts of them. Yet it was regarded as equivalent to neither mother nor father nor to the relation between them: rather it was a hybrid product in another sense, a genetically unique individual with a life of its own. It was only a part of their life, despite the fact that its genetic material was formed wholly of theirs ... Such modernist perspectives had their own pluralizing effect ... Parts in turn thus always appear to be cut off from other larger wholes. (Strathern, 1992a, 93–94)

The picture of Frida's family is unsettling not just because of the depiction of a flow of blood, or of a fetus still connected to its mother yet lying as if on the outside of the mother's body. Nor does the painting just unsettle because of its temporal contradictions (the baby and the child existing in the same space), or irregularities of scale (the giant-like child at the bottom, off-centre of the picture). Rather, the painting is unsettling because the flow of blood/relations does not settle into a whole, unified, singular Frida. There are, critically, not just two parents, and two lots of two grand parents, but two (or possibly even three if one counts the moment of Frida's conception) Fridas present in the space that the painting makes up. Thus the painting unsettles because all its parts do not settle into a whole, a portrait of Frida, the individual. This is reflected in the contradiction between the title of the painting and what the painting depicts;[7] the title declares that the painting is of Kahlo's parents, grandparents and 'I', but the images that the painting keeps juxtaposed depicts two Fridas, not one; two possible I's, not one. Elsewhere Kahlo also portrays more than one Frida in her paintings (see for example, *Two Fridas*, 1939, http://www.fridakahlofans.com/c0290.html). The Fridas in the painting above (a baby Frida, and the child Frida) are depicted as flowing from multiple antecedents – but because of the two Fridas, the painting remains unsettled and unsettling, each person and the part they are playing in the making of the two Fridas, connected, juxtaposed, but distinct and separate.

The assemblage of persons and their connecting ribbon of blood/umbilical cord is set against a landscape that is equally unsettling: it too is made up of two parts, that are connected, but that do not settle into a whole. Like the two Fridas, the landscape is irreducible to *a* body: it forever divides and yet partially connects – the sea (as image perhaps of Frida's father's migration to Mexico from elsewhere) and Mexico, the family home. The painting makes elements of Frida's conception explicit, her multiplicity and heterogeneity, but these parts do not settle into a whole, so that Kahlo does not offer us a simple image of Western plurality, 'a world obsessed with ones and the multiplications and divisions of ones' (Strathern, 1991, p. 53).

Using the idea of a borderline to portray division, and convey a sense in which her body-self is forever in division is frequently painted by Kahlo, for example the painting Self-portrait at the Borderline between Mexico and the US (1932, http://www.fridakahlofans.com/c0110.html) depicts Frida as a borderline that both connects yet holds apart the US and Mexico. In this painting Kahlo portrays a sense of the multiplicity of Frida's cultural inheritance, symbolized by Mexico and the US or 'Gringoland'. Here it must be remembered that Kahlo is painting at the time of the Mexican Renaissance, and the birth of Mexicanism as the celebration of Mexican consciousness (Herrera, 1983; Kettenman, 2002).

In this painting Mexico, on the left, is invoked by the juxtaposition of images of ancient artifacts and monuments. The colors of earth and stone, the images of skeletons and roots, convey a sense of depth, of archeology and heritage, and the mystery of the ideas and beliefs that have gone before. A fierce sun and moon hang inside clouds juxtaposed and yet connected above the arid landscape; at the point of their connection a fork of lightning flashes. So Mexico is being portrayed not just as having an ancient cultural inheritance but also as a space that is in touch with the forces of nature, as raw, elemental, organic, vibrant. In contrast, on the right-hand side of the painting, the US is made up of industry and technology – machines, smoking chimneys and skyscrapers – images of modernity, and instead of the natural forces of the sun and the moon, the sky is dominated by the American flag, a symbol of an imperial, manmade force. Underground, even roots have been replaced by electric cables wired to the machinery above. Frida stands like a statue on a stone plinth carved with words, at the borderline in between these symmetrical images of two distinct cultures, two cultures in which one, the US or 'Gringoland', is at risk of obliterating the material and symbolic life that makes up the other. She is dressed in an elegant 'Western' ball-gown, but with a Mexican hairstyle (see her grandmother in the portrait in figure 1) and holding a small Mexican flag. Frida thus is being made to stand at, and in a sense to stand for what both connects and yet holds apart, these two 'traditions'. And in portraying herself as barely Mexican, Kahlo makes Frida, and thereby her self, stand for the potential obliteration of all that makes up Mexico, and Mexican consciousness, unless of course she, and Mexico, become modern.

As portrayed, then, Frida's parts never quite conjoin to form the pronouns I or me, or into a hybrid whole, the image of the complex individual. The parts are *kept* in juxtaposition; the tropes are not reconciled or reduced. In this way, Kahlo's methods of assemblage and juxtaposition make explicit the complex, heterogeneous nature of reality and selfhood, as at the same time they resist the resolution of part to whole. Kahlo's pictures offer a different vision of what makes up body-persons, for example, the ways in which she depicts bodies and bodily functions.

Kahlo makes explicit the openness, fragility and leakiness of the body-self, as not just object and subject, but also as always potentially 'abject' (Kristeva, 1982): as well as ribbons of blood/umbilical cords and fetuses, there are many pictures in which milk, tears or blood drips. Beck (2006) suggests how this opening up of the body splits open the world as we know it. But I want to press the point that Kahlo does more than this: in many of these paintings, what the flow of bodily substance depicts is a flow of relations, and how persons are made up, substantially as well as figuratively, of these relations. Some of these are 'personal' – such as in the flow of blood that connects Frida with her grandparents and parents, or the *Two Fridas*, to portray a sense of family and relatedness. But some suggest a much broader notion of the flow of relations, and a flow of substance that makes up and nurtures Frida, for example in *My nurse and I, or I Suckle* (1937, http://www.fridakahlofans.com/c0190.html).

The painting mimics portraits of Mary, the Madonna and baby Jesus. And in Kahlo's painting, as in many early paintings of the Madonna and child, an adult Frida's head is painted onto the body of a small child. But the image is made even more unsettling because the baby-adult Frida suckles on the breast not of an exquisite Madonna, but of a sinister, dark masked figure, the nurse. This figure is painted to resonate with an ancient icon that symbolizes Mexico. The breast of the figure at which Frida suckles is painted to make visible the ducts and flow of milk. So that what nurtures Frida, what Frida's body absorbs into itself and grows from, is all the sustaining milk of Mexico itself.

Kahlo, in many different ways, breaches borderlines, such as those that separate the outside from the inside, things from persons, the self from others, the sacred and the profane, the past from the present, and thereby some of the foundations of the integrated, discrete body-individual. And yet she does not offer us a picture of a divided body-self. On the contrary, she illuminates a different vision altogether: a vision in which she refuses to allow Frida to be reduced to a singular perspective, a singular category, or even to some story of multiple realities. In this sense, at the same time as Kahlo portrays her own reality and her 'self' as made up of many parts, these parts are only partially connected. She preserves the contrast between the different worlds these parts conjure up as irreducible.

Kahlo's portraits offer us a way of imagining self that resists the very notion of subsuming self to a singular, categorical identity. Like Probyn, Kahlo puts Frida 'outside belongings' (1996) in the trivial sense of being subsumed to social or cultural categories, such as male or female, Mexican or American, child or adult, human or animal, self or other: she depicts self as made up of all of these things simultaneously, but in ways that do not settle comfortably into a hybrid whole.

In making the abjectivity of her fractured and fragmented body explicit, Kahlo paints something usually hidden. Kahlo reveals, even unconceals (Heidegger, 1996), not just the existential fact of embodied ambivalence and its fragmentation (Ankori, 2002), but all the work that goes into the perspective that produces the figure of the individual as an undivided, integrated, self-contained solid. The fragility of, and the extraordinary effort and machinery it takes to hold all the fragments together to produce an image of a whole, is portrayed in *Broken Column* (1944, http://www.fridakahlofans.com/c0480.html).

At face value, this is certainly a portrait of cyborg-Frida.[8] Frida's face looking at the onlooker (her self? us?) with clear, dark eyes, is difficult to read, it is ambiguous, as it is in many of her paintings.[9] The torture and the pain are conveyed by the image of her body pierced like St Sebastian's by nails and the tears that flow from her eyes. But Frida's look penetrates: she is not going to turn away from the horror of her pain, and in a sense she challenges the observer of the painting to also look at the pain of being Frida in the face. In the picture Kahlo depicts Frida's broken spine as a broken stone column, a symbol of solidity associated for me with Greek architecture and the columnous ideas of civilization's foundations. Here these foundations are portrayed as quite fragile. So that it is not just the solidity of Frida's individual body that is being undermined by the fractured and broken 'spinal' column. Civilization is the central column that held Frida's body upright and that Frida embodies (and of course it is the distinctive mark of the human to have walked upright). This is one more aspect of what Kahlo is making Frida's body-self portray: her own fractured and broken state of being portrays how the very foundations of civilization, and her distinctive humanness, are so easily undermined. Kahlo paints her body as embodying civilization, held together and 'up' by the machinery of the medical corset, painted in such a way that resonates with an image of a straightjacket. The mood of the painting is reinforced by the landscape, itself bleak and dry, and fractured into parts.

Kahlo portrays multiple, unstable Fridas as embodying and as made up of many heterogeneous parts. These parts are both connected to Frida, and yet some are in a sense, like the broken column, painted as distinct, as painful. The parts that make up Frida, that are and yet are not Frida, are of different kinds. They include images of members of her family, of things that evoke her Mexican heritage, and US and 'Western' consciousness. Frida is portrayed then as made up of many others, not just her biological relations, but of many different others, for example her husband Diego Rivera.

In *Diego and I* (1949, http://www.fridakahlofans.com/c0575.html), Frida depicts Diego Rivera's face as her third eye; Diego's third eye is an eye. In this painting, Diego is not just in Frida's thoughts or a part of her consciousness; Frida actually embodies Diego. This substantive relationality is not easy, it is painful and unsettling: again Frida weeps.

In her paintings, then, the figure of Frida is not just in a flow of relations, it is *made up* of a flow of relations. In addition to portraying the relationality of being, Kahlo's portraits also trouble the usual methods for fixing identity by assigning persons into social and cultural categories. As well as keeping in play her ethnic plurality (as Western and Mexican, Jewish and Catholic) Kahlo depicts a sense of ambivalence by playing with symbols of Frida's femininity and masculinity. In *Self-Portrait With Cropped Hair* (Figure 2), for example, Frida is portrayed in a suit, having just cut off her long hair. Kahlo messes with

Figure 2: *Self-Portrait with Cropped Hair (1940) Frida Kahlo. Digital Image ©
2008, The Museum of Modern Art, New York/SCALA, Florence. © 2009, Banco
de Mexico Diego Rivera & Frida Kahlo Museums Trust, Mexico D.F. / DACS*

the aesthetics of body-self relations – at the same time as she paints her feminine
beauty – her breasts are perfect, her face and figure exquisite – she persists
in depicting the heaviness and masculinity by accentuating her moustache or
her famous 'unibrow' or 'monobrow'. The monobrow or synophrys has been
traced in Western thought to developmental and personality problems. For
example, Lombroso (1895) connects the monobrow to a lack of the proper
bodily symmetry associated with the perfection of the white Western body, and
as evidence of the criminal personality. Most people see it as an aesthetic
problem – they pluck it, wax it, in order to settle their brows into distinct parts.[10]
For me, Kahlo's insistence on the monobrow is a further indication of her
refusal to let the images of Frida settle into the image of an individual, and
another example of her ferocious courage.

Kahlo does not attempt to settle opposing features as hybrids but holds their
difference apart. For example, the Fridas of the *Two Fridas* look alike but are
only partially connected, they hold hands and are linked by a tiny river of blood,
and their dresses overlap at the hem. Frida's different faces are not quite blank,
they stare out, poised, but what they convey is a site of difficulty and pain: the
blood, for example, flows out of herself as the gringo bride (*Two Fridas*) or as
tears in *Diego and I*.

Critically, in her shifts in extension Kahlo shows both an adding on and a doubling of parts, as an adding on and a doubling of relations (Latimer, 2001; Latimer and Munro, 2006; Munro, 1996, Strathern, 1991, 1995): not as a dialectical relation of thesis, antithesis and synthesis, but as something almost incommensurate, and *irreducible*. This is different from a simple reproduction of the relation of part to whole that underpins so much Western thought and that Strathern has helped us to understand as embedded by notions of kinship. There is no synthetic effect: people and the many Fridas and things remain juxtaposed, only partially connected.

The individual

In this chapter I have set out to show how Kahlo's paintings unsettle many of the dominant body-self divisions that allow us to see the body-self as an individual: person-category, inside-outside, self-other, mind-body. Instead she creates Frida as made up of many diverse parts of others, which, while they are partially connected, are portrayed as irreducible and 'non-coherent' (Law, 2004). This is not to detract from the individuality and uniqueness of Frida, and the powerful vision of reality that Kahlo's portraiting of self portrays. Rather it offers us a different vision of embodiment, persons, self and reality than that embedded in the notion of the individual as a singular, unitary subject.

This vision is not of a divided self, Laing's schizophrenic (1998 [1960])[11] or Nietzche's (1878) *dividuum*.[12] Nor is it a vision of hybridity: Frida does not coalesce into a body multiple (Mol, 2002), a composite of multiple, heterogeneous parts (Harraway, 1991). Rather, Kahlo offers us a vision that unsettles the perspective that can reduce all the parts to a hybrid whole. She offers a vision of reality and self that preserves all the pain and the wondrousness of non-coherence, of resistance to being subsumed to a single social or cultural category (such as female, human, adult, wife, Mexican), of being *in process*, of being *bodied*. So that Kahlo offers us a perspective through which a notion of the dividuality of personhood can come into view. What this vision helps to make explicit is all the work that goes into reducing being to the figure of the individual, and the individual-society duality, that underpins not just the biopolitics of modern forms of social organization, but most social theory.

The relation between the integral, contained, defined body and the individual helps perform the figure of the subject, and of the autonomous and possessive individual, a cultural figure that underpins most contemporary forms of social organization in the West (Skeggs, 2004). Critically, the way we think of the body in Euro-American cultures is constituting us as discrete persons, as a somebody rather than an anybody or a nobody. It does this by performing the body as integral and unitary, with an inside and an outside, and as distinctive and unique to an individual. This way of imagining the body helps to produce the very notion of self as a subject, as well as the possibility of the Other, as that which is outside, and apart.

Social philosophers and anthropologists, such as Deleuze and Foucault, have helped us to understand that social relations connect to 'ideas' of the body and to how these ideas perform ideas of our 'selves' as persons. For example, the individual is deeply connected to ideas of a specifically human nature (Habermas, 2003), one that involves the possibility of agency, responsibility, autonomy, subjectivity and choice (Strathern, 1988, 1992a) and that can possess both cultural and economic capital (Skeggs, 2004), and that can be in a relation to society in ways that accord particular rights and obligations (Parsons, 1951).

Alongside this idea of the individuated body-person runs the paradoxical and parallel seam of Western thought that detaches rational knowledge from the body: the individual at moments of choice, and autonomous decision-making, to be rational, must have knowledge from a singular, undivided perspective, a perspective that stands outside the plane of personal (that is bodily) action (Latimer, 2007; Strathern, 1988, 1991, 1992a). Western ideas of knowledge rest upon an idea of perspective as a form of distance. It is this 'detachment', this 'seeing' things from a standpoint that is removed from the plane of action, that facilitates an objective, and therefore clear and distinct, view of 'what is'. To have such a singular perspective man (sic)[13] must be able to *disembody*:

> Many features of contemporary knowledges – knowledges based on the presumption of a singular reality, pre-existent representational categories, and an unambiguous terminology able to be produced and utilized by a singular, rational, and unified knowing subject who is unhampered by personal 'concerns' – can be linked to man's disembodiment, his detachment from his manliness in producing knowledge or truth. (Grosz, 1993: 205).

In these ways the integral, discrete body is what helps to create the figure of the individual, but the individual, to be truly human, and transcend their bodiedness, must be able to 'disembody'. The human, distinguished by the fact of consciousness, is much more than the sum of bodily parts. This is one of the paradoxes of dominant body-self relations.[14]

Contemporary challenges to the idea of an undivided body-self emphasize the multiple ways in which the body is performed and enacted, and emphasize its instability, hybridity and heterogeneity. For example, humans can be shown to be in extension with prosthetics in ways that make explicit their hybridity as 'cyborg' (Haraway, 1991). But even here, where the multiplicity and heterogeneity that makes up bodies is made visible, body-selves, however hybrid, seem to settle into an individuated body or as Mol suggests '*the* body multiple' (2002). That is, at moments the multiplicity and heterogeneity is reduced to a hybrid body-self, its heterogeneous parts reconciled, into an individuated, solid, undivided self. Kahlo offers us a different vision of self and reality.

In/Dividuality

Strathern (1992a, 1992b) in her work on Melanesian and Euro-American thought, shows that even though the latter believe that bodily substance is made up of parts coming from biological kin, this substance settles into a unique whole, 'the individual', an undivided self. Melanesians on the other hand imagine persons as made up of the parts of others, never to settle completely into wholes but forever in extension, partially connecting and disconnecting, to produce a notion of persons as 'dividuals'. Strathern's description of dividuals, like Kahlo's portraits, seems to me to stress a completely different vision from the one offered by the notion of the body multiple, or cyborgs. Specifically, this is because dividual beings are not hybrids:

> Far from being regarded as unique entities, Melanesian persons are as dividually as they are individually conceived. They contain a generalized sociality within. Indeed, persons are frequently constructed as the plural and composite site of the relationships that produced them. The singular person can be imagined as a social microcosm. (1988: 34)

I want to suggest therefore that at the same time as Kahlo portraits her self, her portraits also perform dividuality as an alternative vision of personhood to that which dominates Western thought and the biopolitics of social organization. Here it must be stressed that conceiving of persons as dividual is neither an individual simply in division, nor a divided self, nor is it simply a way of making explicit the hybridity that makes up the figure of the person.

For Euro-Americans, selves in division are anathema, partly because of their ambivalence. We are used to thinking of people at a borderline, who are betwixt and between categories, neither one thing nor another (for example, neither a he or a she, or black or white), as dangerous. Similarly, those persons unable to maintain the appearance of unity and containment, integration and closure, especially the separation between the inside from the outside, and the self from the Other, are deeply problematic. These kinds of body-selves are abject (Kristeva, 1982), they are ambiguous, they leak, are penetrable, and their parts keep fragmenting and coming into view *as* parts: they make visible the space between the object and the subject. A body-self that is explicitly in division is deeply problematic (Laing, 1998 [1960]), its dis-integration unconcealed, mad, polluting, desperately in need of making whole again. Divided body-selves are for Euro-Americans like dirt, 'good to think' (Douglas, 1966).

On the contrary the idea of dividuals deconstructs the very object-subject, self-other relations that underpin our forms of social organization. Indeed the idea of the dividual deconstructs the idea of the subject-self and the perspective that underpins the individual-society relation itself. Kahlo's portraits do not make visible the multiplicity and heterogeneity of what makes up body-persons simply to settle them into either an idea of a hybrid or a self in division. Rather by making all the parts that make up Frida present, partially connected yet not reduced to wholes, Kahlo undoes the notion of the individual and dominant body-self relations. Let me explain a little further what I mean drawing on the ideas of the surrealists and the genre the *cadaver exquisite* ('exquisite corpses', also known as 'exquisite cadaver' or 'rotating corpse').

Cadaver exquisite is a method by which words or images are collectively assembled to make up an image of a whole figure whose heterogeneity, ambivalence and multiplicity is made blatant. Each part is authored by a different collaborator-artist. Each collaborator in the project adds to a composition in sequence, either by following a rule or by being allowed to see the end of what the previous person contributed (a bit like the game of consequences). The irony is that all these heterogeneous parts can be reconciled and reduced into a whole by settling them into a recognizable form; in the case of the *cadaver exquisite* in Figure 3, this form simulates the body of a person. In this sense, the *cadaver*

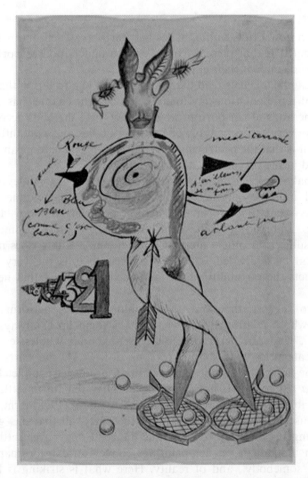

Figure 3: *Exquisite Corpse, 1926–27, Man Ray, Yves Tanguy, Joan Miró, Max Morise. Digital Image © 2008, The Museum of Modern Art/SCALA, Florence.*

exquisite resembles Mol's body multiple: the ways that at moments a perspective (in this case that of a human figure) can settle all the fragments and heterogeneous parts that make up bodies-persons into an integrated, if hybrid form, an 'individual'. Critically, although elsewhere Kahlo has produced several exquisite corpses with colleagues and friends in a series of drawings, she never adopts this kind of assemblage as a constant motif in her paintings. Kahlo's Frida rarely settles entirely into *a* body multiple, into a *cadaver exquisite*, a corpse. Rather, Kahlo's method of keeping parts in juxtaposition offers us a vision of relationality, of partial connection, of persons as the 'plural and composite site of the relationships that produced them'.

Discussion

I have shown how Frida Kahlo makes her portraits of self and reality. I have explored what it is that these portraits can be understood as portraying and have examined some of their effects.

While it can be taken as read that Kahlo works in a tradition that defies any possibility of representation, my focus in the current chapter has been on the particular methods of her portraiture and how these methods accomplish and put into play very different ways of knowing bodies and very different ideas, about what it is that the portraying of bodies can be made to mean, from those encapsulated in the very idea of the individual.

Kahlo makes explicit how bodies and persons are made up of fragmented and multiple substances and parts. At the same time as Kahlo's self portraits seem to perform the relation between the body and the self as unstable, ambiguous, ambivalent, undecideable – at moments abject, object and subject, at others none of these things – Kahlo does not leave us with a vision of a divided self. This is because it is the very perspective that constructs the possibility of an undivided subject-self that her paintings trouble.

I want to suggest, therefore, that Kahlo's pictures perform an idea of 'dividuals', whose relationality is what makes them up as always in 'partial connections', who can never be entirely settled into wholes, especially not the social categories that so pin persons down. All the parts that make Frida up, the flows of substance and relations, are never completely reducible into either *a* self, or an I, however hybrid. They remain unsettled, at some level irreducible, and yet connected and, to use Law's (1998) term, in tension. In a sense, as her paintings celebrate all the parts, all that has gone before in the making up of Frida, of her inheritance, Frida never settles into the image of an individual; yet her paintings convey an extraordinary powerful vision of a 'somebody', and of reality. Here what is striking is how Kahlo makes reality, not multiple realities, but reality as made up of and out of the many worlds and people, past and present, that she keeps in juxtaposition in her paintings.

So I want to suggest that Kahlo's portraits make explicit the divided nature of embodiment, of being forever in division, not just as her own reality, but as a perspective, a way of knowing being. Unlike the Melanesians for whom dividuality is the source of potency and power, dividuality because of its alterity to the individualism of Euro-American thought, is painful, unsettling and is, I suggest, a part of the pathos that Kahlo's painting performs. Here, Kahlo's portraits do not just offer us an existential insight into being bodied as lived, as central to lived reality, but into a way of knowing bodies that both resists and makes clear all the work that goes into humanism *as a perspective*, and as a way of unknowing being: a way of unknowing the body, not as an undivided self, which gives a perspective that forces the body into a representation of the individual as undivided, as a whole, however hybrid, and as able, in some extraordinary way, to transcend its bodiedness. Understanding body-persons as dividuals, however momentarily, helps illuminate all the unknowing of the dominant perspective it unsettles – all that would reduce persons into wholes. Instead, persons, like Frida appear in Kahlo's vision as creations.

Notes

1 Many thanks to all those colleagues and post graduate students at both the Knowing/Unknowing Bodies colloquium and at the Social Theory Seminar *In/dividual* or who have read the chapter, for their comments and suggestions, especially Jamie Munro, Rolland Munro, Nigel Rapport, Michael Schillmeier, Dimitris Papadopoulos, Trudy Rudge, Bev Skeggs and Marilyn Strathern.

2 'This characteristic of Dasein's Being – this "that it is" – is veiled in its "whence" and "whither", yet disclosed in itself all the more unveiledly; we call it the "*thrownness*" of this entity into its "there"; indeed, it is thrown in such a way that, as Being-in-the-world, it is the "there". The expression "thrownness" is meant to suggest the *facticity of its being delivered over*.' Heidegger, 1962.

3 In 1961 the Museum of Modern Art mounted the exhibition *The Art of Assemblage*. Curated by William Seitz, this exhibition marked the first time the term 'assemblage' was put into popular use and also the first time 'assembled art' was recognized for its importance in the context of modern art. Seitz set out to refine the definition of 'assemblage' in order to 'cover all forms of composite art and modes of juxtaposition'. The exhibition was significant in that it presented 'assemblage' as one of the two most important innovations in modern art, the first being 'abstraction.' (Zwirner and Wirth Assemblage exhibition) (http://www.zwirnerandwirth.com/exhibitions/2003/1103Assemblage/press.html)

4 'The author is a subject of enunciation, but the writer – who is not an author – is not. The writer invents assemblages starting from assemblages which have invented him, he makes one multiplicity pass into another.' (Deleuze and Parnet, 1987: 51–52). In the current context, for writer, read painter. Kahlo extends and extends her method of portraiture by assembling and juxtaposing all the relations that make up Frida to the point of making the iconographic figure of Frida almost absent, as in the painting *What the Water Gave Me* (1938) in which the parts of Frida's body that we see in our perspective of being Frida lying in the bath, are her bare feet, and yet the painting is full of other parts that are Frida (http://www.fridakahlofans.com/c0270.html).

5 In the painting *Moses the Nucleus of Creation* (1945) Kahlo makes explicit how she is recreating the creation story with her embryo-'self' centred in the split open nutshell.

6 The fetus is another motif of Kahlo's. One aspect of her biography that makes this motif even more poignant is that Kahlo lost a baby during pregnancy and could not have children.

7 As with Magritte's '*Ceci n'est pas une pipe*'.

8 'A cyborg is a cybernetic organism, a hybrid of machine and organism, a creature of social reality as well as a creature of fiction. Social reality is lived social relations, our most important political construction, a world-changing fiction.' Harraway 1991, http://www.stanford.edu/dept/HPS/Haraway/CyborgManifesto.html.

9 I have noted how in painted portraits people rarely smile. In photographic portraits people usually smile. A famous exception is the Mona Lisa.

10 For other examples of how the monobrow has become a site of resistance see http://unibrow.blog.com/ or http://www.unibrowclub.com/.

11 Robert Young (1966) in his review of *The Divided Self* gives this succinct account of Laing's theory here: 'we are given the following picture of the origins and phenomenology of schizophrenia: The inner core of a person is his "self". The self is in the world and relates to the world by means of its body. Most people – most of the time – feel basically safe in the world; Laing calls this 'primary ontological security'. Some persons, however, become ontologically insecure, ie, they feel persecuted by reality itself. We are not clearly told how this occurs, though the life experiences in his case studies make it plausible that they would feel this way; but one is still left wondering why others with similar experiences did not become schizophrenic. The man who becomes schizophrenic becomes preoccupied with preserving rather than gratifying himself; the ordinary circumstances of living threaten his low threshold of security. His dread of his own dissolution into non-being becomes so great that the self retreats into a central citadel; by being unembodied, it seeks to transcend the world and hence to be safe. The self becomes dissociated both from its own body and from the whole external world of people and events. It is thereby precluded from having a direct relationship with real things and real people; it relates instead to objects of its own imagination and memory. Its own bodily experiences and actions become alien – part of a false-self system. Thus, the self becomes 'a relationship which relates itself to itself' (Cf. *supra*). This relationship sustains an illusion of omnipotence and freedom within (and only within) the circle of its own shut-upness in fantasy. The psychotic's freedom consists in being inaccessible. Action is the dead end of possibility. It scleroses freedom. Laing concludes that there is one basic defence in every form of psychosis: 'the denial of being as a means of preserving being'.

12 Nietzsche suggested that the basis of man's morality is a form of 'dividuum', this is where man (sic) is divided in himself:

Moral of the people as Selbstzerteilung
57.
Morality as the self-division of man. – A good author whose heart is really in his subject wishes that someone would come and annihilate him by presenting the same subject with greater clarity and resolving all the questions contained in it. The girl in love wishes that she might prove the devoted faithfulness of her love through her lover's faithlessness. The soldier wishes that he might fall on the battlefield for his victorious fatherland, for in the victory of his fatherland his greatest desire is also victorious. The mother gives the child what she takes from herself: sleep, the best food, in some instances even her health, her wealth.

Are all these really selfless states, however? Are these acts of morality *miracles* because they are, to use Schopenhauer's phrase, 'impossible and yet real'? Isn't it clear that, in all these cases, man is loving *something of himself*, a thought, a longing, an offspring, more than *something else of himself*; that he is thus *dividing up* his being and sacrificing one part for the other? Is it something *essentially* different when a pigheaded man says, 'I would rather be shot at once than move an inch to get out of that man's way'.

The *inclination towards something* (a wish, a drive, a longing) is present in all the above-mentioned cases; to yield to it, with all its consequences, is in any case not "selfless." In morality, man treats himself not as an **individuum**, but as a **dividuum**.

[Terms of Scholastic philosophy: *individuum*: that which cannot be divided without destroying its essence, *dividuum*: that which is composite and lacks an individual essence.]

13 In many ways we have to understand that the individual is an invention of very specific masculine ideas of being.

14 Agamben (2002) draws out a double paradox here – classical and religious texts portray how humans in the moment of their return to paradise, are restored as animal, because it is their consciousness that is both a cause and effect of their fall from grace. Currently there is a proliferation of interest in recovering the 'magic' of ourselves as not divided from, but as one of the animals (eg Haraway, 2007) Kahlo of course painted Frida as part human, part deer in the self-portrait *The Wounded Deer* (1946: http://www.fridakahlofans.com/c0540.html).

References

Agamben, G., (2002), *The Open: Man and Animal*, translated by Giorgio Agamben and Kevin Attell. Stanford: Stanford University Press.

Ankori, G., (2002), *Imaging Her Selves: Frida Kahlo's Poetics of Identity and Fragmentation*, Greenwood Press Series: *Contributions to the Study of Art and Architectur*, Westport and London: Greenwood Publishing Group.

Beck, E.T., (2006), Kahlo's world split open, *Feminist studies*, 32(1): 54–81.

Collins, J., (2005), *Introducing Derrida*, London: Icon Books.

Deleuze, G., (1997), *Essays Critical and Clinical*, translated by Daniel Smith and Michael A. Greco. W. W. Norton and Company, Incorporated.

Deleuze, G. and Parnet, C., (1987), *Dialogues*, New York: Columbia University Press.

Douglas, M., (1966), *Purity and Danger*, Harmondswoth: Penguin Books.

Foucault, M., (1979), My Body, This Paper, This Fire, *Oxford Literary Review*, 4(1): 9–28.

Frida Kahlo Fans. http://www.fridakahlofans.com

Grosz, E., (1993), Bodies and Knowledges: Feminism and the Crisis of Reason. In L. Alcoff and E. Potter (eds), *Feminist Epistemologies*, pp. 187–216. London: Routledge.

Habermas, J., (2003), *The Future of Human Nature*, translated by Hella Beister and William Rehg, Cambridge: Polity Press.

Handprint Entertainment, Lions Gate Films, Miramax Films, Ventanarosa Productions (2002), *Frida*, Director: Julie Taymor. Screenplay: Clancy Sigal, Diane Lake, Gregory Nava and Anna Thomas. Based on Hayden Herrera's *Frida: A Biography of Frida Kahlo*.

Haraway, D., (1991), A Cyborg Manifesto: Science, Technology, and Socialist-Feminism in the Late Twentieth Century. In *Simians, Cyborgs and Women: The Reinvention of Nature*, pp. 149–181, New York: Routledge.

Haraway, D., (2007), *When Species Meet*, Minneapolis: University of Minnesota Press.

Heidegger, M., (1962), *Being and Time*, New York: Harper & Row.

Heidegger, M., (1996), The Question Concerning Technology. In D.F. Krell (ed.), *Martin Heidegger. Basic Writings. Revised and Expanded edition*, London: Routledge.

Herrera, H., (1983), *Frida: A Biography of Frida Kahlo*, New York: Harper & Row.

Kettenman, A., (2002), *Kahlo*, Köln: Taschen.

Kristeva, J., (1982), *Powers Of Horror: An Essay On Abjection*, New York: Columbia University Press.

Laing, R.D., (1998 [1960]), *The Divided Self: An Existential Study in Sanity and Madness*, Harmondsworth: Penguin Psychology.

Latimer, J., (2001), All-consuming passions: materials and subjectivity in the age of enhancement. In N. Lee and R. Munro (eds), *The Consumption of Mass*, Sociological Review Monograph, Oxford: Blackwell Publishers.

Latimer, J., (2007), Diagnosis, Dysmorphology and the Family: Knowledge, motility, choice, *Medical Anthropology*, 26: 53–94.

Latimer, J. and Munro, R., (2006), Driving the Social. In S. Bohm, C. Jones and M. Pattison (eds), *Against Automobility*, Sociological Review Monograph, pp. 32–55, Oxford: Blackwell.

Law, J., (1998), After Meta-Narrative: on Knowing in Tension. In Robert Chia (ed.), *Into the Realm of Organisation: Essays for Robert Cooper*, pp. 88–108, London: Routledge.

Law, J., (2004), *After Method: Mess in social science research*, London: Routledge.

Lawrence, T. E., (1997), *The Seven Pillars of Wisdom*, Hertfordshire: Wordsworth Editions.

Lombroso, C., (1895), *L'Homme Criminel*, Felix: Alcan. (two volumes).

Mol, A-M., (2002), *The Body Multiple: Ontology in Medical Practice*, Durham, North Carolina: Duke University Press.

Munro, R., (1996), The Consumption View of Self: Extension, Exchange and Identity. In S. Edgell, K. Hetherington and A. Warde (eds), *Consumption Matters*, Sociological Review Monograph, pp. 248–273, Oxford: Blackwell Publisher.

Nietzsche, F., (1878), *Human All too Human. A Book for Free Spirits*, 11: 35–70. (Friedrich Nietzsche Menschliches, Allzumenschliches I II. Zur Geschichte der moralischen Empfindungen 35–70) http://www.textlog.de/21634.html accessed May 2008.

Probyns, E., (1996), *Outside Belongings*, New York: Routledge.

Parsons, T., (1951), *The Social System*, New York: Free Press.

Skeggs, B., (2004), *Class, Self, Culture*, London: Routledge.

Strathern, M., (1988), *The Gender of the Gift*, Berkley, CA: University of California Press.

Strathern, M., (1991), *Partial Connections*, Maryland, USA: Rowman and Littlefield Publishers Inc.

Strathern, M., (1992a), *After Nature: English Kinship in the Late Twentieth Century*, Cambridge: Cambridge University Press.

Strathern, M., (1992b), Parts and wholes: Refiguring relationships in a postplural world. In A. Kuper (ed.), *Conceptualising Society*, London: Routledge.

Strathern, M., (1995), *The Relation*, Cambridge: Prickley Pear Press.

Strathern, M., (2004), *Commons and Borderlands: Working Papers on Interdisciplinarity, Accountability and the Flow of Knowledge*, Wantage: Sean Kingston Publishing.

Tate Modern 2005 http://www.tate.org.uk/modern/exhibitions/kahlo/roomguide.shtm

Young, R., (1966), The Divided Science, reprinted from *Delta* No. 38, Spring 1966: 13–18. http://www.human-nature.com/rmyoung/papers/paper72h.html

Zwirner and Wirth, (2003/4), Assemblage. http://www.zwirnerandwirth.com/exhibitions/2003/1103Assemblage/press.html

Bodily chiasms[1]

Hugo Letiche

Preamble

The theory of the body I want to explore here, assumes that researcher and researched are part of the same flesh of the world and can be understood in radical conjunction and not in duality. An interview is examined, first from the lifeworld (nursing) research paradigm and thereafter on the hand of Merleau-Ponty's concept of the reversibility of touching and being touched, wherein 'subject' (who touches) and 'object' (who is touched) are radically interrelated and co-constituted. Merleau-Ponty develops his reflections on this radical interaction as the 'chiasm'.

Although investigating the 'chiasm' can be seen as lifeworld research, the more common lifeworld approach only leads to rich description, which lacks the radical relational understanding of Merleau-Ponty's insights. I believe that acknowledgement of the chiasms of interrelationship reveals complex processes of enfoldment taking place between researcher and researched, writer and reader. All of them are enclosed in what Merleau-Ponty called the enfoldments or flesh of the world; which makes it very difficult to determine who touches whom and who is touched by whom. Research, when it tries to see, interpret and study the other, focuses on the visible of touching and being touched; but these inherently carry with them the invisible of the same actions. The consequences of these relationships for my study of a specific elderly woman are explored here.

Introduction

Healthcare organization does not seem to know how to 'care'. For instance, healthcare organizations for the elderly meet, better or worse, the basic instrumental needs of feeding, cleansing and clothing those they 'care' for, while the expressive, existential and lifeworld needs of the 'cared-for' are largely ignored. The needs of 'care' are largely worked into the abject. Care has to address mortality, physical existence, and the body itself. But 'healthcare' mostly hides, marginalizes and represses the elements of the body such as blood and excrement or urine, which transgress cleanliness or threaten propriety. Being forced to face the sick, maimed, dismembered or rejected body is traumatic – it threatens the 'subject' (Kristeva, 1982). 'Care' if existentially attuned to the needs of the cared-for, has to address the 'no longer being the same subject' of the abject. The non-care that abjects the abject, or represses the space of the abject, is characterized by the existential refusal of the problems of the cared-for. Such non-care demands a robust alternative to the abjection of care.[2]

The philosophical and ethical work involved in developing an existential concept of 'care' evokes a vast oeuvre.[3] Examining the research of 'care' specifically in healthcare includes, as a beginning, Arthur Kleinman and Arthur Frank (Kleinman, 1989; Frank, 2002). Research methodological themes include (auto-)ethnography, storytelling and narrativity – that is, at least Carolyn Ellis, David Boje and Yannis Gabriel (Ellis, 2004; Boje, 2001; Gabriel, 2000). Obviously, all this terrain could never be covered carefully enough in a few pages. Therefore I pick one assertion and focus on that and its implications.

The one assertion is that in care, body (materiality) and self (consciousness) *fold in double envelopment*, crossing into one another. This claim distances me from the objectivist or behavioral approaches. If bodies and selves are enfolded in mutual co-construction, then there is no researcher (subject), who is outside the relationship from the researched (object), and there is no consciousness (subjectivity) outside of bodily materiality (objectivity). Objectification of the mind/body relationship will not grant insight into the particular event or experience of self and other, or body and consciousness. There is a long phenomenological tradition of researching body and self, or care and otherness in nursing studies. But my assertion, drawn from the late Merleau-Ponty, handles self/other and flesh/relatedness, in a different way from that tradition.

In the mid 20th century, (phenomenological) existential psychology tried to elucidate the fundamental existential qualities of the client or other. For instance, efforts were made to work out the Heideggerian concept of *Dasein* or the throwness of being-in-the-world in terms of descriptive experiential categories. These efforts focused on making aspects or dimensions of human presence visible. At best, they led to an anthropology of existence; but their implicit theory of the social, by stressing the uniqueness or unicity of individual existence, did not match the *Zeitgeist*. Existential psychology was neither utilitarian nor led to a single theory, for instance of behaviour or of society. The emphasis on existential autonomy, severely problematized the role of the therapist – who is the therapist to make existential choices for the client by, in effect, trying to knead the being of anOther?[4] In addition, the individualizing effect of studying forms of lived-existence, or of being, raised issues of the role of the social. If one begins to study existence with the individual, one gets locked into that abstraction or aggregation level and is never really able to re-access the social, collective or political levels. All of these issues beset (phenomenological) existential psychology. What was a relatively small stream of study in psychology became only all the more marginalized.

As Michael Crotty (1996) has asserted, there is a form of 'new American phenomenology' in nursing studies, making use of the tradition of existential psychology, which espouses naïve assumptions of individual self-aware autonomy. This research proposes an unsophisticated exercise in empathy and involvement, locking the researcher and researched into common-sense assumptions and perspectives. The research is focused as close to everyday practice as is possible, confirming the 'natural attitude' as the point of departure. This entails engagement in everyday activity without questioning the norms, power relations, values and assumptions of practice. Husserl's intent was to separate unreflected upon daily existence from rigorously examined action (Husserl, 1970). Crotty asserts (admittedly very polemically) that the 'new American phenomenology' has in effect betrayed the central purpose of phenomenology.

David Silverman has attacked lifeworld approaches to research as a Romantic perversion (Gubrium and Silverman, 1989; Atkinson and Silverman, 1997). Silverman believes that we are living in the 'interview society' wherein repeated displays of (pseudo-)self are all too common. Research as confessional pretends to authenticity while it merely repeats stereotyped social conventions. Silverman sees that research that tries to get close to the text of the other betrays the agenda of classical social science. Marx, Freud, Weber and Durkheim all claimed that naïve direct perception reveals less than does theory-driven analysis. Currently, everything from deconstruction to lifeworld research, from postmodernism to autoethnography, questions this. Silverman is right when he claims that the repetition of the text of the researched, with the researcher denying her or his role in evoking, editing and (re-)presenting that text, is very sloppy work indeed. But Silverman's tirades against the contemporary (neo-) or (post-) Romantic embrace of self, identity and authenticity as key values, are themselves merely tendentious polemics. Valuing the self may be controversial, but it demands serious, careful philosophical inspection. For my part, I accept Silverman's call for methodological care, but remain open to (neo-) or (post-) Romantic inspiration.

Even well-respected research tends to study the researched through a phenomenological or lifeworld perspective, but without problematicizing the researcher reflexivity or perception. The researcher, in effect, assumes an objectivist stance. For instance, Eileen Jones Porter shows sophistication in her studies of widows, but seems oblivious to her own role (Porter, 1995). Or Jan Savage, in her reflection on participant observation, is obviously well-informed and reports sensitively on her own self-reflexivity as (non-)nurse, but without revealing much of anything about her patients (Savage, 2000). Likewise, Jocalyn Lawler is sensitive to epistemological/methodological issues, but stays one-sidedly nurse directed (Lawler, 1991, 1998). The researchers focus either almost solely on the researched or almost entirely on themselves, but (radical) relatedness is not achieved.

Hugh Silverman (1984, 1987) offers a way out of the excessively dualist categories of the researched versus researcher, or the descriptive versus hermeneutic, or the 'interview culture' versus critical social science, or 'humanist psychology' versus bracketing the 'natural attitude'. Descriptive phenomenology, inspired by Husserl, has as its ambition the 'return to things as they are' – ie it is focused on knowing what is researched. Hermeneutic phenomenology focuses on the researcher's assumptions and on the pre-structures of knowledge. Hugh Silverman suggests developing the *in-between* of the researched and researcher, the assumed and the studied, the hermeneutic and the descriptive. At issue is the self or identity of the researcher and the researched. Research neither affirms nor denies self – self develops between consciousness and other, circumstance and awareness, possibility and system.

In effect, micro-histories of self, where one focuses on interaction, relationship and co-existence, are my subject matter. Studying relatedness or doing research from a self-related and self-relating perspective is, epistemologically, very difficult. How does one write about and account for one's own presence, at the same time? This amounts to an effort to touch and be touched both at once, which Merleau-Ponty saw as, at least, very problematic if not almost impossible. In a research of relatedness, the nature and quality of relationships is crucial. In such an enterprise, Ricoeur has asserted that forgiveness, doing justice to the other and the ethics of relationship, have to dominate (Ricoeur, 2004). These are the sort of criteria that play a central role in my investigation.

Concretely, my effort to come to terms with an interview with a woman who had a stroke, forms the backbone of the text to follow. I (so-called) 'know' that there has been brain damage. Therefore, I supposedly can describe her (knowing the nature of her brain damage) as someone who can no longer (adequately) construct and maintain relationship(s). Her ability to do the social, as it is normally done, supposedly has become impaired. I can describe her as someone where person and world touch one another in a way that (many) potential affordances do not operate, while a few seem to overwhelm the rest (Burkitt, 2003). For her, the social and physical environment supposedly offers fewer possibilities (affordances) than they offer someone who has not had a stroke. But all of this assumes objectification – that is, that the other really is an object of science. If we bracket such 'knowing' and engage with the interviewee, then we must wonder what circumstances really do or do not invite her to do, or how persons or objects call her into action, or what any of this means for me as researcher.

At this stage, I must address the famous turn to language in social science – is the interview just a social semiological construct? Am I only studying so many textual cultural artifacts? Merleau-Ponty's claim of *body and self folded in double envelopment* invalidates, I believe a language-based constitutive approach to lifeworld, as is asserted in much social constructivism (McNamee and Gergen, 1999; Shotter, 1993). I see two obvious ways to interpret the interview: (i) social constructivist and (ii) phenomenal / bodily. The social constructivist description would focus on 'doing the social' as a series of subject/object constructs wherein self, world and meaning are created via linguistic articulation and interpretation. Persons represent and share 'world', while 'world' is posited to be a communicative artifact.

To research such an assumption, I would need to focus on discourse or conversation to see how the interviewee constructs self/world, subject/object, I/

other, relationships and identities. I would, for instance, focus on how the interviewee has evidently partially lost her ability to participate in the standard, socially necessary, constitutive process of dialogue. It could be assumed that her brain damage impairs her ability to successfully 'do' speaking and listening, looking and defining, declaring and doing. While her physical abilities to speak and listen are intact, she has, it seems, (in part) lost the ability to place herself (pro-)actively into the spoken or texted world. She hears the words but does not join into the social praxis or activities that the verbal world normally demands. She can speak and listen, but the processes do not lead to consensus, agreement and relationship. Languaging, for her, is not a means of joining-in, taking-part or doing-what-she-wants-to-do. The link between languaging and intentionality has been weakened. She speaks as an observer and a rebel, but not as a social participant. Examples of the interviewee's way of 'doing' the social will come, in the later sections of this writing. Her languaging just does not seem to achieve a socially shared world with and for her. Studied semiologically, she comes to be defined as a *lack* – ie as a lack of successful social construction and languaged intentionality. But I find such a social semiology very one-sided; it focuses on the social production of the signs of the researched, to the exclusion of everything else. What about the researcher? What about the lack of materiality or the hyle of relationship?

My investigation will be grounded in a 'what is' – namely an interview of an hour with a woman of seventy-four, called here Hendriënne.[5] My point of departure is lifeworld investigation and not existential phenomenology. The originatory task is to see or perceive the other, not to reflect upon or connect to the being or Being of the other. The task is decidedly ontic – ie grounded in the lived world of human existence. It has the ambition to be phenomenologically rigorous – ie. not to repeat commonplaces or to reproduce the 'natural attitude', but to be radically perceptually observant of the other. Because the point of departure is seeing or perceiving the other, an interview is used which was not done by the writer. The interviewer and the interviewed are well known to me but I am not out to investigate my existential social relatedness or shared being (or Being) with them. I want to see or perceive the lifeworld of the interviewed. Humanist empathy or psychological intimacy are not my goals. I will begin the encounter with the woman interviewed with a phenomenological lifeworld investigation, and then I will radicalize the investigation by turning in earnest to Merleau-Ponty's concept of chiasm. For Merleau-Ponty, perception, awareness and consciousness are made up of the same flesh of and as the world (Merleau-Ponty, 1968). Body and knowing enfold one another in their common flesh. My task is to make these as yet cryptic assertions clear and convincing and to explore their implications.

Viewing and re-viewing the (CD of the) interview, I have noted that Hendriënne seems to remember many things, but attaches little or no intentionality to her memories. She recounts short often quite dramatic incidents, but as if there were no links either between the incidents themselves, or between the incidents and herself. Everything appears to be on the 'outside' and apparently there is no link to the 'inside'. 'World' is a given without intentional import. But are the concepts I am now using to observe Hendriënne in this way adequate? Contrastingly, we can try to understand Hendriënne as a series of foldings:

> There is, for Merleau-Ponty, a single Being. Our world is of that Being, and we are of our world. We are not something that confronts the world from outside, but are born into it and do not leave it. This does not mean that we cannot remove ourselves from the immediacy of its grasp. What it does mean is that to remove ourselves from that immediacy is neither the breaking of a bond nor the discovery of an original dichotomy or dualism. What is remarkable about human beings is precisely our capacity to confront the world . . . while still being a piece of it.
>
> To grasp this remarkable character, it is perhaps worth recalling Gilles Deleuze's concept of the fold. The world is not composed of different parts; there is no transcendent . . . the world is one . . . being is univocal. This oneness is not, however, inert or inanimate. Among other things, it can fold over on itself, creating spaces that are at once insides and outsides, at once different from the continuous and with one another. (May, 2005: 522)

Late in his career, Merleau-Ponty focused very much on the 'flesh' of being/ Being – or the being of 'to be' or the ontic quality of 'being' (Merleau-Ponty, 1968). He argued that the right hand that grasps the left hand is alternately the perceived and the unperceived term. Perceiving has to be unperceived to perceive. If perceiving perceives itself, it stops to see almost anything else. The self that perceives is always at a distance from whatever it perceives. *Chiasm* is the term Merleau-Ponty used to name this the principle of the alternation, or the two-sidedness, of relatedness. One is both perceived and perceiver, body and world. But if the subject is both sides to the duality, the subject can at the same time be neither. If I am self and other, I am not really self or other at all. I am relatedness or in-between. Relatedness or interaction creates radical ambiguity in identity. Normally we divide subject and object, self and other, researcher and researched into mutually opposed categories, and then we allow them to 'communicate' or 'interact'. Presupposed division operates as a hidden assumption to what is foregrounded. Only because we have committed the act of division is the so-called act of relationship possible. Merleau-Ponty tried to find a form of relatedness that is not merely an artifact of the subject's own assumptions.

Can I perceive Hendriënne and myself as situated embodied consciousness? How can I manage the dialectic of the seen and the seer? Her 'worlding of the world' is, for me, adumbrated. Who she 'is' is sketchy; what I see is partial. How she – that is, her body and language, perception and action – makes meaning seems to be a different 'self/world' from the one I am used to. I need to investigate her expressional action to see what poetry – that is, what tone of feeling, sentiment and affect – her 'being' contains (Balazic, 2003). Hendriënne's way of inhabiting immanence may not be 'average', but that does not make it any less a thematization of being, which is legitimately open to study.

Firstly, I will attempt a rather traditional phenomenological interpretation of the Hendriënne interview. The descriptive text will familiarize the reader with the interview material, without yet engaging in the specific theoretical assertion(s) I wish to make. Secondly, I will attempt the phenomenal bodily interpretation of the flesh of Hendriënne's world. The chiasms between body and expression, self and other, perception and awareness, will then be explored. I will try to demonstrate the attention to the being of being and/or of Being, that really is needed for me to appreciate Hendriënne's enfolding and embodiedness.

Hendriënne's *lifeworld*

In the study of 'care' in healthcare, the (post-)phenomenological focus on individual forms of existence has found a current niche. As already noted, Crotty (pretty much rightly) has accused some of the 'new phenomenology' of rather naively assuming the freedom, individuality and autonomy of the subject. But the work I respond to here is much more careful than that. For Crotty is, I believe, on the right side of the methodological divide. This work is phenomenological, in the sense that it tries to 'see' or to 'perceive' the other. It is not an invitation to the undisciplined or associative outing of researchers' or carers' feelings or sentiments. Quite the opposite, it strives to achieve an ethically self-aware careful description of the other's lifeworld. Theory is used to set an agenda of lifeworld themes that deserve to be examined. I now propose, with this healthcare lifeworld tradition, to familiarize ourselves with Hendriënne.

Leslie Todres has worked in health and nursing studies in a (neo-) phenomenological tradition of lifeworld analysis. The categories he uses to study the lifeworld are:

- How the human body occurs,
- How the co-constituting of temporal structures of past, present and future occur,
- How human mood or feeling pervades and partially organizes experience,
- How human spatiality occurs wherein things have a 'place' of distance, nearness and relevance to self, others and other things, and
- How the quality of interpersonal relations occur: presence and absence, active or passive. (adapted from Todres, 2001)

Thus he calls for the examination of embodiment, temporality, mood or emotional attunement, spatiality and intersubjectivity (Todres and Wheeler, 2001; Todres *et al.*, 2007). In effect, Peter Ashworth's phenomenological description of the lifeworld, repeats the same categories and adds selfhood, project and discourse (Ashworth, 2006). Making use of these lifeworld categorization(s), I now do the first description of Hendriënne.

Embodiment

Hendriënne is carefully and conservatively well dressed. Her hair is tastefully cut and coloured. She is not explicitly feminine in her movements, humour or self-presentation. The female interviewer appeals to her sense of sisterhood at one point in the interview, but Hendriënne does not react to this appeal. Likewise, the interviewer gives her a kiss on the cheek towards the end and Hendriënne again gives no response. She does not reciprocate nor does she withdraw. She does nothing, as if the appeal to physical bonding or emotionality had not touched her. Hendriënne expresses herself bodily primarily through a box of Camel cigarettes that she turns repeatedly in her right hand. With her hands, she is very nervous – repeatedly hitting the box of Camels with her left index finger, then turning the box round and round and hitting it on the table in front of her with her right hand. She also sharply taps the fingers of her right hand on the table. At the same time, her voice is measured, totally in control, reserved, and very professional – she is a retired bookkeeper. It is almost as if her hands and her voice come from two separate embodiments.

Temporality

Hendriënne's sense of time seems to be cyclical. She begins with a story of having thrown at least twenty eggs at another resident of the same apartment building for the elderly. Hendriënne was angry because the other woman supposedly had told stories about her, which were not true. Later in the interview, Hendriënne tells that she had been accused of throwing a flowerpot from the second floor, down at another resident on the street level – it is left somewhat in the middle if it is a true allegation or not. Hendriënne repeatedly reports having shouted 'Debilitated, imbecile, idiot' at different fellow residents. When talking about such shouting, her eyes light up and a hidden joy can be perceived. In general, her muted expressivity makes such tirades hard to imagine. But late in the interview, she reveals that her father was on the wrong (Nazi-German) side in the war and the theme of treachery returns. All her reported anger at other elderly residents is directed at disloyalty, deceitfulness and not being trustworthy. But at the end of the interview, she clarifies that her oldest sister had been a Muf whore (a woman who had sex with German soldiers during the occupation). Her father had been unreliable. She's had no contact with her five brothers for years. When her mother was going demented during the 1990s, she was the only of the ten children who visited regularly. She describes three situations – one now in the home for the elderly; one ten years ago when she alone of the children visited her mother; and one during the Second World War. Each of the three situations centres on being, or not being, loyal. She voices her anger most strongly over disloyalty in the present, where the issues of trust are actually the least powerful. Each time, narratives of trust and betrayal and of being together and alone are re-told.

Mood-as-atmosphere

Hendriënne's mood is one of (dis-)loyalty. She tells how for several years after work, she took the train everyday to visit her mother, who was in her nineties and demented. She reports that she laughed a lot on the train and often enjoyed a few drinks at the bar (pub) in the retirement home after seeing her mother. Apparently she gave herself permission to enjoy herself after having repeated the ritual of visiting her demented mother. Hendriënne voices no frustration or aggression towards her mother, casting herself as the perfect caregiver. She complains that now she is never asked to take part in any social goings-on. In the centre for the elderly there are all sorts of activities and possibilities; such as little trips. Hendriënne complains that she is never invited to join in. She very obviously feels socially isolated and sorry for herself. She moans, for example, that the new director of the choir does not like her and that she therefore does not sing anymore. The interviewer is a bit startled: 'But I saw you today at the choir practice!' Response: 'I did not sing.' Interviewer: 'Well let us say you did not put your heart into it.' She evidently had taken part in the choir practice. The sense of isolation, loneliness and rejection, is very powerful, whatever the daily social routine actually is.

Spatiality

Hendriënne perceives the apartment building for the elderly as an enclosure – she rarely goes out. The building is designed to bring the normal world inside and for the residents to move outwards into the surrounding neighborhood, as much as they can. Hendriënne has no desire to move, either outwards or inwards. For her, space is stable, continuous and closed. Other cities and places are outside of her world – part of an otherness in which she is no longer engaged. The space defined by the apartment complex, seems for her to be characterized by the residents who gossip and more often than not, malign one another. There is also the Director, to whom everyone complains about experienced injustices. In Hendriënne's account, the Director sounds like a father with a troupe of misbehaving children. Hendriënne does not seem to have strong feelings about her own apartment. She never voices a sense of abode or of individual spatial belonging. The interviewer tries to get her to attach a sense of 'houseliness' to her own furniture and things – that is to define a personal sense of place, but Hendriënne refuses. The only living space she acknowledges is the apartment centre's bar (pub) and restaurant, where social interaction occurs.

Sociability

Hendriënne always reports relations as if they were a bit scandalous. One man who lives in the apartments, she reports, watches in the restaurant for half eaten dinners and then appropriates them whenever possible to eat them up. Relationship is constantly her theme. She is always talking about what the one person has to do with the other, and often what they have to do with her. But her stories are always about matters being off- or out of- balance. As in her story about a nurse who tried to arrange a cat for Hendriënne, but the cat turned out to be a stray that was terrified by the apartment building and by people in general. The animal ambulance had to be called to take it away; but the ambulance personnel were also afraid of the cat, which hissed violently from under the coffee table. Hendriënne lost her patience, snatched up the cat, gave it a slap on its nose and presented it to the animal ambulance driver. On the one hand, Hendriënne speaks quietly and in a very disciplined manner; on the other her stories form a theatre of the absurd. Her tone of voice and manner do not match her content.

Selfhood

Hendriënne feels rejected and unaccepted. She repeats over and over how loyal she had been by repeatedly visiting her mother when no other family member did so. But she has no contact anymore with any of her nine brothers and sisters. The interviewer invites Hendriënne at least four times during the interview to help distribute coupons for free drinks at an occasion planned for the following week. Each time Hendriënne acts as if she has not heard the invitation and repeats that she does not know if she will have a role to play or will be invited to do something. Hendriënne speaks as if she is the victim of sociability, never the originator. In her text, she observes and judges, but she does not take the initiative. She is very social in the sense that relationships and betrayals are the stuff of her existence. But she is not at all social, in the sense that she has no sense of participating with others in anything bigger than immediate moments of chance interaction.

Project (or goals in life)

Hendriënne is not committed to anything outside of her immediacy. She does watch television but does not read. She has no children and no (contact with) her family. Since her mother died, she is alone. She used to water the flowers in the apartment's atrium and clean up the tables. She says that she is no longer asked to do these things. From the past, she reports that her father sometimes hit her mother and that she had intervened and threatened to hit him back if he continued. But this solidarity does not seem to have led to feminism or any broader form of commitment. If Hendriënne had ever had any more wide-ranging sense of purpose, it was not voiced in the interview. She had never been religious and makes no mention of politics. Gossip and deception appear to define the horizon of her social existence.

Discourse

In Hendriënne's speech, there is almost no cause and effect. Either she is not interested in why things happen, or she does not observe their causality. People constantly do things, but it never seems to enter her mind to understand why they do what they do. Speech is not linked to speech acts, other than as swearing at one another. She does not talk about mutual comprehension, dialogue or understanding. People scold and swear at one another – they gossip and talk behind each other's backs. There's no sense of kindness, tenderness, or care in the speech that she reports. What is said, supposedly, is not very socially uplifting or constructive. With words, people in her world seemingly constitute relations that are stereotyped – as if determined by fixed characters. Relationships are dynamic in the sense that there are conflicts, but not in the sense that there is growth, development or change. Language has little or no agency – people in Hendriënne's text are not moved by text, do not change via what is said and are not deeply touched by others. The compassion of speaking is overwhelmed by the *commedia dell'arte* of all the minor disputes, jealousies and rivalries.

The fold, chiasms and flesh of the world

While this rendition of the interview material is not downright 'wrong', it is, I believe, also not really 'right'. I have objectified Hendriënne; she is described more as an existential entity than as a dynamic set of processes. This is in part because of the nature of the interview. Hendriënne was in a research situation where the pre-assumed roles were clear: the interviewer asked the questions and Hendriënne answered them. But however hard she tried, the interviewer could not engage Hendriënne in a real conversation. Hendriënne was not open to any such interaction. Hendriënne actually, subtly, had total control of the situation. She combined apparent verbal passivity and a constant threatening nonverbal tension, by tapping her fingers and playing with the pack of cigarettes to create continuous ambiguity. Likewise, she spoke quietly in a reserved manner and was very controlled, while celebrating swearing, throwing things and other forms of (thinly disguised) aggression. She assumed the explicit role of victim and the implicit role of the executioner. The paradoxes of her self-positioning and the way that she hid behind her text, only to re-emerge when least expected, were all more or less lost in the lifeworld description. Lifeworld research focuses on being – that is, on who the person studied *is*. But this existential focus is grounded in an assumption or pre-structure where in the study of individual *being* is thought to be the most revelatory or appropriate approach to the study of the other.

I want to argue that the implicit rejection of *non-being* and prioritization of *being*, actually destroys the radical relatedness of emergent processes and imprisons the analysis in unproductive dualities. In existential phenomenology, it is the shadow of non-being in each assertion of being that makes Being important. The conflict between non-Being and Being, inauthenticity and authenticity, aliveness and anxiety (for death) is really the motor of the analysis. The Subject only exists foregrounded to the background of the Object. The Self exists juxtaposed to the Other. Mind exists as a negation of (mere) Body. In the description, Hendriënne existed as not-the-interviewer, not-the-researcher and not-the-reader. The more that she was isolated from others, the more 'identity' she gained. But the research process made her into a 'freak' – ie someone unique, exceptional and very-Other.

The current lifeworld paradigm for healthcare research illustrates the problems to which I wish to point. Key terms of analysis for lifeworld research in healthcare have been defined as: openness, encounter, immediacy, uniqueness and meaning (Dahlberg and Drew, 1997; Dahlberg *et al.*, 2001). While 'openness' sounds like a fundamentally humanizing value; there is a snake in the grass. Who is open to whom? If the researcher, as is assumed in much of the literature, is being told to be (more) open to the researched, we are merely trying to manipulate the shutters on a very traditional construction. Supposedly researchers look, and the researched are looked at. Researchers are called upon to allow 'what is' to appear to them. More humanist approaches add openheartedness to the call for open-mindedness. Methodologists call for 'genuine insight' via 'true and open questioning', into the experiences of the researched. The construction of self/other relationships supposedly revolves around a sort of 'openness', which is intended to arrive at matters 'as they really are'. The researcher is called upon to enter the world of the researched. Thus the researcher is portrayed as receptive and blank and in effect is defined as pure openness. And the researched is pure closedness or object.

The other qualities of lifeworld research – encounter, immediacy, uniqueness and meaning, go in the same direction. The researcher is called upon to be ethically concerned with the being of the researched. The researcher is to be present with intense immediacy, in order to achieve disclosure from the researched. Uniqueness refers to identifying, the specific unicity or uniqueness of the other who is researched. Meaning supposedly results from research wherein observation is free from pre-assumptions, allowing the essence of the other and her/his circumstances to be researched. Such a concept of meaning is obviously hermeneutically naïve and shows a lack of critical self-reflexivity, just as Crotty criticized. Such research probably does more justice to the researched than traditional positivist or rationalist research does, but it is deeply dualist, assuming a researching subject who existentially examines an object of investigation. All the attention to empathy and openness only serve to define the researcher all the more as Subject, and thereby paradoxically to confirm the researched as Object.

The theory of the body I want to explore here assumes that researcher and researched are part of the same flesh of the world and need to be understood in radical conjunction and not in duality. My assertions will be inspired by Merleau-Ponty's *The Visible and Invisible*, thus by a landmark text of phenomenology, but a text which I believe the lifeworld movement, for instance in nursing studies, has insufficiently cited or applied (Merleau-Ponty, 1968). For Merleau-Ponty, the perceiving body:

. . . is made of the same flesh as the world (it is a perceived), and moreover that this flesh of my body is shared by the world, the world reflects it, encroaches upon it and it encroaches upon the world . . . This means a sort of reflectedness, it thereby constitutes itself *in itself* – In a parallel way; it touches *itself*, sees *itself*. And consequentially it is capable of *touching* or *seeing* something, that is, of being open to things in which it reads its own modifications. (Merleau-Ponty, 1968: 248–249)

Openness has here a very different connotation; it is a principle at once of sameness and dissimilarity, of difference and repetition. In difference, there is inherently repetition – difference is a form of comparison between the one rendering and the other. If there is no repetition, there is no comparison and, thus, neither sameness nor difference. For there to be repetition, there has to be difference. In total sameness, there is only oneness or holism; repetition requires a first, a second, a third . . . – that is an element of difference that makes the distinction between various instances perceptible. Likewise, sameness and dissimilarity are intertwined concepts, where the one implies dimensions of the other. The necessary commonality of relationship, wherein terms touch and support one another, is called the *flesh of the world* by Merleau-Ponty. There is difference but continuity and identity as well, which are not one another's logical opponents but form complementary components of a singular being.

In terms of Hendriënne, she is constantly creating relationships by denying them. She relates to her surroundings via the denial of belonging. She is present to others as a refusal to join, merge, identify or fit in. She touches us who watch the CD of the interview with her stubbornness, inflexible attitude and denial of some deeper hurt. Supposedly, her feelings centre on being asked to water the flowers or to clean off the tables; but the flashes of emotional lightening that she periodically emits imply a frustration, anger and savagery, which most of the time is not really accounted for. She is constantly (at least partially) self-referential in how she drums her fingers on the table. She seems totally oblivious as to whether the interviewer sees or hears her pound her finger tips on the table. It does not seem to be a gesture that is meant to be seen or heard by anOther, but a way of feeling contact with herself and her own body. She is feeling something with her fingers and hitting at something with them. In effect, she is constantly feeling and attacking, sensitive and aggressive, relating to the other and pushing the other away. And the paradoxes remain unaddressed and unresolved. She *is* visible and invisible:

> The human body is the sensible become reflexive, the flesh folding back on itself: the visible that sees itself, the tangible that touches and can touch itself, and the audible that can hear and hear itself. . . . this chiasm or reversibility of the seeing and the visible, the touching and the touched, is always imminent . . . (Burkitt, 2003: 328–9)

Hendriënne remains imminent: that is, almost present, or on the verge of arriving, or nearly at hand. She seems preoccupied, not yet quite arrived, never entirely present throughout the interview. She sits the whole time in the same chair but gazes about in the air several times, as if not entirely sure where she is. In the interview, she never gives explicitly of herself. You are never quite sure exactly how, or if, she is or is not present. Her presence is deeply ambiguous and unresolved. The interviewer struggles to make Hendriënne construct presence – that is, to stage an 'I am here' and 'This is what I have to say' and Hendriënne refuses. When the interviewer gets too intrusive or close to her, Hendriënne lights up a cigarette that she snuffs out as soon as the danger of being cornered is past. She does not actually smoke the cigarettes, so much as flees into lighting them, when asked to perform a 'self' that she does not want to perform. She lights up many cigarettes but actually smokes none of them. A whole collection of less than half smoked cigarettes piles up in the ashtray. As soon as she feels safe, and no direct question is being addressed to her, she puts out the cigarette.

The chiasm is the crossing over of the touching and the touched, the seen and the see-er. The hand that touches is reversible and can become the hand that is touched. The sentient (actor) who looks is invisible, and the sensible or the looked at, is visible (Crossley, 1995). Throughout the interview, Hendriënne struggles against acknowledging or dealing with the invisible. She does not want to be part of a see-er / seen relationship. She wants her visibility, as her own perspective, without having to enjoin the invisible other's (interviewer's) gaze. But, is her limited, personal, idiosyncratic view of life, or being, 'true'? If it is inadequate, what is it inadequate in relationship to? Hendriënne's stories of swearing matches with fellow residents seem awfully juvenile for a woman of seventy-four. Her constant criticism of everyone she meets sounds misanthropic. From other observations, I know that her way of talking during the interview was characteristic of her speech.

Do I make an assumption about how she ought to be that has the right to overrule how she actually appears? Do we accept the primacy of the visible – that is, Hendriënne without a thoughtful 'self' or a reflexive project, or any real attachment to 'wisdom'? Do we accept the flesh of divergence, wherein our expectations inter-relate with her claims and our attempt to find meaning in the interview conflicts with her self-negating anger? She is visible but only visible because the interviewer and I as researcher are the invisible that see her. If one reverses the situation and we become the seen or visible and Hendriënne the observer; all that happens is that the visible and invisible change positions. The structure of visible and invisible stays the same. Merleau-Ponty's basic metaphor for visible and invisible is that of touching and being touched:

> When I touch my right hand with my left hand, the object right hand has the singular property of also sensing itself. Yet the two hands are never with regard to one another, touched and touching at the same time. When I press my two hands against one another, it is not then a matter of two sensations that I would feel together, as one perceives two objects in juxtaposition, but that of an ambiguous organization in which the two hands can alternate in the function of 'touching' and touched' (PP 93/109)

What Merleau-Ponty describes in this passage as alteration, he will later (in The Visible and the Invisible) describe as reversibility . . . he denies, both (a) that the touching and being touched are radically disjunct and (b) that they are simultaneous or coincident. He (argues) instead that there is an essential ambiguity, an alternation or reversibility in which the touched hand feels itself touching and vice versa. (Dillon, 1983: 369)

I can coincide neither with Hendriënne nor with her interviewer, nor can the reader coincide with Hendriënne or with me. Difference, distance, discontinuity and ambiguity pursue us all. In so far as there is identity, it is identity of the in-between, or within-difference, but without rupture or total disjunction. Our relationship to Hendriënne feels as if it is not good enough. Her immanence seems partial, incomplete and disjointed. She does not self-evidently unfold or open up in our presence. However, if we, as the invisible see-er, and she, as the visible seen, reciprocate one another – ie are alternately the touching and the touched, then we seem to be implicated in something incomplete, partial and unfulfilled. Merleau-Ponty's metaphor for such a relationship is that of flesh to flesh, on the model of one hand touching the other. Merleau-Ponty's 'flesh of the world' is the in-between where visible and invisible, sentient and sensible, touched and touching meet. There is incompletion, doubt and no closure between the one and the other. And there is the folding of the same on the same, and of the different on the different, and of the same on the different – that is, of flesh on flesh. Hendriënne is something sensible for me, but what sort of sentient am I, when studying her? In the interview she is visible to me, but what sort of invisible do I form when I am trying to see or perceive her? As already stated, I am not trying to study an existential relationship between the researched and the researcher, but I am trying to understand the act(s) of perception in studying the sensible.

The relation of body to world in Merleau-Ponty's *The Visible and the Invisible*, is a relationship of flesh to flesh, wherein there are no breaches but manifold folds. And this all occurs on a pre-individual or (pre-) I-centred level. There is a difference between 'me' shaking your hand and either of us touching our own hands. Between any two of us, there can be intertwining and (en-)folding, but not identity. Between Hendriënne and me, the relationship is not symmetrical. I have watched the CD of the interview many times; she has only occasionally met me. The structure of our relationship is very partial and incomplete. But all perception involves multiple levels flesh. Between Hendriënne and me there is, as always, flesh touching-seeing-feeling itself. And there is on an enormous number of different levels flesh in touch with flesh. Perception involves multiple series of relationships flesh – in this case, within myself and between myself and Hendriënne. I perceptually am enfolded in the flesh of myself, and in that of the relationship with her. But what does awareness of this pre-reflective connectedness contribute to understanding? It does imply that 'we are both flesh of a unitary world and not monadological transcendental egos each constituting a world of his {her} own in which he {she} reigns supreme as original creator and final judge of truth and value,' which is qua research methodology and epistemology a crucial assertion (Dillon, 1983: 381). But what difference does an epistemology of flesh of a unitary world, concretely make to my research perception?

In effect, we cannot take distance from Hendriënne as easily as I have tried to do. She asserts disjunction and disconnectedness, relationship as alienation and bonding as separation. She dominates the interaction and the interview by denying the possibility of shared relations. She is, in her words, as she is with her fingers, very obviously, constantly feeling, touching, hitting and recoiling. Focusing on the feeling of her touching, she is uninterested in the table or box as such. Her folds are self-enclosed, shutting out the other. But I as observer, what do I do about being folded out of the interaction? The interviewer kept trying to get readmitted to Hendriënne's perceptual fold, but to no avail. Should we just accept exclusion; should we protest, get angry, or insist? Hendriënne told us that she constantly evokes those reactions; they just feed into her mechanisms of closure and (self-)rejection.

Hendriënne denies the reciprocal relationship with anOther of touching and being touched, of speaking and being understood, of speaker and listener. She attacks the reciprocity that Merleau-Ponty refers to as *chiasm* (Low, 2001, 2007). Hendriënne makes the double envelopment of self and other, fairly inoperative. The fold is denied, frustrated, disrupted. If we conceive of relationship and consciousness as a 'fold in the fabric of being', then Hendriënne is trying to close tight the opening of the fold. We need to be touched in order to touch – touching is a relational process. If the folding back onto oneself is excessive, and the folding outwards to relationship is denied; then the linked processes of awareness, speech and affection will be jeopardized. If the inside and the outside of the fold overlap; the opening onto otherness is jeopardized. The two sides are held together by mutual implication. Hendriënne produces a refusal of the anOther, but the anOther has thus been invoked.

In a fold, two dimensions are connected and cross over one into the (an)other. But whichever side of a fold one looks at it hides other sides – it is impossible to look at all sides of a fold. Every fold has its visible and invisible. One can never perceive one's own perceiving – the chiasm applies to the reversibility of touching and of being touched, seeing and being seen, researching and being researched. At any instant, the visible is the one or the other, but never both at exactly the same moment. If Hendriënne's text and my observing are the two sides of the fold, what further invisibles are in operation? We did not meet in a fold open to relationship. Meeting is always deferred in consciousness, first to the one awareness or perception and then to the other. Meeting never really takes place; relationship, movement and instability just keep repeating themselves. Was my reluctance to be enfolded very present? Was Hendriënne willing to betray betrayal as a dominant theme? Is the interviewer's relationship with Hendriënne very different from what I thought it was? Was the reader already implicitly present when I watched the video, so that the reader's fears have all along played an invisible role?

The open field of being is very slippery and slips easily away, especially from consciousness. We only capture a glimpse of Hendriënne wherein self and other do not fold into an unproductive closure or remain estranged. The meeting is not lived-through, there is little shared duration; she makes verbal gestures but actually there is little more than that. Merleau-Ponty believed that perception and language, self and other were enfolded, one into the other; and defined as a chiasm like touching and being touched (Low, 2007). My in-between with Hendriënne was very one-sided. Does the interview define a form of human phenomenal failure – did the chiasm of relatedness fail? The reversibility of visible and invisible, of touching and being touched, of subject and object – or the commonality of enfolding and of the in-between is unachieved. Relationship for Merleau-Ponty simply *is*, but what about when relationship is more *not* than it is?

For Merleau-Ponty, 'at root perception is non-personal and non-linguistic, involving our intercorporeal ties to others and to world' (Burkitt, 2003). The self-other relationship is primary and all the rest comes later. The chiasms of self and other, language and identity, speech and comprehension are all self-evidently to be assumed (Evans and Lawlor, 2000). Relationship is prior to consideration, the fold enfolds before consciousness arises. Through different embodied folds, relationship is always present. But the invisible can encroach on the visible and the visible can alter the invisible. There is no absolute antimony between the one and the other. Though we are of the world, we are not the world. In the embodied in-between, relatedness can remain ill-achieved, the chiasm can be unstable, weak, incomplete and untrustworthy. In the interview with Hendriënne, I seem to miss the primary relatedness and to be lost in all the rest. If I deny the enfoldment and impose the structure of researcher/researched via subject/object differentiation, I can ask if perhaps Hendriënne's ability to do the social, as I define it, has been impaired: that is, (i) perhaps she cannot 'properly' construct relationships, and/or (ii) perhaps in her way of being, she and world no longer touch one another (in a positive or productive manner)? But if I assume the enfoldment of being with Hendriënne, I have to admit that I have become stymied in a failure in relatedness; however that has come to be. Faulting Hendriënne for the failed chiasm is a very one-sided way of dealing with responsibility, and a rather cheap way out. Assuming the failure of her openness does not take Hendriënne's 'being' really into account and merely protects me as the knowing subject.

Concluding: gaps in the chiasm

Analyzing an interview with Merleau-Ponty's concept of the chiasm forces me to examine relationality. The interview becomes one of many folds in an on-going process of sameness and repetition, difference and identity. Enfoldment is pure process – always ongoing, proceeding and moving further. Thus my desire to 'know' the interview, or to perceive what Hendriënne said, meant or represents, is very problematic. How do I define and sustain the here and there, the Hendriënne and the not-Hendriënne? How do I define and fix the visible; and not disappear further and further into the tumbling movement of the invisible? The principle of the chiasm, or of the unlimited reversibility of the visible and invisible, points to how Hendriënne's interview cannot be stabilized, as this or that sensible. Every sensible implies a sentient, every seen requires a see-er. The chiasm of perception enfolds the interviewer with the interviewee, the writer with the interview, and the reader with the text. Each element involves touching and being touched.

In time, there is enough stability that each element remains reasonably identifiable, but the movement from the one to the other is continuous. How the folds enfold in time or duration becomes a crucial issue. As already described, Hendriënne's perception of time seems to be circular, turning around themes of loyalty/disloyalty, loneliness and anger. The effect of this circularity is extremely claustrophobic – all meanings return to betrayal, conflict and self-pity. Merleau-Ponty assumed a world of the being-of-openness. where folds move towards awareness, perception and involvement. But Hendriënne's enfoldment retreats from engagement, openness and the other. I find it very uncomfortable to be touched by her and spontaneously I have little desire to touch her back. I am afraid of being enfolded in a logic of betrayal, existential disappointment and regrets. I can claim that because she has had a stroke, her embodiment is not really congruous with mine, but this is not really a justification for not being and/or not wanting to be touched.

The research focus has flipped; it now focuses on my ability, preparedness and acceptance of touching. This is the consequence of the chiasm or principle of reversibility – the site of research flips from the point of origination, to all the other sites enfolded in the investigation. 'Hendriënne' becomes the possibility, willingness and ability of openness of the interviewer and of myself as writer; and of you as reader. Hendriënne was present in the interview as refusing open positive or mutual presence, which is a paradoxical form of presence. She is visible as not-visible, sensible as in-sensible. Is the case of Hendriënne enormously exceptional, perhaps because of her stroke? I doubt it. Admittedly most of the elderly I have interviewed in my research were perfectly happy to perform sociability or to do the social for me, and the desired mutual enfoldment of positive openness was enacted. Hendriënne may simply have been more 'authentic' than most. She certainly 'touched' me, in the emotional sense of touching or of being touched. But this brings us back to the theme of degrees of touching, or to the quality of the invisible. For Merleau-Ponty, we are always already in the presence of the perceptual or the touched and the world imposes vision (seeing) or touching on us. But what meaning does that presence or tactility really have for us, and how does one assume that vision or affectivity?

I think it is justifiable to assert that interview data always operates in the chiasm of reversibility, and that the processes of touching and being touched are always occurring, though often not acknowledged or described. This means that the invisible is always present, whatever fold is chosen in the research. Who assumes when, how, and why that touching is present and in which position of touching or of being touched the research is conducted? The risk of an endless regression into the invisible, and into the invisible of the invisible, etcetera, looms. Behind how I am or am not touched by Hendriënne, there are always other events and expectations, interactions and assumptions, folds and relations.

Merleau-Ponty extracts himself from the dangers of total entanglement in the folds of folds, or the tactility of touching, etcetera, by asserting the being of time or of duration. Things just are; and they pause, evolve, change and disappear at a tempo that permits persons to see, observe, comment, and write. The flesh of the world makes the human sort of consciousness possible (Low, 2001, 2007). Hendriënne, for instance, comes into relation with me and passes out of my attention; it is just like that. Do I have to take or want to take responsibility for the relationship? That is unclear. But people come and go; situations present themselves and disappear. Phenomenal existence just is.

The question has to be posed – how do I assume the enfoldment of touching and being touched, which the flesh of the world brings me? Merleau-Ponty appeals to 'perceptual faith' as the necessary pre-reflective acceptance of our own situatedness – ie as the willingness to be enfolded, as we will be enfolded. I do not know exactly what will touch me, or what it will feel like to touch it back. That knowledge or dimension is invisible and spread out amongst different sites – the interviewee's, the interviewer's, the writer's, the reader's. The lifeworld research paradigm, when it assumes that researcher openness is the key to good investigation, and that the researcher can make a simple choice to be open, misses the point. Real openness brings some visibility but also lots of invisibility. To be touched is immediately afterwards to touch, without any assurance that the relationship will be rewarding, constructive or especially valuable. To be inside the folds makes all judgments or control over the research uncertain. Merleau-Ponty is right; there really is no place outside of the flesh of the world. Research is all about bodies being touched and touching; it involves an unending chiasm of visibility and invisibility. It is the known/unknowing of bodily relationships. And it entails blind faith in what it *is* to be willing to touch and to be touched. It is not research technique that counts but faith in the being of touching and of being touched; and I do not always have that faith.

Notes

1 Based on research funded by ZONmw, the Dutch research institute funded by the Ministry of Health.
2 My book *Making Healthcare Care* (2008; Charlotte NC: IAP) focuses on these issues.
3 I think of work from Heidegger to Merleau-Ponty to Deleuze; from Levinas to Jean-Luc Nancy; and from Honneth to Todorov (Heidegger, 1962; Merleau-Ponty, 1962, 1969; Deleuze, 1995; Levinas, 1969; Nancy, 2000; Honneth, 1996; Todorov, 2002).
4 AnOther is a neologism of Levinas (1969) that stresses the otherness of the other.

Hugo Letiche

5 The interview was done by Dr Topsy Ross, May 2007 as part of a ZONmw funded research project into choices and choosing amongst the elderly. 'Hendriënne' is not the interviewee's real name.

References

Ashworth, P., (2006), Seeing oneself as carer in the activity of caring: Attending to the lifeworld of a person with Alzheimer's disease, *International Journal of Studies on Health and Well-Being*, Vol. 1: 212–225.

Atkinson, P. and Silverman, D., (1997), Kundera's Immortality: The Interview Society & the Invention of the Self, *Qualitative Inquiry*, Vol. 3 no 3: 304–325.

Balazic, (2003), Embodied Consciousness and the Poetic Sense of the World, *Substance*, 32.1: 110–127.

Boje, D., (2001), *Narrative Methods*, London: Sage.

Burkitt, N., (2003), Psychology in the field of being Merleau-Ponty, Ontology and Social Constructionism, *Theory & Psychology*, Vol 13 no 3: 319–358.

Crossley, N., (1995), Merleau-Ponty, the Elusive body and carnal sociology, *Body & Society*, Vol 1 no 1: 43–63.

Crotty, M., (1996), *Phenomenology and Nursing Research*, Melbourne: Churchill Livingstone.

Dahlberg, K. and Drew, N., (1997), A lifeworld paradigm for nursing research, *Journal of Holistic Nursing*, Vol 15 no 3: 303–317.

Dahlberg, K., Drew, N. and Nystrom, M., (2001), *Reflective Lifeworld Research*, Lund: Studentlitteratur.

Deleuze, G., (1995), *Difference and Repetition*, New York: Columbia University Press.

Dillon, M.C., (1983), Merleau-Ponty and the reversibility thesis, *Man and World*, Vol 16: 365–388.

Ellis, C., (2004), *The Ethnographic*, New York: AltaMira.

Evans, F. and Lawlor, L. (eds), (2000), *Chiasms*, Buffalo: SUNY Press.

Frank, A., (2002), *At the Will of the Body*, New York: Mariner.

Gabriel, Y., (2000), *Storytelling Organization*, Oxford: Oxford University Press.

Gubrium, J. and Silverman, D., (eds), (1989), *The Politics of Field Research*, Sage: London.

Heidegger, M., (1962), *Being & Time*, New York: Harper.

Honneth, A., (1996), *The Struggle for Recognition*, Cambridge MA: MIT Press.

Husserl, E., (1970), *Crisis of European Sciences*, Evanston Ill.: Northwestern University Press.

Kleinman, A., (1989), *The Illness Narratives*, New York: Basic Books.

Kristeva, J., (1982), *Powers of Horror*, New York: Columbia University Press.

Lawler, J., (1991), *Behind the Screens*, Melbourne: Churchill Livingstone.

Lawler, J., (1998), Phenomenologies as research methodologies for nursing, *Nursing Inquiry*, Vol 5: 104–111.

Letiche, H., (2008), *Making Healthcare Care*, Charlotte NC: IAP.

Levinas, E., (1969), *Totality & Infinity*, Pittsburgh: Dusquesne University Press.

Low, D.B., (2000), *Merleau-Ponty's Last Vision*, Evanston Ill: Northwestern University Press.

Low, D.B., (2001), Merleau-Ponty on Truth language and value, *Philosophy Today*, Spring: 69–76.

Low, D.B., (2007), Merleau-Ponty's Philosophy: Method & Ground announced, *Phenomenological Inquiry*, Vol. 31 (prepublication manuscript kindly provided by the author).

McNamee, S. and Gergen, K., (1999), *Relational Responsibility: Resources for Sustainable Dialogue*, Thousand Oaks CA: Sage.

May, T., (2005), To change the world, to celebrate life, *Philosophy & Social Criticism*, Vol 31 no 5–6: 517–531.

Merleau-Ponty, M., (1945), *Phénoménologie de la Perception*, Paris: Gallimard.

Merleau-Ponty, M., (1962), *The Phenomenology of Perception*, London: Routledge.

Merleau-Ponty, M., (1968), *The Visible and the Invisible*, Evanston Ill.: Northwestern University Press.

Nancy, J-L., (2000), *Singular Plural*, Stanford CA: Stanford University Press.

Porter, E., (1995), The life-world of older widows, *Journal of Women and Aging*, Vol 7 no 4: 31–46.

Ricoeur, P., (2004), *Memory, History, Forgetting*, Chicago: University of Chicago Press.

Savage, G., (2000), Nursing intimacy: Ethnography and healthcare, *BMJ*, no 321: 1400–1402.

Schotter, J., (1993), *Conversational Realities*, London: Sage.

Silverman, H., (1984), Phenomenology: From Hermeneutics to Structuralism, *Research in Phenomenology*, Vol. 14 no 1: 19–34.

Silverman, H., (1987), *Inscriptions: Between phenomenology and structuralism*, New York: Routledge & Kegan Paul.

Todorov, T., (2002), *Imperfect*, Garden Princeton: Princeton University Press.

Todres, L., Galvin, K. and Dahlberg, K., (2007), Lifeworld led healthcare, *Medicine Health Care and Philosophy*, Vol. 10: 53–63.

Todres, L. and Wheeler, S., (2001), The complementarity of phenomenology, hermeneutics and existentialism as a philosophical perspective for nursing research, *International Journal of Nursing Studies*, Vol. 38 no 1: 1–8.

Section 2
Moving Worlds

The body in time: knowing bodies and the 'interruption' of narrative

Rolland Munro and Olga Belova

It was her voice that made
The sky acutest at its vanishing.
She measured to the hour its solitude.
She was the single artificer of the world
In which she sang. And when she sang, the sea
Whatever self it had, became the self
That was her song, for she was the maker. Then we,
As we beheld her striding there alone,
Knew that there never was a world for her
Except the one she sang and, singing, made.

(*The Idea of Order at Key West*, Wallace Stevens)

Our concern in this chapter is with occasions when bodies shoot into prominence. Moments that take the form of *breaks* in narrative, wherein bodies unexpectedly find their comportment to be out of line. Moments in which stories about the world fail, such that bodies find they can no longer sustain their recessive posture. Moments in which bodies make themselves present until a new narrative direction is found and a new form of comportment adopted. If any credence is to be given to these moments, it is clear that circumstances could vary enormously from slipping on ice to falling in love. More potently it would include moments in which anyone might describe their world as 'turned over' rather than merely 'turned around'.

As these remarks imply, we go along with assumptions that tie bodies to narrative. Far from setting out to deconstruct bodies as subject to iterations that leave them 'inscribed', the aim is to balance these well-rehearsed ideas with the observation that life is interpolated by 'calls' upon the lived body to undertake a host of different activities. So not only do the authors stop short of conflating inscription with incarceration, as over-zealous readings of Foucault might have us do, we imagine body as *motile* to the very different worlds it helps bring into being. Alongside the picture of the body as a creature of habit and the bearer of culture, we are inserting a reflexivity of body as ever ready to shift shape and character to the materials of whatever world appears.

Departing from conventions about embodiment, we situate body as a 'register' of the *interruption* of narrative, as much as we see it acting as the medium of its inscription. The interest is therefore less with durations of time in which bodies 'follow' knowledge, having fallen in line with one narrative or another, and more with those moments in which bodies appear to step outside of narrative, so to speak. Moments in which bodies *take place*; foregrounding themselves, if fleetingly, rather than remaining recessively as background. In a loss of narrative, body is literally awestruck or dumbstruck; so much so that time horizons appear foreshortened and the immediacy of sense data comes more directly upon someone. Unlike Bergson (1965: 152–153) therefore, who notes how details of the past overwhelm attention to the future in moments of danger, we do not assume that such moments put us in touch with a more real form of time. It is equally plausible for people, freed up from anticipating the future, to notice the materials that surround them in greater detail and so experience a sense of time being arrested.

In what follows we explore 'the body in time' in preference, say, to investigating 'the time of the body' (cf Hodge, 1998). As such, the authors are as much interested in the *puncturing* of narrative as in its punctuation and therefore trace time as discernable as a gap between stories. Yes narrative helps divide up the experience of time into periods, horizons that seem within grasp, but it is breaks in narrative that give value to time. So, rather than focus on bodies working themselves invisibly into a smooth succession of one event following another, in ways that privilege illusions of continuity and decision, we insist on bodies irrupting; as incarnate to the phenomenology of the event.

The phenomenology of the body

Merleau-Ponty (1974) provides a strong philosophical position that seeks to recognize the strengths of the 20th century turn to language, but still accords a rightful place to the body. For him, language is part of our general capacities to survive, reproduce and enhance the quality of our experience. In this section, we first elaborate this point but then draw attention to the way in which different forms of iteration create *multiple* inscriptions within the body. So much so that the crucial issue for us is not that of the body knowing how to go along with any particular narrative. The issue for body is more one of knowing with which particular 'world' to fit.

Understood in terms of what Heidegger calls our 'thrownness', language has interpenetrated all each of us does, long before anyone 'wakes up' to questioning who or what we are. As such language 'goes before', so to speak, and thus already forms our fields of action. Embodiment *as* language already exists:

> I do not need to visualize the word in order to know and pronounce it. It is enough that I possess the articulatory and acoustic style as one of the modulations, one of the possible uses of my body. I reach back for the word as my hand reaches towards the part of my body which is being pricked; the word has a certain location in my linguistic world, and is part of my equipment (Merleau-Ponty, 1974: 180).

For Merleau-Ponty, body is the fount of speaking; it is through the act of embodying language, articulating it, giving it sound, space, and time that body comes alive and speaks to others.

It has long been recognized that language cannot exist as a simple *addition* to the body, with speech merely representing thought. Indeed, as Merleau-Ponty argues, we often do not know what our thoughts are unless we articulate them, and we do not quite know what the thing is until we recall its name: 'It is through expression that we make it [language] our own. The denomination of objects does not follow upon recognition; it is itself recognition' (1974: 177). Without suggesting that things have no prior being before linguistic existence, such matters affirm that the word, 'far from being the mere sign of objects and meanings, *inhabits things and is the vehicle of meanings*. Thus speech, in the speaker, does not translate ready-made thought, but accomplishes it' (Merleau-Ponty, 1974: 178, emphasis added). We would not be able to understand ideas unless we had body and sensibility, and unless they were given to us as a carnal experience (Merleau-Ponty, 1968: 150).

Where we, as authors, want to be careful here is over any holistic interpretations, presumptions that language becomes one with the world it helps to form; for presumptions that imply body is fully articulated and absorbed into this totality. This is the major point on which we insist: that there are any number of 'worlds' that grant being to body. So, equally, there are any number of possibilities open for different forms of comportment. This is not though to argue for multiple realities, at least in any strong sense of there being parallel universes, or deny the plausibility of certain forms of social hegemony. Given humankind is a 'world-forming' creature (Heidegger, 1962), it is rather to accept a *plurality* of 'worlds' more or less along the lines that Wittgenstein argued the existence of language games.

As already emphasized, the issue for body is which world? With which world is one to comport oneself? For much of the time, this question seems settled and the body becomes recessive as is discussed in the next section. Our position in this paper however is one of radical doubt that there ever could be a totality within which we can live, work and interact. Far from seeking a single essence, as Sartre has indicated, the existential question is more the immediate one of *interpreting* where we stand in the here and now. This involves constantly 'reading' the world for its possibilities and so forming plausible narratives about it as a means of going on in life.

Hence interpretive work is not just a question of language games; it is also a matter of bodily experience. In the moment of whatever is happening, any narrative not only takes over, as is often assumed, but also narrative itself is taken over by the body, as it seeks to go along with the way things are going and see how things turn out:

> . . . whether one is offering an elaborate philosophical discourse, asking the price of a beer, or laughing out of joy, the body is the medium of expression . . . the body becomes thought, the body inscribes meaning in a texture of experience by which

it speaks – not in words but in movement and in a tendency toward expression (Silverman, 1981: 125).

Language, then, is a way to 'sing' the world; not in a naïve onomatopoeic way but by extracting its 'emotional essence' (Merleau-Ponty, 1974: 187). The question for body is always: which narrative? Which world is one to sing?

Getting in line

Ahead of exploring the body in time, something needs to be said about how body *disappears* from everyday matters by getting 'in line' with narrative. A start on this detour can be made by recognizing how stories *inform* bodies, putting us, so to speak, 'in form'. This process begins with nursery rhymes in childhood (see also Bruner, 1990). Ahead of his fall, Humpty-Dumpty sits on the wall, exactly the kind of place where he shouldn't. Hansel and Gretel are drawn by smells of cooking into the very kitchen in which they can be popped into an oven. And Little Red Riding Hood is already in bed with the wolf before the disguise of Grandmother is cast off.

In this way stories, no less than more prescriptive forms of discourse, can be considered as helping create a *disposal* of the body (Munro, 1996b; 2001); ways in which bodies can be said to absent themselves by getting 'in line' with social and organizational narratives. In order to make the world a place in which walls are safe to sit on, stories instruct one to sit still and keep well back from the edge. So that the world of the kitchen is made safe, one learns that ovens, however delicious their smells, are hot enough to cook one for supper. And as for young girls getting into bed with someone pretending to be their grandmother, enough said!

It is not hard to find types of narrative that continue to play this role of advising adults how to comport themselves within everyday life. Salutary tales, for example, are passed around the office and the shop floor about what can happen. These not only help guard the unwary from becoming entrapped within difficult situations; they position people ahead, for instance to 'read' bosses *as* sites of power and machinery *as* places of accidents. It is thus not only the more systematic and rational forms of narrative that induce a docility of the body (Foucault, 1970; 1977; see also Latimer and Munro, this volume). Stories too have their instructional and directing properties, even if their guidance is typically ambiguous and indirect.

In understanding how body 'disappears' from institutional arrangements, there seems little to be gained by eschewing narrative altogether. For it is as if stories conspire to create a 'forgetting' of bodies; helping body to align these into whatever kind of institutional movement, conduct or action is deemed to be appropriate. For much of the time, as Leder (1990) notes, body is simply out of view: buried so deep within narrative, as to be out of sight; or so evident (like the eyeball) as to be taken for granted. Thus on occasions when body shoots into prominence and 'stands in the way', it turns into an 'obstinate force interfering with our projects' (Leder, 1990: 84). This has led Leder (1990) to coin this kind of re-presencing, or re-membering of the body as 'dys-appearance' rather than re-appearance, using the Greek prefix 'dys' to stress its dysfunctionality.

As Gimlin (2006: 701) notes in a study of women undertaking cosmetic surgery, such bodily re-member-ing has the affect of removing anyone 'from the activity in which we are engaged, alienates us from the social world and forces us into the limited sphere of the body'. For many, moments in which body re-presents itself may seem occasional, if unwonted and inconvenient. For others though more drastic action is undertaken. Thinking of Chris, a 41 year old nurse and avid jogger who had undergone breast reduction surgery to obviate the steady stream of jokes, Gimlin argues that the body becomes the target for efforts, both 'hermeneutic and pragmatic', aimed at re-establishing what Leder (1990: 86) calls the body's 'absent presence'.

Temporalities of the body

Perhaps with an eye on accounting for the recessive body, there have been many attempts to distinguish between stories and narrative. Gabriel for instance argues that narrative is a factual description of an event while a story is a personal, emotional account of an experience:

> Stories are narratives with plots and characters, generating emotion in narrator and audience, through a poetic elaboration of symbolic material. This material may be a product of fantasy or experience, including an experience of earlier narratives (Gabriel, 2000: 239).

As authors, we understand what Gabriel is getting at, but think his definition – in seeking to find the eternal properties of stories – over-essentializes any difference with narrative.

Stories seem to bring us to life, in a manner of speaking. Yet there is perhaps less of a distinction to be made between story and narrative that might be thought. Specifically any quality held to make a story good or bad, authentic or fraudulent, can be applied to narrative in general. Which is to say that when stories are heeded, and taken on board, body *becomes* the 'character' in a 'plot', to adopt Gabriel's definition. The plot maps the landscape in which body is to comport itself; and, in turn, body takes on the character that helps form this reading of the world.

It would be important, nonetheless, not to overlook differences in temporalities. For instance, stories in the form that each passes on and recites to another incorporate an internal sense of duration quite distinct from any durée elicited by narratives that body has already made its own. So this emphasis opens up the possibility of discriminating, say, between *timescapes* belonging to stories, as these get told and passed around, and *time horizons* created by their eventual inscription into body practices. Yet in terms of this chapter the present object is to do more than acknowledge durations in which time is experienced as continuous, periods when body appears to go 'backstage'.

Our aim is to draw attention to these interstices between narrative; these moments in which there is a lack of either story or narrative appear to be overlooked. For example, while Cunliffe *et al.* (2004), point out the embodied nature of narratives and press a need to study how experience is constructed in time and space, these authors still fall short of exploring what is happening when body can no longer get in line and 'follow' a narrative. All too easy to efface, these fleeting moments are nevertheless just when *body* appears to register time in its immediacy.

If, as surmised earlier, bodies try to get 'in line' with the very *interpreting* of world, then so to all intents and purposes 'world' appears as body disappears. Until, that is, whichever story body is following 'fails'. The disposal of body can be thought to work only until body is surprised. Surprised, perhaps, by being caught 'out of line'; by finding itself in an inappropriate form and at odds to a 'world' that had been predicted or anticipated.

The body, we are arguing, is only ever really called to attention, and reminded of its need to fall 'in line' at the very moment when durée is interrupted. Body comes 'front stage' in those moments when time gets folded up – when time is experienced almost as a *loss* – when there is, specifically to what has previously been 'taking place', no more time. We have time, as Valentine the computational mathematician in Stoppard's (1993: 94) play *Arcadia* astutely notes '. . . till there's no time left. That's what time means'.

Body and time

Some additional remarks should help elucidate this conumdrum about time being experienced in terms of its loss. Bodies do not just 'learn' to move, loping and even groping along with narrative. Bodies are also subject to what is commonly called 'affect', the seemingly spontaneous and sudden response from bodies finding themselves *out of place*.

On one hand, drawing on theory, we can argue that body is *anchored* in a very special form of time, narrative time. Activities and projects create temporal horizons that overlap with Western notions of 'linear time', just ahead of the past and just before the future. This form of time, like language, is more of a way for bodies to keep their hold on the various 'worlds' that beset us. And, of course, when body and clock time seem to run together, all seems well with the world.

In this matter we can return to Merleau-Ponty, who suggests that it is the phenomenological lived body that registers presence. As he notes, time arises from our relation to things: 'There are no events without someone to whom they happen' (1974: 411). Time only becomes such when it is attended to: 'Time exists for me only because I am situated in it. . .I cannot see it, just as I cannot see my face' (1974: 423–424). If time did not have its roots in the presence of living body and therefore its past, it would no longer be time but eternity.

So body captures and makes time present. A living, experiencing body becomes the centre of Merleau-Ponty's phenomenology of temporality:

> It is as much of my essence to have a body as it is the future's to be the future of a certain present. So that neither scientific thematization nor objective thought can discover a single bodily function strictly independent of existential structures, or conversely a single 'spiritual' act which does not rest on a bodily infrastructure. Moreover, it is essential to me not only to have a body, but to have *this* body (1974: 431, emphasis in original).

Precisely. It must be *this* body that participates, and no other. But what we also emphasise, more than Merleau-Ponty might, is just how much what we call 'this body' shifts and reshapes. And mutates, taking up other forms of materials, as it seeks to go along with whichever 'world' it finds itself within.

Anyone's involvement with 'world' is not only spatial, through motion, vision or touch; each body is also present to the world temporally. This is to say that by placing body at the centre of primary experience, each can no longer think of time as linear, objective and universal. Rather time is punctuated by a 'world-shifting' that is alluded to by what we are calling *affect*. Moments in which 'place' has changed, not simply because I have moved on; but because my very chance to 'go on' as before has vanished. This break in narrative heralds the moment in which 'there is no time left', as Valentine noted above. In my reading of it, 'world' itself has changed.

Moving the body

One interesting, and overlapping, way of articulating the relations between temporality and embodiment is through the notion of 'e-motional re-turning' (Mazis, 1993). In taking up body as an affective space that moves in time, Mazis argues: '*In emotion one comes back to the old as always altered but still there as somehow turned around, and with this revelation I am too turned around as moved, moved again to where I've been, but moved to a new place in returning*' (1993: 27, emphasis in original).

What Mazis calls 'e-motion', suggests an affinity of embodiment with movement. Mazis notes that the etymology of 'feeling' goes back to the Icelandic meaning 'to grope' and indicates the way in which 'the body moves forward gropingly into the world, not as self-sufficient, not as holding a meaning already to be signified . . . But rather as touching things in order to be touched back' (Mazis, 1993: 30). Body instances the shifting enmeshments of person and world, a circular moving of body from one form of relational extension to another that obliterates conventional divisions of subject and object, or active and passive. This circular movement of body and world does not end up in us 'getting nowhere' as logic has it, but comes to 'place' anyone in ever new beginnings, new connections and meanings.

Imagine a male employee hearing about bad losses made by a company. He is 'moved' by the news while sitting upright in the chair: 'moved' from the position of comfort and stability a moment ago to fear of losing the very job that has put him in this chair. This movement, however, is not merely 'internal':

> something has pulsed between the man and his world, towards children at home, towards his uncertain job, perhaps, towards the plight of working men in his region, perhaps, and so on, towards the depths of his world and then back to him (Mazis, 1993: 23).

As noted earlier, the perception of world changes when body is 'moved'. In a similar way, re-turn can be about the past that again becomes present: I think I am no longer angry with a colleague but when I arrive at work and see him, anger overtakes me and I am angry with him 'all over again'.

The power of body's movement in time is not simply to give new meanings to the world but also in its sense of 're-turn' to the base where one has been or stood until that moment. It is a transport of the body to what has been and yet feels new. Through these e-motional re-turnings each person thus learns also to 'carry' affect. Our argument here is that affect doesn't just happen in the present, or stay in the past. Rather, just as logic can be perceived as a 'truth-preserving' machine, so bodies appear to 'preserve' affect.

The allure of stories in their immediacy is that they keep things moving: the past is given a new basis, or recollected in a different way. Such is the experience of Proust's protagonist in *Swann's Way*, whose melancholic sense of being-in-the-world is turned over into an 'all-powerful joy' by the taste of a madeleine cake dipped in a cup of tea. As he attempts to connect this surge of joy into a concrete memory, he finds all his intellectual efforts to remember fail to bring it back. Nor do the materials alone do much for him, further mouthfuls simply having receding effects. Yet, suddenly, when he has all but abandoned his efforts, he finds himself immersed in the world that once gave rise to the sensation: his aunt giving him tea and cakes, streets of the village where he spent his childhood, its markets and people, arise before him, in their minute, painfully accurate detail. His movement in time is performed through affect, remembered and carried in his body, which re-turns him to the past now made present. This flow of time, as well as Proust's famously intermittent narratives, is made abrupt and punctuated by transports of body. It is 'this power of transformation, the ability to convey the endless unfolding in the established sense of things' (Mazis, 1993: 26) that characterizes one form of the movement of our bodies in time. With a re-turn of emotions, it is also judgments, meanings, and situations that turn around.

Affect and exchange

We want in this chapter to understand how time *registers* with the body. This brings us back to stories being 'sourced' and 're-sourced' by the body. Many stories, we surmise, begin and end with bodies as these emerge, crumple and elaborate. This is not to deny that other stories, like those of crucifixion and resurrection, might be more about the transmutation of substance. Our concern, though, is with knowing when bodies undergo movement and experience; with noting how they 'register' any displacement of their narrative alignment.

Stories are excited, we suggest, by bodies re-member-ing themselves; by their very *coming into presence*. This is to say, alongside 'effects' being generated by the mass of bodies bumping into each other – in line with David Hume's analogy with billiard balls – bodies may also make *themselves* felt. The centrepiece perhaps is the notion of affect. Affect is often experienced in the form of shock, shame and embarrassment; and sometimes as moments of awe, elation and euphoria. Far from being 'forgotten', as can happen when the body gets 'in line', the body is literally *re-membered*.

In regard to the notion of relational extension (see Latimer and Munro, this volume), perspective is 'exchanged' as much as materials. This implies one can never simply return to a lived experience but only re-turn it, re-live it in a different way. Re-turning is going to an origin (body) that never was. The notion of 'e-motional re-turn' allows Mazis to convey the movement of body in time and ways in which past is rewoven into present and future through bodily and emotional experiences.

Approximating to what Latimer and Munro (this volume) term *switches* in 'extension', these e-motional re-turnings are a common experience. Such re-turnings do not have self going 'in' and 'out' from a common origin, but would have each person moving, as Munro (1996a) has also outlined, from one form of extension to another, from one emplacement to another. Whether in the context of institutional or everyday life, anyone who remembers past events never feels exactly the same about them. The event takes on slightly different meanings in the light of other events that have happened since; circumstances shift as does the here and now.

So, too, with a story. Stories can help 'move' one on, moving body from one set of attachments to another. The affect may feel the same, but the form of relational extension is necessarily different. Whereas before the body might have been 'moved' by events, now it is 'caught up' in the story. 'Moved' by what Mazis calls e-motion, and what we are calling *affect*, body moves not only in the past, but also in present; especially when body finds itself in a different position to what has been anticipated.

Here it is worth emphasizing that there are two very different kinds of 'movement' in play. On the one hand, there is *mobility*, a kind of spatial effect where it is bodies themselves that are understood to be in motion. So that the mobility of labour, for example refers to a geographical movement of bodies; and social mobility, for instance, refers to shifts upward and downwards in status and social class. Thus, where bodies shift their attachments spatially to different 'parts' of the globe, or between different layers of stratification, the world itself is understood to remain more or less the same. Geometry, and time with it, is more or less held constant.

On the other hand, there is *motility* (Munro, 1996a, 1999; Latimer, 2001). This is where 'affect', the shift in state of bodily repose, seems to alter the very fabrication of the world. One minute one is in a certain place; and the next, one finds oneself somewhere quite other than one had thought. It is for this reason that we interpolate Meleau-Ponty's emphasis on 'this body' differently from him. For us, body is never fixed, never quite the same. As a knowing thing, body is never arriving; body is always in process of finding out how to be; moving along, reshaping itself as it moves 'world' with it.

Discussion

Bodies, as has been explained, get 'in order' when they fit in with stories in circulation. In the lull of narrative, they become recessive and almost disappear. When they are unexpectedly expulsed, however, they propel themselves into presence. At this point, for much of Western life, they become 'matter out of place' (Douglas, 1966). This is the key point we want to make. More generally, it might also be suggested that bodies re-member themselves – come into presence – whenever their flow is incorporated into something, or else is interrupted in some way. So that in moments of shame or embarrassment, the body becomes 'present-to-hand': the body looms into view, viscerally separate and disjunct from the world with which it fitted before.

Affect, in contrast, *punctualizes* attention to the body. So that when something unexpected 'takes place', body may find itself no longer 'with the action'. As with Heidegger's (1962) example of hammering in nails to build a roof, the hammer (and the hand holding it) only comes into view at the moment when the action of hammering fails. There is a pause, an emptiness, to be filled by questions such as 'what happened?' Hammering ends and questioning begins. One story is replaced by another. Similarly, whenever the movement of the body is impeded, its 'stop' is to be explicated and accounted for. So, too, when 'transports' of the body are accomplished; these, too, have to be explained.

At the edge of a story then is this 'falling out' of the body with time. We should be careful though not to suggest any priority here about which comes first, stories or the breaks in narrative. Arguably, stories are called for (even if they remain unspoken) whenever the body is impeded, or freighted into another time and place. This 'accounting' for a displacement of the body may be what gives rise to a story in the first place. When stories themselves, as it were, 'take place', they can distract from moments in which bodies and time have viscerally become disjunct.

Yet stories, in their telling, may also *dis-member* the actual experience; as much as they can ostensibly re-*member* it. The story never becomes the representation of experience. At best it acts as an evocation of bodily experiences. What matters in the telling of a story, from the perspective of the more contemporary anthropological schools of thought, is not its accuracy or closeness to the event – its reporting of the event as it happened (see also Czarniawska, 1997) – but the creation of a sense of movement and aliveness in the listener. But to focus only on such issues is to miss our point.

Our argument is that bodies can become 'nervous', even agitated, whenever they find themselves out of line, whenever they find themselves, so to speak, 'out of place'. Polkinghorne (cited in Czarniawska, 1997: 19) captures something of this aspect of events being 'out of place':

> When a human event is said not to make sense, it is usually not because a person is unable to place it in the proper category. The difficulty stems, instead, from a person's inability to integrate the event into a plot whereby it becomes understandable in the context of what happened . . . Thus, narratives *exhibit* an explanation instead of demonstrating it.

To be 'out of place' is also, momentarily, to be 'out of narrative'.

When the unexpected 'takes place', bodies may need to be soothed, placated, restored. This is when stories come into play. Sometimes stories may be required to fill in the moment of interruption, to mask the stall in the chain of events, the gap between essence and existence. But for us, shifts in stories also suggest a 'crossing over' over bodies – an exchange of perspective and parts – in order to accommodate a new plot.

In our line of thinking, stories *exhibit* material experiences of bodies as these knot together, fold into other bodies or fumble past each other. The power of stories thus lies not in their meaning as understood, either in terms of what Frege calls 'reference' or what Saussure calls 'signified'. What matters instead is the 'movement' that stories elicit. It is relational extension – our being-in-the-world – that changes. In a more commonsense mode, one can say something has meaning when each finds oneself 'moved' in some way, as in the shock of discovering that the friendliness of the workplace is not what it seemed, or in awe of a particularly spectacular sunrise. In these moments – affect – it is our 'grasp' of world that is altered in some way.

Conclusion

An emphasis on narrative puts the knowing body fairly at the centre of culture and social action. At the heart of the disciplines of sociology and anthropology, as Chris Shilling remarks, lies a key assumption:

> . . . that human actions are not determined by animal instincts but can be intentional, meaningful and ethical, and are intimately related to the agentic creation of ritual orders and social systems underpinned by moral orders (Shilling, 2007: 11).

Such a view recognizes, with Heidegger, that humankind is a 'world-forming creature'. As such body is always at the *disposal* (Munro, 2001) of any such world. Body, whatever this is, has to get 'in line'. And has to get 'in line' from moment to moment.

What Shilling (2003) also calls the 'mindful body' has to articulate with worlds as it finds them. Unfortunately the pressing importance of body getting 'in line' has long been obscured by thinking of bodies as creatures of habit, a tendency captured in a sociological emphasis on routines and repetition. Where time is made constant, this articulation of 'body' and 'world' is accomplished without difficulty. People, however, no longer live, and perhaps never did live, in the kind of holistic society dreamt up the structural functionalists. Where modernists dream of a universal 'best' way of doing things, the moral codas of today put choice as paramount. The homeostasis of system thinkers like Talcott Parsons appears long gone.

In this analysis of body and time, we moved away from notions of knowing bodies by stressing, instead, 'interruption' in narratives. For the knowing body has to do more than merely keep in line. Body has also to arrange and organize itself in ways that read, as well as reflect, the narrative shifts in 'world'. As *that* which is expected to organize and comport itself properly, as *that* which is expected to be mindful of where it is and find the 'way' proper to itself, body has to recognize not only how it is to get 'in line' but *when*. To 'dress' itself accordingly, body has first to know which world it is to 'address' (Munro, 2008).

Moving 'worlds' (what others might call perspectives) involves *motility*, the way in which shifts in readings call upon body to alter its relational extensions in line with material underpinnings and cultural understandings. This is to say more though that suggesting problems for bodies arise in the face of cultural relativism and technological proliferation. What is missing from sociology, we suggest, is a more distinct emphasis on what we are calling the body in time. The issue for body is always to know under which particular set of cultural understandings, or material underpinnings, 'this body' is to arrange itself.

References

Bergson, H., (1965), *The Creative Mind*, translated by Mabelle L. Andison, Totowa, N.J.: Littlefield Adams.
Bruner, J., (1990), *Acts of Meaning*, Cambridge, Mass.: Harvard University Press.
Cunliffe, A.L., Luhman, J.T. and Boje, D.M., (2004), Narrative temporality: implications for organisational research, *Organization Studies*, 25(2): 261–286.
Czarniawska, B., (1997), *Narrating the Organization: Dramas of Institutional Identity*, Chicago: University of Chicago Press.
Douglas, M., (1966), *Purity and Danger: an Analysis of the Concepts of Pollution and Taboo*, London: Routledge.
Foucault, M., (1970), *The Order of Things: An Archaeology of the Human Sciences*, London: Tavistock.

Foucault, M., (1977), *Discipline and Punish*, London: Routledge.

Frank, A.W., (1990), Bringing bodies back in: a decade review, *Theory, Culture & Society*, 7: 131–162.

Gabriel, Y., (2000), *Storytelling in Organizations: Facts, Fictions, and Fantasies*. Oxford: Oxford University Press.

Gimlin, D., (2006), The Absent Body Project: Cosmetic surgery as a response to bodily dis-appearance, *Sociology*, 40 (4): 699–716.

Heidegger, M., (1962), *Being and Time*, translated by J. Macquarrie and E. Robinson. Oxford: Basil Blackwell.

Hodge, J., (1998), A small history of the body, *Angelaki*, 3(3): 31–43.

Latimer, J., (2001), All-consuming passions: materials and subjectivity in the age of enhancement, in N. Lee and R. Munro (eds), *The Consumption of Mass*, Sociological Review Monograph, pp. 158–173. Oxford: Blackwell.

Leder, D., (1990), *The Absent Body*, Chicago: University of Chicago.

Mazis, G.A., (1993), *Emotion and Embodiment: Fragile Ontology*, New York: Peter Lang.

Merleau-Ponty, M., (1968), *The Visible and the Invisible*, Evanston: Northwestern University Press.

Merleau-Ponty, M., (1974), *Phenomenology of Perception*, London: Routledge and K. Paul,.

Munro, R., (1996a), A Consumption View of Self: extension, exchange and identity. In S. Edgell, K. Hetherington and A. Warde (eds), *Consumption Matters: the production and experience of consumption*, Sociological Review Monograph, pp. 248–273, Oxford: Blackwell.

Munro, R., (1996b), Disposal of the Meal. In D. Marshall (ed.), *Food Choice and the Food Consumer*, 1995a, pp. 313–325. Glasgow: Blackie,

Munro, R., (1999), The Cultural Performance of Control, *Organization Studies*, Vol. 20, No. 4: 619–639.

Munro, R., (2001), Disposal of the Body: upending postmodernism, *Ephemera: Critical Dialogues on Organization*, Vol. 1, No. 2: 108–130.

Munro, R., (2008), Identity: culture and technology, in Margaret Wetherall and Chandra Talpade Mohanty (eds), *Handbook of Identity*, London: Sage.

Proust, M., (1913–27), *Remembrance of Things Past. Volume 1: Swann's Way: Within a Budding Grove*, translated by C.K. Scott Moncrieff and Terence Kilmartin, New York: Vintage.

Shilling, C., (2003), *The Body and Social Theory*, 2nd edition, London: Sage.

Shilling, C., (2007), *Embodying Sociology*, Sociological Review Monograph, Oxford: Blackwell.

Silverman, H.J., (1981), Merleau-Ponty and the interrogation of language. In J. Sallis (ed.), *Merleau-Ponty, Perception, Structure, Language: A Collection of Essays*, pp. 122–141, Atlantic Highlands, N.J.: Humanities Press.

Stoppard, T., (1993), *Arcadia*, London: Faber & Faber.

Strathern, M., (1991), *Partial Connections*, Savage, Maryland: Rowman & Littlefield.

Telling silences: unspeakable trauma and the unremarkable practices of everyday life

Megan Warin and Simone Dennis

Introduction

This analysis focuses on epistemological and methodological issues that arise when working with exiled communities. In particular, we investigate the complex dynamics of ethnographic negotiation between ourselves as social anthropologists and a group of Persian women migrants in Australia. This diasporic group, who are predominantly Bahá'í, share not only a common historical identity, in which religious law was unfavorable to women, but also profound experiences of suffering and alienation following their exile from the Islamic Revolution. As with many 'refugee narratives', stories of suffering and trauma for Bahá'í are tightly bound up in 'bodies of knowledge', both in the performance of embodied memories of persecution and in the intimate knowledge that Islamic authorities collected about them and their families. In engaging with an ethnography of violence our dilemma was how to negotiate these powerful and emotively charged processes of elicitation without resorting to psychological, psychiatric or indeed anthropological understandings of 'opening up'. The intertwined theoretical and methodological approach we take in this chapter allows us to examine the ways in which traumatic memories are enfolded and transformed into mundane and creative practices of ordinary life, thus diverting from understandings of memory and embodiment that rest on social constructivism.

The chapter begins with an ethnographic encounter that points directly to the difficulties of attempting to elicit or construct narratives with migrant Iranian women. Ethnographic techniques of inquiry (such as recording family relationships, tracing movements and enquiring about practices of faith) alerted us to the fine lines between our research methodology and past experiences of threatening surveillance. Not willing to reproduce these disempowering and traumatic relations, and redirected by the women's telling silences, we became attuned to an embodied style and modality of memory-making and to the specific, gendered situations in which trauma is remembered, forgotten and re-remembered. We began to understand how trauma was individually and collectively embodied and performed in the unremarkable practices of everyday lives, through ordinary, domestic and creative practices. Examining the embodied experience of trauma in and through everyday, gendered practices means that the intertwining processes of bodies and memory takes analytic precedence over attention to narrative or symbolic outcomes.

In attending to an embodied style and modality of memory-making, this analysis critiques the privileging of a Cartesian metaphysics that has led to a universalizing tendency to rationalize, emplot and ultimately objectify and explain trauma. In the light of the 'multiple and fluid possibilities of differential embodiment' (Price and Shildrick, 1999), and specific Iranian conceptualizations of the body, we question how a body 'knows' its past, present and future. How do these women embody and remember traumatic social history? As Ram argues in her studies on Indian dance in immigrant contexts, to carry history in one's body does not necessarily mean that one has intellectual access to this kind of social history (2005: 127). Bodily knowledge is not discursively constructed or represented, but is actively engaged with through tacit knowledge, or what Casey refers to as habitual bodily memory (Casey, 1987). For these women (who had learnt to mute emotion), we are interested in their bodies' capacity to conceal, reveal and restrict meaning, and the constant working and reworking of bodily meaning through the aesthetics of everyday practice. This is a specific phenomenological 'labour of investigation' that restores us to a sense of the past, not as history, but as vitally present in the bodies of actors in the present (Ram, 2000).

Ethnographic intrusions

As we walked into the sitting-room, we saw the now familiar bowls on a low glass table; Persian pistachios, apricots, biscuits and sweets in brightly coloured wrappers, and a bowl of rock sugar crystals (*nabad*) for sipping hot, black Persian tea served in transparent glasses. The Persian *ta'arof* involves not simply the serving of tea, but the rituals of politeness and deference which mark social relationships in Persian society (Beeman, 1988; Harbottle, 2000) and the 'sweetening of relations' (Warin and Dennis, 2005: 166). Taraneh, a young Persian women of 25 years of age, motioned with her hand for us to sit on the end of an oversized, white leather sofa, and she settled into the adjoining sofa, patiently waiting for our questions.

This was not the first time we had met Taraneh, as she had been a part of a Persian women's group with whom we had already been conducting fieldwork in Adelaide and Toowoomba, Australia. It was, however, the first time that we had been invited to her small apartment. Our research focuses on memory and migration amongst Bahá'í women, and in particular how everyday practices (such as embroidery, painting and cooking) give meaning to place and home, and to the processes of remembering, forgetting, and the making and remaking of memory. Our fieldwork has been conducted in stages (2004 and 2006) and in well established Persian migrant communities in Australia, in community kitchens and art rooms in migrant centres, in Persian grocery shops, Bahá'í centres, participants' sitting-rooms and kitchens, and local performative spaces (such as the migration museum and a world music festival) in which the women ran Persian sweet making and embroidery classes (Warin and Dennis, 2005; Dennis and Warin, 2007).

The opportunity to talk with these women, both in groups and individually and in a variety of contexts, was important in the telling, performance and rhetoric of memory. In some cooking and painting classes, individual women were teaching others, and we could not ask them sustained questions while they were otherwise engaged. Additionally, some women preferred to speak to us alone, since the possibility of betrayal or the misrecognition of an enemy often ran deep among those whose survival had once depended on their capacity to leave objections and protestations unsaid. This was the case for some women, even as they attended classes with women that had been through similar experiences. Our travelling between these different 'fields' reflects our approach to memory, in which we focus on the back-and-forth movement between the small and large, between the intimate and the social, and 'how private experience and public narrative mutually inform each other' (Lambek, 1996: 241). Memory, like migration, is a constant relationship of movement, of disconnecting and reconnecting the past and present.

Following polite and informal conversation about photographs displayed in the sitting-room (including her recent wedding, her grandmother's effigy, and pictures of the Bahá'í prophet Abdul Bahai), we asked Taraneh if we could tape record our conversation. She declined, stating that she didn't like the sound of her own voice. She did consent to us writing some notes in our open field books. Shortly into our conversation about her journey to Australia from Iran, we asked Taraneh if we could map out a family tree to have a record of the social relations that she was describing. This proved to be a pivotal moment in our engagement with Taraneh and the project as a whole.

Genealogies in anthropology are standard methodological tools for eliciting information about social relationships, and include not only those relations of blood and substance, but other forms of social relatedness that fall outside biological lineages (Carsten, 2000). Taraneh and her five siblings were raised by her *madar bozorg* (her grandmother) as her mother and father were busy managing a food manufacturing company in Tehran. 'Family', Taraneh stressed 'are very important to Bahá'í people' and she joked how she doesn't have more Australian friends as she spends all of her time with her family. After the Islamic Revoultion of 1979, and the increased persecution of ethnic and religious minorities such as the Bahá'í, Taraneh's parents were told that they could no longer sell food to Muslims, and were jailed for a short period. Taraneh continued her schooling in Iran, but when she wanted to go to university she was barred because of her religion, and the family fled to Pakistan, arriving in Australia three years later when Taraneh was 19. As with all the Bahá'í families we work with, members of Taraneh's family are part of the Persian diaspora (what they colloquially refer to as the 'brain drain') and are located around the world, in (but not exlusive to) the US, Canada, UK and Australia.

Although Taraneh was politely answering our questions, her responses were measured and often started with a noticeable moment of silence. It was when we asked to draw a family tree that she stopped and turned the questioning to us: 'Why do you need all this information about my family?' The weight of what we were doing suddenly struck us.[1] Our ethnographically innocent questions about her family, how long her grandmother had stayed in Iran to look after her mother, dates and names of births, deaths and marriages and journeys of migration, were revealed to be personally threatening, reminiscent of past questioning in Taraneh's life that had been anything but innocent. We were chronicling what Taraneh valued most in her life and, by eliciting information about her family, were recreating a terrifying set of power relations in which past vulnerabilites were laid bare. We shifted in our seats and put our pens down. This unintended ethnographic replication of the relationships of power that were part of the context of flight from Iran in the first instance required us to look closely not only at our engagement with these women but, equally, at the ways in which traumatic memories were otherwise expressed, communicated and understood.

In their book on the anthropology of indirect communication, Hendry and Watson (2001) suggest that anthropology is a lot like espionage,

> . . . a shifty business carried out by individuals regarded by the general community with suspicion . . . people with language skills so thoroughly trained and prepared by special tutors, dropped into foreign environments and given the task of finding out important, often secret, information . . . their primary aim is to work with significant individuals who have the required information and elicit it from them (2001: 1).

While we would agree with those theoreticians who have long argued that ethnography is much more than the simple one-way collection of information (see, for example, Crapanzano, 1980; Kondo, 1990) and that it often involves advocacy and 'a dance of carefully chosen communications' (Ewing, 2006), the espionage analogy is an apt one for our blind spot.

Our informants (itself a word that they questioned)[2] belong to a faith that proposes a unity of religions, and the succession of divine gods (thus denying that Muhammad was the last prophet and fundamentally challenging Islamic beliefs). Since its inception in the 19th century, followers of the Bahá'í faith have been persecuted for their 'heretic' beliefs and have been subject to exclusion, imprisonment and execution (most notably by the Shah's secret police – the SAVAK). It was, however, during and after the Islamic Revolution of 1979 and the installing of tighter Islamic laws that the Bahá'í experienced new levels of overt discrimination and violence. Under the new regime, Bahá'ís were 'denied education, stripped of title, land and businesses, and denied the constitutional protection granted to other religious minorities [such as the Jews, the Christians and Zoroastrians]' (Humes and Clark, 2000: 27). As the Iranian Nobel peace author Sherin Ebadi writes in her account of post-revolutionary Iran, revolutionary guards tapped phones, followed people and asked questions about families (Ebadi, 2006). Bahá'í people, and the minutia of their everyday lives, were specifically targetted in this new regime.

Maryam spoke of her shock as she realized that her wedding photographs were not among the few possessions she was able to salvage after her home was burned to the ground by revolutionary guards. She explained that the regime would often take pictures found in Bahá'í homes in order to identify other targets, whose homes would be destroyed in turn. The trail of loss and terror was revealed to Maryam over the weeks and months after her own home and possessions were destroyed as she received news of the fates of her wedding guests whose houses were burned, whose pictures were seized, and whose lives were often taken. In this way individual experiences of loss, shock and fear were commonly experienced and communally awaited. Again, our enquiries about photographs displayed on Tareneh's wall unwittingly reproduced a fear about how knowledge of families and faith could be abused. As recently as March 2006, a United Nations report informed the world that Supreme Leader Ayatol-lah Khamene'i instructed a number of government agencies, including the revo-lutionary guard and the police force, to 'identify and monitor, in a highly confidential manner, members of the Bahá'í faith in Iran' (*The Independent* 2006).

It is in this political context that the Bahá'í women involved in our project lived in and later fled from Iran. While their exposure to, and their stories about violence differed, the women recounted how violence entered their everyday lives. Worlds became dominated by anxiety, terror and despair (Jenkins and Valiente, 1994: 166) and bodies witnessed the deaths of or harm to loved ones, and experienced physical trauma. Violence violated their bodily knowledge, and in doing so, permeated what was 'known and familiar with uncertainty and fear, making the body itself alien and unfamiliar' (Becker *et al.*, 2000: 321). Azita described her constancy of terror: 'I lived in fear all the time. You never get used to it. I would fear the telephone as every time I picked it up it would be news of a friend or family that had been killed or executed.' Constant terror means that bodies, in Heidegger's terms, are no longer 'ready to hand' or taken for granted in their everyday forgetfulness or familiarity. Bodies, and particu-larly female bodies, become highly reflexive and attention is paid to everyday comportment in public spaces, of how one walked, the folds of a chador, the direction of a glance, or the correct expression of emotion.

In post-revolutionary Iran, bodies became markers of political loyalty as the Islamic state mandated sadness, grief and mourning as the appropriate demeanor of its citizens and the paradigmatic emotional tone for contemporary public life (Good and Good, 1988). As the Good's noted in their early ethnographic work in Iran, 'People in Iran are sad (*ghanmgin*) because of the system, history, dic-tatorship. They cry easier than they laugh. It is because of the culture; it is deep' (Good and Good, 1988: 43). Celebrations (such as weddings and *No Ruz*, a celebration of Persian New Year), were suppressed, and dancing, singing and musical performances held quietly and surreptiously behind closed doors. Bodies and their emotive performances are thus deeply implicated not only in

Iranian definitions of selfhood but also in the social orders and political structures of the State; they carry and express a certain, sad valence.

Zarowsky (2004) argues that 'emotion is critical to creating, reorganizing, reinforcing and mobilizing the moral webs on which both individual and collective survival depend' (2004: 189). Following Zarowsky, we argue that the emotional experiences and emotional expressions of migrant populations cannot be conflated with psychiatric analyses or post-traumatic stress disorder. Indeed, to assume that emotions of sadness and grief – *gham o gosseh* – are immediately translatable to discourses of psychopathology is problematic, as it misses how these emotions are elaborated in much wider discourses of Iranian emotional life.

Assembling fragments

Initially, we did not directly ask our participants about their experiences of violence, as we did not want to participate in what Cuellar (2005: 159) refers to as an economy of subtraction, in which voices of survivors become commodities in a transnational network of [academic] prestige. For Sontag, such a preoccupation on our part with the horrors of suffering could fuel a 'culture of spectatorship' (2004), or a 'pornography of violence' (Daniel, 1996), that works to immunise and numb responses. In a slightly different vein, Zarowsky (2004) warns against only focusing on the 'rut' of 'the refugee experience', in which the collective narrative of persecution and trauma becomes somewhat divorced from the context of the lived experience of that persecution and trauma.[3] Moreover, we did not want to focus on a revolution that, whilst profoundly traumatic and life changing, could potentially become a marker of fixed identity. Yet the Revolution was a 'critical event' (Das, 1995) and an inescapable aspect of our participants' worlds, so the question then became, how might we engage with such violence?

Over time participants alluded to, suggested and occasionally recounted in specific detail, experiences of horror that were unimaginable in experiential terms to us. They spoke of sustained terror, of the brutal execution of family members, beatings, kidnappings, the beating to death of children, witnessing murders, the dissolution of families as children fled to Pakistan across deserts at night, repeated raids of homes where all books and photographs were confiscated, threats, and continued surveillance. Such violence was not simply physical, but embedded in psychological, symbolic and structural violence.

It was not often that women spoke openly and spontaneously about these experiences. Only two women have at length, and over many sittings, told us 'their stories'. Samerah, responding to a question about how she and her two daughters had come to settle in Toowoomba, Australia, began to speak of the circumstances under which she had fled Iran. The group of 11 other women sat and listened quietly as she told of her experience, punctuating her story with the silent assurances of occasional nods. But as Samerah came to particularly traumatic aspects of her journey, she began to weep, and could no longer continue speaking. Other women then stood and supported Samerah's body as she wept, and then told parts of her story on her behalf. Samerah's story was told in short installments by women who knew it well. The women spoke Samerah's story in pieces that began and ceased with specific incidences of trauma, with knowledge of her story as one they knew as Samerah's story, and one they knew just as well as their own. Samerah herself wept, rested, and moved into the conversation at times to offer the details of her experience. By the time Samerah's story had been told, 12 women who had previously been positioned on chairs spaced at regular intervals around the large meeting room at the Bahá'í centre were clustered together in one of its corners, and the voice of one persecuted woman took on 12 forms.

This narrative, told in 12 voices issuing from one clustered corporeality, was not a common experience in our fieldwork and clearly marked the experiential distance between us and these women. More often, when questions were asked about the circumstances of leaving Iran, conversations turned sharply to the weather or silences hung between us. One woman, after many years in a new homeland, asked us not to record any details that might implicate her in the public domain and allow her to be traced or contacted by the Iranian police. Following the Revolution, an outspoken family member had been executed in Iran, and she feared that any connection might make her children vulnerable to a similar form of violence. This muting of violence is the conundrum that those researching this topic cannot avoid. Violence, Harstrup (2003) suggests, is a slippery term, as 'victims of violence are silenced, and the anthropology of violence is trapped in its very unintelligibility' (2003: 309). Azita told us 'Iranian people don't like to talk [about the Revolution]'. Others stated that the inability to express experiences in words explained why 'Persian people are reserved, we are not able to talk . . . we have to live in a different skin'.

There is a striking difference between the telling and telling silences of these women's broken journeys and, more familiar, rhetorical narratives of persecution. There is no Bahá'í 'grand narrative' about the flight from Iran post 1979, as there is for, say, Jewish Holocaust survivors or Kosovo refugees from the early 90s. There is no formal avenue where testimonies are sorted, ordered and constructed,[4] there is no Truth and Reconciliation Commission hearings, no UN war crimes tribunals, no demand for legal evidence. While there is a growing media campaign (in the UK, for example), it is overshadowed by concern with Iran's nuclear status. It would be inaccurate, however, to say that there is no collective memory of suffering – it is embodied and expressed not through the public telling of narratives, but through the minutiae of everyday, and often domestic activities, that enfold and refashion memories of loss and violence.

As ethnographers we had to disentangle ourselves from the persuasion to emplot, tell and represent memories, as found in the 'intellectual habit of dichotomizing mind and body' (Jenkins, 1998: 124), and standardized psychological and psychiatric formats (Kleinman and Kleinman, 1994: 711). We shifted our attention away from an expectation of temporally ordered narrations of 'what happened to me', to a processual and creative engagement with the world, in which memory revealed itself. This involved a labour of investigation[5] into the constant working and reworking of memory through everyday 'sensory qualities, emotional registers and styles' (Carsten, 2007: 91) of embodied practice.

The everyday enfolding of memory making

The cultural forms in which these women expressed their emotions are not simply defined by narrative or linguistic genres, but manifest in the commensality[6] (Seremetakis, 1996) and diffuseness of everyday, domestic practices, in the patterning, tastes, smells and sounds of cooking, embroidery, painting, poems, and telling of children's stories. We have already detailed these practices elsewhere (Warin and Dennis, 2005; Dennis and Warin, 2007), but what is important for this analysis is acknowledging the intimate connection of ordinary activities with the creative enfolding and refashioning of memory. Fractured social relations of kin and political histories are sewn by knowing fingers into symbolic patterns that link landscape, people and place, and are then displayed on walls in homes, put to use as functional items in the domestic house (such as cushion coverings and tablecloths), kept rolled in safe corners of the house, and given to sons and daughters when they move away from home.

Empson, in her analysis of the ways in which memory informs different forms of sociality among the Buryat of Mongolia, similarly highlights the ways in which domestic items, such as embroideries and photographic montages, make present those who were physically absent or silenced by the socialist period. She argues that 'daughters-in-law in marital homes had to find alternative media through which to express their intentions and desires, as they were often unable to do so explicitly' (2007: 67). They achieved this by lacing the inside walls of people's homes with embroideries (2007: 58), these objects thus serving as vehicles by which women could narrate stories about themselves to others (2007: 77). One of the participants in our study transformed her house into an art gallery, complete with professional picture railings, in which she displayed her own art work of Iranian landscapes with hidden, human figures from a post-revolutionary Iran. Embroidery and art (particularly Persian miniatures) were, as Empson suggests in her ethnographic work, 'objects in the household [that acted as] enlivened containers or sites' (2007) that literally recalled and brought memory to life.

In the painting classes we observed, which were run by an experienced and established female Persian artist, the women painted thin layers over thin layers, attended to the tiniest of details, and glued on small bejewelled birds, feathers and fabric details to lend the works a three-dimensional air. The carefully attended details produced, over hours, over classes, chromatically and stylistically harmonized relationships between beautiful Persian women (and sometimes their male lovers) and the painted landscapes they inhabited. Central to these paintings were 'traditional' Persian miniature motifs of doe-eyed animals, majestic birds, flowers and musical instruments (often the *kamancheh*), all pointing to the poetic (and intimate) relationships between the senses and 'nature'.

Painting these 'natural' Persian scenes in new Australian lands also tapped directly into Iranian understandings of the *hal*, each body's unique state (Loeffler, 2007). The *hal* is one entity that constitutes a body's physical, mental, social and spiritual state, and is extremely susceptible 'on all fronts to internal and external influences and stimuli' (such as emotions of fear and fractured social relations). Loeffler notes that spending time in 'nature', listening to the burble of a fountain and the singing of birds, brings calm and is restorative of the interconnectedness of physical and mental strength (2007: 109). For the women painting these images in the class, such harmony had been violently interrupted by the circumstances under which they had left Iranian landscapes. Yet via the process of painting calm environments and soundscapes, the *hal* can be remembered and manipulated to preserve health.

Persian stories and poems were also central to this recalling and reproduction of memory. Several women in our project talked of the well-known Persian children's story, *The Little Black Fish* (1968) written by Samad Behrangi. The story, told through the voice of an old fish speaking to her children and grand-children, is said to be an allegory, 'a protest parable about the oppressiveness of conformity to government rules" (Fischer and Abedi, 1989: 32, see also Fischer, 2004). In this sense it produces another story other than that which is read, a story that displaces political themes onto apparently apolitical figures. Many of the women in our project remember being read the story by their mothers in their homelands of Iran, and in turn, reading the story to their own children in Australia. Away from the potentially dangerous ears of the other Persian women in the painting group, Tala talked of this book in whispers, suggesting it was a political text that was not so subtly concealed through a children's parable. Azita, who asked us how we knew about this book (and in doing so, checking to understand *what* we knew about this book), recounted how she no longer has a copy: 'I used to read it to my children pre-revolution, but after the revolution you could be executed if you were found with a copy. It is about a fish, a leader, it is short, only about 30 pages long. How you read it depends on who you are. Do you know about the author? He was drowned in the Aras river. He was a very good poet . . . he was young.'

The everydayness of traumatic memory

How is one to understand or interpret the embroideries on the wall, the Persian paintings and stories like *The Little Black Fish*? Whilst there are numerous theo-retical frameworks for understanding the specific relationship between memory and trauma (from a variety of disciplines), much of the literature that deals with traumatic memories takes the Husserlian philosophical positioning of a subject explaining an external, objective world as a narrative through which a subjective understanding of the world can be expressed, and externalized.

Psychiatric and psychological accounts of memory, as Das and Kleinman note, 'are engaged in documenting, describing and diagnosing post-traumatic stress disorder and other distressing consequences of . . . brutality (2001: 1). A clinical diagnosis of post-traumatic stress disorder explains how traces of the past erupt into the present, in which the locus of the experience is taken to be the mind of the individual. Young argues that 'this [clinical] narrative in which trauma moves through memory to eruption in symptoms depends, in turn, on modern Western conceptions of the self as constituted through continuities of memory' (Young, cited in Breslau, 2004: 116). Kleinman and Desjarlais continue the critique, arguing that the Diagnostic and Statistical Manual of Mental Disorders (DSM-IV) emphasizes that the 'traumatic event is outside the range of usual human experience' (Kleinman and Desjarlais, 1995: 179). As the women in this project (and Das' latest work on the descent of violence into the ordinary) attest, 'the downright common, even routine experience of political trauma in many parts of the world . . . [means that such an interpretation] sounds suspiciously ethnocentric, even provincially middle class and middle Western' (Kleinman and Desjarlais, 1995).

While it is not our intention to examine the wide field of anthropological literature on memory, we do highlight one dominant field in which individual life stories are 'recalled and narrated . . . [thus allowing anthropologists] to explore how memory plays an important role in the construction of the person and the creation of different forms of subjectivity' (Empson, 2007: 59).[7] Dossa, for example, in her work on 'ethnographic narratives' from migrant Iranian women in Canada, uses storytelling to 'retrieve [bodily] knowledge' (2002: 355) and shift powerful biomedical discourses of psychiatric diagnosis towards culturally specific terms of 'emotional well-being'. Becker, Beyene and Ken (2000), in their analysis of Cambodian refugees' experiences of the Khmer Rouge regime, argue that bodily experience is accessible via the externalization of narratives: 'Narrative is a means through which embodied distress is expressed . . . the narrative process enables the narrator to develop creative ways of interpreting disruption and to draw together disparate aspects of the disruption into a cohesive whole' (2000: 322–3). As Kleinman argues in his often cited work on illness narratives, people accommodate pain by constructing culturally viable meanings for it (Leavitt, 1995). These narratives are actively and consciously constructed literary works, in which plot lines, core metaphors and rhetorical devices are drawn upon (Kleinman, 1988).

If we were to draw upon these constructivist frameworks of Cartesian metaphysics in the analysis of memory and embodiment, we might interpret the reading of *The Little Black Fish* and the other creative practices described above, as a means through which the Persian women 'fashion a world of meaning and relevance for themselves' (Weiner, 2001: xiii). In recreating an aesthetic of beauty and poetics which is located in pre-revolutionary temporality, emotional pain associated with the displacement of migration passes into metaphor, and is mediated into a recognizable cultural form. This 'self-actualization' is a familiar Western therapeutic discourse, of positing an articulation or narrative of pain outside the body, in which self and other are radically separated. In this dualist combination of physical depth and corporeal superficiality, inner turmoil is drawn out of the body through psychoanalytic techniques of 'opening up'.

For the Bahá'í women in our project, this interpretation of memory and trauma obscures a number of important cultural differences concerning the ways in which bodies are known. In a recent special issue of *Body & Society* (focusing on Islam, health and the body), the editors note that Cartesian metaphysics do not translate easily to Islamic traditions, which emphasize a mind-body-spirit unity (Tober and Budiani, 2007: 6). Loeffler argues that 'Iranians are quite skeptical about a system . . . that dissociates mind from body and categorically ignores, if not dismisses, all traditional knowledge' (2007: 111). Iranian conceptions of the body rest on the *badan* or *tan* (the physical body) which is composed of organs and parts performing specific functions. These organs are also the site for emotions. The physical heart, for example (the *qalb*), has a semantic relationship with the emotional heart (the *del*) (ibid: 107). Thus, when the women in our project described how their 'hearts were squeezed' when recounting traumatic memories, they are referring to heart distress (*qalbim narahatdi*), and the heart's capacity to express emotion – in this case sorrow, sadness and grieving (see Good, 1977).

In Iranian medicine and everyday health practices, the focus is not so much on the *badan*, as on the constitution of the body (the *hal*). Allopathic medicine and Iranian understandings of the body thus present problems for the universalizing templates of diagnostic categories. A Cartesian knowing of the body also presents problems for investigating the complexity of memory-making.

In terms of theorizing memory, we borrow from Weiner's (2001) sustained polemic against 'social constructivism', in which he argues that such a view obscures the relationship between revealing and concealing. Whilst not dealing with bodies and knowledge, (but more broadly with the usefulness of Heideggerian hermeneutics to anthropology), Weiner raises two points that are relevant to our argument. The first is that rather than reveal or objectify a system of meanings about trauma, it is the everydayness, the forgetfulness, of these activities that render them meaningful. It is precisely because of their everydayness, that they become enfolded into bodies, thus concealing an objectivist interpretation. Weiner, citing Kant, describes this process:

> Humans do not encounter the objective world, but a world in which the patterns and possibilities of its accessibility are provided by total experiential, apperceptual matrix, what Kant called schematism, which we have conventionally labeled 'culture'. What Bourdieu has pointed out to us, however, is how readily humans accept this environed world as the objective one. In taking this objectivist stance, as Bourdieu calls it,

humans conceal the cultural specificity of that objectivism. Heidegger would say that we fall away from knowledge of that experiential apperceptual apparatus through the attitude of everydayness. (Weiner, 2001: 59)

Thus, in their very domesticity and everydayness, the stitching of patterns and colours, the reading of children's stories, poetic painting of romantic miniatures (as well as fine cooking and patterning), conceals and reveals the memory of trauma. For some women in our project, the specific process of embroidering enabled painful memories to be tightly stitched into the fabric (Warin and Dennis, 2005). It is through the process of sewing (and not the outcome) that sadness is remembered and forgotten, revealed and concealed. These practices are not conscious and intentional works of elicitation, but what Merleau-Ponty calls 'practical knowledge' (1964: 89), knowledge that is skillfully practised by knowing fingers, or 'habits of hand'.

Secondly, in focusing on a construction of narrative, the sociocentric properties of creative memory work are lost. Focusing on the products (the embroidered pieces, the finished artwork, the story) is to rest on representations, on the objective signs of social meanings. These are only moments in an ongoing process. A phenomenological approach is drawn to the practice of the event (of bodies coming together to taste and sip, to hand sew, and smell the aroma of paints), and not to what lies after it. Such an approach is concerned with the embodied processes of recalling and remaking memory, not (only) the outcome of remembering.

Empson's (2007) work comes close to the nuanced ways we suggest in which memory reveals and conceals itself. Empson eloquently brings to life the importance of photographs, embroideries and pieces of people (such as umbilical cords and children's locks of hair) concealed within Buryat household containers. The photographic montages are 'fixed site[s] inside the house which anchor meetings between groups of people who may be absent from each other for parts of the year' (Empson, 2007: 65). In contrast to the photographs, embroideries (which are sewn by women in the evenings as a creative endeavour), present 'female biographies and life histories'. In her discussion of rebirthing, of how souls of the deceased are made visible in children's bodies, she acknowledges the 'revealing and concealing of knowledge and the different ways in which this knowledge is then reproduced and communicated to others' (2007: 77).

Whilst we do not agree with the constructivist interpretation of photographs and embroideries as simply 'biographical objects' (2007: 77), Empson suggests that people's bodies work as channels that allow people actively to create new relations with the living through the appearance of the dead. It is the 'doing' (rather than triggering of a recollection through mnemonic sign) that shapes the way people interact with each other. It is precisely this emphasis on the creative *processes* involved in the recalling and refashioning of memory that this paper argues is central to the everyday, sensous practices of memory making.

There is an ethnographic lesson to be learned here, too. If memory is performed in and through processes, then this calls for a specific ethnographic engagement. Cultural practices of memory (of making and undoing) intersect with a specific mode of ethnographic engagement to yield particular under-standings (of trauma). These intersections offer up an alternative to the ethno-graphic presentation of the substantive content of migrant lives. This alternative is resultant of the particular ways that these women communicated their experi-ences of trauma, feeling trauma, and remembering and forgetting trauma in the context of Australia, and the *specific ethnographic mode we began to opera-tionalize in response to these communications*. The women did not offer up their stories in the terms of historical narratives; there was no straightfor-ward revealing of 'what happened to me'. Passerini similarly suggests that 'when trying to understand connections between silence and speech, oblivion and memory, we must look for relationships between traces, or between traces and their absences; and we must attempt interpretations which make possible the creation of new associations' (2003: 236). These new assocaitions happen between body and voice, where 'memory is gendered, and women's memories and silences offer different continuities and repetitions through the specificities of their experience in different times and spaces' (Passerini, 2003: 248).

Conclusion

The possibilities for the migrant women with whom we have worked to narrate their traumatic experiences straightforwardly were constrained. These constraints were often experienced as a bodily heaviness that we could best intuit as the opposite experience of unburdening in and through the sharing of a difficult or traumatic experience in words. For the few women who did talk about their experiences of suffering, they said that talking, rather than expunge emotion, was 'suffocating' and 'made them heavy'. For others, the direction of words towards the weather outside, the way the wind was 'getting up' or the 'unseasonable shower heading our way', might not be understood as the end of the telling of experiences of trauma to interested anthropological ears, but the re-direction of our anthropological attention to the sensual processes in which trauma was revisited. In particular, our ethnographic attention to domestic activity, which itself enfolds the past and present of, and provides a vehicle for, the memory and the expression of trauma (through speech and performance), was transformed by the indication that narrative accounts of past experiences of trauma were unavailable. Our attention to other areas of these women's domestic and everyday lives has revealed trauma to be for these women an ongoing experience that is continually 'done' – not simply remembered as passed, but actively forgotten, remembered, revised, re-remembered.

It is through coming together to paint, cook, and sew, that memories of suffering are replayed, recited and reworked in the play of subjective life. It is in these gendered and shared activities between women, and between mothers and children, that traumatic memories are enfolded in the practices required of the project – in the stitching, the shaping and tasting of sweets, the painting of tiny strokes, and the mouthing and sounds of words as hands touch and turn pages. Through these activities, the phenomenological immediacy of trauma is transformed, enfolding that which lies outside of speech and reason, into a semiosis of culture. It involves bodily processes outfolding into social spaces, and reciprocally, enfolding culture into the body (Kleinman and Kleinman, 1994).[8] Traumatic memory does not appear in neat, told narratives, but belongs to a diffuse, inchoate, embodied world in which experiences of the past are reauthored and retold through the presence of gendered bodies.

In privileging the embodied processes of remembering and forgetting, we offer an alternative to simply recording and presenting the content of migrant lives as 'stories'. Our analysis pivots on intertwined philosophical and ethnographic modes of engagement, between the ways in which bodies of knowledge were collected by us (and Iranian authorities), and how these women enfolded this knowledge into embodied, everyday practices. Once we became attuned to our own methodological deployment of violence (through collecting detailed information about participants and their families), we turned our attention to the processes of mundane and repetitive aspects of everyday life. The processes of remembering and forgetting trauma, itself subject to a particular muting or even silencing in narrative form, found presence in and through the habitual projects and processual activities of these women's daily lives.

Notes

1 In documenting the anti-Tamil riots in Sri Lanka, Daniel similarly notes how the 'very words "project," "informants," "information," "interview," "evidence," "description" took on new and terrifying meanings' (Daniel, 1996: 3).

2 One participant asked us if we intended to use the word 'informant' in our published work, mindful of the ways in which it can lead to unequal relations of power that we unintentionally invoked. This knowledge of power relations spans both Iranian politics and those that characterize our discipline in the absence of reflexive speculation – that might often only mean something to the anthropologist. Our participants are educated people who are aware of some of the literary devices we consider as disciplinary specialists.

3 As Zarowsky (2004) also suggests, 'poetic symbolism' of trauma places specific emphasis on the importance of nuancing institutional political understandings of trauma in and through individual embodied experience, so that the embodied experiences of many do not come to be characterized as 'the refugee experience' of an entire people.

4 We thank Professor Michael Carrithers for this observation.

5 Similarly, Carsten, in her work on adoption reunions in Scotland, refers to this process as 'interpretive labour' (2007: 86).

6 Seremetakis' (1996) concept of commensality extends beyond the social organization, consumption and exchange of food and drink to the exchange of sensory memories, emotions, substances and material objects that are embedded in shared histories.

7 Other examples from this constructivist field of memory include Hoskins (1998), Küchler (1987) and Radley (1997).
8 Grosz, in her book *Volatile Bodies* (1994), uses the model of the mobius strip to highlight this relationship of interiors and exteriors, for the mobius strip has the capacity to twist into each other, not as a combination of physical depth and corporeal superficiality, but as three dimensional.

References

Becker, G., Beyene, Y. and Ken, P., (2000), Memory, trauma and embodied distress: The management of disruption in the stories of Cambodians in exile, *Ethos* 28(3): 320–345.

Beeman, W., (1988), Affectivity in Persian language use, *Culture, Medicine and Psychiatry* 12: 9–30.

Breslau, J., (2004), Cultures of trauma: Anthropological views of posttraumatic stress disorder in international health, *Culture, Medicine and Psychiatry* 28(2): 113–126.

Carsten, J., (2000), (ed.) *Cultures of Relatedness: New Approaches to the Study of Kinship*, Cambridge: Cambridge University Press.

Carsten, J., (2007), (ed.) *Ghosts of Memory; Essays on remembrance and relatedness,* Oxford: Blackwell Publishing.

Casey, E., (1987), *Remembering. A Phenomenological Study*, Bloomington, IN: Indiana University Press.

Crapanzano, V., (1980), *Tuhami: Portrait of a Moroccan*, Chicago, University of Chicago Press.

Csordas, T., (1994), (ed.) *Embodiment and Experience: The Existential Ground of Culture and Self,* Cambridge: Cambridge University Press.

Cuellar, A., (2005), Unraveling silence: Violence, Memory and the limits of Anthropology's craft, *Dialectical Anthropology* 29: 159–180.

Daniel, V., (1996), *Charred Lullabies: Chapters in an Anthropology of Violence*, Princeton: Princeton University Press.

Das, V., (2007), *Life and Words: Violence and the Descent into the Ordinary*, Berkeley: University of California Press.

Das, V., (1995), *Critical Events: An Anthropological perspective on Contemporary India*, New Delhi: Oxford University Press.

Das, V. and Kleinman, A., (2001), Introduction. In V. Das, A. Kleinman, M. Lock, M. Ramphele and P. Reynolds (eds), *Remaking a World: Violence, Social Suffering and Recovery*, Berkeley: University of California Press.

Dennis, S. and Warin, M., (2007), Domestic temporalities: Sensual patterning in Persian migratory landscapes, *Indo-Pacific Journal of Phenomenology* Vol. 7 (2).

Dossa, P., (2002), Narrative mediation of conventional and new 'mental health' paradigms: Reading the stories of immigrant women, *Medical Anthropology Quarterly* 16(3): 341–359.

Ebadi, S., (2006), *Iran Awakening*, New York: Random House.

Empson, R., (2007), Enlivened memories: Recalling absence and loss in Mongolia. In J. Carsten (ed.), *Ghosts of Memory; Essays on remembrance and relatedness*, Oxford: Blackwell Publishing.

Ewing, K., (2006), Revealing and concealing: Interpersonal dynamics and the negotiation of identity in the interview, *Ethos* 34 (1): 89–122.

Fischer, M. and Abedi, M., (1989), Revolutionary posters and cultural signs: Middle East Report 159, *Popular Culture* 29–32.

Fischer, M., (2004), *Mute Dreams, Blind Owls, and Dispersed Knowledges: Persian Poesis in the Transnational Circuitry*, Durham, NC: Duke University Press.

Good, M. and Good, B., (1988), Ritual, The State, and the transformation of emotional Discourse in Iranian Society, *Culture, Medicine and Psychiatry* 12: 43–63.

Good, B., (1977), The heart of what's the matter: The semantics of illness in Iran, *Culture, Medicine and Psychiatry* 1: 25–28.

Grosz, E., (1994), *Volatile Bodies: Towards a Corporeal Feminism*, Indiana: Indiana University Press.

Harbottle, L., (2000), *Food for Health, Food for Wealth: The Performance of Ethnic and Gender Identities by Iranian Settlers in Britain*, New York: Berghahn Books.

Harstrup, K., (2003), Violence, suffering and human rights: Anthropological reflections, *Anthropological Theory* 3(3): 309–323.

Hendry, J. and Watson, C., (2001), *An Anthropology of Indirect Communication*, London: Routledge.

Hoskins, J., (1998), *Biographical Objects: How Things Tell the Stories of People's Lives*, New York & London: Routledge.

Humes, C. and Clark, K., (2000), Collective Baha'i identity through empbodied persecution: 'be ye fingers of one hand, themembers of one body'. *Anthropology of Consciousness* 11(1–2): 25–34.

The Independent (2006), 14th April http://www.independent.co.uk/opinion/letters/letters-bahai-persecution-in-iran-474056.html accessed 4/10/06

Jenkins, J., (1991), The State constructions of Affect: political ethos and mental health among Salvadoran refugees, *Culture, Medicine and Psychiatry* 15: 139–165.

Jenkins, J., (1998), The medical anthropology of political violence: A cultural and feminist agenda, *Medical Anthropology Quarterly* 12(1): 122–131.

Jenkins, J., and Valiente, M., (1994), Bodily transactions of the passions: *El Calor* (The Heat) among Salvadoran women. In T. Csordas (ed.), *Embodiment and Experience: The Existential Ground of Culture and Self*. Cambridge: Cambridge University Press: 163–182.

Kleiman, A., (1988), *The Illness Narratives: Suffering, Healing and the Human Condition*, New York: Basic Books.

Kleinman, A. and Desjarlais, R., (1995), Violence, culture and the politics of trauma. In A. Kleinman (ed.), *Writing at the margin: Discourse between Anthropology and Medicine*, Berkeley: University of California Press.

Kleinman, A. and Kleinman, J., (1994), How bodies remember: social memory and bodily experience of criticism, resistance, and delegitimation following China's cultural revolution, *New Literary History* 25(3): 707–717.

Kondo, D., (1990), *Crafting Selves: Power, Gender, and Discourses of Identity in a Japanese Workplace*, Chicago: University of Chicago Press.

Küchler, S., (1987), Manangan: Art and Memory in a Melanesian Society, *Journal of the Royal Anthropological Institute* 22(2): 238–255.

Lambek, M., (1996), The Past Imperfect: remembering as moral practice. In P. Antze and M. Lambek (eds), *Tense Past: Cultural Essays in Trauma and Memory*, pp. 235–54. New York & London: Routledge.

Larrabee, M., (1995), The time of trauma: Husserl's phenomenology and Post-Traumatic Stress Disorder, *Human Studies* 18(4): 351–366.

Leavitt, S., (1995), Suppressed meanings in narratives about suffering: A case from Papua New Guinea, *Anthropology and Humanism* 20(2):133–152.

Loeffler, A., (2007), Individual constitutions vs universal physiology: Iranian responses to allopathic medicine, *Body & Society* 13(30): 103–123.

Merleau-Ponty, M., (1964), *Signs*, Trans. Richard C. McCleary. Evanston: Northwestern University Press.

Passerini, L., (2003), Memories between silence and oblivion. In K. Hodgkin and S. Radstone (eds), *Contested Pasts: The Politics of Memory*, New York: Routledge.

Price, J. and Shildrick, M., (1999), *Feminist Theory of the Body: A Reader*, New York: Routledge.

Radley, A., (1997), Artefacts, memory and a sense of the past. In D. Middleton and D. Edwards (eds), *Collective Remembering*, London: Sage.

Ram, K., (2000), Dancing the past into life. The Rasa, Nritta and Raga of immigrant existence. Special issue of *The Australian Journal of Anthropology*: 261–74.

Ram, K., (2005), Phantom Limbs; South Indian dance and immigrant reifications of the female body, *Journal of Intercultural Studies* 26(1–2): 121–137.

Seremetakis, N., (1996), *The Senses Still: Perception and Memory as Material Culture in Modernity*, Chicago: University of Chicago Press.

Sontag, S., (2004), *Regarding the Pain of Others*, London: Penguin.

Tober, D. and Budiani, D., (2007), Introduction: Why Islam, health and the body? *Body & Society* 13(3): 1–13.

Warin, M. and Dennis, S., (2005), Threads of memory: Reproducing the Cypress Tree through sensual consumption, *Journal of Intercultural Studies* 26(1–2): 159–170.

Weiner, J., (2001), *Tree Leaf Talk: A Heideggerian Anthropology*, New York: Berg.

Zarowsky, C., (2004), Writing trauma: Emotion, ethnography and the politics of suffering among Somali returnees in Ethiopia, *Culture, Medicine and Psychiatry* 28: 189–209.

Knowing body, knowing other: cultural materials and intensive care

Paul White

Introduction

The body has been perceived, theorized and related to in a variety of ways as made explicit in the introduction to this monograph. Such interest has been represented through a host of conceptualisations of the body such as the sick body (Frank, 2001; Scarry, 1985), the cyber body (Pitts, 2003; Haraway, 1991), the abject body (Kristeva, 1982), the absent body (Leder, 1990), the productive body and consumptive body (Falk, 1994; Munro, 1996; Latimer, 2001), the docile body (Foucault, 2002 [1972]), dormant bodies (Williams, 2005), the body as both subject and object of medical attention (Zaner, 1985), the gendered body (Butler, 1993), the stigmatized body (Goffman, 1986 [1963]), as well as in relation to bodily techniques, inscription and pedagogics (Mauss, 1973 [1934]; Bourdieu, 1977; Shilling, 2007). For the most part the body within these readings is taken as central, yet is read in relation to the experiential, the technological, the political, the visible, the existential, the performative and the interactional body. All of these readings of the body are visible within the place and space of intensive care, through its relation to critically ill patients themselves, their families, health care staff, medical technologies and organizational practices.

Drawing upon an ethnography of intensive care, this chapter traces the cultural materials through which a body becomes known at different points of hospitalization within an intensive care unit; beginning with the means through which bodies requiring intensive care are made knowable, from a point prior to admission, through admission itself (including endotracheal intubation to facilitate mechanical ventilation), and on to extubation. Through a process of becoming embedded within intensive care, physically and culturally, the means through which the body can be read proliferate. The bodies that enter intensive care are read from a certain position. Tacit assumptions that underpin readings of the critically ill body are unconcealed in relation to the cultural practices of intensive care. Following Strathern (2004), Latimer (2004, 2007), Munro (1999, 2005) and Latimer and Munro (2006), this chapter traces how bodies are unknown and made known through bodying forth cultural materials as a particular way of 'knowing' the body. From this perspective, the social world is understood in relations of extension to such cultural materials, just as self and other are also read in relations of extension to cultural materials (Strathern, 2004; Munro, 2005). It is in this respect I aim to make visible the means through which bodies, and by implication self and identity of the critically ill, are read in relation to such materials. Specifically, I present some of the ways that bodies within intensive care become known in relation to available cultural materials at different points of time during a period of admission to intensive care.

The aim here is to reproduce an ethnography of intensive care and the relations to the body that emerge from it. The point of reference to the body is taken from a witnessing of bodies in both conscious and unconscious states (as a consequence of general anaesthesia), with the body relying upon life-sustaining technologies of and in intensive care. The perspective of such a point of reference is not necessarily that of embodied subject, although embodied subjects emerge, nor that of material objects of the fleshy carnal body, although such a body emerges also. The aim here is to make explicit how bodies come to be known or, in turn, unknown within a particular cultural space at different periods of admission. It is argued that understandings of the body are bodied forth in relation to cultural materials (Strathern, 2004; Latimer, 2004; Latimer and Munro, 2006) and the means through which this is accomplished and some of the accomplishments of the cultural materials that are bodied forth will be made explicit. The cultural materials themselves demand a particular way of seeing and being, through their appropriation, and the accomplishments of such appropriation can be seen as a demanding relation (Munro, 2004). By this I mean that the cultural materials, by being both in extension to and in relation with, demand a particular way of seeing in relation to such cultural materials. In short, I hope to illuminate the means through which bodies are made visible as a particular point of perception in different ways (with different consequences), as well as the mundane means through which bodies are read within intensive care. In some small way, the means through which such revealings of bodies are understood, can be understood and are held (Latour, 1987) to be understood on a cultural level will be explicated. Such revealings and ways of knowing are bound up with the way cultural materials demand our relation to the world. For now I aim to show rather than explain such relations in practice.

Pre-figuring entry to intensive care

The (soon to be) intensive care patient becomes 'known' prior to admission into intensive care in relation to gender, age if particularly young or particularly old, significant pathology, injury or, when such classifying details are unknown, the location in which the incident occurred (such as a particular area of the city or neighbouring town) or circumstances surrounding the patient's requirement for intensive care (such as Road Traffic Accident) often suffice. Further details of who the patient is are generally unknown unless the admission has been planned, as after complex surgery, in which case beds are pre-booked by the surgeon. If the reason for admission or the story surrounding the admission is unusual, such as snow-boarding down an artificial ski slope on a For Sale sign, falling down a lift shaft or a violent attack, this is generally a sufficient level of knowing who the admission may be, and provides a certain premise from which the bed area can be prepared for the arriving patient. To some extent this also allows intensive care staff to indulge in certain assumptions about the person through their readings of the means by which the body has become injured.

The staff of intensive care employ a particular way of figuring patients which rests upon the significance they impute to cultural materials, such as those outlined above. For example, Sharon, a nurse with almost seven years experience in intensive care, is provided with the materials to pre-figure an intensive care patient prior to their admission. Specifically, she was informed of an impending admission that she had to accept (take) from the Emergency Unit (Casualty) by the intensive care Registrar:

> She would be 'taking' a seventy-two year old morbidly obese man with a chest infection who has high blood pressure, peripheral vascular disease, diabetes, is wheelchair bound, has had a stroke, a right above knee amputation, smokes twenty cigarettes a day and lives in a nursing home. He has been intubated (an endotracheal tube has been inserted through his mouth in order to facilitate mechanical ventilation) in casualty and needs ventilation, haemofiltration [renal support] and possibly inotropes (drugs which increase blood pressure). Sharon's response was 'what the hell do they expect us to be able to do for him here?' to which the registrar laughs.
>
> (From field notes)

The negative gloss that Sharon painted of the patient '. . . what the hell do they expect us to be able to do . . .' concerns a host of bodily and social issues. Whilst supportive therapies may be provided to support failing organ systems, Sharon's concern surrounds getting the patient off those supportive therapies and back home again. This patient is perceived to be unlikely to recover from this recent infection owing to complex co-morbidity and may not have been admitted if it weren't for the fact that he was intubated and reliant upon mechanical ventilation. By intensive care's own definition of what it should do and who it should treat, its rules of engagement are predicated upon a notion of 'potentially recoverable disease' (Intensive Care Society, 1997). For Sharon, as with other intensive care staff, this admission has breached the order of what intensive care takes itself to be, because the potential for recovery seems marginal in relation to his co-morbidities. In turn, his admission is seen as a subterfuge, as he has already been intubated and as a consequence now legitimately requires a place in intensive care; in part, he is read as a consequence of this organizational performance of intubation.

Suffice to say, the man she would be 'taking' is read through interpretations of his body, and is rendered knowable in relation not just to pathology but to the fact that his body has been breached with medical technologies (mechanical ventilation) and the means through which he has been made visible to intensive care staff.

The particular set of co-morbidities associated with this patient sets up very specifically for the nurse what sort of body she will be dealing with. The body is also read in relation to a pattern of presumed ignorance of health advice (smoking, obesity), and the bodies prosthesis, an endotracheal tube. When asked by other nurses who she is 'getting' she gives an account of the anticipated patient's history, amusing her colleagues in the process. Similarly the 'For Sale sign snow-boarder' provides a potted history of who this person is, the work involved (which will focus on the body) and gives rise to counter admissions from the other nurses 'I was working with Shana last week and we had a patient come in who . . .'. The body of the 'soon to be intensive care patient' is read from the initial information gleaned from a telephone call and within this, aspects of the person's identity are similarly being read and interpreted by intensive care staff. Intensive care staff read the body (and person) in relation to the only cultural materials available to them at a particular point in time; in this instance, a call from the Emergency Unit.

What is being pre-figured by the intensive care staff is a particular way of reading the body. Identity is recognized through recourse to identifiable action, inaction and the circumstances surrounding a reason for their coming into intensive care. Bodies and persons are being read *in abstentia* through recourse to the context of the admission to intensive care. What will be outlined next are some of the means through which bodies are read in relation to their place within intensive care, legitimate or otherwise. Furthermore nurses, through attachment to a certain cultural material (Strathern, 2004), in circumstances surrounding a 'soon to be intensive care patient', can be seen as producing selves in relation to that cultural material. Although this, as Munro (1996) in his critique of Douglas and Isherwood (1979) points out, always involves exclusion (in this case of non-intensive care staff), whilst demonstrating a certain 'belonging', to intensive care (Munro, 1996) in relation to the sharing of experiences, of different circumstances surrounding intensive care admission. In part, these tales as cultural materials are displayed, shared and appropriated by intensive care staff as a means through which membership is shared and made visible.[1] At the same time, they also make visible how a patient's identity is figured in relation to a multitude of materials, from their pathology and place of residence through to the means through which admission was granted. Indeed the doctors and nurses of intensive care demonstrate how the identities of others are continually figured in extension to an array of cultural materials that make themselves visible at different points in time. This will resurface in the analysis and representation of intensive care shortly, but before that a short excursion shall be made into the means through which critically ill bodies become embedded within intensive care.

Bodies on arrival

On arrival within intensive care, the patient is wheeled into the bed-space and transferred to the intensive care bed. At this point, the patient is still not necessarily a *bone fide* intensive care patient; they have to be 'hooked up' to the monitoring equipment as a means of preparing the body or, as Place (2000) described it, transform the 'sick body' into the 'critically-ill' body. Through the insertion of monitoring devices such as arterial lines, central venous lines, urinary catheters, endotracheal tubes and drains, which puncture, breach and open the body, the body can be made sense of; rendered visible to intensive care staff. Yet the body remains an object of treatment, of assessment; through the body's transformation into intensive care, residual aspects of the person (identity) are apparently stripped away, hidden, deferred as the body becomes *embedded* within intensive care.

> The patient had been transferred to the bed, Elizabeth is now 'sorting out' the patient, taking baseline physiological observations and 'turning her into an ICU patient' through the insertion of various lines and tubes, and hooking her up to the monitor. She is working on the patient's left side whilst the registrar is trying to place an arterial line in her right arm. 'I've got blood on the sheets,' the registrar shamefully admits. 'Don't worry,' replies Elizabeth, 'she's pee'd the bed anyway.' There is a foul pungent smell from the bed area, the registrar and the nurses are busy performing the 'sorting out'.
>
> (From field notes)

From the account of the staff nurse and the registrar in the above quote, who are working together to 'sort out' (transform) the patient, we can glean an idea of the ceremonial order. This particular patient was transferred to the unit from the hospital emergency unit. She was admitted as a result of ingesting a large cocktail of prescription and non-prescription pharmaceutical agents, washed down with a bottle of vodka. This 'reason for admission' provides the intensive care staff with a certain idea of who this person is and as mooted previously, their relative moral worth; what is significant is that the intensive care staff are working from their respective roles. Elizabeth is charting a set of baseline observations from which the patient's clinical condition can be judged over time. The work of intensive care is to make the body visible, intelligible, and indexical to the requirements of the organization and practice of intensive care (Garfinkel, 1967; Benson and Hughes, 1991). In order to accomplish this, the embedding of the patient requires the body to be processed into the fabric of intensive care, to become a malleable object that can be worked upon and in part understood through extension to multiple aspects of what constitutes identity as an intensive care patient. To be embedded is to begin the career trajectory (Goffman, 1991 [1961]) of an intensive care patient, which on transfer to the intensive care bed, generally starts with the insertion of an arterial line.

The patient above, who arrived from the Emergency Unit, did not have an arterial line, so the first duty of the registrar was to insert one. She was trying to insert an arterial cannula in the radial artery; she had failed a few attempts on one side of the patient so had gone to the opposite wrist. The patient was unconscious, sedated with a short-acting sedative infusion, intubated and so receiving mechanical ventilation. Without an arterial line there is little hard evidence for deducing whether the form of mechanical ventilation (if necessary at all) is sufficient, so it is needed promptly. An arterial line will generally be inserted prior to intubation in order to observe blood pressure and assess arterial blood gases to ensure that the body is being appropriately ventilated. The blood gas may also be taken if there is some uncertainty about whether the patient should be ventilated. This generally occurs between the admitting nurse and/or the nurse in charge and the medical staff, who will have undertaken their own assessments of the patient, or call upon others' assessments (such as orders from the consultant intensivist who may not necessarily be physically present). On occasion patients are intubated in the emergency unit by an anaesthetist (as in both cases presented here). In this case intubation was necessary because the woman had stopped breathing as a result of the drugs and alcohol she had ingested. Immediate intubation was necessary and so she was brought up to intensive care without the arterial line.

Through taking and analysing a sample of arterial blood, disputes over the appropriateness of intubation and ventilation are generally settled with the criteria for intubation being agreed between the two parties prior to the analysis. Anaesthetic drugs will be prepared in order to paralyse and sedate the 'body' so that the patient will be have no memory or knowledge of the paralysis. Once the patient is intubated, a portable X-ray will be ordered to ensure that the new tubes are in the correct position. Swabs will be taken from the body to ensure that should Methicillin Resistant *Staphylococcus aureus* be present it can be treated; it also ensures that it did not come from intensive care, an accountability measure. As in the opening portion of field notes (focussing on Elizabeth and the transfer of a patient from the Emergency Unit), the malodorous body will need washing and a change of sheets will be necessary, irrespective of whether or not the patient has 'pee'd the bed'. The body may well need additional large venous access for particularly irritant drugs and over time the amount of equipment in the bed space may accumulate, depending on how 'sick' the body is. The body is now being rendered legible to intensive care staff. It is being made amenable to further treatment of the underlying disease (if appropriate) whilst wholly dependent upon the supportive technologies that sustain it, including the intensive care staff.

The embedding routines are circumscribed in the observation ('obs') chart with each piece of the assessment having a particular place to be written or drawn or 'charted'. The admission forms and handover forms similarly require this information, so it is firmly sedimented as a particular intensive care practice. The body is beginning to be manipulated as a form of representation to fit the chart and the chart itself can be seen as a way in which the practices around the body become ordered (Hirschauer, 1991; Heath and Luff, 2000). Often changing the observation chart is used as a specific tool in order for changes in practice to become concretized (Chatterjee *et al.*, 2005). In common with the example of the male admission in the previous section, Elizabeth has admitted a patient who may or may not be an 'appropriate' admission to intensive care, by its own terms. However, both patients allow a further reading of the patient's identity in relation to all the information that is available to intensive care staff about the patient at a particular point in time. For Sharon, the person is read through extension to the patient's multiple pathology, the relative work that will be involved with the body, the residence of the person and the means through which the person gained access to intensive care. Whilst for Elizabeth the body makes itself visible through its leakages, blood and urine, for a moment the body is objectified and only known in that regard, much as the gaze of surgeon, anaesthetist (Hirschauer, 1991) or intensive care nurse (Kite, 1999), has only a limited perception of the body when performing particular tasks. The perception of the body is akin to a gestalt (Hirschauer, 1991; Strathern, 2004), whereby the gaze is restricted and focussed by the technology, both a normative and normalizing (Foucault, 1989 [1973]; Atkinson, 1995) means through which the body and the person is 'known' as will be explored in the following section. The technologies and orderings of the body produce new material from which the body can be read, as the body becomes embedded within intensive care as an object of attention.

Interpreting the body

Once the patient, or more accurately the body, is 'sorted out', they are not only in an intensive care bed but also embedded into the technology that enters, sustains and surrounds the body. The body has been breached, but it has also been extended into the technologies that have been secured to the strictly corporeal body. The heart's own rate and rhythm is displayed on the monitor, the internal physiological processes are presented as external 'physiological representations' (Place, 2000; Moreira, 2006). The body is now linked to the hospital through the network of piped medical gasses that 'connect' the lungs to the ventilator. Arteries are not only linked electronically to the monitor through a transducer, they are 'anastomosed' to a PVC circuit. Veins are infiltrated by numerous drugs and fluids. Feed comes in from another line to the new nasogastric tube, whilst urethral urinary catheters and on occasion faecal management systems drain the body. Everything going in and coming out is meticulously measured and documented. The body has been manipulated, squeezed, injected, ejected, paralysed, forced and reduced to a mathematical representation of itself; the body has been ordered (Law, 1994; Berg, 1997; 1998). The body is now simultaneously opened, closed, drained, filled and, significantly, it now makes 'intensive care sense', being rendered safe and legible by intensive care staff. The body has now become both physically and metaphorically embedded; an intrinsic part of the intensive care unit. It is through such technologies that the body makes 'intensive care sense', yet the technologies of monitoring, ventilation and renal support transform the way the body can be seen, the technologies are 'in your face'.

> . . . if you em come into the bed area or something (.) very sick on intensive care you can come in you've got em you've got a filter in your bed area (.) you've got your monitor you've got your PiCCO box em all the connections to your PiCCO (Pulse induced Continuous Cardiac Output) wire you might have an oscillator (High Frequency Oscillatory Ventilation) at the back of the bed which is thundering away and sounding like a washing machine on a spin dry cycle at the back so it's all you know so many things going on (.) and it's as you get more used to it you just you forget that they're there you become less aware that it's in your face and you just (.) em you can just em (.) you can just you (.) instead of staring intently at it you can pick up what's going on with everything you become em a bit more aware of any changes and any things that are going on around you.
>
> (From interview with George, staff nurse)

George is referring to being allocated a 'sicky' (unstable critically ill patient) the PiCCO monitor and a specific form of mechanical ventilation referred to as the oscillator. Significantly, he is referring to becoming an intensive care nurse and being able to switch off from the technology and work with the technology without letting it take over his concentration. He can remain vigilant of the representations of the body in mathematical form through the monitoring equipment without being dependent upon it. Changes in condition are noted; he no longer stares intently at the technology. The difficulty for him when coming into intensive care was to see the person over the technology and to be able to deal with the unconscious totally dependent patient. Whilst he recognizes that he is being disciplined into the technology of intensive care, a mode of organizing, seeing, he also recognizes a need to perceive the body beyond the way that technology 'forces' him to see. That is, the discipline of being a nurse within intensive care is far more powerful for him than the disciplining gaze of technology, as he makes explicit below:

> you filter out the technology and you just em see the important bits of it you know (.) em rather than looking at er a ventilator and eh seeing em all the expiratory valves all the filters all the tubing everything else around it you just see the fact that your tidal volumes have dropped you know or em you know somebody's you know you look at the flow diagram on the front and you can see that somebody's starting to take a breath over the top or that (.) your inspiratory pressures are rising or whatever
>
> (From interview with George, staff nurse)

The technology performs an important function, but critically it is at the intersection between body and machine that intensive care staff can commence the work of filtering out that information. Information that is considered useful (deviation from 'normal') or useless (normal breath) is ordered so that the work of intensive care can happen. Perhaps more tellingly, it is through the technology that he gets to know the body better. Through the insertion of numerous lines, drains, tubes and numerous modes of monitoring and controlling it, the body can be understood or becomes legible, yet can also be disregarded. The materials (artefacts) of physiological monitoring enable George to read the body in extension, yet they can be discarded or acted upon at different points. This legibility is further concretized in the way it becomes a fact when written onto the 'obs' chart and associated documentation. But this legibility is in part made possible through recourse to artefacts. The artefacts themselves become cultural artefacts through shared knowledge and understanding of the specific meanings they give forth.

The body, through these artefacts, becomes legible to the staff of intensive care and becomes a shared ground through which the body can be discussed between intensive care staff. Whereas previously, cultural artefacts alluded to through the example of Sharon and the sharing of stories enabled a reading of a person, these putatively 'hard scientific facts' are shared in similar terms. The body is read in extension to another way of seeing, another material, but this time the body is known through extension to the cultural artefacts of technical reading. The body is read through extension to the body's prosthesis of medical technology, being simultaneously incorporated by and extended into the technology (prosthesis), provisionally and at least for a time. The body itself becomes unreliable as a source of information on its own; it is through flow diagrams that the most mundane yet most important things such as breathing are re-read. It is possible to tell when the person (the body) is no longer paralysed as breaths are taken over those delivered by the ventilator and this demands a review of the ventilation. As the body has become joined to the intensive care unit, we can see from George's explanation of 'taking breaths' it is becoming increasingly difficult to separate out that which is bodily from that which is technological. Through these artefacts the work of reading the body becomes enmeshed in the reading of artefacts; the body is read in extension to these artefacts.

> Consultant: I want somebody to do the bloods, x-ray, and sort out all the structural stuff. I want somebody else to go through the notes and get a thorough history, I don't want you to just write down what I've been told, I want you to read back and find out.
>
> (From field notes)

What information is considered reliable and what information should not be trusted is demonstrated by a consultant intensivist who had 'retrieved' a patient from another hospital. Even though the intensive care consultant has discussed this patient at length with the referring intensive care consultant, the facts he holds are not considered totally reliable. He has given an account of the patient to the junior doctors, but his account should not be paraphrased and written up in the medical notes. He demands a thorough history of the patient to be documented drawing from the notes supplied by the referring hospital. This is in part a history of the person, how they came to be in intensive care in the first place and what had happened to the body within the referring intensive care unit. In telling of the body, it is a tale of the organization and practice of the referring intensive care unit; a tale of the embedded body that has been physically linked to another space.

He expects a thorough assessment of the body, as he put it the 'structural stuff', the stuff that will form the foundation for any further treatment. He demands that the body be read and interpreted in a way that makes sense to the organizational idiosyncrasies of *this* intensive care. The equipment and scarification produced from the previous 'home' of this intensive care patient needs to be documented, the old lines need to be removed and replaced with this intensive care unit's equipment. Their critically ill body needs to become 'our' critically ill body. This does not mean the previous intensive care unit is an inferior intensive care unit, more that the body needs to be processed or 'sorted out' in a very particular way so that the body can be presented as 'our new patient' on the consultants' shift 'hand-over' in a few hours time. For reasons of both territory and accountability, the new intensive care requires a 'clean slate' from which to work foreign equipment needs to be removed and replaced with the local equipment. Whilst the work of legibility has been done elsewhere, the body needs to be made locally legible, the 'sorting out' and documentation needs to be done in order for the body to be presented on the ensuing Ward Round legibly. The body is ceremonially incorporated into the organization, as 'our body'.

In order to make sense of the body it needs to be punctured, entered and linked physically and metaphorically to the organization. It receives from the space and expels into the space. This process is tied into a judgement of the body, it is required to give information about itself through interpretive monitoring equipment that are in turn interpreted and made sense of by the staff. Core intensive care texts (eg, Hinds and Watson, 1996) reinforce these physiological representations as either in or out of safe parameters for physiological integrity, yet as a cultural material these representations are interpreted at points of medical uncertainty, invoked or discarded in favour of other monitoring forms (Hirschauer, 1991). For example, a member of the medical staff reviews an arterial blood gas and states that with such numbers the patient is fit for extubation (discontinuation of mechanical ventilation), whilst the nurse points out that the patient has a low level of consciousness and is not 'ready' for extubation. The physiological representation of the blood gas is interpreted and passed over as the risk of failed extubation is too great at this point.[2] Ideas of risk and uncertainty are assuaged by the monitoring practices and supportive therapeutics such as blood gas, but are read in relation to a host of other cultural materials, such as in this case, consciousness level. The body is totally vulnerable; manual and mechanical pressures are exerted on it in order for it to be rendered legible to intensive care staff. So the body is sorted out by being assimilated into the fabric of intensive care, which makes it hard to separate out the points of the body and that of the technology (Place, 2000). Yet the 'hard science' of numerical representations can also be reduced to interpretations during disputes about the appropriateness of treatment.

Following Nietzsche (1968) and Rorty (1979), even the facts are made visible as interpretations; they emerge as the body is read in extension to them. Such interpretations, however remain stable within intensive care as (re)configurations of the body (at least for a time) to discuss such materials (such as the numbers)[3] is to be a member of staff, as with the admission stories alluded to earlier. Such talk discriminates the staff of intensive care from others, yet the strength of such figurings (numbers) as materials of reading 'holds' (Latour, 1987) as a means of working and ordering (Law, 1994; Berg, 1997; 1998). The numbers are seldom disputed (the above example being an exception) simply the means of recording them, as in the case of equipment failure. Intensive care staff are vigilant to the changing nature of the body; but the body is transmogrified into a mathematical representation of itself which further enmeshes it into the technology. In essence the body is processed in order to make sense, yet the 'sense' that such 'representations' are extended into is not always fixed. Such representations can be invoked to legitimate action, such as discharge or extubation, but the relative weight of another material can disrupt the 'truth' of the cultural material. The assumption that underlies intensive care is that a greater level of meaning can be provided by a technical as opposed to a non-technical body. That is, the greater the number of technologies that can record and measure the body, the greater the likelihood that the body can be treated effectively and safely (Latour, 1991). The anti-programme, of physiological instability, for example, cannot be completely accounted for within the programme of multiplying representations of the pathophysiological body; but the body requires embedding within the technical and cultural order for such a proliferation of technologies to be implemented. The body has begun a process of assimilation, to be embedded within the structure of intensive care, to be made technical and representable. Through 'sorting out' (ordering), documenting and (re)presenting the body, it has been rendered legible to the local and specific intensive care unit.

Cultural materials are made available for intensive care staff to read bodies, to pre-figure the person who is due to enter intensive care. Bodies and identity are pre-figured in relation to the available cultural materials of pathology, circumstance surrounding injury and in relation to the way the body 'behaves', physiologically. In turn, identity is always undecided, subject to change and read in extension to such a variety of cultural artefacts. The body in turn becomes embedded within the fabric of intensive care as an object deserving of medical attention and re-figured in relation to the ways in which it can be rendered legible. This legibility rests upon the means through which the body can be manipulated to meet the requirements of the organization of intensive care. The body is forced into a means through which it can be easily read; the body is rendered indexical in order that it meet the format required of intensive care (Benson and Hughes, 1991) as a particular organizational ordering. Such organizational ordering transforms the way that the body is seen. The way the body is seen reproduces cultural (intensive care) assumptions that the sustenance of life comes prior to any other consideration of the patient. Yet, within this the significance of calls to risk and accountability (the blood gas, documenting observations and life supporting technologies) surface as crucial means through which the body can be read, interpreted and understood. The technologies are at times effaced and at times recourse is made to the 'legitimate' reading of the body. Readings of the body are undecided yet within intensive care they need to be settled, they need to hold (Latour, 1987) and be seen and believed to be holding. In part it is through the available cultural materials of blood gas results, as materials that hold that any undecidability is settled. The final issue I will address here, in relation to bodies within intensive care, concerns critically ill bodies that move, interact and make up social life in intensive care.

On being awake

Jean is a woman who had been in intensive care for about two weeks following colo-rectal surgery; she had failed extubation during her intensive care stay. By the time I had met her she had developed her own strategies for attracting the attention of the intensive care staff. This consisted of looking at the person whose attention she wished to attract whilst hitting the side of the bed with her hand. This would be repeated, growing louder until the staff member that she required came over to her. She had a reputation as a 'bed slapper' among the intensive care staff. This could be seen as a means through which intensive care patients are known through their actions; in the flesh as opposed to *in abstentia*. Whilst she was never explicitly referred to as a 'bed slapper' as such, if staff needed to differentiate her from another patient, she could be identified through such action. This occurred during handover, the occasion for allocating nurses to patients in a private space within the intensive care unit when a nurse needed clarification of who exactly Jean was:

> oh you know her, she's the one who keeps slapping the hell out of the cot sides in bed fourteen.

> (From Field Notes)

For patients who are unable to move their arms, such as those with Guillain-Barré syndrome for example, they sometimes attract attention by 'clicking', using their teeth and tongue. Often these new methods are introduced by nurses themselves and suggested as means of gaining attention. Yet this communicative strategy is one that enables further readings to be made of the person, even if such strategies were set in motion by intensive care staff. It is through her actions that Jean is rendered visible and identifiable to intensive care staff. These new means of securing the attention of others seem to work quite efficiently, enabling communication either written or 'mouthed'. Jean however, whether for good or ill, was a 'bed slapper', but sometimes this meant she missed out on something; some everyday aspects of the social were being effaced.

Paul: You seemed to get people's attention easily enough though

Jean: Well, I tapped the side of the bed and the nurses (.) oh they're ever so good (.) they come over and read my lips mostly they get it right and do whatever I need change my pillows or whatever but they just turn around and do something else (.) I know they're very busy but I feel bad that each time they did something for me, I tried to say thank you (.) but by that time they had walked away so couldn't see what I was saying

(From follow-up interview in ICU)

For Jean, the nurses in particular were attentive and 'mostly [got] it right', but this attention came at a price. They were able to do the instrumental things for her and read her lips correctly, for the most part, but something was missing. Doing the normal stuff of being social constituted expressions of gratitude, the everyday conventions of doing being Jean (Sacks, 1984; Hirschauer, 2005) are made visible in a space where doing being Jean is seen as an irritation, within intensive care. The normal social rules no longer apply within intensive care, yet often these conventions are still held by its patients. The irritation the nurses expressed can in part be read as a direct consequence of the proximity Jean shares with the nurses, that with such forced attention, or little respite to civil inattention (Goffman, 1966), there may be a discomfort about continually engaging with another (Garfinkel, 1967), particularly when it interferes with the rigid routines of intensive care work. What can be seen through these accomplishments are the nurses turning and doing something else, be that charting observations, drawing-up intra-venous drugs, discussions with colleagues or whatever. What is being disposed of by intensive care staff are the normal interactional conventions of social life. But then intensive care isn't exactly normal, nor are its conventions. But these abnormal situations of speechlessness, immobility and the difficulty in performing the mundane interaction of social life are normalized, made part and parcel of the cultural milieu of intensive care. As a consequence, the 'normal' conventions of social life that lead to the 'bed slapping' are seen as an irritation. Such a practice, however, demonstrates that intensive care patients are active participants in the social world around them, being actively involved in the reality of intensive care as they see it. The fact that intensive care does not stick to the normal rules of social convention that would require engagement with Jean, for example, demonstrates in part that something else is happening here and perhaps requires explication.

Jean, through her actions demonstrates how the more subtle aspects of social life are entered into and effaced. Such effacement can be read as an effect of speechlessness itself. It is recognized that on one level, Jean could be reflexively engaged with the social world that surrounds her, only the nurses do not respond as those outside of intensive care might do. The nurses are elsewhere doing other things, too busy to engage in contact with her. Metaphorically they avert their eyes from Jean, look away through calls to some other issue, some other task. Equally, Jean's actions could be seen as making visible the deeply entrenched conventions of mundane social life, not only as cultural techniques of the body (Mauss, 1973 [1934]), but techniques of interaction (Goffman, 1959 [1990]). It would appear to take quite a lot of effort, seemingly more than the medical technologies and technologies of effacement for these engrained performances of social life to be lost. As a 'bed slapper', the ways through which nurses engage with Jean are slightly altered; attention can legitimately be shifted away from her as she will alert the staff when she requires something. As has been shown earlier, however, not only are the intensive care staff fixed upon the work through the technology, much like the surgeons and anaesthetists of Hirschauer (1991), but also the work becomes easier when the intensive care staff are not 'helped' by the patient. Indeed some staff emphasize how much easier their work is when the patient is under general anaesthesia. Jean has in part become her action, she is her means through which she is known and makes herself known to others. From the perspective of the nurses dealing with her, she is the 'bed slapper', and one that the intensive care staff find difficult to extricate from the sustaining medical technologies, both as an embodied subject and an object of medical attention.

Jean presents an interactional problem, how to get somebody to notice you in the first instance, how to call attention to oneself without recourse to speech. Perhaps the most obvious example is a wave of the hand; and this is a strategy sometimes employed by the critically ill but often discouraged by intensive care nurses. Logically, through the way that nurses negotiate the bed space this would make an ideal means of calling attention, particularly as nurses are focussed for the most part on and around the body. The nurses are engrossed in a certain way of seeing which focuses on the mouth, the body and those tethering accoutrements of technology. The technology transforms the gaze of the intensive care staff, as mooted previously. However, the numbers of invasive lines which tether the body to the technologies of, for example, syringe drivers and monitors, make the wave a difficult thing to accomplish. The technologies that tether the body have specific effects on bodily performances, from 'wave' to 'bed slapper'. Jean is read in relation to the effects that technologies have upon her tethered body. Waving arms runs the risk of admonishment from intensive care staff should a line or cannula come out. This is particularly the case as arterial lines (for monitoring and sampling blood) and venous lines (for non-irritant infusions) are inserted into the upper limbs. Within such a context, Jean's strategy of gaining attention works very efficiently for her, without running the risk of decannulating the arterial and venous lines. It is however, through extension to the technologies that bind Jean to intensive care that aspects of Jean are made visible to intensive care staff. Jean is figured in relation to the technologies of intensive care, both as an organization and a mode of practising, a normative and normalizing gaze (Foucault, 1989 [1973]; Atkinson, 1995); at the same time she is always read in extension to a multitude of cultural materials, such as the technology of bleeps and whirrs and that of the organizational practices of intensive care.

When I spoke to Jean after she was extubated, finally, she spoke about the fear of not being able to talk ever again. She could not recall anybody telling her that her voice loss would be temporary until the tube came out. Ordinarily, intensive care staff would not explain that the voice loss would be temporary with somebody who has an endotracheal tube in place; this is a concern that is most often associated with those who have had a tracheostomy performed. However this did not stop Jean from worrying about the impact this would have on her life, assuming she would leave intensive care. Permanent loss of speech was something that terrified Jean, this was perhaps made worse by the fact that she couldn't seek, or at least be understood in seeking, clarification over whether or not her voice loss would be permanent. At home, Jean lived with one of her daughters who has cerebral palsy. The intensive care staff were aware of her home life as a carer, that her daughter was staying with another of her daughters and their family and that she had learning disabilities, yet they had no idea of her concerns. Yet Jean's particular fear about her voice loss was that she was her daughter's main carer; she did the talking for both of them:

> Paul: I bet you're glad to see the back of that tube
> Jean: (laughs) I was scared that I would never speak again, my daughter has cerebral palsy and I look after her at home (.) I do most of the talking for her, it's just me and (my daughter) so I was very worried
>
> (from interview on High Dependency Unit)

Like most people, speech was seen as of prime importance in the life of Jean and one that should not be denied. The ability to speak was of the utmost importance for Jean and by implication for her daughter in the conduct of their lives. Unlike most people, Jean was acutely aware of the significance of speech within ordinary social life through her experience of caring for her daughter. This was an aspect of Jean of which none of the intensive care staff were aware. For the intensive care staff, she was able to be differentiated from other patients through her technique of attracting the attention of staff. Jean the mother, Jean the carer, Jean the voice of the household, had no place within the order of intensive care; she was the lady in Bed Fourteen, the subtotal colectomy, the failed extubation, the 'bed slapper', in talk among intensive care staff. She became the actions she performed, but she also provides a good insight into the significance of speech within social life in general and an example of how to accomplish 'pillow-changing' within intensive care.

Having taken a brief look at Jean, and one of her concerns in particular, what is being emphasized is the significance of the means through which bodies and persons are read through extension, unconcealed through a lack of speech. On the face of it, this would appear to be obvious. It is through speech that we negotiate and construct the world around us (Derrida, 1976 [1967]; Ong, 1988) but the finer details of how significant it is, in more mundane social encounters, is exposed through examples such as that of Jean. For Jean, being able to attract the attention of staff becomes a hurdle that needs to be jumped and she develops strategies to achieve this. The significance of speech to her is bound up with her daughter and her role at home as the voice for the pair of them, when this is perceived to be lost 'it just doesn't bear thinking about'. Through such cultural revelations exposed through conversation with Jean, another layer of identity as performed through interaction is made visible. Jean is read in extension of the cultural material of motherhood, carer of a daughter with cerebral palsy in addition to 'bed slapper'.

Final thoughts

Introducing this chapter, I referred to a host of theoretical positions concerning the body and social life. All of these readings would have a legitimate place within this chapter as a means of developing understandings of the body within intensive care. As noted in the introduction to this monograph, it is difficult to delineate the distinctions between cultural processes, cultural inscriptions upon the body and that which is the fleshy stuff of the body. In part this is why these readings are not invoked and the ethnography presented does not draw upon such theories although, as the chapter progressed, the points at which such readings might have proved fruitful will have become apparent. The main issue here however, is that this chapter concerns itself with cultural materials; as a consequence, such theoretical readings of the body themselves can be seen as cultural materials through which the body can be understood. The aim of the chapter is to make visible a number of cultural materials and the means through which they are bodied forth as a strategy of knowing the body that related specifically to an ethnography of intensive care.

Theorizations of the body and embodiment can be applied to any body at varying points of individual and social life and the body in turn is read in accordance with such a theoretical position; as distinct forms of understanding, such theorizations of the body, when applied, focus attention on particular aspects of the body, its performance, its cultural reproduction and inscription. As a consequence, the body is reduced in compliance with a theoretical reading of the body, once a means through which the body can be made visible and understandable, akin to the indexicality of Garfinkel (Benson and Hughes, 1991). The theoretical lens through which the body has been perceived holds its own domain's assumptions (Gouldner, 1971) and as a result acts as a cultural material, in extension to which the body is read, being bodied forth (Strathern, 2004; Latimer and Munro, 2006) within such relations of extension to specific forms of analyses, including this one. Theorizations of the body are reproduced as another means through which the body can be understood, and consequently hold their own cultural accomplishments (Garfinkel, 1967; Callon, 1986; Latour, 1987; Latimer, 2000). The body as a site of theorizing is reproduced recursively through the theorizations, as the theory (as cultural material) is bodied forth as a means through which the body can be understood; and that includes readings of the body that have been demonstrated here. The body in part reproduces the lens through which it has initially been made visible. A reading of Law's (2004) notion of deliberate imprecision, drawing upon Strathern's (2004) work, can be taken as a means through which such theoretical and situational reproductions of the body can be assuaged. Yet in turn I invoke Strathern and Law as a particular cultural material and it is to this idea of knowing and unknowing the body that I have attended to within this chapter.

Throughout this chapter I have made visible how bodies are known and identity is read in relations of extension to cultural materials as and when they are made available. Whilst taking this starting point, however, I have also aimed to unconceal some simple assumptions that underlie readings of others in social life. For example, the body can be read in abstentia, in relation to medical and organizational technologies,[4] in relation to doing being member (Garfinkel, 1967; Hirschauer, 2005), behaviour, expectations, the list not being exclusive. Crucially, the multitude of materials available from which to read the body is endless. The point here is, which cultural material is bodied forth and what accomplishments does such a bodying forth hold for reading the body in intensive care specifically and in social life more generally? Such readings of the body within intensive care enable a repro-duction of the cultural order enabling shared understandings and perspectives to be shared and reproduced. Within intensive care, the body is drawn from an array of materials and is tied in with a demand for a body to leave intensive care, particularly for the body to be in a fit enough state to be weaned from life-sustaining technologies, discharged out to a general ward and back to mundane social life. As a consequence, the availability of materials from which the body can be read are initially fairly sparse, but proliferate in relation to medical technologies, organizational practices, visits by family members (Happ, 2000), physiological behaviours, physical behaviours and so on. Taking inten-sive care as a model case perhaps, the ways in which such cultural materials proliferate is unconcealed, which in turn impact upon how the body is related to and as a consequence 'treated'.

> Structure is replaced by process, systems effects are deleted in favour of human agency, modernism is given over to postmodernism, but the essence of reductionism is maintained. There is always this macho insistence on there being some central motor to movement and change, some basic core from which everything swings and sings.
>
> (Munro, 2005: 262).

Taking an ethnographic space that has as its starting point a reduction of persons amidst an amplification of technology, I aimed to make explicit how intensive care patients are read, and read quite differently in relation to the availability of cultural materials. As the chapter progressed and as the patient becomes increasingly embedded within intensive care I attempted to emphasize how the cultural materials from which the critically ill could be figured multiply. Far from a simple pick-and-mix reading of consumption and production of configurations of identity, the aim has been to demonstrate that seeing through extension to cultural materials reflects a particular engagement. At times such ways of seeing were predicated upon limited information, then in terms of the way the body has been embedded into intensive care, through the technologies of intensive care and the technology of intensive care as a means of ordering the body and the perception of the body. As a consequence, the means through which the body is bodied forth, by intensive care staff in general and intensive care nurses in particular, rests upon the cultural materials in extension to which the body is read. Simply put, this reading of an ethnography of intensive care makes visible the multitude of means through which bodies are figured in extension, in turn having implications for understanding how anybody figures anybody else within social life.

These moments are taken as part of the performance and re-performance of intensive care within one field site, yet through the site the translocation of selves and identities has been made visible in relation to numerous cultural materials that are appropriated and applied in numerous ways. The emphasis I wish to make is not a heterogeneity of selves and identities that pick and choose a moment of unconcealment, more that ideas of the other, or indeed of ourselves are less whole and more part(s). A core self or central motor, as emphasized in relation to the above quote that is concealed and revealed under differing conditions, is not what is being suggested; more that bodies, persons, understandings are always in extension to 'something'.

These relations are bodied forth through cultural materials as prosthesis, such as monitoring technologies, a mode of seeing such as in an organizational context. These relations are made and remade and I have attempted to illustrate the means through which bodies are read at different points within a moral career of being critically ill. The body is always known and unknown in relation to the available cultural materials as well as those that are 'bought into', such as physiological representations. It is in this sense that social life is both known and unknown in relation to those cultural materials that are taken to represent the underlying position from which the world is witnessed and understood, which has implications for how culture is produced and reproduced as a means through which we body forth cultural materials.

Acknowledgements

I would like to thank Joanna Latimer for providing me with the opportunity to present an earlier version of this paper and providing insightful comments of earlier drafts. I also wish to thank Michael Schillmeier for helpful comments to a previous draft of this chapter. Of course, I am most grateful to the staff, patients and families of intensive care who allowed me into the research site and provided fascinating insights into the workings of intensive care. The research was undertaken as part of an Economic & Social Research Council research studentship (PTA-030-2002-00317), with an additional research award provided by the British Association of Critical Care Nurses and I gratefully acknowledge their support. Full ethical and institutional review was secured for this research.

Notes

1 The recourse to such tales can also backfire, however, as different members envisage persons and situations in relation to different cultural materials, a point that will not be elaborated here.
2 A failed extubation refers to extubation (removal of endotracheal tube) and the subsequent need for re-intubation. Failed extubation is seen in a negative light as it runs a greater risk of slow weaning from ventilation (Schwartz, 1997), increasing intensive care length of stay.
3 'Numbers' within the field site referred to the physiological representations, blood chemistry results and so forth.
4 Medical technologies are referred to for reasons of clarity. It is recognized that the material blips and whirrs of medical technology is a an organizational technology.

References

Atkinson, P., (1995), *Medical Talk and Medical Work: The Liturgy of the Clinic*, London: Sage.
Benson, D. and Hughes, J.A., (1991), Method: evidence and inference – evidence and inference for ethnomethodology, in G. Button (ed.), *Ethnomethodology and the Human Sciences*, Cambridge: Cambridge University Press.
Berg, M., (1997), *Rationalising Medical Work: Decision-Support Techniques and Medical Practices*, Massachusetts: MIT Press.
Berg, M., (1998), Order(s) and Disorder(s): of protocols and medical practices, in M. Berg, M. and A. Mol (eds), *Differences in Medicine: Unravelling Practices, Techniques, and Bodies*, Durham NC: Duke University Press.
Bourdieu, P., (1977), *Outline of a Theory of Practice* (translated by R. Nice), Cambridge: Cambridge University Press.
Butler, J., (1993), *Bodies That Matter: On the Discursive Limits of "Sex"*, London: Routledge.
Callon, M., (1986), Some Elements of a Sociology of Translation: Domestication of the Scallops and the Fishermen of St Brieuc Bay, in J. Law (ed.), *Power, Action and Belief: A New Sociology of Knowledge*, London: Routledge & Kegan Paul.
Chatterjee, M.T., Moon, J.C., Murphy, R. and McCrea, D., (2005), The 'OBS' chart: an evidence based approach to re-design of the patient observation chart in a district general hospital setting, *Postgraduate Medical Journal* 81: 663–666.
Derrida, J., (1972 [1984]), Difference, in *Margins of Philosophy* (translated by A. Bass), Chicago: University of Chicago Press.
Derrida, J., (1976 [1967]), *Of Grammatology* (translated by G.C. Spivak), Baltimore: John Hopkins University Press.
Derrida, J., (2006 [1993]), *Specters of Marx: the State of the Debt, the Work of Mourning, and the New International* (translated P. Kamuf), London: Routledge Classics.
Douglas, M. and Isherwood, B., (1996/1979), *The World of Goods: Towards an Anthropology of Consumption*, London: Routledge.
Falk, P., (1994), *The Consuming Body*, London: Sage.
Foucault, M., (2002 [1972]), *The Archaeology of Knowledge*, London: Routledge.
Foucault, M., (1989 [1973]), *The Birth of the Clinic: An Archaeology of Medical Perception*, London: Routledge.
Frank, A., (2001 [1991]), *At the Will of the Body: Reflections on Illness*, New York: Houghton Mifflin.
Garfinkel, H., (1967), *Studies in Ethnomethodology*, Cambridge: Polity.

Goffman, E., (1959 [1990]), *The Presentation of Self in Everyday Life*, Harmondsworth: Penguin.

Goffman, E., (1961 [1991]), *Asylums: Essays on the Social Situation of Mental Patients and Other Inmates*, Harmondsworth: Penguin.

Goffman, E., (1986 [1963]), *Stigma: Notes on the Management of Spoiled Identity*, New York: Simon & Schuster.

Goffman, E., (1966), *Behavior in Public Places*, New York: Free Press.

Gouldner, A., (1971), *The Coming Crisis of Western Sociology*, London: Heinemann.

Happ, M.B., (2000), Interpretation of nonvocal behavior and the meaning of voicelessness in critical care, *Social Science and Medicine* 50: 1247–1255.

Haraway, D., (1991), *Simians, Cyborgs and Women: The Reinvention of Nature*, London: Free Association Books.

Heath, C. and Luff, P., (2000), Documents and Professional Practice: 'bad' organizational reasons for 'good' clinical records, in C. Heath and P. Luff (eds), *Technology in Action*, Cambridge: Cambridge University Press.

Hinds, C.J. and Watson, D., (1996), *Intensive Care: A Concise Textbook*, (second edn), London: WB Saunders.

Hirschauer, S., (1991), The Manufacture of Bodies in Surgery, *Social Studies of Science* 21(2): 279–319.

Hirschauer, S., (2005), On Doing Being a Stranger: The Practical Constitution of Civil Inattention, *Journal for the Theory of Social Behaviour* 35(1): 41–67.

Illich, I., (1991 [1976]), *Limits to Medicine: Medical Nemesis – The Expropriation of Health*, Harmondsworth: Penguin.

Intensive Care Society, (1997), *Standards for Intensive Care Units*, London: Intensive Care Society.

Kite, K., (1999), Participant observation, peripheral observation or apart-icipant observation? *Nurse Researcher* 7(1): 44–55.

Kristeva, J., (1982), *Powers of Horror: An Essay on Abjection*, (translated by L.S. Roudiez), New York: Colombia University Press.

Latimer, J., (2000), *The Conduct of Care: Understanding Nursing Practice*, Oxford: Blackwell.

Latimer, J., (2001), All-consuming passions: materials and subjectivity in an age of enhancement, in N. Lee and R. Munro (eds), *The Consumption of Mass*, Sociological Review Monograph, Oxford: Blackwell.

Latimer, J., (2004), Commanding Materials: (Re)legitimating authority in the context of multi-disciplinary work, *Sociology* 38(4): 757–775.

Latimer, J., (2007), Diagnosis, dysmorphology and the family: knowledge, motility, choice, *Medical Anthropology* 26(2): 53–94.

Latimer, J. and Munro, R., (2006), Driving the Social, in S. Böhm, C. Jones, C. Land and M. Paterson (eds), *Against Automobility*, Oxford: Blackwell.

Latour, B., (1987), *Science in Action: How to Follow Scientists and Engineers Through Society*, Massachusetts: Harvard.

Latour, B., (1991), Technology is society made durable, in J. Law (ed.), *The Sociology of Monsters*, London: Routledge.

Law, J., (1994), *Organizing Modernity*, Oxford: Blackwell.

Law, J., (2004), *After Method: Mess in Social Science Research*, London: Routledge.

Leder, D., (1990), *The Absent Body*, Chicago: Chicago University Press.

Lyotard, J-F., (1986), *The Postmodern Condition: A Report on Knowledge* (translated by G. Bennington and B. Massumi), Manchester: Manchester University Press.

Mauss, M., (1973 [1934]), Techniques of the Body, (translated by B. Brewster), *Economy and Society* 2(1): 70–88.

Merleau-Ponty, M., (1989 [1962]), *Phenomenology of Perception*, (translated by C. Smith), London: Routledge.

Moreira, T., (2006), Heterogeneity and Coordination of Blood Pressure in Neurosurgery, *Social Studies of Science* 36(1): 69–97.

Munro, M., (1996), The consumption view of self: extension, exchange and identity, in S. Edgell, K. Hetherington and A. Warde (eds), *Consumption Matters: The Production and Experience of Consumption*, Sociological Review Monograph, Oxford: Blackwell.

Munro, R., (1999), The cultural performance of control, *Organizational Studies* 20(4): 619–639.

Munro, R., (2001), Disposal of the Body: Upending Postmodernism, *Ephemera* 1(2): 108–130.

Munro, R., (2004), Punctualising identity: time and the demanding relation, *Sociology* 38(2): 293–311.

Munro, R., (2005), Partial organization: Marilyn Strathern and the elicitation of relations, *The Sociological Review* 53(1): 245–266.

Nietzsche, F., (1968), *The Will to Power*, W. Kaufman (ed.), (translated by W. Kaufman and R.J. Holingdale), New York: Vintage.

Ong, W.J., (1988), *Orality and Literacy,* London: Routledge.

Pitts, V., (2003), *In the Flesh: The Cultural Politics of Body Modification*, New York: Palgrave Macmillan.

Place, B., (2000), Constructing the Bodies of Critically Ill Children: an Ethnography of Intensive Care, in A. Prout (ed.), *The Body, Childhood and Society*, Basingstoke: Palgrave Macmillan.

Robillard, A.B., (1999), *Meaning of a Disability: The Lived Experience of Paralysis*, Philadelphia: Temple University Press.

Rorty, R., (1979), *Philosophy and the Mirror of Nature*, New Jersey: Princeton University Press.

Sacks, H., (1984), On doing 'being ordinary', in J.M. Atkinson and J. Heritage (eds), *Structures of Social Action*, New York: Cambridge University Press.

Scarry, E., (1985), *The Body in Pain: The Making and Unmaking of the World*, Oxford University Press: Oxford.

Schwartz, M.A., (1997), Airways management in critically ill patients: Prevention and Management of complications, in M.A. Schwartz and D.E. Matthay (eds), *Complications in the Intensive Care Unit: Recognition, Prevention and Management*, New York: Chapman and Hall.

Shilling, C., (2007), Sociology of the body: classical traditions and new agendas, in C. Shilling (ed.), *Embodying Sociology: Retrospect, Progress and Prospects*, Sociological Review Monograph, Oxford: Blackwell.

Strathern, M., (2004), *Partial Connections* – Updated edition California: Alta Mira.

Strong, P.M., (1979), *The Ceremonial Order of the Clinic*, London: Routledge.

Zaner, R.M., (1985), 'How the Hell Did I Get Here?' Reflections on being a patient, in A.H. Bishop and J.R. Scudder (eds), *Caring, Curing, Coping: Nurse Physician Patient Relationships*, Alabama: University of Alabama Press.

Zussman, R., (1994), *Intensive Care: Medical Ethics and the Medical Profession*, Chicago: University of Chicago Press.

Section 3
Bodies & Technology

Actor-networks of dementia

Michael Schillmeier

Remembrance of things past

> ... my sleep was so heavy as completely to relax my consciousness: for then I lost all
> sense of the place in which I had gone to sleep, and when I awoke at midnight, not
> knowing where I was: I had only the most rudimentary sense of existence ... it always
> happened that when I awoke like this, and my mind struggled in an unsuccessful attempt
> to discover where I was, everything would be moving around me through the darkness:
> things, places, year ... but then the memory, not yet of the place in which I was, but of
> various other places where I had lived, and might now very possibly be, would come like
> a rope let down from heaven to draw me up out of the abyss of not-being, from which I
> could never have escaped by myself ...[1]

Marcel Proust's *Remembrance of Things Past* is a wonderful novel on the
intertwining of space, time and memory. It is very much about non-cognitive
involuntary memory where sensory practices, emotions, bodies and objects
play a crucial role in human life. Involuntary memory draws upon the importance of 'things' that gather people, spaces and times. *Remembrance of Things
Past* unfolds in its extraordinary way an object-centred narrative of memory.
Let us just consider the beginning of the novel where we find the narrator in a
moment of awakening from deep sleep. In this short but highly uncanny moment
of utter detachment from the world, he finds himself in 'the abyss of not-being'.
His *Da-sein* is enmeshed with the 'things, places and years' that have lost their
references; he stumbles within ontological insecurity. Proust's character is
caught in a moment of dementia; it is his object-world though that brings
back slowly but surely the security of being that he could not have achieved
by himself alone.

This chapter is also about the remembrance of things past. More precisely,
it is about the fading, the mixing up and the loss of remembrances and how
people living in a long-term residential care facility experience it. In contrast to
Proust's short moments of dementia, I am concerned with dementia as a 'senior
moment' that happens mostly to elderly people and that still cannot be cured.
In ethnomethodological terms dementia describes a *crisis* of common modes of
social orderings.[2] Differently put: Dementia unfolds a 'cosmo-political event'
(Schillmeier and Pohler, 2006). Cosmo-political events disrupt, question and

alter a) the cosmos of common modes of human social orderings and b) how they are described by relevant (scientific and non-scientific) observers.[3] In effect, cosmo-political events make us slow down the ways we set the limits of how we think, feel and live, since we have to care about the difference and heterogeneity introduced. The consequences of cosmo-political events are political in its most general meaning: they possibly make us do things differently. The work on dementia did affect my own way of (un-)doing scholarly practices. It gave my scientific outlook – to put it all-too pathetically – a 'dementic' twist inasmuch as it deepened the philosophical ethos of taking care of the *questionability* and openness concerning the relations of human and non-human affairs. Moreover, it intensified my uncertainties about 'what' the social *is* and made me realise – more than ever before – that the social does not explain anything but has to be explained by the questionability e(a)ffected by everyday practices.

This chapter brings together the methodology of Actor-Network-Theory (ANT) and the work of the German philosopher Martin Heidegger. I reflect upon dementia along a Heideggerian reading of being-in-the-world by using the heuristic tools of ANT. In the following I engage with Mrs M, who has been diagnosed with dementia, and I reflect upon some discontinuous forms of individual and social being that come along with the intensities of dementia. It has been Mrs M's smart and lucid way of expressing and describing how she is, feels and thinks, her sadness and her humour, her charm and her hidden smiles, her anxieties and her hopes – her humanness I should say – that brought me closer to grasping dementia. In effect, Mrs M enabled me to access and explicate the merits of Heidegger's work and ANT for the study of (dis-)embodied living and for how to open up new spaces of rethinking un/knowing bodies, care and care practices in our everyday life, beyond the hiatus of social and medical models of health and illness.

Actor-networks of remembering

With the introductory quote by Marcel Proust we already saw that 'dementia' has different forms and is – though less dramatic and painful – a common part of our everyday life: the very moment of awakening from deep sleep, the moment his sense of *being-in-the-world*[4] as the effect of related mind/s, body/ies and things, is lost and is to be found again by the pragmatics of remembering. The latter assemble human actions that, for most of our lives, we take so much for granted that we (can) forget to think about them. The idea that we all have our 'demented' moments, or the fact that we all necessarily have to forget in order to remember in the first place, is a crucial feature of the networks that make up remembering.[5] This pragmatic assembles what I like to call actor-networks: *actor-networks of remembering*.

Generally speaking, the notion 'actor-network' tries to capture the idea that actors, human and non-human alike, their abilities or disabilities to do things (feeling, thinking and acting) are the effects and affects of heterogeneous entities. Hence a network is an actor as much as an actor is a network.[6] The description of actor-networks, then, is not about the focus on *relationships of entities as sources*; rather, it tries to follow and describe how actors come into being as the *effect or affects of associating heterogeneous forces of different elements* (eg, minds, bodies, and things). This process of eventful association can be called *translation*. Only through translation does the composite of our world come into individual being, endure and/or change. Thus, actors are translated translators. The elements involved may differ in the ways they work as associates: they can be either 'intermediaries' or 'mediators'.[7] An intermediary 'transports meaning or force without transformation' whereas mediators 'transform, translate, distort, and modify the meaning or the elements they are supposed to carry'.[8]

Memory, as taken-for-granted, can be seen as *the* intermediary between mind and matter that links past, present and future events.[9] Such a process intermediates between the realities of the past and the possibilities opening up for the present and its futures. But memory is also very much an act of mediation inasmuch as it 'brings to the world (. . .) the possibility of unfolding, hesitation and uncertainty.'[10] Hence, one can say that on the one hand it is the very pragmatic of remembering that realizes the (resembling) possibilities given by the (known) past, which – in its most perfected, pragmatic and also most convenient, unthematized way – refers to all the routines we do without having to think about them. Then, memory is the perfect intermediary; it translates the past into the present without transformation and in effect memory becomes black-boxed, invisible. One of the most powerful intermediaries of remembering is our non-sensuous bodily perception.[11] It refers to our – mostly vague and often unnoticed – physiological experience whereby the immediate presence comes into being by conforming to the immediate past: it makes us remember our own self as well as our body (as mediating sensuous perception). In such 'intermediary' mode, memory refers to the process of realization that moves between conformation to the past and limiting the possibilities given by the past.

As the literature on remembering shows, practices, objects and places also operate as crucial intermediaries – less vague but more 'objectified' – of actor-networks of remembering.[12] Actor-networks of remembering, then, do not exist mere mentalist forms of recollection and representation. Rather they visualize the importance of embodied and material actor-networks of remembering: place and body memories. Edward S. Casey stresses:

> [C]oncrete places retain the past in a way that can be reanimated by our remembering them: a powerful but often neglected form of memory. Body memories are not just memories *of* the body but instances of remembering places, events, and people with and in the lived body. In commemoration, body and place memory conspire with co-participating others in ritualized scenes of co-remembering. (. . .) [T]here are few moments where we are not steeped in memory; and this immersion includes each step we take, each thought we think, each word we utter. Indeed, every fibre of our bodies, every cell of our brains, holds memories – as does every physical object outside bodies and brains, even those inanimate objects that bear the marks of their past histories

upon them in mute profusion. What is memory-laden exceeds the scope of the human: memory takes us into the environing world as well as into our individual lives.[13]

With Casey we can say that 'in the case of memory, we are always already in the thick of things';[14] by remembering we do live in extensions: bodies, places and things; and we live the heterogeneity of time: past, present and future. Remembering, then, configures the complexities of the 'time-spaces'[15] we are living. Hence, memory is not a mere recollected mental copy of the past but an act of re-collecting whereby the spatio-temporalities of minds, bodies and things constantly re-relate to each other.[16] Following from that the practices of memory can be seen as modes of *mediation* that actualize something new – opening up times and spaces for a contingent future.[17] Such a process genuinely assembles heterogeneous elements in time and space; and, in effect, innovation, creativity and difference but also individuality and 'objectuality' are achieved. Remembering individualizes the social commonalities of intermediated memory (eg social and individual routines) and introduces heterogeneity and difference. Consequently, as an event, it disrupts, questions and alters the very taken-for-granted forms of common social practice; the mediation of memories mediates social orderings.

Actor-networks of dementia

Dementia occurs when we lack memory as intermediary (or get the latter wrong) and when there is 'nothing' to mediate (see below). Lacking or mixing up memories produces a complicated mess of odd mediators; it complicates the world inasmuch as it *thins out* the thickness of things: living extensions become questionable. These processes, then, homogenize the heterogeneity of different time-spaces as well as multiply the actors/mediators/ intermediaries involved.

This is why scientific rationalities are apt to divide dementia into functional units of accounts, as, for example a purely mental (dis-)ability, a natural source of individuals that is lost or impaired, a mere social construction, a solely human affair . . . etc. The tendency is to give different, self-closed explanations that turn dementia into a mere privation of the nature of the very given, exclusive explanation. For a medical model, dementia is a purely cognitive dis-function effected by bodily malfunctions, a tragedy of individual impairment: the troubled nature of the human being generates and explains the problems that will arise in society.[18] Or vice versa; for social scientists, society explains the nature of dementia. In this vein, social scientists aim to explain cognitive and bodily conditions like dementia as *social* phenomena and not as individual phenomena, bio-medical phenomena, philosophical phenomena etc.[19] Only by excluding the difference of the other perspective (ie natural bodily reasons that explain the reason/effect relation of dementia), is the explanatory power of 'the social' achieved, secured and maintained as a different realm that *in toto* configures dementia.

The problem I see with such a strategy of exclusion is the tendency to treat 'nature' or 'the social' or 'the individual' as detached ontological domains from which either 'nature' or 'the social' or 'the individual' can be explained, observed, or worse, be criticized or ruled out. Such an exclusivist point of view eliminates the possibilities of 'others' (social and non-social alike) to have their own *objecting* voice(s) that may well put at risk the 'safe' position of the methodology of 'nature' or 'the social'.[20]

This chapter proposes a shift from exclusive perspective to inclusive differences.[21] Through inclusive differences, neither the domain of 'nature' nor 'society' nor 'the individual' can function as a self-explanatory force concerning dementia. Inclusive differences highlight instead the associations of human and non-human elements that make up the social relevance of dementia. The concept of 'inclusive differences' displays the societal evidences and experiences of dementia as the effect of concrete practices that are never purely human or non-human, social or non-social, individual or collective. Such a shift refers to 'perspectives' *in the making* rather than to a mode of exclusive *abstraction by given* perspectives.[22]

Accounts of nursing practices as well as interdisciplinary oriented *care studies* sensitive to such a shift are trying to 'dissolve disciplinary boundaries'[23] and highlight the inclusive differences of the 'conduct of care'[24]. Additionally, actor-network approaches have also proved to be a good heuristic to research inclusive differences but do not have a strong impact on care studies. This chapter links care studies with an actor-network approach. What one should expect from an actor-network analysis of dementia is that it follows the traces of 'thick', material objects and actors – human and non-human alike. By doing so it increases the voices of actors and objects that play a role in understanding dementia. But isn't such an approach rather counter-productive, since it is precisely dementia that, as we have said before, *thins out the thickness of things* and in effect limits their potential for action? And indeed, this seems to be the litmus-test for an actor-network approach dealing with the conreteness of dementia. Hence, the chapter unfolds actor-networks of dementia where the 'thinness of objects' plays a major role in fabricating 'thick actor-networks'. This is the moment where the work of Martin Heidegger proved most relevant (see below).

The thinning out of things, by an actor-network of dementia, does not mean that minds, bodies, and things aren't 'there' anymore. Metaphorically speaking, minds, bodies and things become too thin to stand on their own anymore, either as mere social or as natural matters of fact. Demented objects, one may say, 'fall ontologically' and thus change or lose their taken for granted 'factish' [*gegenständliches*][25] and known being. Moreover, they become 'time-less': through demented objects, time doesn't stretch and protract anymore. Demented objects have no past and no future but a *presence* that is *absent*. However, these tumbled, oddly present absent things are far from being a mere standing reserve. Rather, they circulate (as we have already seen with Proust) as highly complicating mediators associating the actor-networks of dementia. Actor-networks of dementia transform the intermediary and taken-for-granted pragmatics of actor-networks of remembering. They turn into mediators, putting at risk the relations of humans and non-humans involved. As mediators the actor-networks of dementia become conspicuous they leave traces.

'What is on hand'? The presence of absence

> Mrs M.(in her night dress walking down the hallway): I am all over the place [*Ich bin ganz ausser mir*] – Good day! With whom do I have the pleasure?
> Marion (filming Mrs M): It's me, Marion!
> Mrs M: Marion, what is on hand (t)here [*was liegt da vor*]?
> Marion: Whereabouts?
> Mrs M: Here, with me and the surrounding [*bei mir und der Umgebung*]!
> Marion: You are here at the (. . .) care centre. It is a home for the elderly and a nursing home.
> Mrs M: A home for the elderly and a nursing home? Why haven't they told me anything about that?
> Marion: I am sure that you must have just forgotten it in this moment since you are nervous.

This is the first sequence of Marion Kaintz's ethnographic film 'Der Tag der in der Handtasche verschwand' ['The day that got lost in a Handbag']. It is about Mrs M who lives in a long-term care facility. She has been diagnosed with dementia and was moved from her flat to the long-term care facility. She, however, doesn't remember *that* or *why* she has (been) moved. In effect, she is regularly terribly upset by finding herself somewhere she doesn't know and doesn't belong to; she finds herself nowhere.

> Mrs M (approaching nervously a nurse on the hallway of the ward; nurse is busy): I wonder if you could help me?
> Nurse (going away): Afterwards, Mrs M
> Mrs M: **Afterwards**? **When** is this?
> Mrs M. (to Marion): Listen, I can do without this. I am going home.
> Mrs M (goes back to her room, which is the last room on the hallway): You see, here it's over here. End of dream. . . .
> Mrs M (looking at the second bed in her room): Is a man sleeping there?
> Marion: It is another woman, your roommate, Mrs N . . .

Mrs M must have been told hundreds of times that she has moved and is now living in the ward. However, it is especially her short-time memory that fails. Mrs M remembers 'the old days' better, but sometimes she forgets about them and/or mixes them up as well. Most of the time she forgets about recent moments, about things just used, the places she was sleeping last night, people she has just met on the corridor, people met while eating or in her room, things she just did or intended to do, etc. Frequently she forgets about her new home and all the people, objects and practices involved. Her new 'home' appears utterly unknown and, consequently, all Mrs M wants to do is to go home to where things happened to be fine. She gets very upset when she thinks that the people around her are rather impolite in the way they deal with her most emotional questions.

With her steady camera, the young filmmaker Marion Kaintz has followed Mrs M over a period of one year. Although Mrs M often forgets about Marion and her camera, they became close allies in observing a world, a world that – as we have already seen – turn more and more into an unknown one. Mrs M (like Proust) struggles with remembering, although in a quite different fashion. Still, in both cases, what is experienced as questionable is the very sense of 'being on hand', of *Da-sein*[26], of existing. Through dementia, Proust and Mrs M are caught in the 'abyss of not-being'[27]. Mrs M's moments and places of dementia, the moments where she plunges into the 'abyss of not-being' multiply during day and night, her struggle with memory becomes a persistent companion in her life. Mrs M appears to be constantly awakening from the Proustian deep sleep with all its 'shifting and confused gusts of memory'[28] and their apparent losses. Her dementia is at an early stage but is slowly getting worse. At the time the film was made, she still reflects upon the very fact that something odd is going on. She struggles while noticing that she is forgetting or mixing things up, situations, friends, practices, thoughts, words, intentions, plans, and herself. To be sure, it is not a permanent situation, some days or nights are better than others; she also remembers some things or some people better than others. Unlike Proust, though, Mrs M is starting to forget the very fact(s) of forgetting or remembering itself.

Disentangled from the temporalities and spatialities of her past and present life-world Mrs M. frequently feels displaced. *Ich bin ausser mir* ('I am all over the place'), she says, which literally translates as *I am outside of myself*. Mrs M worries about what is happening to her, she doesn't feel at home with herself anymore. Outside of herself she becomes absent. She asks Marion the filmmaker a very odd question: 'What is *on hand* (t)here [*was liegt da vor*] (. . .) with me and the surrounding [*bei mir und der Umgebung*]?' Mrs M is concerned about herself *and* her circumambience: her *Da-sein*, her being on hand. She is terrified that her embodied being and her environment is not hers anymore and appears unknown, detached, cut off and nothing but a body *here* and an environment *there*. Herself and the environment: two mere objects that by their present absence *object* to being part of Mrs M's life-world.

Following Martin Heidegger, Mrs M's question concerning 'what is to hand' refers to two modes in which entities are typically encountered in everyday practices: ready-to-hand [*Zuhanden*] and present-at-hand [*Vorhanden*].[29] Mrs M's question articulates a crisis of attachment from those modes of existence. First of all, she feels detached from entities (her body, her surrounding, her domestic environment) 'ready-to-hand', which grounded the ways she has been acting in her world. Rather than being a relationship with a self-present intentional 'subject' and somehow undiscriminated 'objects', the everydayness of ready-to-hand things discloses human existence precisely by how human beings *dwell with* or *live through* others. Being-in-the-world refers to primordial *relations* of human existence: Being-with-others – human and non-human alike – through which these relations gain their own specificity and significance. And memory is precisely what usually reminds us of being-with-others. To be in the world is to remember being attached to others. It presupposes others to be attached, not in an abstract but 'thisly',[30] that is, in a meaningful way.

Mrs M asks: 'What is at hand *here*?' which is a question about spatiality, about her living in extension. She feels displaced because the networks of remembering have temporarily fallen apart, they don't connect properly, they make her forget and mix things up. Mrs M lives in a constant care facility that hardly resembles her former everyday life practices.[31] Everything looks, smells and feels different, has different rhythms and spaces: everything *is* different. Mrs M's troubled short-time memory engenders the very difficulties of feeling at home with herself and her environment. Contexts, routines, situations, people, and things she may still remember through her long-term memories don't match what she is supposed to be at home with now. In the ward, her long-term memories don't contribute to making her feel at home. In the moment of dementia, the recent past that is forgotten makes her stuck in the mere presence-at-hand of things. Mrs M is trapped within the vicious circle of suspicious facts. Hence, not-being at home is constantly at stake:

> Mrs M (approaching a nurse on the hallway of the ward): May I talk to you?
> Nurse: Yes, what? What do you want?
> Mrs M: I am not sure when I am going home tonight?
> Nurse: You are now living here, Mrs M – Ok?!

'Old' habits, as significant and highly specific lived routines and experiences with their incorporated temporalities, spatialities and things are 'stubborn facts' in the moment new habits, routines and experiences cannot be remembered. This seems to be a central problem shared by Mrs M and the way of dealing with it by long-care facilities. Precisely in the moment of dementia, the spatio-temporal specificities of the ward's everydayness are part of Mrs M's crisis of existential orientation. In so far as it seems that these present objects put at risk Mrs M's being-in-the-world, her *Da-sein*, her existence; the significance and specificities of *her* being with others – human and non-human alike – are lost, making her feel nervous, agitated, anxious. And last but not least: Mrs M thinks that nobody has told her that she has (been) moved to such an un-homely place – another incomprehensible matter of fact with which Mrs M is confronted.

Nothing but 'accomplished facts' – the lure of dementia

> Mrs M (drained, anxious, upset): I don't know what to do.
>   I am being confronted with **accomplished facts** and
>   I should be happy with them? I cannot be happy with them!
>   I have – do you hear – I have fulfilled all my duties that have been necessary.
> Marion: You did so.
> Mrs M: Yes, and?
> Marion: Nobody wants to do you any harm.

Mrs M: And **now** [*nun*]? What is happening **now** [*jetzt*]?
Marion: You can stay living here!
Mrs M: '**Stay**' living here? What does this mean?
Marion: You have already been here for a while.
Mrs M: Already for a **while**? And nobody has told me so! How is this possible?

Proust's 'rudimentary sense of being', the ungrounded 'abyss of not-being' as well as Mrs M's anxious question 'what is on hand here' refers to the lack of readiness-to-hand of oneself (mind and body) and the environment. Mrs M is confronted with an odd loss of the safeguard of ready-to-hand embodied practices and things. To be sure: in the moment of dementia she is still with a body but not with *her* body. The same can be said about the surroundings: Mrs M happens to find herself in a present environment that isn't hers. Her body as well as her *Umwelt* are becoming just present-at-hand: they appear as simply detached bodies and objects. 'Present-at-hand' they do not make up the ready-to-hand interwoven relations of human and non-human entities that make up *her* world. She and the environment do not refer to the pragmatics of her times and places of everydayness. These *pragmatics* refer to the more or less silent and non-obtrusive composite of people and things that make up the routines, practices and performances of Mrs M's everyday life: they are ready-to-hand. However present-at-hand, these relations turn into relationships of self-closed, isolated *occurrences* in space and time (eg subjects and objects), or 'accomplished facts', as Mrs M has put it very lucidly. Mrs M sees her embodied being detached from knowing it and sees her environment as mere encapsulated, ungraspable occurrences in space and time.

At the same time, Mrs M doesn't know that she is starting to forget; when she doesn't know, she forgets her forgetting of remembering. In effect, anxiety creeps in. This, then, is not so much a question of cognitive knowing or failing of volition. Rather, it is a matter of *non-knowing*, ie of feeling, of mood, of affection, of *Befindlichkeit*. Caught in the very presence of unknown things she *feels* displaced, alienated, out of tune. Living with the plain presence of bodies and things, she is cut off from the pragmatics of remembering that unravels the multiple extensions to the past and opens up for the future. In her existential crisis Mrs M has no past and finds no future: She doesn't know what to do! She is acting (with)in a very real present-at-hand environment, which, precisely because it is just present, means nothing to her. The present world happens to come from, to be and to lead to into nothing and to nowhere.

Bearing this in mind, Mrs M's questions are not only very precise, but deeply human and social: they enunciate the attunement [*Befindlichkeit*][32] of and with herself *and* her environment. Mrs M's question 'what is on hand (t)here?' is an existential question: being in tune [*Stimmung*] with herself and with her environment is questioned, is out-of-tune [*verstimmt*]. It brings to the fore Mrs M's intimidated, affected and un-homely *Da-sein*, her anxious and uncertain *Befindlichkeit* through which it happened that her world is becoming lost within 'the spell of uncertainty'.[33]

Actor-networks of Angst

Mrs M's embodied and spatial *Befindlichkeit* makes her paralysed, she is at a loss. In the moment where the pragmatics of remembering fail to relate past and future, Mrs M finds herself highly affected, dispersed in an utterly uncanny circumambience. She does not feel at home at all with herself and her surroundings. Both she and her surroundings fail to become (tacitly) known. In effect, Mrs M plunges into ontological uncertainty: she is afraid of (her) nothingness *being* nowhere. This is precisely the *Befindlichkeit* of 'anxiety' [*Angst*]. Being anxious is feeling uncanny and uncanniness [*Unheimlichkeit*] refers to experiencing not-being-at-home.[34] 'Uncanniness', as Heidegger stresses

> . . . reveals itself authentically in the fundamental attunement of *Angst*, and, as the most elemental disclosedness of thrown Da-sein, it confronts being-in-the-world with the nothingness of the world about which it is anxious in the *Angst* about its ownmost potentiality-of-being.[35]

> . . . in the face of which one has *Angst* is not encountered as something definite to be taken care of; the threat does not come from something at hand [*Zuhandenen*, MS] and objectively present [*Vorhandenen*, MS], but rather from the fact that everything at hand and objectively present absolutely has nothing more to 'say' to us. Beings in the surrounded world are no longer relevant. The world in which I exist has sunk into insignificance, and the world thus disclosed can set free only beings that are not relevant.[36]

As the etymology of (un-)canny suggests (canny derives from 'can'), she 'cannot' do anything. Mrs M is roped in uncanniness, nearing the presence of the unknown: unknown bodies, unknown objects; objects that have lost their recognizable voices. It is precisely such *present absence* of the physiological being-in-the world, its troubled *facticity*[37], that brings to the fore the 'questionability' of human *social* affairs. It is the two-fold character of 'questionability' of human social affairs that Mrs M makes us aware of: (1) the *question*ability of human social affairs refers to the deferral of a universal answer to the question *what* human social affairs *are*; and (2) the question*ability* of human affairs alludes to the multiple possibilities of human affairs to enable such questioning in the first place. Mrs M's dementia politicizes, ie disrupts, questions and alters the cosmos of common modes of related individual and social orderings. Subsequently, dementia is asking for new forms of individual and social orderings. Noticeably, Mrs M's *Angst* alludes to the fragility of multiple social orderings (eg hers and the ward's) that mediate human and non-human configurations into the more or less (dis)continuous pragmatics of human everyday life.

The *Angst* through which Mrs M's dementia becomes visible addresses the fragility of our being-in-the-world that is made up of more or less strong ties or associations of affectual, emotional and factual, individual and social, human and non-human configurations. These relations achieve, stabilize, maintain and transform being-in-the-world as specific actor-networks of minds, bodies, and things incorporating the specificities of spatio-temporal arrangements. In its most existential sense Mrs M's *Angst* addresses her potentiality-of-being as the effect and affect of such actor-networks.

Hence, it is the silence of her body and her surroundings, present 'thinned out' objects that 'say' nothing to Mrs M, which assemble her actor-networks of *Angst*. But how, one might intervene, can actors be called actors if they 'say' nothing, if they are utterly alien to, detached from and non-significant to Mrs M? It is precisely the *Befindlichkeit Angst* of Mrs M's dementia that relates *non-related and non-specific objects*. Heidegger notes

> *Angst* is not only Angst about . . . , but is at the same time, as attunement, *Angst* for. . . . That for which *Angst* is anxious is not a *definite* kind of being and possibility of Da-sein. The threat itself is, after all, indefinite and thus cannot penetrate threateningly to this or that factically concrete potentiality of being. What *Angst* is anxious for is being-in-the-world itself. In *Angst*, the things at hand in the surrounding world sink away, and so do the innerworldly beings in general. The 'world' can offer nothing more, nor can the *Mitda-sein* [being with other Da-sein, MS] of others. Thus *Angst* takes away from Da-sein the possibility of understanding itself, falling prey, in terms of the 'world' and the public way of being interpreted. It throws Da-sein back upon that for which it is anxious, its authentic [eigentliches, MS] potentiality-for-being-in-the-world. Angst individuates Da-sein to its ownmost being-in-the-world which, as understanding, projects itself essentially upon possibilities. Thus along with that for which it is anxious, *Angst* discloses Da-sein as *being-possible*, and indeed as what can be individualized in individuation of its own accord.[38]

One can say that the specificity of actor-networks of *Angst* is that they cut[39] the common and taken-for-granted spatio-temporal networks into messy, fractious, stubborn and highly individualized configurations. Whenever Mrs M forgets her sense of place (her embodied self and her environment), she becomes visible as a person with her 'own', ie highly individual problems. Dementia enacts the constant repetition of the individual, the non-remembered, the non-expected, and the non-known. The moment of dementia cuts off Mrs M from the spatio-temporal arrangements and the related pragmatics of remembering that enable the routines of everyday practices. Living with dementia, Mrs M is enacted by the thinning out of memorized and sensed time-spaces that either multiply their past and future (eg the daughter turns into the sister and the sister into the nurse, etc.) or lack any connectivity to provide them with a past and future in the first place (daughters, sisters, nurses, rooms etc. remain unknown). When she mixes things up, her troubled being-on-hand [*Da-sein*] is assembling an ontological multiple world and in effect new mediators re-relate her life-world. When she is within *Angst* she is assembled by the presence-absence of bodies and things, which remain unknown and non-expressible.

Mrs M's *Da-sein* jitters between being-in-the-world, a 'multiverse'[40] of being-in-the-world and non-being. Her times and spaces of everyday life flicker between detached, self-closed relations that have no past and no future and moments where the past is accessible and open to be translated into the future present. In her current phase only the latter facilitate a) the event of intimacy of Mrs M's lifeworld that connects and establishes the readiness-to-hand of present action, people and things, and/or fabricate b) the spatio-temporal stabilities of present-at-hand bodies and things. Mrs M's 'senior situation' shows that the translation of past into a present that *has* future (as intermediation or mediation) is not always a smooth and fast process. Its failing brings to the fore the hard work of constant translation/mediation of memorized and sensed/perceived times and spaces, present-at-hand and ready-to-hand bodies and things, as they come into being *while* being with others, human and non-human alike.

Through dementia Mrs M becomes socially conspicuous; she turns into an event that dwells in a closed form; she 'has' something non-translatable: dementia. Individualized by *Angst*, Mrs M becomes a case, a resident of a long-term care unit, a 'home-less' person, an object of the medial, medical and scientific gaze; she is mother and becomes child, an annoyance for some, pitied by others; she becomes a cosmo-political actor that disrupts and makes us re-think and change our taken-for-granted social orderings. Cut off from the social routines, she appears 'non-social', living in her own world, more or less unapproachable, acting peculiarly, and asking existential questions; in effect she appears helpless, vulnerable, needing to be cared for. At the same time, she lives her own life highly 'independently' and due to its indifference to the ward's life it is this individuating independence that makes her a cosmo-political actor. Hence, paradoxically speaking, it is the non-translatability that translates her into a highly conspicuous and concrete cosmo-political actor.

According to Heidegger, the feeling of uncanniness and the *Befindlichkeit* of *Angst* is primordial to human relations inasmuch as it unravels the ownmost potentiality-of-being in the first place. Following such a reading, the individualizing effect of *Angst* is not only a disturbing fact of individual and social life but also, at the same time, a creative moment that opens up the possibilities (and limits) of the potentiality-of-being. The actor-networks of *Angst* remind us of our mortal being, of being empirically present-at-hand and its *Verfallen* into non-being, its decay, ruin and death. Interestingly enough, this happens to take place alongside a radical breakdown of relations as well as along a radical veiling of the things involved. Mrs M encounters a radical severing of the ready-to-hand relations of mind, bodies and things: they become mere present-at-hand objects. Ambiguously enough, these present-at-hand objects *object* to being merely objects present-at-hand. They turn into risky and virtual ones, silent, ungraspable, veiled objects that refuse to be known at all but nevertheless enact the presence of things. It is precisely by being *non-epistemic objects*, ie non-knowing objects, that they affect us in the most radical uncanny way and lure Mrs M into the pondering of *Angst*.

Affected by the actor-networks of *Angst*, Mrs M's embodied being turns into being just present-at-hand as well. The more she forgets that she is forgetting things the more she is cut off from her ready-to-hand relations with her environment, human and non-human alike. Hence, dementia and the related uncanniness as well as the *Befindlichkeit* of *Angst* reveal the *eigentliche*, the virtual being-in-the world: it is about translations of objects into relations and relations into objects. More precisely, it is about heterogeneous relations of heterogeneous objects as well as about heterogeneous objects of relations which, through processes of translation, constantly appropriate and expropriate their multiple modes of existence. Dementia reveals mediation, the mediation of actor-networks.

The force of silence – care, conscience and guilt

We have seen so far how the *presence of absence* makes Mrs M plunge into unrest and anxiety. She is faced with 'accomplished facts' to which she has no access: they are neither part of her own life-world nor a product of her own decisions. Mrs M feels enacted by those accomplished facts into a *totally institutionalized* world that very clearly does not summon her into feeling at home:

> Mrs M (drained, anxious, upset)
> I am being confronted with **accomplished facts** and I should be happy with them?
> I cannot be happy with them!
> I have – do you **hear** – fulfilled all my duties that have been necessary.

Obviously, living in a long-term care facility, Mrs M has to keep up with rules and routines. Since she forgets about her situation, these appear as modes of punishment for having failed to comply with certain societal expectations. In his seminal study on *Asylums* Goffman defines a 'total institution'

> . . . as a place of residence and work where a large number of like-situated individuals, cut off from a wider society for an appreciable period of time, together lead an enclosed, formally administered round of life. Prisons serve as a clear example, providing we appreciate that what is prison-like about prisons is found in institutions whose members have broken no laws.[41]

We have seen how the mere presence of absence of things imprison her being *(her-)self* so much that she is unable to do anything. Mrs M cannot escape the presence of absence, of things that are devoid of any meaning. This presence of meaninglessness, nothingness, assembles the actor-networks of anxiety as well as the feeling of being punished for something she isn't responsible for. Clearly, Mrs M cannot be happy with such 'accomplished facts'. This may explain why she feels forced to confirm to Marion the filmmaker that she has fulfilled all her duties. Her conscience is calling, she feels guilty.

Marion the filmmaker responds quickly and confirms 'yes, you did' fulfil your duties (she may have had experienced the situation very often during the year filming). Still, it seems that Marion's response does little to relieve Mrs M in her situation.

> Mrs M: And **now** [*nun*]? What is happening **now** [*jetzt*]?
> Marion: You can stay living here!

> Mrs M: **Stay** living here? What does this mean?
> Marion: You have already been here for a while.
> Mrs M: Already for a **while**? And nobody has told me so, how is this possible?

'Yes, but?' she asks and adds right away: 'And **now** [*nun*]? What is happening **now** [*jetzt*]?.' Mrs M remains stuck in the presence of absence of things. Marion's answer that she 'can stay living here' instantaneously brings back Mrs M's dilemma: How is she supposed to stay living here, to dwell in a place that for her doesn't 'exist' and thus is utterly alien? Mrs M becomes even more suspicious when she hears that she has already been 'here for a while'. Nobody has told her so, no person, no thing, no body. And how could they? All these mediators – persons, bodies and things – do not assemble the pragmatics of Mrs M's remembering any more, they have turned into thinned-out, flat actor-networks that don't stretch and protract in time. They have become time-less; utterly unknown and detached, they mediate Mrs M's *Da-sein* into uncanniness and *Angst*. Mrs M feels utterly unhomely, being forced to live in an oppressive place; it is an unknown place where things and people are non-social; 'non-social' in the literal sense of the word: they don't associate, they are silent, that don't speak, they don't communicate, *they don't stay except in their absence*. That's why it seems that for Mrs M the question 'what is happening *now*', is so crucial, especially since nothing seems to stay, to continue *to be* within these thinned out 'nows'. The only 'thing' she feels is uncertainty and the affects of anxiety; the only voice she hears is – as it seems – the inner voice of 'bad conscience', of guilt.

I cannot deny that this scene puzzled me a lot. Not only emotionally, but also how to think about it in sociological terms. The scene is filled with vagueness (anxiety, the presence of absence of bodies and things), with objects that don't object, with actors that act due to their indifference to others, with affects, feelings, emotions, with 'inner voices' etc. All in all, I was confronted with very obscure traces of even more incomprehensible mediators and actor-networks. Heidegger's work might again help to make sense here. The shattered Da-sein of Mrs M unfolded a very special occasion. It not only described the intensities of actor-networks of forgetting; the actor-networks of *Angst* re-described the very conditions of possibility of Da-sein *as* actor-network.

> Mrs M (drained, anxious, upset):
> I don't know what to do.
>
> I am being confronted with **accomplished facts** and
> I should be happy with them? I cannot be happy with them!
> I have – **do you hear** – I have fulfilled all my duties that have been necessary.

Following Heidegger's reading of guilt and the call of conscience,[42] Mrs M's insistence in saying (she wants to be heard!) that she has fulfilled all her duties is more than just a way of reassuring that she lived a societal life through which she has contributed to all the moral and societal expectancies. Rather, the actor-networks of *Angst* assemble the silent call of conscience as a way of self-assurance, an assurance of the very individuality of her being-in-the-world.

Angst 'summons Da-sein into existence, to its ownmost potentiality-of-being-a-self.'[43] The silent call of conscience assembles the conditions of possibility of being able to be guilty in the first place. Through *Angst* the call of conscience is mediated not so much as a form of cognitive knowledge but as an emotional, affectual and utterly vague though rather intense desire of 'wanting-to-have-a-conscience'[44] of Da-sein. The actor-networks of Angst mediate highly individual but heterogeneous forms of knowledge and non-knowledge, which relate past, present and future of minds, bodies and things as confidants and witnesses that make up the potentiality-of-being-herself.

Mrs M's call of conscience is about the question of guilt that asks if she had done something bad or immoral in the past. However, it is also about the possibility of being able *to have guilt* in the first place. Declaring that she has fulfilled all her duties means that that she has fulfilled all the duties within the actor-networks she is belonging to. She was an active part of the network, she says, she was an actor in that network, she herself, she claims, is an actor-network. She owes as much to the network as the networks of her life owe to her. Guilt is a question of owning, of property, of having and not of being. *Being is having the ability to have guilt, is existing*. This is what Mrs M is telling us with her Angst. And the ability of having guilt is enacted by ready-to-hand and present-at-hand actor-networks. If they turn present absent, the *actor-network of Angst* reminds us of our potentiality-of-being and existing as mediated by others.[45] Heidegger stresses

> Uncanniness is the fundamental kind of being-in-the-world, although it is covered over in everydayness. Da-sein itself calls as conscience from the ground of this being. The 'it calls me' is an eminent kind of discourse of Da-sein. The call attuned by Angst first makes possible for Da-sein its project upon its ownmost potentiality-of-being. (. . .) The statement that Da-sein is at the same time the caller and the one summoned has now lost its empty formal character and its obviousness. *Conscience reveals itself as the call of care*: (. . .) The call of conscience, that is, conscience itself, has its ontological possibility in the fact that Da-sein is care in the ground of its being.[46]

The silent mediation of the call of conscience and guilt by *Angst* brings to the fore that Mrs M owes her *Da-sein, her existence* to others – human and non-human alike. The uncanniest cosmo-political event – dementia – reveals *Da-sein* as *care*: the care for human others [*Fürsorge*] and the care for 'fitting' human/non-human relations [*Besorgnis*].

The social – a matter of care

Following some of the traces of Mrs M's dementia we could see that the human world is not a representation of given things but an event of *gathering* – constructing as well as maintaining – *heterogeneous* elements. The process of being human, *dwelling* as Heidegger calls it, gains specificity in appropriation of and to heterogeneity.[47] Following Mrs M's dementia helps unravel mediations – like memory or its loss – that do not just relate human and non-human entities but make up a 'conjunctural event'[48] stabilizing, questioning or altering the orderings and specific spatio-temporal belonging of humans and non-humans.

Obviously this process bears a fragile and delicate set of practices. According to Heidegger it asks for *caring* for the heterogeneous 'other' as they become visible. Only through caring can the differences that appropriate humans and non-humans to one another be given and the heterogeneous other gain its own voice. Moreover, it reminds us humans (mortals) of being 'dwellers' as much as being 'builders' as well, who – in order to be able to dwell – care for, that is, *save* heterogeneity. 'Existing is differing', as Gabriel Tarde[49] has put it, and so is dwelling. Human being as dwelling is 'safeguarding' heterogeneity, difference. Dwelling as saving heterogeneity means 'to set something free into its own presencing'; it preserves 'the other', it spares heterogeneity and makes us aware that we stay with *things*: 'Mortals nurse and nurture the things that grow, and specially construct things that do not grow. Cultivating and construction are building in the narrower sense. *Dwelling*, insofar as it keeps or secures (. . .) things, is, as this keeping, a *building*'.[50]

Through the actor networks of Mrs M's dementia, an ontological ethos of the social became visible: it is the desire that cares for the other, since only through its other (the non-social, the non-human, the individual) does it appropriate its own (human) being. The actor-networks of dementia ask for feeling and understanding of, that is, caring and caring about, heterogeneity. The ontological ethos of the social also denotes an attitude that 'spare[s] and protect[s] the thing's presence in the region from which it presences' (Heidigger, 1971: 181). It gives dementia a voice through and by all the detached, non-related and silent actor-networks involved. This is precisely what dementia has shown through Mrs M's *Angst*: it mediates common ready-to-hand and present-at-hand actor-networks into highly uncommon and individual ones. Through dementia the 'region' of the non-known, the other, the silent is spared and protected as actor-network, and makes visible how dementia 'conjoins itself out of the world'[51] by the heterogeneity of minds, bodies and things. Through the actor-networks of dementia, the very present-absence of things reminds us of the uncanniness of our being as staying with and falling [*Verfallen*] from others and things.

Strangely, forgetting about the conjunctural event of gathering heterogeneous beings brings to the fore the ontological ethos of the social: sparing difference and heterogeneity. As a cosmo-political event, it has been the actor-network of dementia that makes us aware of the human social as caring about heterogeneity and difference; only then is human dwelling possible. Mrs M's 'homelessness' reminds us of that very vividly. Being caught within and affected by the present absence of bodies and things, she feels detached from building/dwelling within *her* world. Through the actor network of Angst she suffers from being attached to thinned out and time-less bodies and things. At the same time, Mrs M appears as a cosmo-political actor, who, through her indifference to common orderings, opens up the possibility of making the others slow down their taken-for-granted practices and care for difference and heterogeneity. It is precisely the pragmatic of remembering and its failures that bring to the fore the ethos of inclusive differences, by which the sociality of humans cannot be thought of without the caring for the other, non-human and non-social alike. Following from that, we cannot describe dementia merely as a social event. Rather, the social itself becomes an event through the cosmo-political agency of actor-networks of dementia and Angst. The latter are highly individual and lack translatability. Still, these networks reconcile the social with the individual by transgressing exclusivist perspectives. Care as a human social matter of concern preserves difference and heterogeneity. This, I suppose, is what this short glance at Mrs M's story tells us so intensively.

References

Bergson, H., (1991), *Matter and Memory*, New York: Zone Books.
Bermùdez, J.L., Marcel, A. and Eilan, N., (1995), (ed.) *The Body and the Self*, Cambridge, Ma./ London: MIT Press.
Callon, M., (1986), 'Some Elements of a Sociology of Translation: Domestication of the Scallops and the Fishermen of St. Brieuc Bay', in J. Law (ed.) *Power, Action and Belief: A New Sociology of Knowledge?*: 196–233, London: Routledge and Kegan Paul.
Callon, M., (1991), 'Techno-Economic Networks and Irreversibilty', in J. Law (ed.), *A Sociology of Monsters. Essays on Power, Technology and Domination*, London/New York: Routledge.
Casey, E.S., (2000), *Remembering. A Phenomenological Study*, second edition, Bloomington and Indianapolis: Indiana University Press.
Deleuze, G., (2002), Bergsonism, New York: Zone Books.
Esposito, E., (2002), *Soziales Vergessen. Formen und Medien des Gedächtnisses der Gesellschaft* [Social Oblivion. Forms and Media of Societal Memory], Frankfurt/Main: Suhrkamp.
Garfinkel, H., (1967), *Studies in Ethnomethodology*, Cambridge: Polity.
Goffman, E., (1961), *Asylums. Essays on the Social Situation of Mental Patients and Other Inmates*, London: Penguin Books.
Grosz, E., (1994), *Volatile Bodies*, Bloomington and Indianapolis: Indiana University Press.
Grosz, E., (1999), 'Thinking the New: Of Futures Yet Unthought', in E. Grosz (ed.), *Becomings. Explorations in Time, Memory, and Futures*, Ithaca and London: Cornell University Press. *The Body, Culture and Society. An Introduction.*
Hancock, P., *et al.*, (2000), Buckingham/Philadelphia: Open University Press.
Heidegger, M., (1971), 'The Thing', in Heidegger, M. *Poetry, Language, Thought*, translated by A. Hofstadter, New York: Harper and Row.
Heidegger, M., (1993), *Sein und Zeit [Being and Time]*, Tübingen: Niemeyer.
Heidegger, M., (1996), *Being and Time*, translated by J. Stanbaugh, New York: State University of New York Press.
Heidegger, M., (2001), *Phenomenological Interpretations of Aristotle, translated by* R. Rojcewicz, Bloomington: Indiana University Press.
Hetherington, K. and Munro, R., (1997), (ed.), *Ideas of Difference: Social Spaces and the Labour of Division*, Sociological Review Monograph, Oxford: Blackwell.
James, W., (2003), *The Will to Believe and Other Essays in Popular Philosophy*, New York: Kessinger.
Kohn, T. and McKechnie, R., (eds), (1999), *Extending the Boundaries of Care. Ethics and Caring Practices*, Oxford and New York: Berg.
Latimer, J., (2000), The Conduct of Care, Oxford: Blackwell.
Latour, B., (1988), 'Mixing Humans and Nonhumans Together: The Sociology of the Door Closer', *Social Problems* 35(3): 298–310.

Latour, B., (2005), *Reassembling the Social. An Introduction to Actor-Network-Theory*, Oxford: Oxford University Press.

Law, J., (1994), *Organizing Modernity*, Cambridge: Blackwell.

Law, J., (2002a), *Aircraft Stories. Decentering the Object in Technoscience*, Durham/London: Duke University Press.

Law, J. and Moser, I., (1999), 'Good Passages, Bad Passages', in J. Law and J. Hassard (eds), *Actor Network Theory and After*, Sociological Review Monographs, Oxford, Blackwell.

Leder, D., (1990), *The Absent Body*, Chicago/London: The University of Chicago Press.

Merleau-Ponty, M., (1962), *The Phenomenology of Perception*, London: Routledge and Kegan Paul.

Merleau-Ponty, M., (1968), *The Visible and the Invisible*, Evanston: Northwestern University Press.

Middleton, D. and Brown, S., (2005), *The Social Psychology of Experience: Studies in Remembering and Forgetting*, London: Sage.

Proust, M., (2006), *Remembrance of the Past*, Vol. 1, Wordsworth: Hertfordshire.

Schillmeier, M., (2007a), 'Dis/abling Spaces of Calculation. Blindness and Money in Everyday Life', *Environment and Planning D: Society and Space:* 594–609.

Schillmeier, M., (2007b), Politik des Behindert-Werdens. Behinderung als Erfahrung und Ereignis [The Politics of Becoming Disabled. Disability as Experience and Event] in Werner Schneider / Anne Waldschmidt (ed.), Disability Studies, Kultursoziologie und Soziologie der Behinderung. Erkundungen in einem neuen Forschungsfeld, Bielefeld, transcript.

Schillmeier, M., (2007c), 'Dis/abling Practices. Rethinking Disability', *Human Affairs* 17(2): 195–208.

Schillmeier, M., (2008a), 'Globalizing Risks. The Cosmo-Politics of SARS and its Impact on Globalizing Sociology', *Mobilities* 3(2): 179–199.

Schillmeier, M., (2008b), 'Time-Spaces of Becoming In/dependent and Dis/abled', *Time and Society* 2/3: 215–231.

Schillmeier, M., (2008c), (Visual) Disability. From Exclusive Perspectives to Inclusive Differences, Disabilty and Society 23(6): 611–623.

Schillmeier, M., (2009), 'Moving Home. From House to Nursing Home', *Space and Culture*, with Michael Heinlein.

Strathern, M., (1996), 'Cutting the Network', *The Journal of the Royal Anthropological Institute* 2(3): 517–535.

Strathern, M., (2004), *Partial Connections*, updated edition, Oxford: Rowman and Littlefield Publishers.

Tackenberg, P. and Abt-Zegelin, A., (2000), (ed.), *Demenz und Pflege. Eine interdisziplinäre Betrachtung* [*Dementia and Care. An Interdisciplinary Account*], Frankfurt/Main: Mabuse Verlag.

von Wedel, U., *et al.*, (2004), *Verwirrung im Alter. Demenzkarrieren soziologisch betrachtet* [*Age-related Confusion. Dementia-Carriers Sociologically Observed*], Wiesbaden: DUV.

Whitehead, A.N., (1955), *Symbolism. It's Meaning and Effect*, New York: Fordham University Press.

Whitehead, A.N., (1978), *Process and Reality. An Essay in Cosmology*, corrected edition, London/New York: The Free Press.

Washing and assessing: multiple diagnosis and hidden talents

Bernd Kraeftner and Judith Kroell

In the following chapter we juxtapose two clinical procedures: 'whole-body-washing' and the SMART-assessment-technique. Both have been developed in the context of the neuro-rehabilitative care setting where people who are physically dependent, medically vulnerable and cognitively impaired spend years of their lives. This juxtaposition, on paper, refers to an 'experiment' in the real world where, among others, multiple medical and nursing diagnostic and treatment practices are carried out to take care of these patients. This experiment was originally initiated to improve the 'knowing' concerning these bodies/persons. However, it might also be considered as a dynamics of unknowing that plays an important role when carers intend to become, together with their patients, talented bodies themselves. Furthermore, this account of events should give an impression of the transdisciplinary involvement of ourselves as members of a research group interested in the exploration of scientific and artistic methods that allow the displacement of issues, questions and positions, and the creation of renewed and surprising arrangements, co-operations and agreements between the actors involved.[1]

Washing the body

The sick room of a nursing home, nine o'clock in the morning: A nurse is about to undertake a so-called 'whole-body washing' of a young man. The 28-year old patient suffers from the consequences of traumatic brain injury caused by a motor-cycle accident in 1998. After 14 months at an early rehabilitation centre, and without evident improvement in his state, he was transferred to the ward of a long-term rehabilitation and nursing unit. He is living there to this day.

He receives nutrition and liquids through a (PEG-)tube that penetrates the abdominal wall and discharges into the stomach. The man is quadriplegic, ie he is totally paralysed. Despite a drug delivery system that continuously administers a muscle-relaxant medicine into the spinal fluid, his extremities show increased muscle tonus. Both hands are clenched to fists. If one tries to move his knee or elbow joints through their range of motion, one feels a strong resistance. He wears a urinary and fecal collection system. Everyday he is transferred to a wheelchair, where he stays for up to four hours. He has no trunk and head control. His general condition is described as stable. In the records, the medical diagnosis reads: 'vegetative state after traumatic brain injury'.

This kind of diagnosis, and the fact that the traumatic event dates back almost ten years, refer to an extremely unfavorable prognosis for this young man (Multi-Society Task Force On PVS, 1994), according to which he should not be alive anymore. He is in good company at this care unit, though. Approximately 35 patients have disproved all prognostic statements and are living on the ward. In this environment, a multi-professional team strives for improving, or at least preserving, the current condition of the patients.

The whole-body-washing follows a meticulous procedure. The nurse has closed the door behind her. She has prepared the washing equipment and adjusted the water temperature. She remains silent and focuses entirely on 'her' patient. She puts a toweling sock over the right hand of the patient and conducts his arm, with supported elbow-joint, to his trunk and starts to wash it. (Figure 1). Then with a careful movement, she guides the patient's hand with the washrag back to the washbowl, dampens the fabric, and again guides the patient's hand, this time to his face. Subsequently, she dries it, brings the patient into a rest position and leaves the room for 20 minutes. After this rest period, she is going to wash the rest of his body. This procedure takes about one hour and should be done regularly.

If one pays attention to the young man's face, it is noticeable that he occasionally opens his eyes and looks in her direction. (Figure 2) Usually, his eyes are almost totally closed so that one gets the impression that he is asleep. During the washing procedure, the care person looks for exceptional behaviours; whether the patient is agitated, anxious, or tensed up, or whether he shows increased breathing frequency or tonicity. She also looks for any changes in these parameters during the washing procedure. From these reactions, she concludes whether the young man feels well or not at any one time. Later, she is going to add her observations to the records.

Of course, the goal of the washing procedure is to clean the body. But there is another reason why the nurse spends almost one hour with the patient. The nursing staff consider this specific way of washing as a treatment intervention that, combined with other interventions like positioning, transferring or sensory

Figure 1

Figure 2

stimulation, should improve the condition of the patient or, at least, prevent its deterioration. Thus whole-body washing can be considered a therapeutic technique that, by means of the administration of environmental stimuli 'by an external agent', should help to promote the patient's arousal and behavioural responsiveness (Giacino, 1996; Steinbach and Donis, 2004). However, in addition to the personal hygiene and treatment aspects of the intimate contact between patient and nurse, this regular washing procedure exhibits another dimension: it can be considered a clinical diagnostic setting.

Becoming talented

What do we understand by a clinical diagnosis or a clinical diagnostic setting? When we accompany the nurse to the small office where the patient records are stored and look over her shoulder when she records her observations concerning the patient, we see that the condition of the patient has been *classified* in terms of NANDA-Diagnoses (NANDA: 'North American Nursing Diagnosis Association'). Along with the number '1.6.1.4' we read that the patient is at 'risk of aspiration'. Furthermore, we find a 'self-care deficit: bathing/hygiene (6.5.2), sensory perception alterations (7.2), activity intolerance (6.1.1.2), bowel incontinence (1.3.1.3), knowledge deficit (8.2.3), impaired social interaction (3.1.1) and social isolation (3.1.2)' among others. This classification is updated bi-annually. We face a combination of predetermined categories intended to reflect the behavioural complexities of the syndrome.

If we continue our investigation and ask the chief neurologist how the syndrome is codified by the *International Classification of Diseases* (of the World Health Organization), we learn that no code exists for apallic syndrome (the German term for the vegetative state) (see also Jennett, 2002). Instead, this syndrome shows a 'heterogeneous clinical picture' that 'disappears behind a bunch of diagnoses' that should represent the syndrome and which, he adds, 'makes any epidemiological data collection extremely difficult'. These examples show that, in most cases, no unequivocal clinical sign or symptom that allows a definite diagnosis of this syndrome exists. (A fact that also holds true for neuro-imaging or electrophysiological techniques.)

Besides the practices of classifying clinical observations according to pre-existing categories, the term diagnosis may refer to the process of *manufacturing* categories. It is about arranging clinical symptoms, signs and (medical) findings: to arrange, in the sense of discerning and discriminating, deciding and attributing. It is a practice that, after it has stabilized, may get a name and become a category (Fleck, 1980 [1935]).

Patients in a vegetative state are experienced as unconscious. This means that any communication is perceived as highly problematic: any sign or behaviour that we perceive, could possibly be a signal or a message. Inversely, any message we suppose to understand, could be a sign that is 'irrelevant'. Regarding the described syndrome, we wonder if the washing procedure or other clinical (nursing) practices may have the potential to produce diagnostic knowledge in the sense that specific and reliable clinical categories can be developed from them. Watching the washing procedure and various other similar clinical activities, one begins to consider these interactions as a complex mutual process of bodily, cognitive and emotional assessments of the respective actors. We assume that we are facing patients and non-patients with the potential to become 'talented bodies/persons' (Despret, 2004) with their various abilities and skills. Thus, we understand the act of diagnosing and the diagnostic-setting as an assessment act of variable duration and intensity. This constitutes or co-produces in a material environment both the assessor and the assessed body/person (Pols, 2005). As the title 'multiple diagnoses' indicates we utilize the term diagnosis not exclusively for medical or nursing procedures but for all kinds of formal or informal assessments one may encounter in the clinical context that we describe. The question then is whether this understanding of a clinical diagnostic process may have any implications for the daily care of severely disabled bodies/persons.

The separation of mind and body?

A few steps from the room where the washing procedure takes place, in a small office on the ward, we recognize different hand-written terms on a flip chart. It reads as follows: (see Figure 3)

This list is a melange of observations, experiences, and interpretations. It is the collaborative result of the weekly meeting of the evidence-based-nursing research team at the ward. The goal of this meeting is to discuss the reactions of the patients to specific or unspecific stimuli and to describe clinical signs and symptoms that may indicate awareness, perception and/or purposeful behaviours, thus, capturing the notion of cognition and consciousness.

This nursing research group works on a pilot study that investigates whether the specific nursing techniques that are applied during washing, positioning, transferring and sensory stimulations, have any effect on the quality of life of patients in vegetative or minimally conscious states.[2]

During the respective meeting, another question is discussed: How, in the clinical routine, does a nurse assess, categorize and document a patient's mental/cognitive changes during the course of the project? A heated debate erupts concerning the right assessment of awareness, wakefulness, arousal, and the classification of behaviour as spontaneous, reflexive or purposeful. The debate culminates in the (almost angry) question: 'Does research mean that mind and body have to be separated from each other?'

So far, only with reluctance, the participants of the meeting have done the categorization and have finally written down these terms on the flip chart. For neurologists, psychologists, and philosophers, these terms may represent quite familiar, albeit, disputable categories. However, for the members of the nursing research team – who take care of these patients on a 24-hour basis – apparently it does not make sense to write down these categories. They state that they 'know their patients' anyway through the constant assembling of non-verbalized 'experiences' of conditions and interactions; and moreover, that this

Criteria for observation:
(subj./obj.)
Eyes: opening, vigilance, visual tracking, eye contact, expression (moods, interest);
Facial expression: relaxed vs. tensed up (mood, muscles), smile, pain, refusal, discomfort, contentment vs. satisfaction, fear, . . .
Oral motor control: purposeful – reflexive, opening–closing, chewing, swallowing, disgorging, tongue pumping; lip pursing;
Head posture: head control, movement restrictions, duration, position, turning towards or away from something, neck muscles, tension vs. relaxation;
Voice: voluntary, involuntary, vocalization, articulation;
Arm: mobility, posture (eg withdrawal), functional restrictions, (muscle) tonus; function (ie duration, independent, following instructions);
Hand: like above, fine motor skills, sensibility;
Trunk: trunk control, posture, defective position, duration, tonus;
Leg/foot: see arm

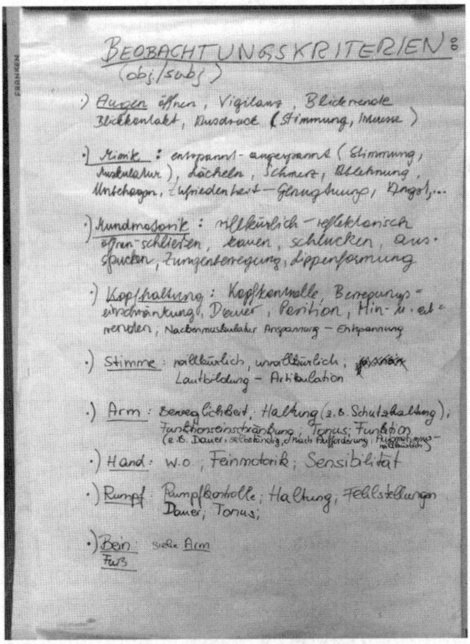

Figure 3

embodied, situated and personal knowledge (Varela *et al.*, 1991) is not describable or expressible, and that they repeatedly have a 'gut feeling' for the patient's condition. If they tried to name it, they would immediately lose something and miss the significant point.

Regarding the conditions of these bodies/persons, it is not difficult to find categories that indeed are made explicit by the nurses and that are verbalized without any reluctance. These categories apparently do not establish an explicit reference to any 'cognitive existence' of the patients. The nurses then talk about 'tensed up/relaxed', 'congested/non-congested with phlegm', 'calm/anxious', 'out-of-tune/happy', 'sleepy/awake' bodies/persons. Nevertheless, these apparently vague and fuzzy categories are important reference points for the exchange of knowledge of about patients among the nursing staff.

For the members of the nursing staff, however, although this experienced knowledge is expressed in sophisticated terms, the explicit naming of respective categories – in contrast to a 'clear-cut and unequivocal' medical diagnosis – often seems banal, futile and superficial. (This self-image mirrors some aspects of discussions concerning the problems related to the implementation of nursing as an area of scientific research: 'If we cannot name it, we cannot control it, finance it, research it, teach it, or put it into public policy.' (Clark and Lang quoted by Friesacher, 1998: 30)

Subjectivity and objectivity

Why was the debate among the nurses so heated? As already indicated, one reason, possibly, is related to the fact that the procedure of a diagnosis, namely the ordering or enacting (Mol, 2002; Dupuy and Varela, 1992) of reality in (separated) parts and categories, does not self-evidently arise from current, everyday nursing practices.

Another possibility may be that we, as participants of the nursing research project, witness the difficult attempt to perform a shift from the emphasis on people's disabilities, to their level of health as it is eg formulated by the *International Classification of Functioning, Disability and Health* (ICF, WHO, 2001). This is a shift that holistic nursing concepts try to account for in the clinical care of patients in vegetative state or minimal conscious state.

From the nursing staff's point of view, the quality of life of patients is related to the attempt to take advantage of the patients' individual resources, by means of 'dialogic interactions with the patients'. This view aims to 'comprehend/ understand' the reality of the patients, without creating a deficit-position for these bodies/persons, within a reductionist perspective. Perhaps the aforementioned reluctance of the nurses to classify the cognitive behaviour relates to attempts to avoid a classifying language (in the sense of a classification-oriented diagnostic set-up). This might then create a reality that does not resonate with the reality of the patients.

Some may be surprised by the attempt of the members of the research project to measure the impact of those concepts on the quality of life of 'comatose' patients. How is it possible to assess the quality of life of a person who cannot be asked whether she or he feels her/himself good or bad, or, whether he or she suffers from pain? What can be done in the face of a person who cannot provide any 'subjective' self-assessment, who cannot be interviewed and/or fill in questionnaires? And, what is more, how is it possible to assess their condition when no 'objective' parameters exist that can be measured and that allow their quality of life to be deduced? How is it possible to grasp 'objectively' the 'subjective' health conditions of people in vegetative states, their level of capacity or of performance, 'from the body, the individual and societal perspective'?

This is an interesting conundrum: while the medical disciplines struggle with the deficits of a syndrome that shows a 'heterogeneous clinical picture that disappears behind a bunch of diagnoses', the nursing discipline feels obliged to measure the health (conditions) of patients that cannot support this endeavour.

How can their 'holistic' approach be achieved? By attempting to link biomedical necessities (thus, organ-related, and more objective), with social and philosophical necessities, (thus, experience-based, and more subjective)? (Hladik, 2007). Can this link be performed by reference to the frequently evoked discrepancy between natural and social sciences or between analytical-methodological and phenomenological-sociological research approaches? Does this mean a combination of the holistic 'good' with the reductionist 'bad'?

We ask ourselves whether this discrepancy actually has to play a crucial role when medicine and nursing take care of bodies/persons and enact with them and other actors multiple versions[3] (Despret, 2001) of this syndrome? Could it be that the relations of versions are too intricate to be forced into a dichotomy? Maybe it is more intriguing to look beyond these extremes and study the logic of a shared 'care for the syndrome'?

An opportunity

Let us return to the mundane care routine at the ward, where oil has been poured on troubled waters. The head of the research project (who is also the head nurse of the ward) shares the doubts of her colleagues, that it will be difficult systematically to document an 'embodied' knowledge / feeling as it is experienced, for instance, during the washing procedure described before. However, on her own authority, she has added the category 'cognition' on the aforementioned flip chart. (see Figure 3) This designates a discreet shift from the description of a shared bodily experience of nurses (and patients), to the evaluation of observations of behavioural changes that could imply a cognitive component of the patient.

In the research project, it is her responsibility to look for existing clinical assessment methods to evaluate the impact of different nursing measures. What is more, her task is to find out if these measures lead to any changes in the patients' condition, that for themselves constitute an improvement. But then the question arises: are these patients aware of themselves – of their bodies and of their situation? To have a self-awareness implies a consciousness and then again one has to ask: to what extent do these patients perceive their surroundings and what do they comprehend? And then, in the context of a clinical research project, it is a consequential step to ask how to discriminate and assess between reflexive, spontaneous or purposeful behaviours. However, with respect to holistic nursing concepts and the respective self-image of nursing, the head nurse is forced to enter a dangerous field.

In the role as a trans-disciplinary consultant, one of us has been following these discussions for almost one year. We conclude that this phase of the research project gives us an opportunity to intensify our research on the intricate relationship between – to put it bluntly – a holistic and reductionist perspective.

An experiment

We take advantage of the situation and venture a risky experiment. We convince the head nurse to attend, together with a researcher, a training course for a

NEUROPSYCHOLOGICAL REHABILITATION, 1999, 9 (3/4), 305–320

The Sensory Modality Assessment and Rehabilitation Technique (SMART): A Comprehensive and Integrated Assessment and Treatment Protocol for the Vegetative State and Minimally Responsive Patient

Figure 4

psychometrical assessment tool called SMART (Gill-Thwaites and Munday, 1999) (see Figure 4). This tool has captured our attention since it was designed specifically for the case-management of difficult situations that may occur in the course of the long-term nursing of patients in a vegetative state or minimally responsive state.

This specific assessment procedure should warrant that bodies/persons, before others make a respective decision for them, get ample opportunity to demonstrate their resources and potentials. This is so that they may possibly free themselves from the definitional clamp of the syndrome called, '(permanent) vegetative state'. This definition sometimes equals diagnosis with prognosis. The key to escaping from this 'prison' then, is to show minimal signs of 'awareness', irrespective of whether it represents the adequate or appropriate key for any patient. Thus, the results of the respective psychometrical assessments may affect the decision of whether or not a patient's life should be terminated by withholding, or withdrawing, life-sustaining treatment, namely the withdrawal of fluid and nutrition. In other words, and expressed with pathos: In the UK, for instance, it can be a matter of life and death.

Within the title of the paper (see Figure 4) the juxtaposition of the terms 'assessment' and 'treatment' especially intrigued us. Practical-clinical action tends to follow a program, step by step. In the majority of cases, this procedure passes from the anamnestic collection of symptoms to the search for and observation of signs, by means of diagnostic measures such as a physical examination or a blood test. The aim of this procedure is to confirm a diagnosis that finally proceeds to therapeutic actions. This is the preferred pathway that, in most cases, is expected to show positive results. But there are situations of high uncertainty, where this two-step logic, (first, to establish a diagnosis and second, to advise a treatment) has to be revised, or at least supplemented by a more circular practice. The process *starts* with a therapeutic intervention and diagnosis follows from these actions. In the medical and therapeutic context, the entanglement of diagnosis and therapy is widely accepted and a common practice (Mol, 2002). For example:

SMART is both an assessment and a treatment tool, since assessment that requires the systematic application of stimuli can also be construed as treatment. (Gill-Thwaites and Munday, 1999: 310)

Although there is the intention of developing an 'objectifying' behavioural assessment tool, the quote confirms our presumption that the authors have conceived of the test in the sense of the second, circular, logic: to assess (to evaluate) means to treat (to stimulate), and to treat means to assess. During a series of sessions, this dynamic circle should create a relationship between patient and assessor/therapist. This diagnostic/therapeutic procedure introduces the assessor in the diagnostic set-up, since only in this relationship both do get the opportunity to use their potentials or 'talents'. (Despret, 2004) In addition, one could say that it is about a behaviouristic procedure that embraces the possibility, that eventually, it is generating the phenomena that it tries to measure. (Stengers, 1993)

From this we conclude that it would make sense to 'import' SMART to central Europe. Why not introduce a diagnostic protocol that is based on a positivistic-behaviourist tradition, to an environment that, at least in the context of nursing, works with methods that are related to constructivist theories like eg that of Jean Piaget (see for example the perception theory by Affolter, (Affolter and Bischofberger, 1996)?

There is another dimension of the endeavour that we call an experiment. This dimension concerns our own role as members of an 'art & science' research group called *Xperiment*! who started to pay attention to the described syndrome: as part of our research, we, as ethnographers/researchers/artists and citizens, intend to take over responsibility for the development of idiosyncratic versions of the ontological patchwork (Law, 1999) as one could call this syndrome. This makes it possible for us not to conceptualize the syndrome as a pre-given (medical) entity but to enrich it by adding our own versions to the medical, nursing, private, administrative, economic, neuropathological, etc; versions that come into being through multiple (clinical) practices.

This implies that we take part in the experiment ourselves. It is the attempt to become part of the reality we entered some years ago. Like the diagnostic set-up of the described assessment procedure, where assessor and patient should interact to refine their 'knowing', we try to establish relationships and interactions between the involved actors (nurses, doctors, therapists, family members etc.) and ourselves that should help to address the issue that is connected with the question: how do *we and those actors* want the assessment/measurement of 'something' that affects the knowing/unknowing of bodies in the described clinical context?

One consequence of this reasoning is that for the implementation of our 'experiment', one of us temporarily leaves the role of a transdisciplinary researcher, in order to become an assessor and together with the head nurse to graduate from the 'SMART' training course. In other words, from now on, we are forced to oscillate between the role of an assessor and that of an assessor of assessment.

Assessing the mind

From washing the body to assessing the mind: altogether, the preparation for the implementation of the assessment tool takes about two years until the first assessments can take place on the ward. And here we are. We are gazing into a small office on the aforementioned ward. It is about 10:30 a.m. and the whole-body washing was finished one hour ago. After the washing, the patient was transferred to his wheelchair and had some rest in front of a switched off TV-set. Then, he was wheeled into the office. Currently, his eyes seem to be closed as if he is asleep. We witness an assessment session: the assessor (a member of the group *Xperiment*!) undertakes the strictly determined and structured assessment procedure called SMART.

By means of a SMART Kit (comprised of various stimuli) the assessor is both observer and therapist: he observes potential behaviours and simultaneously intervenes by presenting a set of stimuli in order to test the patient's sensory modalities (visual, auditory, tactile, olfactory and gustatory) together with her/his abilities in motor activity, functional communication and wakefulness.

As already pointed out the aim of the assessment is to find out if, and to what extent, the patient is able to perceive; whether he is able to show purposeful behaviour or develop a yes/no code; how many cues are necessary to wake him up and how long he is able to stay awake etc.

For ten minutes, the assessor has observed the patient without being active himself. He assigned any behaviour to a specific code and made several entries on a form. Then, according to the sensory modalities, he started to present specified stimuli. Now he presents a toothbrush at the patient's eye level. He asks the young man to focus his gaze on this object and, subsequently, to follow the toothbrush with his eyes, as soon as it starts to move. This task is part of the assessment of the visual modality. In the photographs, we do not note any reactions (Figure 5). It is very difficult to determine whether the patient sleeps or whether he looks via a narrow palpebral fissure in the direction of the toothbrush. Possibly, he observes the assessor.

The second picture series show two wooden blocks in the hand of the assessor. The noisy banging of the blocks is part of the assessment of the audio modality. Again, the patient does not show any clear reaction to the intervention (Figure 6).

At the end of the session, the assessor will write down that the patient showed wakefulness during the session, but hardly stayed awake.

Washing and assessing are two procedures that, at first glance, appear quite different. In the first case, washing, we see two people in close physical contact

Figure 5

Figure 6

that forms part of an everyday-life experience. In the second case, assessing, we observe one person engaged in a structured observational task that, for the other person, takes place in an unusual manner. Nevertheless, a closer look may reveal similarities in the goals of the procedures.

For instance, during washing, the nurse guides the hand and arm of the patient to his trunk and face so that he becomes aware of his own body – its surface and its boundaries. It is an attempt to establish a kind of *self*-awareness of the body/person. In the second case, the assessment tries to conduct a mental training that pays attention to any manifestations or traces of an *environmental*-consciousness of the patient. Thus, in both cases, the person's consciousness plays an important role in the aim of the intervention. Furthermore, both procedures attempt to create a standard environment that helps to develop the patient's level of capacity and performance.

In addition, both procedures refer to concepts of structured 'sensory stimulation' that are based on the recognition that sensory deprivation may have an adverse effect on mental functioning (International Working Party, 1996). It is comprised of a systematic program of sensory input, sometimes aimed at specific senses (Jennett, 2002). However, its effectiveness is difficult to estimate (Giacino, 1996). There is some evidence, though, to suggest that sensory 'regulation' could influence the recovery pattern (Wood *et al.*, 1993). Nevertheless, these principles remain contested (Lombardi *et al.*, 2002). Apart from the diagnostic setting of the assessment procedure that follows a more traditional stimulus-response paradigm, the washing procedure of the vegetative patients integrates various nursing concepts that could be called sensory stimulation in a broader sense (Zieger, 2003a). Finally, this reference to a sensory stimulation/regulation concept explains that both interventions follow a long-term approach: what for the washing procedure, in most cases, seems to be self-evident, might be surprising in the case of the assessment procedure, where serial assessments/treatments blocks (eg comprised of ten sessions) are conducted over months.

Assessing assessing

Why did we call the introduction of a behavioural assessment tool into a holistic-oriented nursing environment a 'risky' experiment? One reason for this is that we run the risk of transforming the participants (we are talking here not only of the patients but also of the nurses, doctors, therapists, family members etc.) into accomplices of our own research agenda. This means forcing them to become mere testimonials for our interest in order to enact other versions, differences or practices beyond the traditional dichotomies as they are eg 'objective vs. subjective', 'holistic vs. reductionist'. In other words, we might fail to create a 'set-up' that gives participants in the experiment the opportunity to develop and unfold their own potentialities or talents that qualify for new and surprising enactments.

Second, there may be another risk: that we get trapped between the fronts of the seemingly contrary, operating logics, of nursing and medicine. This is a fact that in the worst case may force us to leave the field of our investigation. Two incidents at the beginning of our experiment seem to confirm our apprehensions: during the 'SMART assessor training course', the head nurse realizes that, at least from the perspective of care concepts that are applied at the department and the care unit, she has entered a dangerous field. On the occasion of dealing with the SMART technique more closely, she starts to doubt if her colleagues at the ward will accept the application of this assessment. Historically, this is not difficult to understand, as these fragile bodies/persons depend on superior professional care. The head nurse has spared no effort to help establish, at least national, care standards. These standards assure the well-being and quality of life in regard to the 'human being as a whole', who, under all circumstances, must remain in 'the centre of all efforts'. Hence, the caregivers at her ward are urged to feel responsible for these patients and to protect them 'from any kind of noxious stimuli'. As mentioned above, in order to meet these claims, a specific combination of nursing concepts is consistently implemented.

During the training course, the head nurse becomes familiar with the testing of the auditory modality, which involves the administration of loud sound. For this purpose, outside of the visual field of the patient, and approximately one meter from her/his right and then left ear, two wooden blocks are repeatedly banged against each other, thus causing a sudden and almost painful loud noise (see Figure 6). Any reactions to this intervention are thereby carefully observed and subsequently written down. And this is exactly what nurses understand, among other things, as noxious stimuli.

During a break, the head nurse expresses her disagreement, and declares that this test is not appropriate for use on the ward. Given the danger that our experiment fails before it has even begun, we develop a 'Paracelsian' reasoning. We state that whether or not something is noxious or beneficial, depends on the dose. Furthermore, we argue that, compared to other unpleasant procedures patients undergo during their every day life of being nursed, the wooden-blocks test is not so bad.

She insists on her viewpoint. A tough and passionate discussion follows. She says that she has seen too many patients being transferred from other wards, in deplorable conditions: horrible and ulcerous bedsores that expose the bones beneath; bodies that become stiff like a piece of wood when being slightly touched; sweating when there is the slightest noise in the room; a facial expression showing unease and anxiety when a foreign person approaches the bed; permanent motor agitation or opisthotonus (abnormal posturing) when lying in the bed; and excessive amounts of bronchial mucus. She continues saying that when these patients are transferred to the ward, the consequent employment of the nursing concepts induces a very remarkable metamorphosis after a few weeks: sweating, mucus production and muscle spasticity decreases; decubital ulcers heal; the bodily posture relaxes; and startle responses become infrequent. The patients have become confident in 'their' nurses who take care of them. 'We treat them as human beings. How should I advocate an intervention that could jeopardize the patient's trust?' The nurse is a spokesperson for the patients. What can we reply? We make an attempt. We point out that this may be right, but during the application of 'therapeutic nursing' there may occur situations where a beneficial procedure can cause side effects that may affect the relationship between nurses and patients negatively. There are, for instance, the kinaesthetic transfer techniques that may have caused some of the bone fractures that have occurred in the past. Of course, we are talking of highly osteoporotic patients but this does not mean that a kinaesthetic transfer, 'per se,' is beneficial or harmful.

The break is over and there seems to be no compromise. We start to wonder if we will fail at an early stage. But then we remember the starting point of the discussion: Why is this technique being applied at all? It concerns the question of whether patients who cannot hear are constantly misdiagnosed. The suspicion or the knowledge that a patient cannot hear is important information, since it affects further therapeutic interactions with this patient (Andrews *et al.*, 1996).

In fact, we have become advocates of a medical approach, as the application of 'noxious' auditory stimuli helps to reach a diagnosis. This may include interventions that are hurtful or entail side effects. The aim is to collect information that guides the next steps for treatment. The insight, that the *withholding* of a noxious stimulus, could eventually prevent a patient from fully developing his potential, is, finally, the convincing argument for the head nurse.

The second incident, that indicates the risk of getting trapped between the fronts, is the reaction of the chief physician to our intervention. What for the head nurse has been almost too 'hard' a procedure, seems, for the neurologist, to be too 'soft' a procedure. He points out that he misses the neuro-pathological background of this assessment. He critically adds, that this assessment method is a 'tool,' that tries to gather information by 'subjective' means. However, he continues, it would be nice to 'harden' these observations, by means of correlating them with clinical findings and neuroimaging techniques. Of course, he refers to a neuroimaging study that shows promising results concerning the detection of conscious awareness in patients who are assumed to be vegetative (Owen *et al.*, 2006).

The neurologist's reference to the hard sciences reminds us of Isabelle Stengers and her thoughts on boundary techniques of the emerging medical discipline(s), vis-à-vis charlatans. She points out that medicine succeeded in establishing acceptance, especially for those therapeutic effects that also combat the cause of diseases. This definition implies that scientific-medical practice tries to find out how the ill body discriminates between 'real' and 'fictitious' cures. The difference between a body and an experimental system, namely the characteristic of the living body that is capable of making a 'fiction' such as a placebo effect 'real', that means effective, is for medicine a parasitical, disturbing effect (Stengers, 1993: 40).

In this case, we take a more holistic position. During the discussion with the chief physician, we point out the following ideas: within neuro-sciences; anatomical, neuro-pathological examinations and their tendency to allocate the nature of a complex function like vision, hearing or memory, to the presence and the proper function of circumscribed parts of the brain have been criticized time and again; that is easy to correlate the position of a brain lesion with the loss of a certain function but this does not mean, inevitably, that the location of this tissue-lesion is the responsible carrier of a function; and that the functioning of the brain and body as a whole is important for the functioning of the sensory modalities (Foerster, 1997). Furthermore, the neurologist should know, from his own experience, that there are patients who, according to the visualization of brain activities, actually should not be alive. These patients are quite able to (re)act in sophisticated ways on a physical-vegetative level, so that behavioural categories like purposeful, spontaneous or reflexive, sometimes, become questionable. Although the chief physician expresses his doubts, the discussion ends with his commitment to support the implementation of the new assessment technique.

The next phase of our experiment started with the official implementation of the assessment tool of the 'evidence-based-nursing' research project during summer 2007. Currently it is still underway, and we would like to present some intermediate results.

Intermediate results

Washing, assessing and communicating

The preliminary, most important, result for us is the fact that a lively discussion has started on the ward about the differences, commonalities and commensurability of versions of bodies/persons and/or the syndrome. In the clinical routine, such a discussion is seen more as a luxury problem, a problem that, nevertheless, can play an important role in the course of conflicting encounters between for example a medical, a nursing or a family version of bodies/ persons or the syndrome.

The fact that there is a discussion at all, has to be seen within the background of the permanent struggle for personal resources, which aims at establishing and maintaining appropriate nursing standards in the long-term care of these severely disabled bodies/persons. In the majority of cases, in long-term neuro-rehabilitative care, where patients spend six to eight years and more at special-ized units, attempts are made to preserve an initial condition that is presented on admission to the ward. Only in the best case can an 'improvement' of this state be accomplished. Any striving for improvement becomes an illusion when quantitative, but also qualitative, shortcomings in human resources (for differ-ent reasons), are accompanied by the physical-psychical and also economic distress of family members. Most of the persons involved are aware of the resulting danger of a therapeutic nihilism. The fact that our experiment opens additional options for diagnostic and therapeutic re-orientation may be one reason why it is appreciated.

Another experience should also be mentioned. As suggested earlier an inter-vention of this kind implies unforeseen problems. Our experiment occasionally enabled a dynamic between the nursing staff and the medical staff that ques-tioned the a priori positive relation and the close cooperation between those disciplines. Maybe this is also related to the fact that the introduction of the assessment procedure is considered an initiative of the nurses that has enabled them to start a research project that hitherto has not played a very prominent role during clinical everyday life. However, this critical situation has changed through sustainable self-reflection of the persons involved, and some diplomatic activities from our side.

Time and lack of time

A formal assessment requires a structured observation and interaction with the patient – and that needs time. In order to carry out an assessment with one patient, this technique demands that the assessor dedicate, within a three-week period, ten sessions, of 60–90 minutes, exclusively to this patient. In a similar way to the whole-body washing, this means *being alone* with one patient, and finding time that is exclusively dedicated to explore (learn more about) the condition of the patient.

Busy nursing people experience wresting this time from their daily nursing duties as a hard struggle. Interestingly, thinking about the temporalization or time management of 'holistically' conceptualized clinical care-routines, that should put the 'human being' into its centre and that should spend as much time as possible with these patients necessitates an 'objectifying' procedure. This type of nursing understands itself as therapeutic nursing, beyond the mere fulfilment of basic needs like feeding, cleaning and keeping warm. The discussion about the new assessment technique challenged this self-image. It became evident how much time is actually dedicated to this basic care instead of to therapeutic care practices, such as the whole-body washing that we described at the beginning of this article. Like the new assess-ment technique, this could also be designated as a diagnostic/therapeutic practice.

Legitimate observations

Certainly, the staff members working at the described health care site are used to the obligation to fill in preconfigured lists, tables and forms that should guide, structure and record their activities over time. Nevertheless, during the team meetings of the research project, advantages and disadvantages, the related expenditure of time and the fear of being controlled by 'the organization', are repeatedly discussed when the issue of data collection and the need to put those data down on paper comes to the fore. Furthermore, as we have seen, the formation of categories leads to emotional discussions.

The formal behavioural assessment procedure requires the assessor to classify his or her observations and subsequently to enter them into a hierarchical checklist of behavioural categories. Although this comprehensive list contains many pre-given categories, of course, it cannot be exhaustive. Accordingly, observations cannot be classified, but exactly this fact shows that, nevertheless, *any* observation can be documented and integrated into another part of the assessment. This has made it possible to discuss the 'manufacturing' of categories that did not exist until then.

Furthermore, the implementation of the SMART-assessment demonstrated the role of the legitimacy of observations. Its systematic demand for observations demonstrates that the multi-disciplinary team endow some observations with higher legitimacy than others. We do not refer to observations of signs and signals that may require medical or nursing training. It is about inconspicuous and discreet signs that patients are able to show in daily, mundane situations. Sometimes, these signs do not make it into an official documentation because it can make a difference who observes them: a doctor, a therapist, a registered nurse or a caregiver, a civil servant or a member of the cleaning staff.

The same holds true for the legitimacy of observations made by family members. The multidisciplinary team considers them indispensable 'co-therapists' (Steinbach and Donis, 2004). But, until our experiment, nobody thought of involving them as 'co-diagnosticians', since the SMART-assessment requires them also to write down their observations. It is interesting to note that there is a high consistency between observations of professional and lay diagnosticians. Regarding the family members, this is a remarkable observation since the professionals frequently complain that the relatives, in many cases, are either too optimistic, or too pessimistic ie that there is a mismatch between realities.

Surprisingly this mismatch of realities also holds true for the professionals: the results of 'formalized' assessment and the 'subjective feeling' for the potentials of the bodies/persons show differences: potentials and abilities have been, on both sides, under- and overestimated. In other words, washing and assessing, seen as different diagnostic set-ups, could possibly complement each other in finding more realistic pathways between (therapeutic) euphoria and nihilism.

Every day life and 'ethico-economical-rehabilitative' considerations

The experiment has (further) intensified the consideration about the possible – until then, frowned upon – distribution of resources. As already mentioned, time and again, even condition-preserving care measures cannot be assured for all patients. This implies that the decision of who should receive appropriate (therapeutic) care would privilege some patients, and at the same time, discriminate against others.

For this reason, until now, the scarce nursing/therapeutic resources have been distributed evenly to all patients. The introduction of this assessment tool (and the fact that this implies providing additional resources) led to considerations concerning a rotation principle that periodically provides the full repertoire of care measures to changing groups of patients. This quantitative and temporal concentration of treatment measures and the assessment of the respective effects, may help develop more personalized treatment plans. This would account for the fact that not only does the course of the syndrome allow a change for the worse but also there is a chance (called 'therapeutic windows') that patients take advantage of regularly-offered therapeutic interventions and show unexpected and surprising improvements.

This reasoning aligns with a neuro-rehabilitative saying that there are only three principles that, so far, show any effects on a reproducible basis: repetition, endurance and constraint-induced therapies. (Saltuari, 2007)

Everyday life and research

The described discussions and considerations, for the first time, related everyday practices of the nursing staff to neuro-scientific research and some of its more theoretical research questions. From a practical point of view, these research issues become relevant as soon as staff members realize that their prognostic statements and therapeutic decisions are being influenced by the hypothetical answer to the question: How should one envisage the ability of the brain to regenerate on a functional and anatomical basis?

In the context of various therapeutic nursing approaches, issues like 'neuro-plasticity', 'sensory stimulation/regulation' and 'functional neuro-imaging' become especially relevant. In the course of the experiment, members of the nursing research team tried to link their own therapeutic nursing practice to the respective scientific issues. That includes therapeutic methods and interactions that follow 'functional exercising concepts' (Zieger, 2003b) like the 'Affolter' and the 'Bobath' concept, 'Basal Stimulation' and 'Kinaesthetics'. These rehabilitative measures understand the functioning and the organization of the central nervous system in recursive dependence on an active or activated (peripheral) body.

Thus, the group developed a (theoretical) awareness of the fact that any isolated stimulation, via perception 'channels' (seeing, listening, smelling, tasting and tactile sense), probably does not suffice to activate any 'cognition.' Rather, there is the need to create conditions that help to improve any '(self) organiza- tion' of the damaged central nervous system through support and s(t)imulation of complex every day life experiences that integrate the whole body of the patients (Varela *et al.*, 1991; Bienstein, 1991).

It goes without saying that against this background, the possible disadvan- tages of the SMART assessment/therapeutic technique have also been dis- cussed. Namely, that this assessment tool favours, mainly, the cognitive aspects of a patient and this may bias any assessment of her or his abilities: How could emotional, vegetative (the involuntary body functions that are linked with breathing, temperature, digestion, regulation of secretion etc.) or other physical (eg muscular) parameters be integrated?

By the same token the nurses re-evaluated a kind of 'sensory stimulation' that happens mostly carelessly: the habit of endless exposure of the patients to radio and TV programmes in the ward corridors and rooms. They discussed if this could be partly replaced by a structured presentation of selected, and also, biographically meaningful audiovisual stimuli. These discussions aligned with scientific controversies about the effectiveness and non-effectiveness of sensory stimulation/regulation of patients in a vegetative state.

Medicine and nursing

Maybe the relation between medicine and nursing could best be described as ambivalent, multi-layered and complex. As the description of the conflict regard- ing the wooden-blocks test should point out, during the course of the possible implementation of this assessment tool, the responsible representatives of the nursing staff, to a certain extent, had to enter into medical terrain by adopting some aspects of diagnostic-prognostic thinking and transform it into a different appreciation of the syndrome.

Is it possible to observe a reciprocal behaviour of representatives of the medical staff – for example, whether there is a tendency for doctors to adopt holistic reasoning to a certain extent? In the face of prognostic incertitude, the occurrence of this tendency seems to depend on the response they try to give to an intricate answer: are they dealing with extremely vulnerable and fragile patients with a high risk of developing lethal complications (eg recurrent pul- monary or urinary tract infections, systemic failure or sudden death) (Jennett, 2002) or are they managing severely disabled persons that may remain stable and survive for many years and who should be treated as resourceful individuals?

On the ward, one can observe a kind of oscillation between these two posi- tions, depending on the medical specialism each doctor is affiliated with (eg neurologist, internist, general practitioner). However, in the light of limited curative treatment options, for the doctors, a 'holistic' nursing approach is a fact that plays an important role in the care of patients in a vegetative state. Tensions may arise in periods where the caring for the stability of the vital parameters of corporeal organ systems and acute medical procedures start to intervene with the daily therapeutic nursing activities. One of these activities can be the daily transfer of patients out of bed into wheel-chairs and the organization of leisure activities for them. What doctors may see as a risk, nurses may consider as an important part of the quality of life of those individuals.

The situation changes when doctors get interested in spending more time with patients at risk. This interest may also imply transferring patients out of bed because they want to make assessments in a sitting position. This situation occurred when the chief physician, despite his reserved attitude towards this assessment technique, decided to attend the SMART training course together with the ward internist, to learn the assessment technique. It is still too early to say whether or not the intensified interaction between patients and members of the medical staff will influence the aforementioned oscillations.

Our roles: Diplomats?

For more than four years, we have attempted to become familiar with different versions of the syndrome called the vegetative state. Finally, we have also started to craft our own versions and to make some of them public (Xperiment!, 2005). For this purpose, we work with a kind of method-multiple and with the long-term presence in the field of investigation. Of course, the long-term presence, as a prerequisite for their work, is self-evident for ethnographers and cultural anthropologists when they are 'in' the field and concretize their 'research object'.

However, the mere presence is also an important characteristic of diplomats: this presence is about a difference that can make a difference (Bateson, 1972), in regard to the relation to the opposing parties that will, therefore, change themselves. The character of the diplomat is used, among others, by Stengers (1993) and Latour (1999). We feel inclined to look at our activities, in the light of this interpretation. We are frequently confronted with the same questions that a diplomat is asked by his opponents *and* by the party he belongs to: 'Who are you? On which side are you? On behalf of whom, do you speak?' These questions can be translated into other questions: 'Can we (still) trust you?' or 'Can we count on your loyalty?' And then we have to ask ourselves if our activities could be interpreted as a betrayal of confidence; a betrayal of a subject, a discipline, patients, the (holistic or reductionist) perspective or a method etc.

The position of a diplomat becomes more complicated by the fact that he or she belongs to one of the conflicting parties. In his welcome address directed to young diplomats the director of the Diplomatic Academy in Vienna, Jirí Gruša, characterizes diplomats as 'duplicate beings in a duplicate world' ('diploos' meaning folded and doubled things) and states that the most important precondition of diplomats is the 'principal of renewal of personality' (Gruša, 2005).

In this respect, we are no exception. During our work, we have designated ourselves as a research group comprised of members that have specific educational backgrounds or 'origins': eg ethnographer, medical doctor, sociologist, artist. Together, we attempted to find out how the syndrome could be described. Each of us has – if only temporarily and within a certain context – an 'origin'. In other words, each of us, in analogy to the situation in the field that we described before, belongs to a different conflicting party, eg a more 'holistic' or 'reductionist' oriented, a 'realistic' or 'constructivist', or a more 'factual' or 'value-related' party.

Nevertheless, as members of the group *Xperiment!*, we commit ourselves to a work that is committed to Gruša's 'renewal of personality'; that tries to avoid the term of a joint world of reference and that accepts getting in touch and 'being a representative'; that never talks about the 'rational' or the 'irrational'. We are, then, in the sense of Gruša, 'duplicated beings in a duplicated world.' In the acknowledged function as a representative of a 'party' (education, discipline, method, theory), we feel inclined to respect others solely because we 'despise' them; however as 'diplomats', as members of the Research Centre for Shared Incompetence, we do not despise anything or anybody. Neither, however, do we respect the parties or their fixed positions regardless of the name in which they may act.

In this light, we think that our experiment has something to do with the question of whether knowing/unknowing bodies, and in particular the 'unknowing' can be understood in the sense of temporal oblivion: an oblivion due to another difference, another question or another practice that enacts another version of the syndrome, so that the existing syndrome (with its persons/bodies) will be transformed and rendered surprisingly, less predictable, less in the familiar and automatized differences. Maybe this includes – as a side effect – the opportunity to describe those enactments of bodies/persons at a marginalized part of the healthcare system in a more realistic way.

Notes

1 This 'experiment' was developed within an ethnographic long-term project called, 'Research Centre for Shared Incompetence – A Topography of the Possible. What is a Body/a Person?' conducted by the research group *Xperiment!*. This work took place at a specialized ward of a nursing home on the periphery of an Austrian town.

2 The research project, originally, was instigated by the head nurse of the ward and the chief physician of the neurology department. In this group of seven registered nurses and one scientific adviser, one of the members of the research group *Xperiment!* took on the role of a transdisciplinary consultant.

3 We refer to the understanding of 'version' that Despret (2001) uses to describe different and also contradictory practices concerning emotions. By using the term 'versions' she points at the coexistence and multiplicity of different and interrelated practices.

References

Affolter, F. and Bischofberger, W., (1996), *Wenn die Organisation des zentralen Nervensystems zerfällt – und es an gespürter Information mangelt*, Neckar Verlag: Villingen-Schwenningen.

Andrews, K., Murphy, L., Munday, R. and Littlewood, C., (1996), Misdiagnosis of the Vegetative State: Retospective Study in a Rehabilitation Unit, *British Medical Journal* 313: 130–116.

Bateson, G., (1972), *Steps to an Ecology of Mind: Collected Essays in Anthropology, Psychiatry, Evolution, and Epistemology*, Chicago: University Of Chicago Press.

Bienstein, C. and Fröhlich, A., (1991), *Basale Stimulation in der Pflege*, Düsseldorf: Verlag Selbstbestimmtes Leben.

Despret, V., (2001), *Ces émotions qui nous fabriquent – Ethnopsychologie de l'authenticité*, Les Empêcheurs de penser en rond. Paris: Le Seuil.

Despret, V., (2004), The Body We Care For: Figures of Anthropo-zoo-genesis. *Body & Society* 10 (2–3): 111–134.

Dupuy, J-P. and Varela, F.J., (1992), Understanding Origins: An Introduction, *Boston Studies in the Philosophy of Science* 30: 1–26.

Fleck, L., (1980 [1935]), *Entstehung und Entwicklung einer wissenschaftlichen Tatsache*, Frankfurt/Main: Suhrkamp.

Friesacher, H., (1998), Pflegediagnosen und International Classification for Nursing Practise (ICNP). Eine Analyse von Klassifikationssystemen in der Pflege. In *Dr. med. Mabuse 112*, Frankfurt am Main: Mabuse-Verlag GmbH: 33–37.

Foerster, H.v., (1997), *Der Anfang von Himmel und Erde hat keinen Namen – Eine Selbsterschaffung in 7 Tagen*, Albert Müller and Karl. H. Müller (eds), Wien: Döcker Verlag.

Giacino, J.T., (1996), Sensory Stimulation: Theoretical Perspectives and the Evidence for Effectiveness, *NeuroRehabilitation*, 6: 69–78.

Gill-Thwaites, H. and Munday, R., (1999), The Sensory Modality Assessment Rehabilitation Technique (SMART): A Comprehensive and Integrated Assessment and Treatment Protocol for the Vegetative State and Minimally Responsive Patient, *Neuropsychological Rehabilitation* 9 (3/4): 305–320.

Gruša, J., (2005), *International Mission on Diplomacy*, talk on 23 May 2005 at the Diplomatic Academy in Vienna, [Online], available: http://www.da-vienna.ac.at/application/startseite.asp [accessed 24 February 2008].

Hladik, R., (2007), *Pflegekonzepte: Angst und Hilflosigkeit. Theoretischer Hintergrund und Anwendungsmöglichkeiten von Pflegekonzepten in der Praxis*, [Online], available: http://www.pflege.noe-lak.at/dokumente/Netzwerk/Seminarunterlagen.rtf, [accessed on 20 August 2007].

Jennett, B., (2002), *The Vegetative State: Medical Facts, Ethical and Legal Dilemmas*, New York: Cambridge University Press.

International Working Party, (1996), *Report on The Vegetative State*, produced by The Royal Hospital for Neuro-disability, West Hill, Putney, London UK.

Knorr-Cetina, K.D., (1981), *The Manufacture of Knowledge: An Essay on the Constructivist and Contextual Nature of Science*, Oxford: Pergamon Press.

Kräftner, B., Kröll, J. and Warner, I., (2007), Walking on a Storyboard, Performing Shared Incompetence: Exhibition 'Science' in the Public Realm. In S. MacDonald and P. Basu (eds), *Exhibition Experiments (New Interventions in Art History)*: 109–131, Oxford: Blackwell Publishing.

Latimer, J., (2000), Socialising Disease: Medical Categories and Inclusion of the Aged, *The Sociological Review* 48 (3): 383–407.

Latour, B. and Weibel, P., (eds) (2005), *Making Things Public. Atmospheres of Democracy*, Karlsruhe: ZKM & Cambridge MA: MIT.

Latour, B., (1999), *Politiques de la Nature. Comment Faire Entrer les Sciences en Démocratie*, Paris: La Découverte.

Latour, B., (2004), How to talk about the body? The normative dimension of science studies. In M. Akrich and M. Berg (eds), *Bodies on Trial*, special issue of *Body and Society* 10 (2/3): 205–229.

Latour, B., (2006), Was bedeutet es, Anteil zu nehmen? in M. Guggenheim, B. Kräftner, J. Kröll, A. Martos and F. Oberhuber (eds), *Die wahr/falsch Inc. – Eine Wissenschaftsausstellung in der Stadt*, pp. 64–67. Wien: Facultas.

Law, J., (1999), After ANT: Complexity, Naming and Topology, in J. Law and J. Hassard (eds), *Actor Network Theory and After*, Sociological Review Monograph: 1–14, Oxford: Blackwell Publishers.

Law, J., (2004), *After Method. Mess in Social Science Research*, London: Routledge.

Lombardi, F., Taricco, M., De Tanti, A., Telaro, E. and Liberati, A., (2002), Sensory Stimulation of Brain-injured Individuals in Coma or Vegetative State: Results of a Cochrane Systematic Review, *Clinical Rehabilitation* 16 (5): 464–472.

Mol, A., (2002), *The Body Multiple: Ontology in Medical Practice*, Durham and London: Duke University Press.

Multi-Society Task Force On PVS (1994), Medical Aspects of the Persistent Vegetative State, *New England Journal of Medicine* 330: 1499–1508 and 1572–1579.

Owen, A.M., Coleman, M.R., Boly, M., Matthew, H., Davis, M.H., Laureys, S. and Pickard, J.D., (2006), Detecting Awareness in the Vegetative State, *Science*, Vol. 313 (5792): 1402.

Pols, J., (2005), Enacting Appreciations: Beyond the Patient Perspective, *Health Care Analysis* 13 (3): 203–221.

Saltuari, L., (2007), *Robotics – sich gehen fühlen*, presentation at the annual conference on Vegetative State of the Austrian Association for Vegetative State (Österreichische Wachkoma Gesellschaft) in Vienna on 19 October, 2007, available: http://www.wachkoma.at [accessed 3 March, 2008].

Steinbach, A. and Donis, J., (2004), *Langzeitbetreuung Wachkoma. Eine Herausforderung für Betreuende und Angehörige*, Wien, New York: Springer.

Stengers, I., (1993), *L'invention Des Sciences Modernes*, Paris: La Découverte.

WHO (2001), *International Classification of Functional Disability*, [Online], available: http://www.who.int/classifications/icf/site/icftemplate.cfm?myurl=homepage.html&mytitle=Home%20Page [accessed 20 March 2008].

Wood, R.L., Winkowski, T. and Miller, J., (1993), Sensory Regulation as a Method to promote Recovery in Patients with Altered States of Consciousness, *Neuropsych Rehab*, 3: 177–190.

Varela, F.J., Thompson, E. and Rosch, E., (1991), *The Embodied Mind*, Cambridge MA: MIT Press.

Xperiment! (2005), What is a Body/a Person? Topography of the Possible, in B. Latour and P. Weibel (eds), *Making Things Public. Atmospheres of Democracy*: 906–910, Karlsruhe: ZKM and Cambridge MA: MIT.

Zieger, A., (2003a), *Traumatisiert an Leib und Seele – Konsequenzen für den Umgang mit Wachkoma-Patienten aus beziehungsmedizinischer Sicht*, presentation at the annual conference on Vegetative State of the Austrian Association for Vegetative State in Vienna on 24October, 2003, available: http://bidok.uibk.ac.at/library/zieger-traumatisiert.html [accessed 3 March, 2008].

Zieger, A., (2003b), Komastimulationstherapie – was wissen wir? *Neurologie & Rehabilitation* 9 (1): 42–45.

Embodying autonomy in a Home Telecare Service[1]

Daniel López and Miquel Domènech

Introduction

European governments have intensively fostered telecare and telemedicine as an economically sustainable and efficient way to treat the chronic health problems and disorders associated with an increasing ageing population.[2] Telecare, actually, has now turned into a technical solution broad enough to manage many different kinds of problems, from health problems to social problems, and is adaptable enough to take into account individual and very contextual necessities (see Koch, 2006), enabling elderly people to maintain their independent lifestyle as long as possible (see Milligan et al., 2006).

Despite a wide variety of contexts of application and technological features,[3] the average telecare service organizes personal and institutional, as well as formal and informal resources, on a remote basis. These resources range from social services and ambulances to relatives or neigbours who attend the needs of several groups of dependent people living at home. All that is necessary is an alarm device (which can be more or less sophisticated) installed in the user's home and connected to a call centre. There, an operator manages the situation and selects and mobilizes the most suitable resource while speaking to the user and listening to what is going on. For this reason, telecare and in general e-health, has been considered not just as a mere technological device or one care service among many, but as a structurally new way of care delivery that places a high value on autonomy (Percival and Hanson, 2006).

In fact, if telecare is framed in a new logic of deinstitutionalized care-giving (see Bashshur et al., 2000), it is because the autonomy it offers is presented as a result of managing the users' problems as a virtual management of information rather than a hands-on care activity that demands physical intervention at home (Audit Commission, 2004). Given that telecare is introduced as a means to take care of elderly people from a distance, it gives users the feeling that they can maintain control over their lives because they do not have to move to a residence or to another's house to receive the attention and care they need. While management of information has prevalence over hands-on treatment, the possibility of disembodied care arises in which the users feel that their control over their needs could increase, while at the same time any vestige of disciplining their lifestyle disappears. Nevertheless, this is not an ideal scenario for users and caregivers, nor is telecare, in practice, a disembodied care. On the one hand, users and caregivers insist that even though telecare is transforming the way care is delivered, this would not be possible by removing hands-on care – telecare is not a substitute (Percival and Hanson, 2006; Mort *et al.*, 2008). And on the other hand, as Armstrong (1995) and Brown and Webster (2004) have suggested, although the increasing relevance of information in e-health and telecare might imply the possibility of a deinstitutionalization of care delivery and an informatization of the body (see Nettleton, 2004), this does not necessarily result in a disembodied care.[4] Indeed, as we are going to show, specific forms of being an autonomous user are embodied in the functioning of these informational technologies.

Our aim is, specifically, to discuss how autonomy is embodied through the use of a telecare device. What kind of bodies are autonomous bodies? How are they constructed? By means of what practices and materials have they been built up? And by trying to answer these questions, we would also like to critically discuss the idea of autonomy that is implicit to telecare advertisements and policies that foster telecare as a new care solution: autonomy is achieved when disciplining interventions over the body and its habits are not necessary to live safely. In fact, as we suggest in what follows, the use and appropriation of a telecare system implies not only embodiment processes and struggles within it, but also the enactment of different bodies and the emergence of competing definitions and practices of being autonomous when using telecare.

We draw on phenomenology, especially on *The Phenomenology of Perception* by Merleau-Ponty (1962), where body is defined not as an external object or a mental construct, but as a mediator that situates us as a being-in-the-world. Additionally, we draw on other phenomenological contributions concerning how pain (Leder, 1990) and disability (Seymour, 1998) are embodied. Contributions from Actor-Network Theory (ANT) are also taken into account as they enable us to think about the body as a heterogeneous compound where technological and human elements are equally important and as an entity that extends further the individual self. As Moser has said, 'the most recent generation of ANT has moved from "outer nature" to "inner nature", to subjectivity and embodiment, and has demonstrated that inner nature is no less inner than outer nature is outer' (Moser, 2006: 376). Thus our aim is to explore from a relational or material semiotic perspective how autonomy is embodied by telecare users.

To illustrate our point we use empirical material extracted from our fieldwork in a 12-month ethnographic research study in a Catalan Telecare Service. During the study period we were able to carry out participant observation in the alarm centre and to interview technicians, operators, volunteers, users and relatives.

Autonomy in the Catalan Telecare Service

> Our aim is to improve the quality of life of elderly people, making it easy for them to exert their right to live at home, enjoy their daily environment with independence, autonomy, security, tranquility and without feeling alone, in the best possible conditions and for as long as possible.
>
> (Excerpt from the Catalan telecare service pamphlet)

As this pamphlet states, telecare is mainly addressed to elderly people who want to continue living in their own home and in an autonomous way. The increasing risks this lifestyle entails (mainly risk of falling)[5] is compensated by the possibility of continuing to live at home in their way and delaying any decision about moving to a relative's home or a residence. In this sense, telecare arises as a useful aid to promote 'active ageing' (see Malanowski *et al.*, 2008) in a context in which autonomy is seen as a prominent value of ageing (Abellán *et al.*, 2008).

We now look at how users and their relatives talk about autonomy.

> 'Well, let's see . . . my mother is an 87 year old lady, but she looks pretty well and she wants to be independent. So, I suffered a lot because of this, because, of course, very independent means . . . Yes, ok, It sounds very well, but mobility is increasingly . . . is more complicated. In such a way that recently she has fallen twice. And, of course, she shuffles around, then she trips and I was suffering a lot. Well, independent . . . I live outside of Barcelona and then, of course, if she comes to my house . . . she gets bored! At home, she has her neighbours, her friends, her stuff . . . And yes, that's fine, but I was always worried. She tells me: 'Oh! If something happens to me, I have my neigbours and the telephone!' And I say: 'Yes, fine, you have the neigbours and the telephone. And what if you fall in the kitchen? Tell me, how are you going to call anybody then?' And she understood, she understood and she keeps it on her. And furthermore she is very happy.'
>
> (Excerpt from an interview with Inma, a relative of a telecare user)

As this fragment shows, users feel autonomous not because the service allows them to do activities that otherwise would not be possible, but because it enables them to keep under control everyday relationships of dependency (for a discussion about this see, Reindal, 1999). Actually, besides living alone or with someone, living at home entails keeping such dependency relationships. This is why, as the next fragment shows, the decision to contract the telecare service usually arises when there is a possibility of these relationships changing because the user needs more aid and support due to a worsening disease or a fall.

> 'Mrs. Asunción: Let's see, mmmm . . . leaving home . . . I'm talking about my mother . . . because you tell her: 'Mum, what are you doing there on your own? Come to my house, you know you have a room for you'. And she answers: 'Yes, yes, but the railing of your stairs, I mean, is too wide and I can't hold it.'
> Mrs. Encarni: She looks for excuses . . .
> Mrs. Asunción: That's right! I mean, well, 'what do you want us to do, Mum?' and she says: 'Come and live here with me!'

Mrs. Encarni: Ah, yes, that's great!
(they laugh)
Mrs. Asunción: 'No! I can't come, I've got . . . I've got my house, I've got a job, I've got my life set up!' And she says: 'Ah! Of course! And my house it's not good enough, I should take down everything and throw everything away, shouldn't I?' Then I answer: 'Well, what do you wanna do then?' And she says: 'You just leave me here, just leave me here'. And of course, she would have to undo a whole life.'
(Excerpt from a discussion group with relatives of telecare users)

As we can see from the above exchange, the implicit understanding of autonomy has nothing to do with not being dependent on others. Indeed, neither fragment speaks of autonomous users in terms of individuals free to make any decision about their lives. Rather, autonomy is mainly associated with preserving certain dependencies. In this sense, autonomy appears as the result of a group of connected interdependencies that enable/disable certain possibilities of action (see Corker and Shakespeare, 2002; Verkerk, 2006; Sybylla, 2001; Hughes *et al.*, 2005).

In this context, telecare appears as a service that favors autonomy because it preserves the configuration of interdependencies that make a person feel at home. It does not discipline users' bodies.[6] It looks after them without touching them; it just controls their environment.[7] That is, it offers an *ecological care*: it monitors the interdependencies sustaining the user's way of life just in case it is necessary to take control of and mobilize them quickly when the users can not do it by themselves. Thus, when a user contracts the service, the technicians enter information into the database about the distribution of the house, the medicines being taken, the available technical aids, and the neigbours and relatives visiting. All this information is augmented and updated every time the service has contact with the user, relatives, the GP or volunteers.

The bodies of the autonomous telecare users

However, even though it might seem that the autonomy of the telecare users only depends on the capacity of the service to remotely manage the users' care environment (relatives, neigbours, GP, ambulances, etc.), we are going to show that it also depends on how the service turns the user into an active agent (see Willems, 2000). That is, the user must make certain decisions and develop certain actions according to the logic of the service. And the simplest, but also the most important action, is to wear a personal alarm, consisting of a pendant with a red button, and to press it whenever anything goes wrong.

There are campaigns to encourage them to wear it because doing so is very important. 'Take care, because if you fall down at home, then . . . What use is the pendant, if you can't reach the pendant? It's silly!'
(Excerpt from an interview with Antoni, a telecare volunteer)

Indeed, the action of wearing and using the pendant raises the question of what constitutes the body of the user and what it is capable of, and consequently what living autonomously means. Thus, by presenting excerpts of interviews with users and relatives about this topic, we show that the action of using/not using the pendant enacts two different conceptions of the body that change the practice and meaning of autonomy: in one, the body is enacted as being risky and in the other as being vigorous.

To press or not to press

Interviewer: Are you used to using the pendant?
Mrs. Paquita: Well, no, no, no, no. I'm not used to it at all. Well, I mean, sometimes, sometimes, I wear it because they told me to try it, to see how it worked. But I never think about it. Since I don't need it, I don't think about it. And, sometimes I remember, and, I'm sorry, but I think: 'Look, now I have to bother them? Come on! I'll do it tomorrow, I'm fine now!' Well, one night, I thought I needed them, but I stopped myself. I thought: 'it will pass, it will pass, it will pass'. I didn't know what was happening to me, something very strange, anyway . . . I was in bed; I started to breathe heavily, like I was going to suffocate. I wanted to get up but I couldn't. I couldn't get out of bed, I couldn't move. And so that, when . . . I have it on the night stand, so that right away, just by doing this I'm able to touch it. But I thought, it will go away, it will go away and as in fact it did go away, I didn't call. If I call my daughter, if I call her, it's easier for me, because, my daughter's telephone number I know by heart, but what if I'm too nervous and I don't remember it. 'Don't mess up'. And since I think it was 4 in the morning, if I called them (she says weakly) . . . but anyway, what happens if they come and nothing is wrong?, if it has already gone away? Don't worry, don't worry, no, don't call. No, and I didn't call (laughs) and then Joan (the volunteer who twice a month visits her) gave out to me.
Joan: Yes, that happens rather often, there are people who call a lot, and people who don't call so as not to bother, and that is not right . . .
Mrs. Paquita: It's that I'm really sorry to be a bother (laughs).
(Excerpt from an interview with Mrs Paquita, user of the telcare service, and Joan, a volunteer. Mrs. Paquita, aged 82, lives alone in a working-class neigbourhood of Barcelona. She has the help of a Filipino caregiver who stays with her three hours a day)

Mrs. Paquita's experience, rather than being exceptional, is a common case: despite not feeling well, and even feeling she might have something serious, she did not call for help. As opposed to what usually happens in a hospital or certain enclosed or assisted living settings, the telecare service requires that users do something apparently simple for themselves: that they put on the pendant and press the red button if they need help. But this simple gesture turns out to be extremely complicated, since the action of putting on the pendant and pressing the button is not a logical consequence of need on the part of the user.

The anecdote Mrs. Paquita tells us truly reveals that requirements and dangerous situations, as well as the responses entailed, do not have any single meaning. It is as hard to know clearly what is going on within oneself and what to do regarding it. If it had been clearly just a momentary discomfort, Mrs. Paquita would not have had to ask for help. But how long would this discomfort have had to last in order for her to ask for help? It is not clear. And furthermore, how would it have been possible for her to know what kind of problem it was? Is it just a psychosomatic problem produced by stress, a muscular problem produced by a disturbed sleep or a severe health problem such as the sign of an oncoming stroke? It was important to assess the severity of the problem and find out its nature because, only on this basis, not asking for help, phoning and waking up her daughter or pressing the button, could each have been the most suitable response.

Therefore, it is not enough to have a telecare device installed in the house, or to have a 'clear head'. Knowing in which situations the red button should be pressed is the result of a complicated process of incorporation of practices, technologies and discourses. This process models and constructs individuals that evaluate and scrutinize themselves in search of some dysfunction or dis-comfort, that analyze what is happening to them, that are able to determine if they really have a problem and, if they do, to discern if what is happening to them requires the aid of others.

Finally to use the pendant, a complex process is needed that requires household medical technologies, such as a thermometer, blood pressure monitors, drugs or diagnostic tests; assistive technologies such as the telecare pendant or hearing aids; and means of communication like the telephone. But it also requires certain practices. It is necessary that family members remind the users to wear the pendant and not to exert themselves or do risky activities. Check-ups with the doctor also play an important role, as a way to get guidelines to interpret what is happening to them and determine what they can do and what is not advisable. Visits from volunteers from the telecare service are also important. The volunteers remind users that they have to wear the pendant and also advise them when to press the button, and how dangerous it is to do some activities without help. Finally, the calls by the operators, to the users who have not used the service for a while, are important in that they act as reminders of their availability. The operators show them how convenient it is to make use of the device. This can be just to check that the device works or to take the opportunity to ask them how they are getting on. They can ask the users if they have been to a doctor recently, or if there is any change in their health.

All of these practices and technologies appear to go in the same direction: to build up the body as a problematic field. By a continuous self-assessment – that could enable not only the users, but also the relatives, operators and doctors to get to know quickly any kind of threatening disorder – the body becomes some-thing that requires definition rather than being perfectly clear and visible.[8] And this is precisely the problem for Mrs. Paquita. Even though she must know her body enough to know if the situation demands the pressing of the button, at the time she did not know how to be sure about it. She was hesitating all night long: it might have been a temporary discomfort or a serious disease, a breath-ing problem or even a stroke. That is why the operators and managers of the service insist that the only thing the users must do is to take care of themselves and press the button every time they feel something out of the ordinary. 'Whenever you feel something just press' is what the volunteers and operators constantly remind the users. Because users' bodies are regarded as an unstable object, it is necessary for the caregivers, operators and volunteers to actively and constantly keep watch over them through regular check-ups, complementary devices like fall or movement detectors, household medical technologies and frequent conversations about how they feel. Actually, to have a chat with the user is very important because, even though these conversations might seem a waste of time, they are, in fact, fundamental in providing an opportunity to grasp any significant change in the user's health.

Nevertheless, the body is not merely some sort of fuzzy object that is hard to grasp and define but it is a 'treacherous' entity. It must keep itself under constant surveillance, since one cannot be certain that the body will respond as expected when needed to be called upon to do something. In short, as we see in the following excerpts of interviews with users, for family members and operators, the main characteristic of this body is its fragility (see Kvigne and Kirkevold, 2003).

> So she manages well enough with her limitations, but after all she is 90. It's also a process where we are starting to wear her down, you know? Living alone, you have to keep her from her doing a lot of things, I mean, right? But you start telling her, Mama! You can't do that! Don't do it, okay?
>
> (Excerpt from an interview with Marta, a relative of a telecare user)

By taking into account the risks involved in doing particular things, the uncertainty caused by declining health requires increased control over oneself. It requires behaving as if something dangerous could happen at any time; always wearing the service pendant throughout the house (since you never know when an accident will happen); pressing the green button every 24 hours to advise that all is well; calling once in a while to check that all the information is correct and the devices are working well; installing supplementary devices such as fall detectors, in case a sudden fall occurs, or medicine dispensers in case at some moment the users do not remember the pills that they have to take. All of these are self-supervision practices that enact an uncertain and threatening body.

To wear or not to wear

> Interviewer 1: And, why don't you wear the pendant?
> Mrs. Carmen: I don't know, I don't know. I don't know what's wrong, but I don't like it. Now, I've hung it . . . I have a crucifix on the wall behind my bed and I have the pendant there. I do like this (stretch her arm) and I touch it. (laughs)
> Interviewer 2: That is to say, you don't like it because you don't like to wear it?
> I1: Because of aesthetics? Or because . . .
> I2: Because of aesthetics . . .
> I1: Does it bother you?

Mrs. Carmen: Not because of aesthetics! No. Because I know that it is something that has to do with . . . I don't know . . . with illness. Or whatever. Doesn't it? I don't like to wear it. (She laughs)

I2: Right.

I1: That is to say, while you feel fine you prefer to go to the central-telephone and press

Mrs. Carmen: Yes, yes, that's right. Yes.

I1: Or would you prefer making the pendant more . . . aesthetic? More . . . like a piece of jewelry?

Mrs. Carmen: It would be the same. The impression would be the same.

I1: Right

I2: Right

Mrs. Carmen: No, no. There are times that I really wear it, because . . . Do you know when I wear it? When?

I2: When?

Mrs. Carmen: I'm climbing the stepladder

I2: Right

Mrs. Carmen: That's when I wear it.

I1: When you see that there is danger?

Mrs. Carmen: Yes

I2: That is, when you see that there is a possibility of falling down or . . .

Mrs. Carmen: If I might fall down, I wear it.

I2: But when you feel safe, then . . .

Mrs. Carmen: Walking I'm safe. I can fall down, but I don't (she laughs).

> (Excerpt from an interview with Mrs. Carmen, a user of a telecare service.
> Mrs. Carmen, aged 75, lives alone in the centre of Barcelona. She has no contact
> with her family and her only help is the visit of a caregiver twice a week)

However, if autonomy implies wearing the pendant and pressing the button to call for help, why does the user resist wearing the pendant so much? We could answer this question by saying that the user actually resists this embodiment of autonomy, and that, therefore, what they are doing by refusing to wear the pendant is resisting a particular way of understanding how care has been transformed from what was previously the responsibility of family members into a consumer product that can be bought and sold depending on certain individual necessities. We could also interpret the denial of wearing the pendant as an unsuccessful result of the incorporation process of the technology in the daily life of the person. This could be because the device is poorly designed and the person lacks the minimum abilities in order to use it (for example, forgetting that they have it), or simply because the families and close friends do not reinforce the importance of using it to the users (this is actually a matter of concern in usability approaches). Both explanations could be correct but they do not question the reactivity of the action: in the case of not wearing the pendant, it is a reaction of resistance to a social change; the other is a reaction due to a disruption in a process. What we propose is to approach this action as the expression of a conflict among different ways of practising autonomy that imply different ways of embodying it.

Despite the service and the family members insisting that they should wear the pendant at all times – even when they shower – many users decide to put it on and use it only on certain occasions. But why does Mrs. Carmen consider that putting it on implies being ill? Why did Mrs. Paquita prefer to endure discomfort, resist, and put the health of her body to the test before mobilizing her family members or the telecare service? Far from being faced with a reactive practice, which is defined by what it denies, we contend that another kind of body is enacted which necessarily enters into conflict with the body-at-risk we depicted above. Mrs. Carmen does not simply say that she will not put the pendant on, she explains when and how she will put it on (when climbing the stepladder) and this is also the case with most of the users. That is to say, users cannot live all the time with a body-at-risk, constantly watching over themselves. So, as Mrs. Carmen also tells us, she wants to do things without the pendant because her body 'can'. She is able to do her daily chores without worrying about her body.

> She always wants to overcome her limitations. And she says that if some day something is going to happen to her, it's going to happen anyway . . . to get her to understand that she must take care of herself and that she must learn to ask for help is hard . . . my mother does not know how to ask for help.
>
> (Excerpt of an interview with Rosa, a relative of a telecare user)

Actually, most of the users have never pressed the button because they trust their own capabilities to overcome accidents and obstacles. They believe in their bodies' strength. They do not want to focus on the body, on its limitations, and risks. As Mrs. Carmen says, these things make her feel ill, like someone who is not able to carry out her own life.

Phenomenology of the telecare user autonomy

In Mrs. Paquita's and Mrs. Carmen's cases, we have seen that there are two bodies enacted by the use/misuse/nonuse of the pendant. On the one hand, a threatening body-at-risk is enacted and made present through the monitoring activities carried out by the service as well as by the user. On the other hand, a vigorous body is also enacted, one which operates like a node that supports a group of relationships and practices that make up a way of life. But this body should remain in the background.

Phenomenology of the body has shed light on this tension between bodies-at-risk and vigorous bodies. According to Merleau-Ponty (1962), the body is neither an object-in-the-world nor a mental construction. 'The body is a vehicle of being-in-the-world, and having a body is for a living creature to be inter-involved with a definite environment, to identify oneself with certain projects and be continually committed to them' (Merleau-Ponty, 1962: 82). Thus, the body is eminently a mediator, the operator through which a certain way of living becomes possible. The focal point of the inter-dependencies that comprise the way of life of the users. That is why personal hygiene, leaving the house and doing the daily shopping, preparing meals, going outside to talk with neigbours, having visitors in one's own home and taking care of grandchildren are every-day activities in which the body is constructed as an element that sustains them.

However, stating that the body is the vehicle of being in-the-world does not mean that the body is the isolated and individual foundation of any form of action and subjectivity. Actually, the key point of the contributions of Merleau-Ponty (1962) is that they define the body from a relational perspective. It is a medium among things, it connects the elements of the world while being made up of and transformed through those connections. This is why we talk about embodiment. And in this respect the ANT contributions are very important, they enable us to overcome an essentialist or social constructionist conception of the autonomous body (Moser, 2005; Winance, 2006; Schillmeier, 2007). Following the ANT approach, both bodies, the body-at-risk and the vigorous body, are heterogeneous compounds. Or to put it in another way, despite appearing as single units, they are, in fact, *hybrid collectives* (Callon and Law, 1995). They are the result of an arrangement of technologies (eg walking aids, telecare devices, household medical technologies, drugs), spaces (eg handrails distributed around the house), physical disorders (eg osteoporosis or slight deafness), daily habits and practices (eg housecleaning, going for walks or visiting the neighbour) and also other bodies (eg caregivers, neigbours, relatives, medical staff, and volunteers as well as ambulance personnel and policemen). And this is precisely the point. There exists, firstly, an arrangement of elements in which the body is made present as threatening and at-risk, and, secondly, one in which the body stays in the background and supports a way of life. In the first arrangement, the pendant is constantly on the user's body and all the resources are articulated and mobilized through the telecare service; in the second one, the pendant is usually in the drawer or hanging on a wall, in such a way that it is not present all the time, and the resources are mobilized through various actions by the user: visiting the neigbour, calling the relatives or the doctor by phone or finding the pendant to press the button.

Therefore, through the use/misuse/nonuse of the pendant, a conflict between two ways of being autonomous is made manifest.

On the one hand, being autonomous implies challenging the body. The body cannot be constantly problematic; its ontology cannot be so fluctuating. It has to be durable, consistent and strong. And its strength and vigour necessarily depend on the ability to remain in the background of daily actions. For this reason, even though it is stressed that users should not do certain tasks, that they should put on the pendant and notify someone if anything out of the ordinary occurs, practising this type of autonomy requires risking their health and not following this advice. Thus, in order to be autonomous the body must operate as a support for daily actions and not as the object of these actions. It should be enacted as the node through which determined relations between practices, spaces and objects are assured. Hence, it necessarily undergoes concealment, or as Leder (1990) and Akrich and Pasveer (2004) would say, it entails a disappearance of the body. So the users that do not press the button despite feeling ill, far from asking themselves what is happening, instead resist questioning their bodies and emphasizing their fragility, thus safeguarding their world and keeping their lifestyle stable.

On the other hand, there is an autonomy that consists in managing a body-at-risk. To keep living as they wish, the users need to deal with elements that go from the daily routine of wearing the pendant, to giving daily or weekly information about any kind of incident to the operators of the service as well as family members and doctors, to technological devices such us household medical technologies, telecare devices, fall detectors or any other telemedicine technology, through which it is possible to monitor the fragility of the human body and act quickly to avoid a problem. As Brown and Webster (2004) have emphasized, this is something very common in new health technology because it does not work with clear distinctions between health and illness but with probability factors of risk that have to be continuously controlled by their variability and by being related to multiple aspects of life. The individualization of risks does not define a healthy or ill body, or an old or young one. The body is not defined so much by the presence of certain characteristics as by the future scenarios that they imply. In our case, the bodies of the users of the service are defined as being at constant risk. That is to say, by the concrete fragility and vulnerability that singles it out. In fact, the service establishes typologies of users depending on the risk of a particular event occurring. The basic user profile, for example, is a woman over 60 years old that has a high degree of probability of falling and not being able to get up due to a broken femur caused by bone decalcification. This is the reason for designing a medical alarm pendant and insisting that it always be worn. But there are other user profiles depending on the grouping of other features; for example, users with a risk of suffering some type of cardiovascular ailment or critical episode. There is an extended service for these cases where the user, in addition to wearing a pendant must press a button once a day to notify the service that they feel well. In the opposite case, an alarm is activated automatically and it would be treated as an emergency. The device, therefore, operates under the logic of the *somatic individual* (Novas and Rose, 2000): it is not so much about whether the individuals are healthy or not healthy or whether the State provides health services, but about acquiring improved well-being through care that is ever more specific and conscientious of the risks registered in the body.

In this sense, although telecare and telemedicine appear theoretically as technologies that, as Cartwright (2000) states, 'do not so much discipline bodies as offer new and relatively benign ways to organize, assess, compare, and rank bodies in the form of client pools, catchment regions, or populations' (2000: 87), the use and implementation of these technologies enacts a fragile and constantly-at-risk body that requires monitoring care and self-surveillance. For this reason, at the moment in which the users accept having a telecare device in their house, they are close to experiencing what Crawford (1980) has defined as 'the potential sick role'. A state of anxiety produced not only by fear of illness or deterioration, in the form of a heart attack, for example, but also by the responsibility of having to watch over their own personal situation and anticipate a possible problem. For this reason, not wearing a pendant, not accepting the service, is seen as a kind of irresponsibility for their own body and a sign of neglect that must be concealed. In this sense, we may say, following Foucault, that wearing and using the pendant is part of a contemporary technology of self-care (Foucault *et al.*, 2005), because it is a practice that by transforming the body (the elder body becomes a body-at-risk) it makes possible the ability to govern oneself (the elderly person now can live their life securely – see also Willems, 2000).

Conclusion: adjusting autonomies

The first conclusion is that the embodiment of autonomy in a body-at-risk or in a vigorous body does not speak to us of a false autonomy or a real autonomy. The first is neither covered-up dependency that is looking to convert the service into an obligatory first step for an autonomous life of the users, nor is the second really a genuine autonomy because it is based on preserving the capacity of doing things on their own. If this were the case, we would be defining autonomy as the essential feature of an individual body. The point is actually that in both cases autonomy emerges from the articulation of technologies like the pendant, practices like self-monitoring, different bodies like the elderly, relatives, caregivers or volunteers, and spaces like the user's home. For this reason, we think that two forms of autonomy are expressed in the use/non-use of the telecare device. Furthermore, the requirement of wearing and using the pendant can be thought of as a process in which the self-management of a body-at-risk opens up a new kind of 'safer' autonomy that necessarily asks for the cancellation of a life based on the practice of a vigorous body. Nevertheless, the fact that both bodies can be enacted concurrently shows us that the incorporation of the pendant is actually an adjustment process between both (Winance, 2006) and, therefore, is ambivalent: it opens and closes possibilities. This is why the ordinary use of the telecare service is located in between the autonomy that arises from managing a body-at-risk and one that arises from preserving a vigorous body.

In fact, without preserving the vigorous body, the self-management autonomy would not be possible. If it were, we would be confronting a user that is constantly calling the service and demanding the permanent attention of the doctors, and whose habits would break down and become the object of constant self-doubt. We would then be talking about an autonomy that would no longer be embodied in a self and would be totally located in control centres such as the alarm centre of the telecare service or a hospital. For this reason, the telecare service that at the same time insists that they have to put on the pendant and watch over themselves also encourages and promotes an active aging. In other words, the telecare service indeed needs the users to carry on a normal life without overly worrying about what they can and cannot do.[9] Thus the embodiment of autonomy in a vigorous body not only operates as a limit on autonomy based on constant self-scrutiny but also as its condition of possibility.

The second conclusion concerns the feeling of being safe, which is deeply linked with autonomy. The promotion of autonomy is not underpinned on a negative notion of security (ie as the absence of danger), but on a positive one. Being safe does not entail just being completely free from daily dangers, being protected from them. Rather, given that dangers are inescapable and part of life, to be safe has to do with knowing how to deal with them. In this regard, the adjustment of an autonomy based on a vigorous body to another based on a body-at-risk turns out to be a shift concerning the sense of security. The consequence of a self-managed autonomy that results from a vigilant self-scrutiny of an unfaithful and untrustworthy body laden with invisible risks, is the transformation of trust into a never-ending request for a security to which these devices can respond. Thus, whilst in an autonomy based in the vigour of the body, to be safe has to do with the confidence with which one faces the dangers of ordinary life, in an autonomy based in the management of a body-at-risk, trust becomes productive distrust and security is achieved through a systemic and constant supervision. For this reason, using the pendant concerns the issue of adjustment between two processes of embodiment of autonomy, which turns out to be an adjustment between two forms of being safe, two forms of living with and facing ordinary dangers.

Acknowledgements

Thanks to members of the Catalonian Red Cross Home Telecare Service for their support and collaboration. Thanks also to Francisco Tirado, Israel Rodríguez, Tomás Sánchez-Criado, Blanca Callén, Mariona Estrada, Michael Schillmeier, Joanna Latimer, Niza Cassián and Brian McCarthy.

Notes

1 This contribution has been written as part of the PhD Programme of Social Psychology at the Autonomous University of Barcelona (UAB) in the context of a project called 'Psychosocial impact of the technoscientific innovations', funded by the Ministerio de Ciencia y Tecnología.

2 The increase of the European population over 80 (the 'old old'), which consumes most of the health resources, has been forecast to increase about 300% for the period 1960–2020 (Banahan, 2004)

3 See Fisk (2003) for a complete description and history of the emergence of telecare and its different applications.

4 As Mort *et al.* (2008) suggest, the patient centred care ideology that underpins e-health and telecare services promotes and selects specific identities for the patients.

5 Accidents are the fifth leading cause of death in older adults, and most of these fatal injuries are related to falls (Rivara *et al.*, 1997).

6 This is why we could talk about telecare in terms of a control device rather than a disciplinary one (Deleuze, 1995). In this vein, because of its openness and fluidity, rather than an institution, telecare could be considered an ex-titution (Tirado, F.J. and Domènech, M., 2001; López, 2007).

7 It has always been debated as to whether it is a service that renders security rather than care (Fisk, 2003).

8 According to Foucault (1988), this problematization and fragilization of the body is something characteristic of the 'health practices': 'a constant and detailed problematization of the environment, a differential valuation of this environment with regard to the body, and a positing of the body as a fragile entity in relation to its surroundings.' (1988: 101).

9 One of the main reasons why the users are happy with the telecare service is that it enables them to take risks. Although this is seen as a matter of concern for the caregivers and also the users, to have the possibility of taking risks and fall is a way to maintain their self-image (Ballinger and Payne, 2002).

References

Abellán, A., Barrio, E., Castejón, P., Esparza, C., Fernández-Mayorales, G. and Pérez, L., (2008), *A propósito de las condiciones de vida de las personas mayores*, Madrid: Observatorio de Personas Mayores.

Akrich, M. and Pasveer, B., (2004), Embodiment and Disembodiment in Childbirth Narratives, *Body and Society*, 10(2–3): 63–84.

Armstrong, D., (1995), The rise of surveillance medicine. *Sociology of Health and Illness*, 17(3): 393–404.

Audit Commission, (2004), *Assistive Technology: Independence and Well-being*, [www.audit-commission.gov.uk/home].

Ballinger, C. and Payne, S., (2002), The Construction of the Risk of Falling Among and by Older People. *Ageing and Society*, 22: 305–324.

Banahan, E., (2004), The Social/Non-Technical Challenges in Developing to Support Elderly Care (The TeleCARE Experience). In Luis M. Camarinha-Matos (ed.), *Proceedings of the 1st International Workshop on Tele-Care and Collaborative Virtual Communities in Elderly Care, TELECARE 2004*, pp. 136–142. Porto: INSTICC Press.

Bashshur, R., Reardon, T.G. and Shannon, G.W., (2000), Telemedicine: A New Health Care Delivery System, *Annual Review of Public Health*, 21: 613–637.

Brown, N. and Webster, A., (2004), *New medical technologies and society: reordering life*, Cambridge: Polity.

Callon, M. and Law, J., (1995), Agency and the Hybrid Collectif, *The South Atlantic Quarterly*, 94(2): 481–507.

Cartwright, L., (2000), Reach Out and Heal Someone: Telemedicine and the Globalization of Health Care, *Health*, 4(3): 347–377.

Corker, M. and Shakespeare, T., (2002), *Disability/postmodernity: embodying disability theory*, London: Continuum.

Crawford, R., (1980), Healthism and the medicalization of everyday life, *International Journal of Health Services*, 10(3): 365–388.

Deleuze, G., (1995), Postscript on control societies. In *Negotiations 1972–1990*, New York: Columbia University Press.

Fisk, M.J., (2003), *Social alarms to telecare: older people's services in transition*, Bristol: Policy Press.

Foucault, M., (1988), *The Care of the Self*, London: Penguin.

Foucault, M., Gros, F., Ewald, F. and Fontana, A., (2005), *The Hermeneutics of the Subject: Lectures at the Collège de France 1981–1982*, New York: Palgrave-Macmillan.

Hughes, B., Mckie L., Hopkins, D. and Watson, N., (2005), Love's Labours Lost? Feminism, the Disabled People's Movement and an Ethic of Care, *Sociology*, 39(2): 259–275.

Koch, S., (2006), Home telehealth – current state and future trends, *International Journal of Medical Informatics*, 75: 565.

Kvigne, K. and Kirkevold, M., (2003), Living with Bodily Strangeness: Women's Experiences of their Changing and Unpredictable Body Following a Stroke, *Qualitative Health Research*, 13(9): 1291–1310.

Leder, D., (1990), *The absent body*, Chicago: University of Chicago Press.

López, D., (2007), La Teleasistencia Domiciliaria como extitución. Análisis de las nuevas formas espaciales del cuidado. in F.J. Tirado and M. Domènech (eds), *Lo Social y lo Virtual. Nuevas formas de control y transformación social*, pp. 60–78. Barcelona: EdiUOC.

Malanowski, N., Ozcivelek, R. and Cabrera, M., (2008), *Active Ageing and Independent Living Services: The Role of Information and Communication Technology*, Luxembourg: Office for Official Publications of the European Communities.

Merleau-Ponty, M., (1962), *Phenomenology of perception*, London: Routledge.

Milligan, C., Mort, M., Moser, I. and Roberts, C., (2006), *Healthcare at home? New Technologies and responsabilities across diverse European systems and cultures*, MEDUSE Project CIT6-CT-2006-028350, European Commission.

Mort, M., Finch, T. and May, C., (2008), Making and Unmaking Telepatients. Identity and Governance in New Health Technologies, *Science, Technology & Human Values*, 34(1): 9–33.

Moser, I., (2005), On becoming disabled and articulating alternatives. The multiple modes of ordering disability and their interferences, *Cultural Studies*, 19(6): 667–700.

Moser, I., (2006), Disability and the promises of technology: Technology, subjectivity and embodiment within an order of the normal, *Information, Communication & Society*, 9(3): 373–395.

Nettleton, S., (2004), The Emergence of E-Scaped Medicine? *Sociology*, 38(4): 661–679.

Novas, C. and Rose, N., (2000), Risk and the Birth of the Somatic Individual. *Economy and Society*, 29(4): 485–513.

Percival, J. and Hanson, J., (2006), Big brother or brave new world? Telecare and its implications for older people's independence and social inclusion, *Critical Social Policy*, 26(4): 888–909.

Reindal, S., (1999), Independence, Dependence, Interdependence: some reflections on the subject and personal autonomy, *Disability & Society*, 14(3): 353–367.

Rivara, F.P., Grossman, D.C. and Cummings, P., (1997), Injury prevention, *The New England Journal of Medecine*, 337(8): 543–547.

Seymour, W., (1998), *Remaking the body: Rehabilitation and change*, London: Routledge.

Schillmeier, M., (2007), Dis/abling spaces of calculation: blindness and money in everyday life, *Environment and Planning D: Society and Space*, 25(4): 594–609.

Sybylla, R., (2001), Hearing Whose Voice? The Ethics of Care and the Practices of Liberty: A Critique, *Economy and Society*, 30(1): 66–84.

Tirado, F.J. and Domènech, M., (2001), 'Extituciones: del poder y sus anatomías', *Politica y Sociedad*, 36: 191–204.

Verkerk, M., (2006), The care perspective and autonomy, *Medicine, Health Care and Philosophy*, 4: 289–294.

Willems, D., (2000), Managing one's body using self-management techniques: practicing autonomy, *Theoretical Medicine and Bioethics*, 21(1): 23–38.

Winance, M., (2006), Trying Out the Wheelchair: The Mutual Shaping of People and Devices through Adjustment, *Science, Technology and Human Values*, 31(1): 52–72.

Section 4
Absences and Presences

On psychology and embodiment: some methodological experiments

Steven D. Brown, Paula Reavey, John Cromby, David Harper and Katherine Johnson

Introduction

The set of discoloured white plastic canisters sit in rows in the grubby box. She selects two in turn and hands them together to her fellow student. Her friend sighs, shifts on the uncomfortable laboratory stool and holds the canister one in each hand, feeling the weight of the lead shot contained inside. He makes an overly elaborated gesture of comparing the two. A short pause ensues, which feels like much longer to both of them. 'This one is definitely heavier,' he declares, with a distinct tone of weariness in his voice. She jabs at the sheet of paper in front of her with a slightly leaking disposable pen, which, she notes with irritation, has leaked onto her fingers. He hands the canisters back to her, yawning loudly. They both stare at the number of canisters left in the box. So many more left to go.

Generations of psychology students have been bored insensible by this procedure. It involves the repeated presentation of a series of stimuli, typically canisters of varying weight, to the experimental subject. The two test stimuli are presented together and the subject is asked to estimate which is the heavier. Whilst the subject is unaware of their actual differences in weight, the experimenter follows a carefully prescribed schedule, and by amassing a lengthy series of reported differences is able to construct a graphical relation between the actual weight and the subject's judgement of perceived weight. The smallest unit of this relation is known as 'just noticeable difference' (JND) – that is, the minimal judgement of perceived difference that a given subject is able to make. The overall mathematical function in which this relation is explicable is termed 'Fechner's Law'. This law states that the recognition of psychological differences proceeds through an arithmetic series that is correlated to the geometrical series of physical differences. Fechner's law is typically taught in introductory psychology courses because it demonstrates the power of mathematical modelling to render the subjective as measurable, calculable and predictable.

Unsurprisingly, there is more to Fechner's law than is discussed during introductory psychology courses. The law only really seems to hold under limited

circumstances, and even then with some degree of statistical tweaking. Its significance for contemporary psychological enquiry is therefore somewhat limited.
The JND procedure is considered as an historical artefact and pedagogical tool
rather than a 'live' element in current epistemology. It is a way of demonstrating
to students that the business of doing psychology is a serious matter of careful
experimentation and precise statistical measurement. Hence the not-so-secret
reason for its inclusion on many introductory courses is to scare off students
whose view of the discipline is forged by 'popular' or 'self-help' psychology, and
who are correspondingly thought to be unwilling to submit to the rigours of a
statistically driven science. With every canister lift, pen scribble and yawn, scientificity is drilled into the bodies of student psychologists. From the perspective
of critical psychology, the JND procedure can be regarded as a symbol of
everything that is wrong with the experimental tradition in psychology: the
hostility to the arts and humanities, the narrow view of scientificity driven by
jealousy of the clear successes of the methods of natural science (or 'physics
envy'), the unshakeable tendency toward a 'fallacy of misplaced concreteness'
(as Whitehead would put it), and most of all, the oversight of the complexities
of lived, felt, embodied experience.

As a method, the JND procedure appears to have very little to offer for a
phenomenologically oriented account of experience. Indeed, the procedure systematically excludes practically all aspects of how participants engage with it,
save for the sole aspect of making and recording a judgement of the difference
in weight between the two canisters. The repetitive lifting, the work of monitoring and controlling, the experience of being in the peculiar space of the teaching
laboratory, the sheer monotony of taking part in the experiment/demonstration
– all this is formally unimportant. And yet it is precisely these aspects of the
experience which are critical to the pedagogical goals of the procedure. It is
absolutely necessary that students have a physical experience of the arduous
nature of the production of scientific psychological knowledge. It is not so much
that the body is excluded from the science, rather that the contemporary application of the procedure recruits the embodied participant in a very particular
way in order to ground its own intelligibility. The literal *meaning* of the JND
procedure may well be found in the mathematics of Fechner's law, but the *sense*
– what it is to participate, to be exposed to the task – is in the disciplining effect
of numbing, creeping, repetitive boredom.

This is unfortunate because Gustav Fechner, the originator of both the law
and the procedure, had an altogether richer set of concerns. His *Elements of
Psychophysics* is an attempt to grapple with Spinoza's philosophy of immanence
and becoming, which has proved so influential in recent years for social and
cultural studies of the body (eg Brown and Stenner, 2009; Hardt and Negri,
2004; Gatens, 1996; Massumi, 2002). Fechner writes at the historical moment
when philosophy of mind looked to the advances in physiology and neuro-
anatomy, and saw in their experimental practices a new and dramatic way of
staging metaphysical problems. The key problem for Fechner is finding a way
to demonstrate Spinoza's famous reconfiguration of the mind/body problem as

the parallelism of the attributes of thought and extension. Mind and body are no longer distinct transcendental domains, but rather two aspects of a single substance which is experienced as either the mental or the physical in the limited causal powers of the human. In order to translate metaphysics into physics, Fechner reasons that if mind and body do exist in parallel rather than hierarchical relations to one another, then the presentation of objects to the subject ought to be jointly registered. The body will physically respond to the perceptual impress of objects in a way that is directly linked to the recognition of the object by consciousness. Fechner then proposes that this linkage can be specified in mathematical terms.

Whether or not it is the case that such a mathematic relationship is plausible between mind and body (a question that has received a great deal of attention since Fechner's time), what is truly astonishing about the JND experiment is that, to use Isabelle Stengers' (2000) phrase, it opens up a 'new mode of accessing reality'. In the experiment mind and body are *pre-posed*, or stood before us, in a unique fashion. She or he who constructs the JND curve is able to make a claim to have made the body and mind of the subject speak in concert to the questions they have asked of it. The Fechner experiment is, in Stengers terms, an 'event'. It is a scene by which the power is conferred upon nature to confer back on the experimenter the right to speak in its name. In the mathematical relation that emerges, Fechner can claim to have allowed the body to have spoken in a new language, such that it can have told something of what it is and what it can do.

Is this still the case with the contemporary application of the JND experiment? Are bored psychology students also letting the body speak through the medium of canister lifts and pen marks? We do not think so; not because the JND experiment no longer has the sole character of an event. Its methodological innovation has been subsumed into an overarching instrumental concern with fixing the body as a clearly known object of psychological concern. What the body may or may not be saying matters less than the fact that the body can be made to speak. Stam (1998) describes the development of this instrumentality in psychology as following two distinct phases. In the first half of the last century the body was treated by psychologists as an abstract, mechanized entity, which allowed the generalization of notions of stimulus, response, reflex, habit and drive at the same time as it 'managed' subjectivity by reducing it to issues of detailed psychophysical measurement. In the second half of the 20th century this behaviourist psychology declined, to be replaced by a cybernetic systems metaphor where information, signal, noise, difference and feedback predominated. In this new cognitive psychology the body per se became further reduced as the container of mind, its capacities made subordinate to self-regulating control systems. Within this neo-Cartesian conception the body 'has evolved into the sexless hull of the robomind' (Stam, 1998: 4).

The critical response to this treatment of the body is nearly always to reject experimentation per se as an inherently flawed and reductionist procedure (Sampson, 1998; Stam, 1998). Irrespective of Fechner's particular ambitions of creating new forms of access to the body, the experimental tradition which he helped to inaugurate proves itself unequal to handling the lived particularities of embodiment. It makes of the body a mere recording surface for its own theoretical indulgences. In place of experimentation, qualitative methods – in particular discourse analysis – have become the method of choice for critical psychologists (Hepburn, 2006; Hollway, 1989). The attraction of qualitative methods in psychology is that they appear to accord dignity to participants by allowing for a wide range of responses, rather than the pre-established minimal options that characterize experiments (eg judge which canister is heavier; press the button when the stimulus occurs; recall this string of numbers). In particular, by focussing on language as the primary medium through which meaning and social interaction is performed, qualitative methods adopt a model of the person as an expressive being capable of reflecting upon and explicating their own conduct (Harré, 1991).

However, this 'turn to language' in psychology also has a difficulty in engaging with lived experience. The body and its sensed, felt engagement with the world around it is rarely represented as such in qualitative work in psychology. When it is, it must first be converted into either *talk around the body* or as the *embodied grounds of talk* (see Cromby, 2005; Ellingson, 2006; Johnson, 2007; Morgan, 2005). For example, some recent work in discursive psychology has focused on the transcription of crying during social interaction. Analysts have typically noted that a participant was [crying] during an interaction by inserting the comment into square brackets, and where relevant have inserted a [sob], a [sniff] or a [blows nose]. Hepburn (2006) argues perceptively that this transcription practice is inadequate in the sense that it omits most of the interactional organization of crying, the ways in which it is regulated, restrained and released in accord with social cues. In order to engage with these interactional dimensions, Hepburn proposes the decomposition of [crying] into one of seven kinds of *sobbing particles*, elements of transcript precisely timed and denotated to stand for each gasp, sob, snuffle and so on. This transcription procedure then facilitates their analysis as interactionally relevant, situated and occasioned moments readable for their communicative import. Hepburn's points are valid and the strategy yields interesting analytic insights, but the practice she advocates nevertheless remains a formalized, methodologically constrained way of translating embodied experience into language. Since it is precisely a transcriptional strategy, and to this extent purely a refinement of what we do with language in analytic contexts, it leaves the gulf between language and embodied experience intact whilst nevertheless giving the superficial appearance of bridging it (see Del Busso and Reavey, forthcoming; Stephenson and Papadopoulos, 2007).

The problem of finding 'new modes of access' to embodied experience persists across both experimental and qualitative methods in psychology. In this chapter we will describe our own collective experiences working together as a research group exploring the potential of various methodologies to surface embodied experience (see also Gillies *et al.*, 2004 and 2005; Brown *et al.*, forthcoming). We will focus here on the particular challenges and difficulties that these methodologies present, and on our own particular difficulties as analysts in engaging with the materials which result. We will also demonstrate that in taking embodiment seriously we are forced to reconsider the experimental tradition in psychology and its ongoing legacy for the discipline in a new way.

The methodological process of failing to get to grips with embodiment?

The project began in the autumn of 2005 with three female and three male group members. However, one of the female group members left shortly after due to other commitments. The remaining two women had previously been involved in a women-only group examining issues of embodiment. That group had begun to use Memory Work (Haug, 1987) to investigate the experience of sweating and pain (Gillies *et al.*, 2004) and it had also used visual methods to explore the experience of ageing (Gillies *et al.*, 2005). The three men came to the group with some knowledge of, but no direct experience of, the methods. Whilst we shared a background in psychology we were working in a variety of disciplines and institutions.

Given our theoretical preoccupations with the topic of embodiment we were keen to engage an appropriate research method. Memory Work seemed to address our research questions which were to explore embodied experience by delineating key aspects and examining commonalities and differences in our experiences. Willig (2001) notes that Memory Work has allowed:

> researchers to focus on the role of the body in the formation of a sense of self and identity because it works with descriptions of scenes or events that are rich in circumstantial detail. The method is designed to access how a situation was *experienced* rather than how it was explained or accounted for by its participants. Such a focus on 'being in' a situation (as opposed to 'thinking about' it) implicates both body and mind. It provides a way of studying what is sometimes referred to as *embodied subjectivity* (Willig, 2001: 133, emphasis in original).

For the initial task we decided to use memory work methods. Crawford *et al.* (1992) and Willig (2001) note a number of key stages which we followed. They stress the importance of choosing a 'trigger', which is 'a word or short phrase which is expected to generate memories that are relevant to the topic under investigation' (2001: 128). Since our group was newly formed and we were still developing a way of working together, we chose the relatively uncontroversial trigger 'dizziness' and agreed to write one 'positive' memory and one 'negative' memory. The group members wrote memories in the third person and brought them along to a meeting where we discussed each one in turn before engaging in a cross-sectional analysis looking for commonalities and differences. Over subsequent meetings we began to draw out themes from the analytic discussion.

One of the first things we noted was the variety of ways in which (what we thought to be) a relatively discrete experience – 'dizziness' – was interpreted. Some experiences seemed linked to embarrassment or nausea caused by intoxication. Others were either self-induced or accidental. It became rapidly unclear whether we were all focusing on the 'same' type of experience. However, we were able to settle on clear themes, which appeared to cut across the memories. In this sense our approach was fairly traditional and followed the basic analytic pathway of most forms of discourse analysis. Indeed to a certain extent we treated the memories as 'texts' to be analysed. We set about analysis collectively and tape-recorded the session, which was then transcribed so that the materials for analysis comprised both the original memories and the text of the subsequent discussion. One of the first themes we discussed at length that appeared to emerge across the memories was 'control'. Many of the memories seem to involved a sense of 'losing control' whilst dizzy. Take the following:

Dizzy memory (negative)

> He is lying on his bed. He is so drunk that he has not got undressed. He has not even got under the covers. He has vomited twice already tonight and he doesn't want to be sick again. He has put a bowl by the bed just in case. As he is lying there the waves of nausea build. I must keep control or I'll throw up he thinks. But the waves keep getting stronger. Is it better with my eyes open or closed he wonders. He tries each but it doesn't seem to matter. With his eyes open the room begins to spin. With his eyes closed he still feels as though he is spinning but there is no visual reference point to judge this against. He regrets mixing his drinks and not eating enough before the party. He feels embarrassed at having vomited out of the taxi window. He's glad he made it to the bathroom at his friends' house. He hates this feeling, the way it continues to build despite attempts to focus or be still. He feels helpless. I'll get through it, he thinks, I just need to see it through. The room continues to spin. Then he suddenly passes out.

This memory is replete with details of losing control – both of self and body – and of the gamut of feelings that follow, from physical nausea through to helplessness and intense social shame and regret. But loss of control can also be experienced as pleasurable, as in the following:

Dizzy memory (positive)

> She climbed into the cardboard box and sat down with her legs crossed in front of her, arms clasped around her knees. Her sister closed the flaps down, one by one and clamped them together by tucking them under each other. Inside the box it was dark and stuffy. She shuffled around a little and then called 'ready'. Thump, over the box went. She rested on her back, knees to her face. Thump, over again – onto her shoulders, neck twisted, knees over her head. Thump. Face down, squished in the corner. Thump, over again, and again, moving down the red, carpeted, landing towards the top of the stairs. 'Stop, Stop,' she gasped, laughing simultaneously. Thump. 'Please, stop,' she called, weakly, hitting the side of the box. She could hear the creaking of

cardboard as the lid was pulled open. Light shone in. Her sister stood overhead, laughing at the crumpled, distorted heap that was in the bottom of the box. 'My turn,' she said, pulling her out.

This memory depicts a safe environment where a momentary loss of control (the 'stop, stop' and laughter) can be explored. Safety was associated with notions of youth and confidence, the sense that whatever one does everything will be alright in the end. Positive memories also focused on containment (eg the box), of being held or accepted, the other waiting patiently and attentively for normality to return (eg 'my turn'). By contrast, the negative memories were marked with a complete lack of control. Danger or unpleasantness tended to be marked with implications of social and physical isolation, as with the memory of being physically sick whilst alone. The negative memories also had a common thread where the subject felt themselves become the object of the gaze of others, typically depicted as critical or judgemental. Control then acted as a hinge or axis around which positive and negative was distributed. But within this there was some differentiation. We thought there was also an aspect of repetition (the repeated game of rolling in the box, for instance), although across all the memories there was an open question of whether repetition was actively sought or driven by others. Finally, there was an aspect of the pushing of boundaries, the deliberate placing of oneself in a situation where something might occur in a particular way, in order to have an experience of a new or unusual kind.

This type of analysis seemed to be fairly coherent, and appeared to summarize many common threads running through the memories. However we found ourselves rapidly dissatisfied. In subsequent discussion we noted that the analysis had mobilized several commonsense notions, which were to some extent predictable in advance. 'Control' is a fairly general-purpose notion, which can to some extent be used as a descriptor for any form of social interaction. Although we felt that we had surfaced the notion inductively, the notion of control all too readily brings us back to a recognizable grammar of social-psychological descriptions of action that takes us away from the memories themselves. Or to put things another way, we rapidly found ourselves trying to generalise and impose a common framework on the memories, based on commonsense notions, rather than attempt to excavate the specificity and particularity of each memory. In this sense we subsumed the embodied sensations in each memory as instances of generalized recognizable social categories, such as control. We ended up moving away from the very thing we had attempted to study – embodiment – and towards a general framework of social-psychological descriptions.

The difficulty with control reprised in some way an earlier problem encountered by the group. Earlier explorations of memory work and visual methods had aimed to avoid reifying divisions between mind and body by focussing on the specificities of embodied experience contained in the memories and painting produced by group members (see Gillies *et al.*, 2004; Gillies *et al.*, 2005). But during the analysis of the materials, Cartesian assumptions and dualistic modes of explanation appeared to return. Doubtless, as with the example of the 'control' theme, the problem was partly with the status of such assumptions as cultural commonplaces. Cartesianism, like 'control', is part of the psychological grammar of Western sense-making practices around the body. It is scarcely surprising to see it emerging in our own analyses as a means of organizing a disparate set of materials.

In order to address this problem, we decided to create a common shared experience. Our reasoning was that although our particular experiences and memories of the event would vary from person to person, we would at least be analysing the 'same' experience, and therefore have less need to stretch a general theme across diverse events. We settled on a group visit to a luminarium entitled *Amozozo* – an art installation in Nottingham designed by *Architects of Air* (http://www.architects-of-air.com). This was a series of large inter-connected tent-like chambers. It was made out of a fabric which, when seen from the inside and illuminated only by daylight, was very brightly illuminated. We spent about an hour moving through the space together with other visitors. Once again, following the experience we later wrote memories of the event. However, at a subsequent meeting where we shared and analysed these memories, we were intrigued by how, even though we had been in the same place at the same time, our experiences were so remarkably opposed as to throw doubts on whether this had actually been the case. Sharing the experience did not then seem to clarify either the process of memory work or the difficulties in our analysis.

A number of issues visible in the memories themselves illuminated some of the tensions which contributed to the faltering of group cohesion. These included: i) expectations ii) performance against/with others iii) the writing of the memories, and iv) engagement with the task. We will briefly consider each in turn.

i) Expectations

Some group members felt anxiety as to the nature of the task and their position with respect to others. This clearly 'arrested' some of us:

> He feels a bit ridiculous . . . aware that he is copying their actions of a few minutes ago and wonders, briefly, if they are monitoring and comparing what he is doing. Has it been enough time yet?

It appears that such embarrassment surrounding the unclear expectations around the object of the exercise led to a degree of passivity in relation to the other group members; a sense that one should focus attempts in performing group cohesion by mirroring the actions of the others:

> He isn't sure how to explore it but he sees the others experimenting and follows their lead.

This self-conscious move never fully results in a satisfactory engagement with the activity, and very little of the sense of 'being there' is captured, though there are slight references to colour and flickering. Successful engagement is never fully achieved it seems, though the will to do so is clearly there throughout.

ii) Performance with/against others

Although we thought that we were clear about our research questions, our differing experiences and written accounts of them led us to wonder whether there had been a lack of clarity over the purpose of the activity. The next set of extracts suggests that this might only be successfully addressed when there is some alignment work between group members:

> Some conversation about party possibilities [ie possible uses of the luminarium] affirms my own sense of how the place is being experienced. Begin to play . . .

Engagement, through play, seems to follow when there is a sense of common perception (eg on what kinds of activities the space might be suitable for). However, it is not just this ability to affirm one another's comments on the space which helps bring about some sort of cohesion, it is also the sense of mutual physical and spatial orientation, of being together in place. On this occasion, the other visitors to the luminarium acted as a barrier to group cohesion:

> Finding some of the other people there annoying and noisy, wishing the group of us just had the place to ourselves . . .

> He notices the other people in it. He wishes they weren't there, that the group had the place to themselves so he didn't feel so self-conscious.

Here it appears as if 'passivity' (an inability to participate actively) is created by an absence, not of group identity but of group movement. The physical, sensuous nature of the task itself together with the felt relations instituted between group members through accomplishing the task, clearly impacted on the extent to which group members felt they were adequately contributing.

iii) Writing the memories

Difficulties and uncertainties around the process of writing the luminarium memories emerged in subsequent group discussion. For example, a number of us mentioned how difficult it was to remember exactly what occurred, given the gap between the activity and the writing. Of course, writing is itself an embodied activity and we varied in our stance towards it, with some of us taking time over the writing of our memories whilst others wrote up to the deadline of the group meeting. We also varied in what we included in the memories. Willig (2001) notes how memories should aim to be richly descriptive with attention to 'as much circumstantial detail as possible', for example 'sounds, tastes and smells' and with an openness to 'contradiction, conflict and ambiguity' (2001: 128). However, we found that his invitation could be taken up in different ways with some choosing to focus on describing the colours, shapes and texture of the luminarium, based on the shared (although undiscussed) assumption that this was the purpose of the writing task. Thus, this kind of 'peripheral' information on the context of the activity, though entirely relevant may not be what captures our embodied experiences most fully.

v) Engagement with the task

All of the group engaged with the task on some level. For example, one member's rich description of the luminarium's 'warm and sexy dome of red' and her soaking up of the aroma, and another's description of his widening eyes were clear indications that some shift in our perceptions had taken place. There were also descriptions of being 'overwhelmed' by the colours and sensations evoked by their surroundings, whilst one member vividly described how the colours conjured both 'good, and less good' impressions until he was able to adjust and enjoy the different light textures. A group member reported being able to 'melt into her surroundings' in such a way that different 'child-like' memories of enjoying space freely, and without expectation were evoked and embraced. Another described the sense of physical closeness to the others in the group:

> I felt more de-centred . . . [and] felt overwhelmed by the need to make a connection. Connection to the rest of the group. These are people I had known a long time, but hardly touched, just spoken to . . . I felt my body opening up, lying down freely without reservation. The colours in the spaces allowed for a certain anonymity, which provided permission for greater physical intimacy with those around me.

By way of summary, we can see that the process of engaging in the task itself was not incidental to its perceived success or failure. The way that group members physically share the space with and orient towards one another fed through into the memories and the subsequent process of memory work analysis.

Reflections: is embodied research impossible?

In this chapter we have described our own recent experiences as a research collective whose common aim was to explore the possibilities of embodiment research. As we have described, our experiences in this particular case are probably best characterized as 'mixed'. Why should this be so? As we discussed at length in the preceding section, many of the problems may arise from the difficulty of creating an effective shared context in which experience may be adequately reported. As we saw, members of the group differed considerably in the extent to which they felt that the expectation of success or failure in the task allowed them to participate fully. That is, to engage in the experience properly rather than anticipate selectively which features might be reportable at a later date.

Now in a curious way the surfacing of this problem takes us back to the very origins of modern psychology. As historians such as Kurt Danziger (1990) have described it, the division of labour in Wilhem Wundt's Leipzig laboratory – one of the founding sites of experimental psychology in the late 19th century – was done precisely to manage problems such as we have encountered. The Wundtian paradigm takes as its object the contents of consciousness which are to be reported by the experimental subject. In stark contrast to the experimental psychology which would follow, the subject is the most important part of the research since the subject is the 'authority' on their own consciousness. The experimenter then assumes the role of recorder, in effect acting as the amanuensis of the subject. The writing up of the results is seen as another distinct role altogether. But what is interesting about this set-up, Danziger observes, is that all three roles are seen as complementary and as requiring professional training to be accomplished. Only a trained researcher can act as a suitable experimental subject, for example. Moreover in Wundt's laboratory researchers would regularly shift between the three roles.

Wundt's work deliberately excluded the 'higher mental processes'. It sought essentially to clarify what Wundt saw as the basic mechanics of consciousness – perception, recall, recognition etc. Our research has very different aims, seeking to explore more complex forms of embodied experience. And yet we have perhaps ironically ended up reproducing much of the logic of the Wundtian paradigm. For example, the focus on content rather than process or function is strikingly similar. Like Wundt, we have wanted to say that beginning with the reportable contents of experience (broadly defined) is the place where psychology ought to start. What is also striking is that again, with Wundt, we have concluded that trained researchers – in other words, ourselves – ought to take up this task. We have also made distinct the roles of engaging in the experience from recording and re-organizing the experience and finally from assembling the 'data' into a written paper. That we should also have decided that we should all circulate between these roles as the research unfolds retrospectively is hardly surprising, given our reproduction of Wundtian logic.

Thus some of the practical problems we have been describing – such as the difficulty of maintaining group cohesion, the dilemma of separating experiencing from reporting, and the collective problem of knowing what (if anything) to publish and how to accomplish a final written text – might be said to emanate directly from the 'primal scene' of experimental psychology (ie the Wundtian Leipzig set-up). But does that also mean that the conceptual problems we have been grappling with are similarly derived from an experimental tradition?

We want to explore this by considering an example taken from another great early psychologist. William James tells the following invented story: a child reaches curiously towards the flame of a candle. She feels sudden burning in her fingers and snatches her hand back. What has just happened? The most obvious way to grasp this example is to break it into component parts. There is a candle, emitting warmth and light. The child's sensory system picks up these sensations, which attract her conscious attention. She moves her hand forward to explore, but instantly experiences a new sensation – pain – which triggers off an automatic motor response. We might then want to seal this example by adding something in about learning or reflection. Indeed this is what James does in his 'motor theory of consciousness', where he has conscious reflection entering into human action only secondarily, as the means of making sense of our acts post-hoc.

James' logic is strikingly different to that of Wundt. In the Leipzig set-up the body is more or less invisible, since it is merely the 'container' of consciousness. But for James the body is significant because it mediates between the environment and thought. The body drives thought into space, it is what realizes our conscious plans and intentions. In this way what is interesting about embodiment is not the body per se, but rather the precise ways in which this shifting surface of bodies and things (ie fingers, hands, flame and candle) is 'loaded up' into consciousness. The body is interesting in so far as it realises our goals and plans. It is this broad view of embodiment that we have been seeking to explore.

John Dewey (1896) makes use of the child-candle example in his classic essay 'The reflex arc concept in psychology'. Dewey's statements about psychology are in dialogue with William James, whose *Principles of Psychology* had made cautious experimentation, coupled with a 'functional' approach to human action central. Dewey is no armchair philosopher, but someone interested in descriptions of human action which explicate its organization (Dewey speaks of 'co-ordination'). In this sense Dewey is writing against Kant and the Kantian tradition of restricting knowledge merely to hypothesizing general conditions of experience against a backdrop of things-in-themselves (*noumena*) which elude any complete knowledge. Like James, Dewey wants to avoid the Kantian dead-end for psychology but, unlike Wundt, he is seeking to do so not by focusing on the contents of consciousness but by emphasizing instead the planful, goal-oriented quality of human action, such as that the world is knowable with reference to the projects we enact in relation to it.

Dewey's essay begins by taking aim at the 'reflex arc' concept. This is a 19th century term which makes sense of the relation between stimulus and response by postulating that environmental objects trigger sensations which give rise to motor responses. The child touches the candles, feels pain and snatches her hand back. Defined in this way, the body is a vehicle for movement in which stimuli are linked to an array of motor responses. The chaining together of these stimulus-response patterns into complex patterns of 'behaviour' would become the basis for operationalism (but crucially Dewey is writing before a general category of 'behaviour' was invented as a way of packaging up – and hence neglecting! – all of the problems which are attendant on understanding the chaining of environment with human action). As Dewey notes:

> It is not a question of making the account of the process more complicated, though it is always wise to beware of that false simplicity which is reached by leaving out of account a large part of the problem. It is a question of finding out what stimulus or sensation, what movement and response mean; a question of

seeing that they mean distinctions of flexible function only, not of fixed existence; that one and the same occurrence plays either or both parts, according to the shift of interest; and that because of this functional distinction and relationship, the supposed problem of the adjustment of one to the other, whether by superior force in the stimulus or an agency *ad hoc* in the center of the soul, is a purely self-created problem. (Dewey, 1896: 364–5)

The relationship between stimulus and response outlined in the reflex arc is not sufficient. It is not sufficient because it treats both as entities that are separable in both principle and practice, and then takes the problem to be how to connect them together. But for Dewey neither can be assumed to have an independent existence. What does it mean to say that some entity acts as a 'stimulus'? It can only mean that we are already starting to treat it with respect to the possible forms of stimulation that it might have on the body. In other words, we have started our analysis from the varieties of sensation that might obtain, not the stimulus itself. Thus the meaning of the stimulus is a matter of 'distinctions of flexible function'. A given stimulus is relevant in terms of the possible sensations it might engender, which are themselves only understandable in the context of what kinds of actions the body is already engaged in (eg the candle flame burns because it is 'unexpected' perhaps, but the flame which singes us as we press close to the fire does not burn in the same way because it is already loaded up into a pattern of planful action).

Dewey then goes on to argue that, in a sense, it is the response that defines the stimulus. Because we only encounter the 'stimulus' with reference to possible sensations, and these sensations are themselves only understandable with reference to the possible 'responses' we are engaged in, it makes sense to say that the flow of our current and anticipated actions (ie response) actually determines or lends value to our perceptual acts of engagement with the world (ie stimulus). So psychology has a 'self-made problem' based on the conceptual muddle of trying to separate and establish a causal link between a single complex of perception-action-engagement where every term is interdependent.

What is interesting here is that Dewey is developing a language that emphasizes interdependency. There are no clear-cut distinctions between subject and object, stimulus and response. We should instead be concerned with complexes of action. Contrary to the Kantian position, and all that would follow in cognitive psychology, Dewey is not interested in describing the conditions of possible experience – that is, what sorts of things have to be in place to have any kind of experience, irrespective of context – but rather the conditions for a concrete, given experience. Take the following:

In other words, sensation as stimulus does not mean any particular psychical *existence*. It means simply a function, and will have its value shift according to the special work requiring to be done. At one moment the various activities of reaching and withdrawing will be the sensation, because they are that phase of activity which sets the problem, or creates the demand or, the next act. At the next moment the previous act of seeing will furnish the sensation, being, in turn, that phase of activity which sets the pace upon which depends further action. Generalized, sensation as stimulus, is always that phase of activity requiring to be defined in order that a coördination may be completed. What the sensation will be in particular at a given time, therefore, will depend entirely upon the way in which an activity is being used. It has no fixed quality of its own. The search for the stimulus is the search for exact conditions of action; that is, for the state of things which decides how a beginning coördination should be completed (Dewey, 1896: 368).

The language that Dewey uses is intended to cut across the usual distinctions we would be tempted to make. In particular it emphasizes reversing our usual sense of sequentiality – what comes first (the stimulus) is projected backwards from the sets of activities we are engaged in. We might say that it is only after having been burned by the candle that the child reconstructs the sequence to have been 'reaching-withdrawing' from the perspective of the activity that has been interrupted. But, as we take it, Dewey's point is that this is precisely a reconstruction, it is not the only possible description. The stimulus becomes seen as stimulus only after the action complex has entered into a certain phase (Dewey calls it a shift between two quale – only after we have passed the threshold of one to the other can we look back and impose a sequence of causes). If we take this insight back to our own work, we will be forced to conclude that the separation of reporting/recording from experiencing (ie the Wundtian set-up) will always create difficulties because it is literally a shift between two different action-complexes, and hence the relationship between experience (crudely 'response') and what experience is about (even more crudely 'stimulus') will be completely altered. To coin a crude metaphor, a shift between action-complexes completely re-shuffles the deck of values and significance with respect to experience.

Now, we also hear in all this the echo of another interesting philosophical position. In a mechanistic universe we can impute effects from causes (hot candle, burning, snatched away hand). But for the worlds that psychology describes we can only impute causes after effects, and then only as provisional descriptions of possible conditions for some action. To go back to the candle again, it is only once we ask 'what changes have been brought about as a consequence of the child burning their fingers? What activities were interrupted?' that we can then go back and say that there is some causal chain that brought about this change, this transformation. We can never do so in advance because we have no idea of what would follow. Or to put this in another way, there is a difference here between providing descriptions of the conditions of possible experiences (anyone who touches a candle will follow roughly the same pattern of stimulus-responses) versus providing descriptions of the conditions of actual, concrete experiences. For example, this particular girl, thinking of the time when her mother lit the candles on her brother's birthday cake, found herself reaching towards the flame, feeling first the warmth, then her hand coming too close, a slight pain, snatched her hand away, and wanted to run to her mother, but felt embarrassed in case her brother would hear and tease her, so wrapped her fingers in the palm of the other hand and hoped that no-one would see. The conditions of this would then be a description of the family relationships, the emotions around the brother's birthday and how the family celebrates such events, along with a description of the concrete set-up in the home in which the event takes place. To describe such a chain could potentially lead us into wider questions of gender, childhood, domesticity and so on. But any descriptions of these conditions would be purely provisional and would have to be argued for and against.

Our methodological practice has then most definitely concentrated on the concrete rather than the abstract. But, in Dewey's terms, we have done something odd in our analysis. We have tried, in the dizziness work, to hold 'dizziness' still as something like either a class of stimuli (a set of sensations) or a set of responses (a set of actions). We did this – admittedly in an arbitrary sense – as the means of comparing the memories. But whatever dizziness is (it can jump places as stimuli or response, depending on where we choose to stop the process we are describing), depends entirely on the 'action-complexes' in which it is embedded and the thresholds between them. It is not entirely clear to us how one might go about describing such transitions. But it would have to be done from the perspective of an unfolding process or a 'becoming'. This might include 'becoming anxious', 'becoming intoxicated', 'becoming sisters'.

We might also conclude that one of our errors has been to treat the memories in terms of the conditions of possible experiences (ie look for common themes etc), rather than first describing the conditions of these actual, concrete experiences, and only then, on that basis, looking for how these wildly diverse sets of conditions and subsequent experiences might communicate (or not) with each other. Again, we are not clear what form this latter analysis might take other than to say that it all depends on working backwards and trying to elucidate what is or is not a part of each concrete experience, rather than invoking common terms before having done this (eg the word 'control' would not be seen as having any particular analytic purchase in advance, but might return as a set of concrete conditions about becoming liberated or becoming restricted).

Third, and finally, specifically with the luminarium task, it seems to us that we tried to hold the 'stimulus' still, on the very sound basis that if we all shared the same inputs to experience then we might be in with a chance of understanding how our bodies were recruited into those environmental conditions. But again, following Dewey, we can see that the stimulus and the response aren't the places to begin, because both are determined, or at least get put into place, according to the projects and 'action-complexes' in which they are embedded. To think of researching embodiment in this way then means beginning not with triggers, nor with specific analytic goals in mind, but instead with the action-complex itself. With sisters rolling boxes, moments of shame-filled illness, anxious researchers looking to one another for guidance and support. And with bored students comparing canisters.

In a curious way, the history of psychology affirms the relationship between experiment and experience. In French, the phrase 'faire un experience' means both to 'have an experience' and 'to conduct an experiment' (see Lapoujade, 2000). In their work, albeit in very different ways, Fechner, Wundt and James all explore this relationship. Experience, like an experiment, requires a set of specific concrete conditions, a setting up or 'pre-posing'. We have discovered for ourselves some of the complexities involved in such setting up. But experiments, like experiences, exceed their own conditions. There is always more that occurs in a psychology experiment than is marshalled together in the analysis (think again of the variety of feelings and sensations of the bored students or the researchers desperately seeking a common experience in the luminarium). It seems to us that the psychological is to be found precisely in the interplay between these two terms – between the setting up, the conditions, and the elaboration and reworking of these conditions. What we are seeking is not 'in' the body, any more than 'self' is in the mind or the brain. It is in the way that embodiment acts as a connective, a way of making and breaking relations within action-complexes. Fechner was right, but with this crucial corrective: the JND curve is less important than what happens when a participant takes the canisters in both hands.

References

Brown, Cromby, Harper, Johnson and Reavey, (forthcoming).

Brown, S.D. and Stenner, P., (2009), *Psychology without Foundations: Mediation, Constructionism and Critical Psychology*, London: Sage.

Crawford, J., Kippax, S., Onyx, J., Gault, U. and Benton, P., (1992), *Emotion and Gender: Constructing Meaning from Memory*, London: Sage.

Cromby, J., (2005), Theorising Embodied Subjectivity, *International Journal of Critical Psychology*, (15): 133–150.

Danziger, K., (1990), *Constructing the Subject: Historical Origins of Psychological Research*, Cambridge: Cambridge University Press.

Del Busso, L. and Reavey, P., (forthcoming), Moving beyond the surface: young women's embodied experiences in everyday life, *Feminism & Psychology*.

Dewey, J., (1896), The reflex arc concept in psychology, *Psychological Review*, 3: 357–370.

Ellingson, L.L., (2006), Embodied Knowledge: Writing Researchers' Bodies Into Qualitative Health Research, *Qualitative Health Research*, 16(2): 298–310.

Gatens, M., (1996), *Imaginary Bodies: Ethics, Power and Corporeality*, London: Routledge.

Gillies, V., Harden, A., Johnson, K., Reavey, P., Strange, V. and Willig, C., (2004), Women's collective constructions of embodied practices through memory work: An exploration of memories of sweating and pain, *British Journal of Social Psychology*, 43: 99–112.

Gillies, V., Harden, A., Johnson, K., Reavey, P., Strange, V. and Willig, C., (2005), Painting Pictures of Embodied Experience: The Use of Non-Linguistic Data in the Study of Embodiment, *Qualitative Research in Psychology*, Vol. 2(3): 199–212.

Hardt, M. and Negri, A., (2004), *Multitude: War and Democracy in the Age of Empire*, New York: Penguin.

Harré, R., (1991), The discursive production of selves, *Theory and Psychology*, 1: 51–63.

Haug, F. (ed.), (1987), *Female Sexualisation*, London: Verso.

Hepburn, A., (2006), Getting closer at a distance: theory and the contingencies of practice, *Theory and Psychology*, 16(3): 327–342.

Hollway, W., (1989), *Subjectivity and Method in Psychology.* London: Sage Publications.

James, W., (1957), *The Principles of Psychology*, New York: Dover.

Johnson, K., (2007), Changing Sex, Changing Self: Transitions in Embodied Subjectivity, *Men & Masculinities*, 10(1): 54–70.

Lapoujade, D., (2000), From transcendental empiricism to worker nomadism: William James. Pli, 9, 190–199.

Massumi, B., (2002), *Parables for the Virtual: Movement, Affect, Sensation*, Durham, NC.: Duke University Press.

Morgan, M., (2005), Remembering Embodied Domination: questions of critical/feminist psy-discourse on the body, *Theory and Psychology*, 15(3): 357–372.

Sampson, E.E., (1998), Life As An Embodied Art: The Second Stage – Beyond Constructionism, in B.M. Bayer and J. Shotter (eds), *Reconstructing the Psychological Subject: Bodies Practices and Technologies*: 21–32, London: Sage Publications.

Stam, H., (1998), The Body's Psychology and Psychology's Body, in H. Stam (ed.), *The Body and Psychology*: 1–12, London: Sage Publications.

Stengers, I., (2000), *The Invention of Modern Science* (translated by D.W. Smith), Minneapolis: University of Minneapolis Press.

Stephenson, N. and Papadopoulos, D., (2007). *Analysing Everyday Experience: Social Research and Political Change*, London: Palgrave Macmillan.

Willig, C., (2001), *Introducing Qualitative Research in Psychology*, Buckingham: Open University Press.

Bodily knowing as uncannily canny: clinical and ethical significance

Fiona K. O'Neill

How might the body *know*? There is something distinctly *uncanny* about the *canniness* of our bodily being that becomes especially apparent when our bodies are taken beyond what we are accustomed to; when they become ineffectual or interact with, and are supported by, techniques and technologies.

Between writing and editing this chapter, I too have had some salient experiences of the un/canniness of an unaccustomed embodiment. I know my breast has been removed, I can see that; but it was not until I wore a bra with a 'softie' (a basic foam prosthetic breast) that I began experiencing the un/canniness of what and how I 'know'. Wearing the 'softie' meant that for the first time in nearly three months the inside of my upper arm was being 'brushed' by my (now 'prosthetic) body', a sensation I had not consciously been aware of before surgery. This movement was giving me contradictory feedback that I had a breast where I knew I did not. My knowing and seeing that I've had a mastectomy remains in contrast to these bodily experiences which still hold to my original accustomed embodied beliefs and to the trauma my chest has experienced.

My experience, and those that are offered here, draw attention to the usually uncannily canny body becoming uncannily unusual, echoing Sacks's (1986) association between Wittgenstein's *On Certainty* 2004 [1969], the uncanny and bodily knowing. That is, finding oneself questioning that which should not be in question; namely the accustomed familiarity of one's embodied experience, which until then has in most respects been taken for granted, and to all intents and purposes has been below one's awareness.

Whatever one's accustomed embodiment may be, when this is disrupted and/or 'supported' by medical intervention, then expressing one's bodily knowledge of these experiences is not necessarily easy or *de rigueur*. Indeed expression may signify social deviance and provoke oppression, making this an issue for medical sociology, disability studies (Thomas, 2007) and bioethics alike.

So, the following considers the possible nature of *bodily knowing* as being a *canniness*, a know-how, an *ur*-trust, an ontological security in bodily being in the world. What is offered is the possibility of effectively acknowledging and engaging with bodily knowing in order successfully to appreciate all that 'the bodily' can tell us. To do this a transdisciplinary approach has been taken in order to provide a rigorous foundation for these aims. A case is made for acknowledging the validity and significance of *bodily knowing* as being clinically and ethically on a par with the 'evidence base' of medicine and ethics.

The possible nature of bodily knowing, embodied belief

In everyday language to say we *know* something may or may not imply the use of rational, reasoned facts of the matter. Philosophically, however, a distinction is made between rationally *knowing* something epistemically and having a *belief* in something non-epistemically, each having a different relationship to the experience of said 'something'. Importantly, for this discussion, the value placed upon *knowing* and *believing* depends upon one's point of view, one's philosophical leanings. Wittgenstein (1969) elicits this distinction in discussing issues of certitude. Common sense tells us that we have hands, but Wittgenstein argues that this does not constitute an evidence-based rational 'knowing'. For him, our bodily awareness is first and foremost a non-epistemic, non-propositional *belief* in our embodiment.

> Bit by bit there forms a system of what is *believed*, and in that system some things stand unshakeably fast and some are more or less liable to shift. What stands fast does so, not because it is intrinsically obvious or convincing; it is rather held fast by what lies around it. (Wittgenstein, 1969: 144, my emphasis)

For Wittgenstein, this *belief* in things that stand more or less unshakeably firm comes from the accumulated, confirmatory bodily experiences of our being in the world allied to the language with which our embodiment is expressed. And importantly, it is these beliefs which underpin our fundamental sense of certitude, echoing the embodiment work of Merleau-Ponty (1962, 1968), Leder (1999).

This embodied belief, 'knowing this is my body' is therefore something that for the vast majority of us can be relied upon, taken on trust. It is 'an unapprehensive, uncalculated, nonconscious trust' (Moyal-Sharrock, 2004: 194). Such *ur*-trust, unlike our struggles with epistemic trust, normally cannot be doubted, it 'is not a mirror-like reflection of the world; not the truth about the world, but our trust in it' (Moyal-Sharrock, 2004: 199). Epistemology may claim to know the *truth about the world* with veracity but, in the end, it is founded upon individual and communal *trust in the world*.

Hence, one can say that epistemic knowledge develops from experiences and observations that are reflected upon including evaluation, inference and learning, that producing reasoned facts that are 'known' to be trust*worthy*. Whereas, *ur*-trust, our bodily canniness, develops from experiences that are not usually reflected upon, where there is little or no evaluation, inference or learning. The

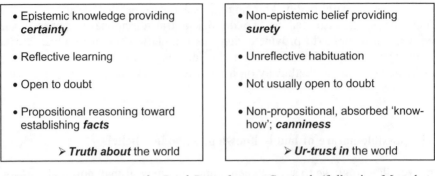

• Epistemic knowledge providing **certainty**	• Non-epistemic belief providing **surety**
• Reflective learning	• Unreflective habituation
• Open to doubt	• Not usually open to doubt
• Propositional reasoning toward establishing **facts**	• Non-propositional, absorbed 'know-how'; **canniness**
➤ **Truth about** the world	➤ **Ur-trust in** the world

Figure 1: *Appreciating the Dual Basis for our Certitude* (following Moyal-Sharrock, 2004).

continuity of confirmatory experiences from the world, others and ourselves, induced through conditioning and habituation (but not argument) leads to a 'belief in', which *takes things on trust* (Moyal-Sharrock, 2004: 193–4). Therefore the *worthiness* of such *ur*-trust is not an issue.

> [*Ur*-trust] is a trust that is not *experienced as trust*, but rather shows itself in the absence of mistrust – that is, in our *taking-hold* of something, *directly*, without any doubts – the way we take hold of a towel. Trust here is better described as the *utter* absences of distrust – . . . It is an *excluder concept*. . . . It is recessive – a background, default and unconscious certainty. (Moyal-Sharrock, 2004: 197)

Before my mastectomy I had no epistemic need to *know* that the brushing against my arm indicated that I had a breast; yet bodily I *believed* in and trusted such feedback to avoid injury and the like. Now the feedback from wearing the prosthesis may well protect it, yet it also provokes confounding un/canny experiences.

It is this juxtaposition of the trustworthiness of rational facts as truths 'about the world' and the embodied *ur*-trust, without doubt, which we have 'in the world' that demonstrates the different forms of certitude with which we all operate. We are *certain* of the facts which we *know* because if we have doubts they can be propositionally tested, as in the approach of evidence-based medicine; whereas the *surety* which comes from being in the world is 'beyond a shadow of a doubt', its veracity and trustworthiness is not the sort of thing which usually (as a rule) is questioned. 'This unquestionability of the body, its certainty, is for Wittgenstein, the start and basis of all knowledge and certainty' (Sacks, 1986: 42–3). Whatever we are bodily habituated to becomes foundational and will not usually be doubted. However, such embodied belief/bodily knowledge, its un/canniness and surety, can be at odds with evidence based practices.

Examples of un/canny bodily knowing

Before discussing in greater depth the significance of *ur*-trust a few examples may help demonstrate the potential scope for our un/canny bodily knowing; remembering that modern medicine is now seeking to utilize our 'fleshy' bodies and biotechnologies in ways which were untenable some sixty years ago (O'Neill, 2007a, 2007b).

Using hearing aids

Hearing in many respects is considered a secondary sense to that of vision for humans. However, it is the intermodality of hearing with vision (and our other senses) that affords us many of the skills we might consider to be purely one or the other. For example, to a degree we all lip-read so as to fill in the missing gaps in our auditory information. Likewise sound orientates our vision, from infancy. However, normally we are unaware of how our individual, let alone our intermodal, sensory inputs sustain us in the world (BBC Radio 4, 2005: online).

When Charlie moved from a single standard to two digital hearing aids he experienced the following:

> I do notice, when I switch them (digital hearing aids) on in the morning, an immediate sense of location of my 'self' within an environment of small sounds, which is 'not there' without their help. . . . I switch on say the right 'aid' and am immediately aware of tiny sounds on that side of me. I switch on the other aid and there is then a sense of all-round awareness that is lacking otherwise. . . . This level of awareness diminishes as time passes during the day – but does not completely disappear. When the battery fails (they do this quite suddenly) in one aid there is an immediate sense of 'loss' – comparable to the original 'gain'. (CMC research participant: O'Neill, 2007c).[1]

And similarly Jo, using two standard aids, notes:

> At a deep level, I am more aware of the fact there are things going on all around me that I am unaware of – [without and even with the aid] . . . But I know that I miss a lot of things . . . (CMC research participant: F.K. O'Neill, 2007c)

In fact becoming aware of these orientating sounds draws the individual's attention to the uncanny canniness of their embodiment (and potentially to the canny uncanniness of the technology). As Charlie notes when first using his new digital aids:

> [I]nitial surprise at the loudness of my own voice (. . .) the rustle of clothing, the rattle of the computer keyboard (and the car) and other high-frequency sounds. My brain (assumedly) has adjusted my sensitivity to these sounds over the last two weeks and, though I can hear them, they are no longer as prominent and surprising. . . . The moment of switching the aids on (one before the other) provides a sense of location (or 'situatedness') within a sound-scape of small sounds that is really quite startling even after some months of experience. (CMC research participant: F.K. O'Neill, 2007c)

Here, it is the overt mimetic success of the aids which draws his attention to the uncanniness of his being in the world. On several occasions Charlie makes reference to his brain adjusting to or compensating for the 'new' sensory input. He demonstrates an awareness of the normally taken-for-granted orientating effect of sounds and of the withdrawal of this 'hearing', and in this case the technologically supported effect.

Hearing therefore orientates one in the lifeworld's 'sound-scape' enabling one's engagement in that lifeworld; this orientation usually falls below one's active perception. Our embodied habituation to the parameters of the everyday lifeworld takes-for-granted the 'know-how' of our canny intermodality which we continuously draw upon.

Loss of proprioception

The knowingness of the body from its sensory intermodality is starkly exhibited with the loss of proprioceptive sensations as with Sacks's *disembodied women* (1986). Proprioception is the unconscious, effectively effaced, perception of whole and partial bodily orientation and movement derived from inner bodily sensations, particularly pressure feedback, from muscles, gut, blood vessels and the like. It is highly intermodulated with tactile, vestibular, visual, and aural sensations. Loss of proprioception draws attention to the significance of one's 'body schema' for bodily knowing; as discussed by Gallagher and Cole (1998).

> The body schema is not a perception, a belief, or an attitude. Rather, it is a system of motor and postural functions that operate below the level of self-referential intentionality, although such functions can enter into and support intentional activity. The preconscious, subpersonal processes carried out by the body-schema system are tacitly keyed into the environment and play a dynamic role in governing posture and movement. (Gallagher and Cole, 1998: 132)

It is the body schema's activities which afford the lack of a need for constant bodily awareness; so the body can withdraw from our immediate attention. And if one becomes habituated to a medical technology, accommodating to its support, then it too will become withdrawn within one's body schema and, to varying degrees, from one's active perception (Ihde, 1990; Crossley, 2001).

The loss of proprioception and with it the unity of one's intermodal body schema is an uncanny experience. Un/canny, in the sense that it is disquieting in and of itself and in what it suggests. Loss of proprioception particularly highlights the hidden nature, the *canniness* of the customarily habituated body. This bodily surety with which the vast majority of us are endowed is something which few of us ever become fully aware of, let alone have cause to doubt (except, say, when one gets a numb leg and then pins and needles). It usually goes without question that our bodies will perform actions as we proceed through everyday life. This canniness will usually not provoke propositional questioning, nor can it easily provide epistemic facts. However, the surety with which one 'believes' in things that are not normally in doubt, has a conviction which suggests to rational minds that it should be epistemically provable and therefore knowable (hence neuroscientific research efforts).

Chimerism in transplantation

The examples given above discuss bodily canniness for gross physiology. However, our immunological responses to things that are other than self, be they viruses, bacteria, fungi, saliva, sperm or tissue transplants, may be considered a cellular canniness. Generally speaking the body reacts to the intrusion of foreign material, identified as such at the cellular level, with zero tolerance. Immunologically there is an ongoing 'questioning' and 'negotiation' of what is and is not 'biologically-self' (Tauber, 1994; Walsh and Bunce, 2001). It is this keen, or canny, immunological sense of biological-self that underdetermines our very existence from the moment of conception.

Transplantation of tissues from one individual to another who is not genetically identical (and on occasion even one who is genetically identical) provokes host body and donated tissue immunological responses. The usual scenario for organ transplantation is that the recipient will need a personalized complex of biochemical intervention, primarily immunosuppressants, to allay the rejection of the organ they are hosting.

However, in the late 1990s Thomas Starzl made a significant discovery, namely transplant immunological chimerism. He studied several liver and kidney transplant recipients who had had good function from their grafts for some 30 years since transplantation. What was unique about this group was the fact that for a significantly prolonged period none of them had required any form of immunosuppressant treatment to support the donor organ, and showed no signs of rejection. What Starzl found were dendritic cells* derived originally from within donor bone marrow, which appeared to have migrated from the donor organ into the recipient (and to a degree vice versa). It is this migration of cells that had 'conferred' *immunological privilege* between the donor organ and the recipient host. This tolerance of 'recognized' foreign entities, by the host body and the donor organ alike, forestalls rejection; whilst maintaining an immunological response to other entities deemed foreign to both organ and recipient. Starzl discussed his findings with his participants, reporting the following response:

> Thus, organ allograft acceptance was associated with the *cryptic persistence* of a small fragment of extramedullary donor marrow, including stem cells. . . . These cells had been assimilated into the overwhelmingly larger immunological network of the host. . . . The discovery was *instinctively* understood by most patients to whom it was explained, and it had a *surprisingly great emotional impact*. The point was not lost that the physical intimacy of the donor to the recipient was greater than anyone had imagined. It was closer and more lasting than that of a gestational fetus with its mother. The women applying lipstick in the morning was touching that unknown cadaveric male donor of 30 years ago whose live cells were everywhere in her own

*Dendritic cells are specialized cells originating in bone marrow, that help regulate the immune response.

tissues. She was not the recipient of an organ only. *The realization was usually moving, and it was invariably sobering.* (Starzl, 2000: 10, my emphases).

Here again, in these unusual transplantation cases, we find the uncanny canniness of our embodiment. Uncanny, in the sense that it is disquieting in and of itself and in what it suggests. When one is made aware of how the body acts ordinarily and extraordinarily, then what has been *grasped* in pre-reflective acts of everyday living, becomes a disquietingly uncanny issue for reflection. We bodily 'know' that our bodies make immunological negotiations for our well-being. We epistemically know that transplantation requires immunosuppression. And those who exhibit the immunological privileging of transplant chimerism have grasped *instinctively* that their bodies have somehow biologically re-negotiated their well-being. Nonetheless, when the 'facts of the matter' are brought to their attention, they still have the disquieting impact of the covert enmeshment of the strangely-familiar, where the un/canniness of the body has been revealed.

So, when we talk of bodily knowing, we are making reference to an embodied non-epistemic appreciation of being in the world, that is pre-reflective and pre-conscious; a grasped understanding which is strangely-familiar, which can be revealed into the world of rational discussion, but provokes a distinctly disquieting response, at least in the first instance. It would seem we may only just be touching the tip of the iceberg when it comes to the ways in which the body un/cannily underdetermines our being in the world and therefore our ability to rationally comprehend it. (Just consider the bodily effect of someone talking about nits: there is no rational reason for almost instantaneously wanting to scratch one's head.)

The 'rationale' for bodily knowing: toward an appreciation of the un/canny

When uncanny things happen we normally dismiss them as too silly, too spooky, too disquieting. However, appreciating expressions of the un/canny can provide new perspectives on issues of certitude, truth and trust; not only clinically, but ethically too.

The canny and the uncanny

Canniness comes from *can*, as in 'to be able'; as in 'having a canny knack'. It is not about book learning but the way in which the human body, as much as the mind, is skilled in certain activities. Such activities do not lend themselves to verbal explanation and are generally acquired or *grasped*, as Wittgenstein (1969) notes, through hands-on practice. This echoes Mauss's discussion of *body techniques*, as he says 'The English notion of 'craft' or 'cleverness'' (1979: [1950] 108; see also Crossley, 2007). Historically, blacksmithing and midwifery (the canny wife) are exemplary canny crafts. Such overt canniness, however, can be considered distinctly uncanny, as if supernatural; this perception played its part in the prosecution of the witch-hunts.

The most celebrated exposition on The Uncanny, *Das Unheimliche*, is the 1919 paper by Freud; where even he struggled to find effective articulation of his own experiences. Nonetheless, our awareness of the uncanny has a long history, from ancient myths through Shakespeare to movies like *Toy Story* (1995) or *The Matrix* (1999).

Freud (1955 [1919]) highlights three key aspects to the uncanny: the fact that it is an experience of something that is both strange and familiar, something that has been revealed and that usually remains hidden, and that linguistically and experientially uncanniness and canniness are profoundly entwined.

> Thus, *heimlich* (homeliness, canniness) is a word the meaning of which develops in the direction of ambivalence, until it finally coincides with its opposite, unheimlich. *Unheimlich* is in some way or other a sub-species of *Heimlich*. . . . *Heimlich* in a different sense, as withdrawn from knowledge, unconscious . . . *Heimlich* also has the meaning of that which is obscure, inaccessible to knowledge. (Freud, 1919: 226, my inclusion).

Significantly, although the linguistic emphasis differs throughout European languages, the sense that the un/canny is about the hidden, bodily 'known', yet not 'rational', is consistent. Such that the un/canny always provokes anxiety, *a certain disquiet*; wherein there is a *certainty* regarding one's disquietude whilst underscoring the *uncertainty* of its origins. It is this *certain disquiet* which is often so difficult to articulate fully and hence is so readily dismissed.

Characteristically, the uncanny is a revelation of a covert enmeshment of strangeness with familiarity. Indeed at a mundane level, as familiar as we are with our own bodies, when revealed we still find our bodily-ness, our skilled physical 'know-how', strange; as it is this which withdraws from our perception through our bodily habituations (Merleau-Ponty, 1962, 1968).

Doubt where there should be none

As discussed earlier, rationally we may claim to know the *truth about the world* with veracity, but in the end this is founded upon individual and communal embodied *trust in the world*. In some respects, the development of bodily knowing and our *ur*-trust in the canniness of our bodies within the world is best explained through R.D. Laing's (1960) work on *ontological insecurity*. One's ontological security comes from the 'self-validating data of experience' (Laing, 1960: 43). From birth onwards our bodily experiences establish how an individual comes to appreciate their embodiment in relation to others and the world, their sense of 'the self made flesh'. Or as Wittgenstein notes:

> We teach a child 'that is your hand', not 'that is perhaps (or probably) your hand'. That is how a child learns the innumerable language-games that are concerned with his hand. An investigation or question, 'whether this is really a hand' never occurs to him. Nor, on the other hand, does he learn that he *knows* that this is a hand.

We each have a life-time of accumulated experiences (including those language games) which (re)validate or otherwise the mutuality of our individually being in the world. One's ontological (in)security underdetermines one's *ur*-trust. The ontologically secure person will therefore rarely reflect upon, nor doubt, their embodiment.

Taking this one step further, as Shilling (2001) has noted regarding Durkheim and Mauss on embodiment:

> ... in order for any society to exist the life of the group must become 'organised within' individuals. These body techniques remain vital within modernity because their transmission involves an 'education in composure' and rationalisation congruent with a specialised society. (Shilling, 2001: 334)

Ontological security and one's embodied *ur*-trust provide the individual with the canniness, the composure, to function communally. Loss of one's bodily composure can, therefore, leave one personally and socially vulnerable at best (consider, say, urinary incontinence) echoing Goffmann's *Stigma* (1968). One may endeavour to explain what is happening, yet real understanding, acceptance and guidance is most forthcoming from those who have had similar un/canny experiences; validating the role of expert patients across medical practice.

It is from this embedment in our bodily *ur*-trust in ourselves and the world that we gain our canniness and from there we can reason epistemically. Therefore, what needs to be considered are the effects of medical techniques and technologies, alongside the treatment of the body, upon an individual's established ontological security. The bodily experience of illness may question an individual's *ur*-trust. Illness provokes doubts, where hitherto there was no cause to doubt. Revelations of the uncannily canny body, let alone the uncanniness of illness and medical technologies, can be disquieting. This can leave an individual questioning not only the epistemic foundations for their reasoning but also the ontological foundations for their being and, therefore, their ability to reason, just when they may need to make significant treatment decisions.

The refusal to acknowledge dependency upon bodies and technologies

Not only do bodies and technologies withdraw from our perception through habituation and in effect cease to be doubtable, we may also find that we in fact prefer not to be made aware of our un/canny dependence upon our bodies and any technical support. As Jo discusses:

> I take care of my body (or try to) and care about it, but I just expect the bits of my body to do their job, fulfil their function, not 'take care of' me. . . . I don't think of them (body parts) 'worrying' or 'caring' about me. . . . Perhaps it would be good for me if I did? . . . If I think about it in less 'anthropomorphic' terms, yes I do feel that my aids take care of me. Just as my skin protects my inside bits (other examples from body parts). . . . They (glasses, hearing aid) work in collaboration with my eyes and my ears. . . . I think some of the stuff I was saying in the first couple of paragraphs

is about being 'in denial' – *I don't actually want to acknowledge my dependency and articulating the fact* that they (glasses, hearing aids) do take care of me means I do have to admit that I am dependent upon them, and increasingly so. I don't like to feel helpless, vulnerable, reliant. I want to be, and feel, self-sufficient. And that is where the divide between organic body parts and technological aids becomes clear. I couldn't see if I don't have eyes – but that doesn't make me feel 'dependant' upon my eyes. (CMC research participant: F.K. O'Neill, 2007c).

Here Jo ably draws that important distinction between the usually unquestionable surety of one's body: 'I just expect the bits of my body to do their job'; and the questionable certainty we 'in fact' have about our bodies and any technical support we may use. The dependability of a body (or technology) comes into stark contrast when illness or dysfunction reveals fallibility. One's dependency upon the withdrawn body (and medical aids) is potentially something, as Jo says, which one will not want to acknowledge. Indeed as the body is usually beneath question and beyond doubt, then why should one acknowledge it? But the fallibility of bodies and technologies highlights our habituated unquestioning dependence upon them; hence we may exercise denial to protect ourselves from feeling 'helpless, vulnerable, reliant'.

Psychologically, the juxtaposition of private moments of objectivity and the public articulation of denial is a major factor in our ability to cope with illness, technology and living with constraints; notably discussed in relation to dialysis and transplantation (Curtin *et al.*, 2002; Fricchione *et al.*, 1992; Beard and Sampson, 1981). The reinstitution of the unquestionable, dependable, un/canny body (and potentially technical aids within this) in order to regain a sense of control and surety, is inevitably going to be in tension with a probable medical need, at least initially, to acknowledge illness and technical support; and the later need to re-establish one's embodied ontological security.

Appreciating un/canny bodily knowing

Can an appreciation of un/canny experiences be useful? Well, in Jo's case she feels she has an uncanny knack of knowing what is wrong with her faulty hearing aid. Having been to the audiologist several times and being *sure* it was the amplifier at fault the following was reported:

I had felt from the start that this (the amplifier) was the problem, but no one was listening to me (perhaps they are all deaf too?) This time (her third visit) a fault was detected, and I was issued with a new amplifier. . . . I was experiencing fuzziness, a crackling swishing sound – like a radio that's not quite tuned in or picking up interference . . . It was also similar to the imperfect output I was getting from the speaker of my rather antique music system. . . . I couldn't see how this kind of background 'interference' noise could be produced by the . . . tubing or ear mould (which had initially been replaced). . . . Further the problem was progressive. (CMC research participant: F.K. O'Neill, 2007c).

Although Jo is obviously using strong analogies with inductive reasoning, based on her understanding of how electronic amplification works, to explain this experience, there is still a sense that she was just 'sure' it was the amplifier in the first instance. The uncanny effect of the fault came from its mimetic failure, its inability to act as if it were part of the body into which it had been habituated.

Just as the loss of proprioception is disquieting, this uncanniness can also support an individual's rehabilitation, as with Christine; Sack's *disembodied women* (1986).

> 'I can't feel my body. I feel weird – disembodied.' (44). She had, at first, to monitor herself by vision, looking carefully at each part of her body as it moved, using an almost painful consciousness and care (47). 'I've already noticed' . . . 'that I may "lose" my arms. I think they're one place, and find they're another. This "propriocep-tion" is like the eyes of the body, the way the body sees itself.' (46). But then – and here both of us found ourselves most happily surprised, by the power of an ever-increasing, daily increasing, automatism – then her movements started to appear more delicately modulated, more graceful, more natural (though still wholly depen-dent on use of the eyes) (47). Christine learned to . . . conduct the usual business of life – but only with the exercise of great vigilance, and strange ways of doing things (49)(Sacks, 1986).

The loss of *ur*-trust in her body is certain and remains disquieting, 'I feel my body is blind and deaf to itself . . . it has no sense of itself' (Sacks, 1986: 49). This is an uncanny experience revealing the canniness of the body which hith-erto has been withdrawn from her reflection; whilst also querying her ontologi-cal security (Sacks, 1986: 51–2). Yet, this revelation is one which is both strange and familiar. And it is the canny familiarity of her previously *ur*-trusting embodi-ment which she references in her efforts to overcome her loss of proprioception. She actively reflects upon the un-doubtable canniness of the body, in order to use her other senses. Christine, as with similar cases, is left learning to orientate herself primarily through visual perception, thereby regaining a semblance of normality.

Acknowledging and engaging clinically and ethically with the un/canny

> We are unaware of how canny we are and how we are canny, until the uncanniness of our canniness (and of our technologies) is brought to our attention' (F.K. O'Neill, 2007c: 221).

The un/canny in clinical practice

How might the un/canniness of the body be engaged in clinical practice? Well, in the first instance it is an issue of awareness rising. All too often in medicine the un/canny can be dismissed as it provokes a response of being either too silly or too spooky. What needs to be appreciated is that paying heed to experiences and expressions of the un/canny is not superstition but an open-minded (dare one say late Wittgensteinian?) scepticism.

When one experiences the un/canniness of the body through illness, dysfunction, or the use of a supporting technology, one may struggle to articulate that experience and to understand what it is about. As has already been noted, the uncanny is renowned for being difficult to put into words without recourse to phrases which conjure the supernatural. And the social fear of invoking anything suggestive of superstition, especially in a place full of scientific endeavours, can itself deter communication. It is all too easy and understandable for us to dismiss our experiences as silly or spooky, retreating form acknowledgement into denial. The importance of non-verbal communication skills in such situations is all too obvious.

If practitioners can acknowledge and actively engage with the two modalities of certitude we operate with in everyday life, namely our knowing *certainty* in the truths we learn *about the world* and the usually unquestionable *surety* we accrue as our *ur*-trust *in the world*, especially in our bodies, then potentially they can use these modalities to support patients when experiencing and expressing un/canny moments. (And of course many of our best nursing staff and other practitioners cannily do this 'without question' or realization).

Take rehabilitation. As the word suggests, it is a reinstating of the skills one had, one's habitus; concomitant with this one might hope to regain certitude in one's body and potentially its prosthetic support. As one of Wainwright, Williams & Turner's research participants noted:

> The worst thing is not that you are injured; it's the coming back through the reha-
> bilitation . . . psychologically it's horrendous because you have no confidence what-
> soever, as you have something that's bothering you. The body is in a good state by
> now, but it doesn't feel like it used to and it takes forever to go back psychologically
> to where you were. (Wainwright *et al.*, 2005: 54)

This 'not feeling like it used to', the disquietude that remains within a physically rehabilitated body, speaks to the need for more than just regaining one's certainty in the truth about one's body, but also the time and care it takes to (re)establish the surety of one's *ur*-trust in one's embodiment and potentially its technical support; as highlighted in Wainwright's paper.

The disquietude that a patient can experience when one's body (and supporting technologies) does not function as expected, can take an individual beyond rational arguments. The effect of revealing the un/canniness of the body, as in the cases discussed, may be insignificant to profound. What is common is the need for patients to be facilitated in their communications; especially when language is hard to find or verges on the unacceptable. Expressions of the uncanny may well be indicative of an individual's need for further medical attention, or emotional support. When profoundly experienced, individuals may need to be reassured of, and given time to, regain their capacities to make judgements; as they may experience a profound if temporary loss of ontological security.

Expressions of the un/canniness of the body are not restricted to patients; practitioners will also have moments when they too experience the un/canniness of their own and other's bodies and technologies. As early as 1906, Jentsch (1995[1906]) noted how practitioners become inured to the uncanniness of their profession. Acknowledging their uncanny habitus may help practitioners appreciate their own embodied professional *ur*-trust.

It is worth remembering here that rehabilitation has its own political economy which may seek to perpetuate dependency and 'facilitate the prosthetic disguise of impairments' (Thomas, 2007: 43 & 61). My own experience of being 'fitted' for a 'natural' silicon breast form has been an eye-opener, by turns humourous and daunting. From my ongoing National Health Service entitlement to two breast-forms per breast removed, to the amusement of having a personalized nipple created, and the reality of if, when, with what and for how long one might manage to wear said prosthesis. Whether 'going commando' or wearing the prosthesis, both still provoke personal and social disquietude. Just as one of the participants in *How to Look Good Naked* notes: it is about the prosthesis not yet feeling part of you physically or emotively (Channel 4: 20.5.2008).

The un/canny in ethical practice

Does the un/canny have ethical significance for modern medical practice? Throughout Wittgenstein's *On Certainty* the un/canny engages with issues of trust. However, being non-propositional, difficult to articulate, referencing the supernatural, the un/canny does not at first sight lend itself to rational ethical discussions, unless of course you take Wittgenstein's view of ethics.

> Our words used as we use them in science, are vessels capable only of containing and conveying meaning and sense, *natural* meaning and sense. Ethics, if it is anything, is supernatural and our words will only express facts; as a teacup will only hold a teacup full of water and if I were to pour out a gallon over it. . . . [T]o write or talk Ethics . . . (is) to run against the boundaries of language. (Wittgenstein, 1965: 7 & 12).

In the 2002 Reith lectures, entitled *A Question of Trust*, Onora O'Neill discussed the possible causes of mistrust and the importance of trust with regard to, amongst other things, informed consent. In the fourth lecture, *Trust and Transparency* (O. O'Neill / BBC Radio4 online 2002), she makes several points regarding the process of trust. These include: the need to be able to check the veracity of the information we are given, this is not just about access to alternative sources for verification, but the ability to sift through, decipher and check appropriate information when we are often overwhelmed by indistinguishable information and misinformation; and then the need beyond this to check and verify the credentials of those providing the information. With this in mind, O'Neill suggests that the ability to establish trusting relationships with those who provide such information and services may be difficult in a world that has less time and actual (as opposed to virtual) space in which to establish a 'traditional' face-to-face relationship of mutual respect that can be actively tested for its degree of trustworthiness.

We see in Onora O'Neill's discussion a typically modern ethical emphasis on the importance of having information and being able to test its veracity, including its source, in order to be able to trust in its certainty. In other words, propositionally tested information provides us with *truths about the world.* O'Neill, in passing, draws attention to the fact that our trust in the people who inform us is just as significant to the process of trusting as is the veracity of the information itself. In effect it is suggested that the trustworthiness of individuals and institutions effectively underdetermines the veracity of information. O'Neill notes that trust comes from (habitually) being with others, her 'traditional relations', as with 'family, friends or colleagues'.

In traditional relations of trust, active inquiry was usually extended over time by talking and asking questions, by listening and seeing how well claims to know and undertakings to act held up. (O. O'Neill, BBC Radio4 online 2002: Lecture 4: *Trust and Transparency*).

And in the next lecture she goes on to state that:

Informed consent [as a given permission] is therefore always important, but it isn't the basis of trust. On the contrary, it presupposes and expresses trust, which we must already place to assess the information we're given. (O. O'Neill, BBC Radio4 online 2002: Lecture 5: *Licence to Deceive*, my inclusion).

What 'bodily knowing' adds to this emphasis on active enquiry toward epistemic veracity to provide a sense of trustworthiness is the role of *ur*-trust. *Ur*-trust underpins not only the process of developing epistemic trust in the credentials of informants and the building of trusting relationships, it also has a role in an individual's ability to make judgements and decisions.

As noted earlier, the *certain disquiet* that experiencing the un/canny can provoke, can lead to a disruption in one's ontological security. At these times individuals may find it profoundly difficult to assess the information and informants they encounter; for they may well be experiencing a loss of (*ur*)-trust in themselves, and therefore in their ability to judge and decide. Indeed, can an individual who feels they can't (*ur*)-trust their own judgement be expected to form a trusting relationship with informants and then assess the information they have been given? This is not to suggest that all those who have moments or long-term experiences of *a certain disquiet* have lost their autonomy and require a proxy. But it does suggest that those who are experiencing the *shadow of doubt where there should be none* may well need a particular kind of understanding, emotional support, reassurance and time to be enabled to engage with informants and information in a way that would truly constitute the process of informed consent which O'Neill is discussing. For both the 'informed' and the 'consent' will require an *ur*-trust in one's embodiment and the world.

Could it be that the present personal and social experiences of mistrust in professionals and institutions, which Onora O'Neill is addressing in these lectures, reflects a move away form the tacit acknowledgment of our common bond of embodied *ur*-trust, through say a pejorative emphasis on evidence-based protocols? A critique of O'Neill's position might be to ask 'do we only trust in truths' in order to be *certain* as she emphasizes, or might certitude also require 'an *ur*-trust in our canniness' in order that one might also feel *sure*?

The upshot: addressing evidence-based practice

If these examples and arguments have provided a case for appreciating the un/canny and our *ur*-trust in our 'bodily knowing', then it is hoped that both clinical and ethical practice in medicine might work toward more readily acknowledging the un/canny as a significant aspect of patient care and thus avoiding unnecessary harm. Evidence-based medicine and evidence-based ethics have, possibly unwittingly, detracted from the significance of 'bodily knowing' for both the patient and practitioner. As *evidence* suggests a requirement for proof, it focuses our understanding of medical care on propositional *truths about the world*; potentially omitting our *ur-trust in the world*. Just as Onora O'Neill sees deception rather than a lack of informational transparency as constitutive of a crisis in trust, this chapter sees a lack of acknowledgement of our 'bodily knowing', our canniness and *ur*-trust as constitutive of the *certain disquiet*, even mistrust we experience with purely evidence based clinical and ethical protocols.

If the aim of medical practice is to acknowledge and support an individual's needs in the round, then we must accept the need to acknowledge and support patient's *ur-trusting belief* in their bodies and the world. And when appropriate, assisting them in articulating and appreciating any un/canniness they may experience, before expecting them to test the *evidence* of truths about their bodies and the world they now find themselves within.

Note

1 Quotations from CMC (computer mediated communication – email correspondence) research participants are verbatim, retaining all typographical presentation except font style and size. My editing is shown by . . . and my inclusions are in [square brackets].

References

BBC Radio 4 online (2005), *In Our Time – perception and the senses*, presented by M. Bragg, 28 April 2005. http://www.bbc.co.uk/radio4/history/inourtime/inourtime_20050428.shtml [accessed on 12 November 2008].

Beard, B. and Sampson, T., (1981), Denial and Objectivity in Haemodialysis Patients: Adjustment by opposite mechanisms. In N.B. Levy (ed.) *Psychonephrology 1. Psychological factors in hemodialysis & transplantation* (pp. 169–175), New York: Kluwer Academic, Plenum Publishers.

Channel 4 20.5. (2008), *How to Look Good Naked: series 3 episode 15* (online video clip http://www.channel4.com/video/how-to-look-good-naked/series-3/episode-15/painful-adjustment_p_1.html [accessed on 12 November 2008].

Crossley, N., (2001), *The Social Body: Habit, identity and desire*, London: Sage.

Crossley, N., (2007), Researching Embodiment by way of 'Body Techniques', *Embodying Sociology*, Sociological Review Monograph (pp. 80–94), Oxford: Blackwell Publishing.

Curtin, R.B., Mapes, D., Petillo, M. and Oberley, E., (2002), Long-term Dialysis Survivors: a transformational experience, *Qualitative Health Research*, 12(5): 609–624.

Freud, S., (1955 [1919]), Das Unheimliche / The Uncanny. In *The Standard Edition of the Complete Psychological Works of Sigmund Freud vol1 xvii (1917–1919)*, London: James Strachey.

Fricchione, G.I., Howanitz, E., Jandorf, L., Kroessler, D., Zervas, I. and Woznicki, R.M., (1992), Psychological Adjustment to End-Stage Renal Disease and the Implications of Denial, *Psychosomatics*, 33(1): 85–91.

Gallagher, S. and Cole, J., (1998), Body Image and Body Schema in a Deafferented Subject. In D. Welton (ed.) *Body and Flesh; A philosophical reader*. pp. 131–147. Oxford: Blackwell.

Goffmann, E., (1968), *Stigma: Notes on the management of spoiled identity*, Harmondsworth: Penguin Books.

Ihde, D., (1990), *Technology and the Lifeworld: From garden to earth*, Bloomington: Indiana University Press.

Jentsch, E., (1995 [1906]), On the Psychology of the Uncanny (trans. R. Sellars), *Angelaki*, 2(1): 7–16.

Laing, R.D., (1960), *The Divided Self: a study in sanity and madness*, London: Tavistock.

Leder, D., (1999), Flesh and Blood: a proposed supplement to Merleau-Ponty. In D. Welton (ed.) *The Body: Classic and contemporary readings* (pp. 200–210), Oxford: Blackwell Publishers.

Mauss, M., (1979 [1950]), *Sociology and Psychology: Essays* (trans. B. Brewster), London: Routledge & Kegan Paul.

Merleau-Ponty, M., (1962), *Phenomenology of perception* (trans. C. Smith), London: Routledge.

Merleau-Ponty, M., (1968), *The Visible and the Invisible*, C. Lefort (ed.), (trans. A.Lingis), Illinois: Northwest University Press.

Moyal-Sharrock, D., (2004), *Understanding Wittgenstein's On Certainty*, Basingstoke: Palgrave Macmillan.

O'Neill, F.K., (2007a), Fashioning Flesh: Inclusion, exclusivity & the potential of genomics. In P. Atkinson, P. Glasner and H. Greenslade (eds), *New Genetics, New Identities*, London: Routledge.

O'Neill, F.K., (2007b), The Raw and The Vital: Medical technologies and Aristotle's *psuchē*. In D. Janes (ed.), *Back to the Future of the Body*, Cambridge: Cambridge Scholars Press.

O'Neill, F.K., (2007c), *Uncanny Belongings: Bioethics and the technologies of fashioning flesh*, Lancaster University, PhD Thesis, August 2007.

O'Neill, O. / BBC Radio 4 (2002), *The Reith Lectures 2002: A Question of Trust*, Lectures 1–5 as transcripts or recordings at http://www.bbc.co.uk/radio4/reith2002/ [accessed on 12 November 2008].

Sacks, O., (1986), *The Man Who Mistook His Wife for a Hat*, Basingstoke & Oxford: Picador.

Shilling, C., (2001), Embodiment, Experience and Theory: in defence of the sociological tradition. *Sociological Review*, 49(3): 32–344.

Starzl, T.E., (2000), The Mystic of Transplantation: Biological and Psychiatric Considerations, in P. Trzepacz and A.F. Di Martini (eds) *The Transplant Patient: biological, psychiatric and ethical issues of organ transplantation*, Cambridge: Cambridge University Press.

Tauber, A.I., (1994), *The Immune Self: Theory or metaphor?* Cambridge: Cambridge University Press.

Thomas, C., (2007), *Sociologies of Disability and Illness: Contested ideas in disability studies and medical sociology*, Baskingstoke, Palgrave Macmillan.

Wainwright, S., Williams, C. and Turner, B., (2005), Fractured Identities: Injury and the balletic body, *Health: an interdisciplinary journal for the social study of health, illness and medicine*, 9(1): 49–66.

Walsh, I. and Bunce, M., (2001), HLA Typing, Matching and Crossmatching in Renal Transplantation. In Sir P. Morris (ed.) *Kidney Transplantation: principles and practice* 5th edn. (pp. 135–158), Philadelphia, Penn: WB Saunders & company.

Wittgenstein, L., (1965), A Lecture on Ethics, *The Philosophical Review*, 74(1): 3–12.

Wittgenstein, L., (2004 [1969]), *On Certainty*, Oxford: Blackwell Publishing.

Filmography

The Matrix: The fight for the future begins (1999) Written and directed by A. and L. Wachowski, produced by Warner Bros.

Toy Story: The toys are back in town (1995) Written by Lasseter *et al.*, directed by J. Lasseter; produced by Disney Pixar.

232

Beyond caring? Discounting the differently known body

Trudy Rudge

> The social actually gets into the flesh, and unless we take account of this, we cannot account for the extent to which socio-historical realities affect us psychically, and how we in turn act in ways that produce and reinforce them. We also need to address the problem of how we come to experience ourselves as contained entities, contained in terms of energies and affects. (Brennan, 1993: 10)

From this ethnographic study on a burns unit it was clear, when talking with the men and the nurses who care for them, that patients return to the outside world after treatment to a qualitatively different life. Very few of their family or friends can understand how the experience of trauma and subsequent treatment has altered them, and this lack of comprehension often extends to those who provide treatment. Such a lack of comprehension leads to feelings of uncertainty for everyone involved. The processes of care tend, due to the way that medical treatment objectifies patients, to focus more on surgical repair of the skin to the detriment of confounding effects on identity and embodiment. The focus on medical treatment is understandable, even taken for granted, as the highest priority. Moreover, to contain uncertainty, it becomes less threatening to disavow and contain emotions under the certainties of medical treatments and their seeming objectivity.

Patients who are burnt and the nurses who care for them destabilize our sense of security as each reminds us we are vulnerable. Their embodiment is integrated in action and activities to accomplish what is needed to be done to re-cover skin and to recover from its subsequent trauma. Exploring mutual embodiments of nurses and patients brings into view another position on caring that does not discount the familiarity of 'unknowingness' of bodies. On one hand, I ponder how burnt bodies are thought about in health care, fuelled as this is by assumptions (what is known) from health care professionals as to the experience of burns. I trace how, in the bodily trauma of burns and the grafting of new skin, it is assumed that patients' bodies become a 'body unknown'. Particular bodily functions associated with skin are over-determined. On the other hand, I examine how the care of burnt people is a specialized form of care and is provided by nurses who have learnt to care for burnt people sometimes by working on units such as the one that is part of this study or sometimes by undertaking specialist education in intensive care or plastic surgery. To explore how this care is undertaken I present the embodied practices of nurses as they provide care for these people, to expose how bodies, knowing and unknowing, produce a particular kind of caring that takes account of the intertwined embodiment of nurses and re-covering patients.

The body in this case

Merleau-Ponty (1968) famously noted that in all his prior work on embodiment and perception, he remained entrapped in the mind/body dualism. In this critique he admitted that his own work on perception as emerging from the body as its null point, and its resultant cognitive focus, did not overcome the mind/body split. In his re-working of his thinking on the body, Merleau-Ponty suggested that embodiment be imagined through the idea of flesh, as a chiasmatic relation between bodies, parts of bodies and our relationship to our and others' bodies. Such a re-thinking suggests that embodiment is accomplished intersubjectively; an heuristic for comprehending the situation of the care of people with burns. While their flesh is made visible through the burn and the burn treatment, its effects reverberate intersubjectively – through the language which constitutes the treatment – in the experience for the patient and the nurse.

Skin is the embodied tapestry that is the body's largest sense organ (Podolsky, 1987; Connor, 2004). It contains us, keeps us from leaking except at specific points, prevents infections, maintains our sense of embodiment through proprioception, assists with regulating our temperature, acts as a point of attachment, senses our environment, gives out messages, does some of our excretion. However these multiple functions of skin are denied in the view of western philosophy and the science of skin care, where skin has come to convey and is constitutive of our unitary state, metaphorically representing our containment as individuals (Jackson, 1983; Kirmayer, 1992; Rudge, 1997; Connor, 2004). This understanding is metonymic and portrays the skin as mere surface. Further, I would argue that it is such a view on skin as cover which affords modern surgical treatment as *the* treatment of possibility. In counter-distinction to such a view, a psychoanalytic reading of the centrality of skin to development of the ego by Anzieu (1989) suggests that skin holds many affective and emotional meanings because of its more than skin-deep metaphorical meaning. Anzieu coined the term skin-ego to suggest how integral skin is to identity formation in his Lacanian reformulation.

It is my contention that as a result of the rupture of the tapestry of skin, a liminal space opens for analysis. Rupture of this boundary destabilizes the mind/body split that Shildrick (2002) asserts medicalized discourses use to exclude the entry of abnormal and monstrous bodies into their calculus of treatment. Moreover, in using this paradigmatic split, medical discourses seek to control and contain the uncontainable, such action leading to oppression and suppression of the aberrant effects caused by trauma and burns. Moreover, unless there is an interruption of the opposition of the monstrous to the normal in the care of trauma, normative ordering of health care prevails, with the potential of failure to acknowledge the complexities entailed in recovery. An analysis using the concept of abjection shows how, despite its containment, this primer emotional defence is never fully expelled, neither subject nor object, but resident in a liminal space in-between the social, emotional and personal structures of human experience. Abjection and its defences of disavowal and sublimation remain as both a reminder of, and a threat to, the precarious status of the closed and unified self.

From such a perspective, subjectivity formed in the dynamic structures of the emotional is always already contaminated by abjection's archaic memories.

> It is something rejected from which one does not part, from which one does not protect oneself as from an object. Imaginary uncanniness and real threat, it beckons to us and ends up engulfing us. (Kristeva, 1982: 4)

Therefore it is important in any analysis of bodies which is located in the ambiguous and liminal space of the abject, where the normal/monstrous, mind/body dualisms are transgressed, to explore how abject positioning affects care and understandings of embodiment (see Douglas, 1966; Kristeva, 1982; Shildrick, 2002). In exposing the operation of the binary normal/monstrous, in burn trauma and burns nursing, through an exploration of the abject body and abjection, the hope is to destabilize what can be thought of as either the unknown/known body.

Assumptions about the person in each case

The event for patients

It is no surprise that when skin's bounded corporeality is ruptured by a trauma such as a burn, a cascade of events occurs. First there is the trauma itself; then life-threatening situations resulting from fluid loss, tissue toxicities and burnt airways; the shock ensuing from pain screaming from the millions of damaged nerve endings, or more worryingly not, due to deeper burns; nightmares and hallucinations from a combination of sub-acute high temperatures and the pain relief needed to dim pain; and abject horror accompanying every day of treatment until nearing exhaustion, worn out by the constancy of the daily round of dressings, the person is re-covered.

In other papers (Rudge, 1998; 1999; 2003) I have detailed how, in this round of activity, each severely burnt person lost their sense of identity and security, moved along haplessly on the roller coaster of treatment. The treatment regime of surgery alternating with dressings or graft care,[1] as well as the need for them to slowly take over their care through on-going education and motivational work, structures everyone's time on the unit. As time goes on, each person is expected to take their part in the care of their skin, washing the burns with their hands so they exercise their hands, moving about in their bed while they can; and then staying still or stabilized as they must not move their newly grafted areas. A formerly strange set of activities becomes familiar and then routinized as the care of their new grafts and healed skin is taught to them by the nurses working with them. As this regimen becomes more familiar, what was their 'normal' daily life gets lost, and their sense of security in the outside world is now replaced by vulnerability, uncertainty and many unknowns.

Nurses' embodied practices

Nurses' bodies are educated to undertake the care of people in places such as the burns unit by the development of skills and an ethical comportment of acceptance of human frailty, not to mention sheer stupidity that brings the patients to the unit. Nurses, like the patients, undertake a rite of passage, experiencing in caring for people with burns a similar fall into chaos. The nurses in this study had all come to the ward as registered nurses (some with previous experience as students) or as enrolled nurses. Some had undertaken specialist training in intensive care nursing, yet others were undertaking graduate nursing education or other forms of education such as arts degrees. The learning and knowing about skin, damage from burns and the treatment with dressings, grafts, skin biopsies, skin cell slurries and cloned skin and other forms of plastic surgery undertaken as a part of the treatment and replacement of skin required after a burn is largely learnt through 'on the job' training or in nursing parlance, hands-on training.

Many of the nurses tell a similar chaos story as their first experience of the unit when the ward was full with people who had major burns. At such times, nurses are called upon to care for acutely ill people, some of whom may die. They are also called upon to inflict pain and encourage patients to work through pain to maintain their mobility. The nurses' work with skin, cleaning burnt and newly healed skin in showers or bed baths, undertaking graft care[2] and the replacement of dressings are key components of their work, very little of which gets into the medical record, the only record or knowledge about such work is recorded on the patients' bodies with success of healing and grafting (Rudge, 2003; 1998). Patients and nurses acknowledge that nurses' work walks out of the unit on the patient's body (Rudge, 1997). Many nurses in the unit where this study occurred were very experienced burns nurses, yet others had only up to three years experience after graduation. Such a shortfall in mid-range nurses is common in the nursing workforce as nurses in the medium range leave nursing or move to other professions. The effect on the climate of the unit of the lack of middle ranges of experience leads to splits in the cohesion of the unit, where the more experienced nurses are put under strain to both educate *and* work. This leads to junior staff often feeling excluded and unsupported particularly when workloads and intensity increase when the unit is at capacity.

The community of burnt men

The data for this chapter were collected during an ethnographic study of a burns unit where unlike most other forms of care in contemporary health care, patients can spend an extended time in hospital. The determination of time in hospital varies according to the total burn surface area (TBSA) and the depth of the patient's burns. Time as an in-patient varied from 6–24 weeks in hospital, correlated with the extent and depth of the burn in each case. The inclusion criteria for the study was a burn accident varying between TBSA of 25–50%, because beyond that treatment can take a very long time or there is a greater likelihood of death. In more recent times, some rehabilitation of the patients occurs in other wards or rehabilitation units in other locations, but until 'cover' is achieved patients remain in the unit. The researcher observed wound dressings 3–4 times a week for each patient. The study took 14 months because there was an extended period with no suitable patients admitted to the unit. The last 4 months occurred in summer with an increase in numbers and severity of burns. There were no female patients who met the protocol during the time of the study. This is a common occurrence, as women are often admitted for burns either as a result of assault or due to burns from domestic accidents that occur when they are elderly and confused.

The trauma of burns: outside of normal

The psychological and psychosocial effects of severe burns on the individuals who are burnt are exhaustively documented in the burns and burn rehabilitation literature (eg Duncan and Driscoll, 1991; Madjar, 1997; Yu and Dimsdale, 1999; Adcock *et al.*, 2000; Menzies, 2000; Brych *et al.*, 2001; Patterson and Jensen, 2003; Williams *et al.*, 2003; Weichman and Patterson, 2004). Such discussions provide evidence of the effects on body image, self esteem, social and intimate relationships and trace problematic paths, through to rehabilitation, for some personality types into their former social and occupational status. The driving force for burns care is the need to cover the body again with a complete skin, either through surgery or the promotion of skin healing through dressings, skin slurries or cloned skin (Rudge, 1997). Hence, the fatal effects of infection, respiratory distress and renal failure from dehydration due to fluid loss are largely avoided in contemporary treatment regimens.[3] In the literature about burns there are seldom descriptions by burn victims (or survivors) of the events of the burn. Their feelings about treatment remain captive to descriptions constructed by psychometric testing and observations about pathology that are centrally about them, not about what they have experienced.[4] Being burnt is one of the many things that rightly terrifies us (as these are testament to the bombings in Bali, the July bombings in London, plane crash stories from Indonesia or in Australia, bush fire stories told about others and in the media).

As these data below indicate, if it does happen, the conditions, the time and how it felt, and continues to feel, are remembered/known with great clarity (see also Tulloch, 2006; Hicks, 2007). As Glen recounts being overrun by a bush fire:

> I could feel the heat through my clothes, we were running but the fire was all around us – I fell over, I got up once – I fell down again! This time I just lay there all curled up – you know how they talk about finding people all curled up – but I kicked myself up and forced myself to run – otherwise I was dead!

His clothes were the protective uniform worn by voluntary rural fire services personnel. His story is about a bushfire patrol that went wrong. He knew that he could have died as he ran back to the fire truck that was also surrounded by the bushfire that had overtaken their originally safe position. His legs and hands were severely burned, his hands saved a little by his putting them into water bags while his fellow volunteers fought the blaze around them. Not until this crisis was over did they notice his condition and Glen was airlifted out.

The accompanying horror of being burnt is augmented by a growing suspicion that the effects of the burn may interrupt what was otherwise a sure and certain life story, bringing into question one's longevity – or certainly surfacing this as a pre-occupation. So, as Alan said:

> My life is never going to be the same again. I'm never going to be certain about anything again. I mean if I had been really thinking about it I shouldn't have gone in there. I should have run away. . . . I mean in the first shock of the burn, when I was sitting there waiting for [my brother] to get the fire out, and it was burning my legs still. I could feel it, I mean you don't know the effect that will have on you. . . . The body must have taken some hammering. The body must have been through quite a bit with it really. I mean you don't know that even though you didn't feel much of the pain, but your body still went through it . . . At sixty years of age this is something I didn't need to happen. . . . It's made me think of retiring . . . I want to enjoy my life.

Vulnerability and uncertainty: normalizing connection

The loss of skin, with its accompanying loss of a sense of boundedness, brings with it an acknowledgement of vulnerability unknown prior to this – it also opens up a sense of connectedness, where vulnerability strengthened connections to family and concern for friends and fellow sufferers (Rudge, 1997). While their brush with death horrified them, their sense of openness and community was heightened. As their sense of separateness faded, with their bodies, so they attested to a new sense of their responsibilities to others:

> What can I say – it is just stupid that I am here. I feel so guilty to my wife and kids – they nearly lost me, and now I have to get my hands and muscles back – I have just faded away . . .

Just as their social situation was different, so was their surety about their bodies. In terms of the theme of this collection, in their final interviews each thought that recovery was a process that contained both the known and unknown. As patient Glen talks about the familiarity/unfamiliarity of his skin:

> I mean I touch this bit [here he touches a grafted section of his arm] and I can feel it and it's sort of like you'd think it would be – but then I touch this bit here [touching an unaffected part of his arm] and I know it's different, um, it's sort of tingly, not like skin at all really – like rubber with some sort of sensation. No, it's not like **real skin**.

Or, as Phil expressed this:

> I mean I have to think about whether I can **pick up** a glass of milk – whether **I need to put** my other hand under it. How I am going **to shave myself** because it is **hard to hold** the razor. How **on earth** I'm going to get the toothpaste out of the tube. . . . And I'm like **an old snake**. . . . you wouldn't think that you had **that much skin** on your **whole body**. I mean, they've taken bits off there, and bits from here and here, and you think, well, where's the rest of the skin coming from? You think that your **whole body is falling apart**. Soon, you'll be **just a blob on the floor**!

With Phil, we begin to grasp the possible positions for a person who is burnt – from the mundane difficulties of the day-to-day, to the frustrations with formerly skilled activities made impossible, to his wonder about the plasticity of surgical techniques, to the destabilization of a boundary he had always counted on, to an abject fear of formlessness. Clearly, little of this experience is absolutely unknown to Phil. What *is* difficult for him is the powerlessness he experiences each day, and the vulnerability he now feels as a constant presence.

Phil was burnt doing his job as an owner/mechanic used by a road-side emergency agency for at-the-side of road emergency repairs. In his telling of his accident he emphasized that he was safety conscious and vigilant. He had done all the checks and yet as he leaned over the hot engine, fuel leaking on to the engine exploded. He knew how to put out the flames but nothing could save him from the flames he had breathed into his body in the shock of the explosion. Over the next 36 hours, as a result of his swollen trachea[5] he had a respiratory arrest and was ventilated by a machine until the swelling subsided and the subsequent pneumonia had resolved. He knew what had happened, and hated the uncertainty. In an attempt to win back control, he played nurse off against nurse until they tended to leave him to himself and not teach him what he needed to know to look after his donor sites and newly grafted skin. He was a treatment failure, back within 30 days of discharge with infected grafts and contractures[6] because of his refusal to care for himself. He was profoundly depressed, requiring medication to treat this. He then spent an extended time in a rehabilitation hospital, all paid for by the occupational safety insurance company. To my knowledge, several years post burn, he has not returned to work except to supervise the work of others; his uncertainty and abjection prevailed. The nurses all recognized they had failed him.

Nursing burnt men

Tales of Gothic horror: normalizing monstrosity

Nurses portray their first days and weeks in the unit as underpinned by a sense of chaos and confusion. Nurses who agreed to participate in the study were permanent members of staff in the unit and were beyond their first staff nurse year. Each openly expressed their horror at seeing and smelling burns on admission, the first dressing, the first time in burns theatre and their first times watching graft care (Nagy, 1998; Adcock *et al.*, 2000). One nurse talked about it as being 'like a war zone', or in a more overt expression of the horror as a baptism of fire:

> When I first got here, it is so totally unlike any other area of the hospital. My first experience, of being in the Unit, was going straight to theatre, to observe a patient being debrided. And that burn was a 90% burn and I just remember it being incredibly **hot** and **everyone** had a limb. There were about **24** people in there, a couple of anaesthetists, some student nurses, and two teams of scrub nurses. . . . And being **in there** was a real eye opener. I just thought what am **I in for**?!. . . . I just remember seeing a lot of blood, and all the skin areas that were burnt were **very black** and I just thought that **this is the most horrific thing** I have ever seen. Just for a moment – I thought – Am I going to **cope**?

While the men told survival stories using a more matter-of-fact reportage style, nurses highlighted the gothic horror aspects of their experiences. Like the nurse above, they represented themselves as 'in' the unit, often having nightmares and emotional responses such as crying every night at home. Slowly, each nurse learned to manage their response to this horror, although such management was never entirely successful as some patient situations broke through their control. Also at times of high workload when the unit was full with numbers of people with extensive burns, nurses found such times very stressful and likely to re-awaken their earlier feelings. Their narratives highlighted the kinds of transitions they made in becoming a burns nurse. Each recounted a journey that marks out burns care as different but they also highlighted how, in coming to terms with the injuries they see as part of this, the daily dressings and surgeries came to be considered as 'normal'. All of this was necessary to be able to adjust to working in the area. As one nurse put this:

> Because it's just such **a horrific area** to work in, **visually**, I sort of tend to deal now with the wound, and then wrap it up and they're a person again.

And as another nurse put this she responded to the patients and their wounds by 'steeling myself for each dressing, just take several deep breaths and get into it'.

Nurses related that working in a unit where people are under long-term care was different from other parts of nursing, where nurses and patients are not long in each others' company. Allen (2004) suggests that nurses' work has changed significantly with shortened lengths of stay, yet units such as burns units, where long-term care is needed, continue to exist. Moreover much of the care and the body work in the unit was done by registered nurses even though the daily wound dressing could take anything from 30 minutes to 3–4 hours. Many of the nurses recounted tales of agency or replacement nurses being afraid to work in the area because of the horror associated with burns care *and of* the nurses who worked there. Nurses pointed out at their final interviews, that other nurses wondered in admiration how they do such work, while simultaneously they are horrified that any nurse could undertake the work. Thus nurses who do the work in burns units are both admired and feared. As Grosz (1994) points out about feminine subjectivity, such a paradoxical positioning, that is being both reviled/valorized, may be two sides of the same coin. In such a situation nurses are positioned as abject by the work that they do, and they take up this position in order to accomplish the necessary horror of the tasks of wound and graft care. Indeed working in a burns unit requires different nursing subjectivities, but one thing in particular situates this form of nursing as 'unique'.

Getting the practised eye

> This is really different to ICU.[7] You can't just sit at the end of the bed and take obs [observations]. You have to really understand the kind of men we get here. . . . And like them. (Nurse)

> Well if I was thinking about what you had to do after someone had been burned this is exactly what I would think would happen except that I thought that they put plastic skin on you. I didn't realize that when they did the grafting that they took skin from you and put that over the grafted area. I thought plastic surgeons put plastic on you. Didn't think that they would use your own skin. Amazing! (Patient)

As the nurses talked about their work with patients' skin and graft care, it is easy to see why nurses can work in such a place despite its earlier horrors:

> But with burns and grafts, you can **every day**, see it healing and you're a part of that healing in the way that you care for it. Especially, if you get a graft . . . sometimes we get to lay skin, if you laid that bit of skin and it's going beautifully, it's really good!

Such a statement positioned the nurses and their work as integral if not central to the process of wound and graft care. Their ability to embody the practised eye is measured as important as to how well the treatment turns out. Many nurses also reported how good it felt when their clinical knowledge expands, showing how expertise came to contain their sense of chaos and uncertainty. For instance:

> I really liked it when I got really good at knowing how to assess the depth and extent of the burn, how to tell if it [the burn] was going to extend because of the type of burn, how to accurately assess if they had airway involvement.

In taking such a position, this nurse exemplified how nursing is a knowledge-based practice (see Gordon and Nelson, 2006). Nurses held their work in high esteem, openly acknowledging how their work made a difference, once they attained that practised eye. The power/knowledge in this eye is both disciplined and disciplinary (see Foucault, 1977). As a senior nurse talked about learning the distinctions needed for good graft care;

> And trimming[8] the graft is something that they just don't recognize that something needs to be done, if they haven't seen a demarcation line, they don't know a demarcation line, it's not that they aren't doing it right they just don't see it for what it is, and so they might not even say to somebody come and have a look at this . . . because they might just see it as a bit of bruising. I mean because I hear that all the time there's a bit of bruising. Unless you really know what bruising looks like, most times it's not bruising but a bit of clot that needs to come out. So, trimming's a real problem.

She highlights the practised eye required to observe some detailed differences between skin, burns and the natural history of the 'taking' graft. The learning of burns nursing is portrayed as 'hands on', through recognition of what is unknown, actively diagnosing when information and support is needed, seeking out information when uncertain, with a focus on the visual aspects of learning.

The metaphor of the practised eye conveys the meaning of learning in the unit, as a chiasmaic relationship between the eye and what is usually termed 'hands on' learning common in nursing education. The practised eye is the 'hands-on-eye' – a multiplicity of sensory perceptions linked to clinical knowledge, partially obtained through supervision by experienced senior nurses who pass on such knowledge and experiencing the care of grafts and burns – which develops into the governed and governing eye (Holmes and Gastaldo, 2002). The practised eye is liminal in that it is located across the texts of nursing, embedded in nursing's history and context, working across the embodied spaces of wound care practices in a burns unit. It is a location where the flesh of inter-subjective relations (Merleau-Ponty, 1968) allows nurses and patients a place to work together for the patients' recovery. Also, the chiasmic relations portrayed in the figure of the practised eye speak of embodied skilful practice that crosses onto and re-situates itself as the re-covered patient's body. This embodiment of skilled nursing was recognized by the patients as they all talked with admiration of their grafted skin.

> I remember in one shower, one of the nurses, I can't remember her name, got really stuck into it and took all the scabs off and really cleaned it up. And I thought 'they don't look too bad!'

Or even Phil saying, 'I sort of look at my hand and I've had the glove on all the time, and I think, 'they've done **a fantastic job**! . . . they've done a **top job!**'

Discussion: minding the body

> Our corporeality is part of the corporeality of the world. The mind is not merely corporeal but also passionate, desiring and social. It has a culture and cannot exist culture-free. It has a history, it has developed and grown, and it can grow further. It has an unconscious aspect, hidden from our direct view and knowable only indirectly. . . . Its conceptual system is limited; there is much that it cannot even conceptualize, much less understand. (Lakoff and Johnson, 1999: 565)

At the outset, Brennan reminded us how important it is to know how the social gets into the flesh; Merleau-Ponty and Lakoff and Johnson further remind us that that flesh is mentalized, known imperfectly through intersubjectively sharing experience of that embodiment. This study of care by nurses of people with burns shows what is at stake should an ethics of care become disembodied. If embodiment and the emotional containment are objectified, then both the intellectual and affective capacities of caring are denied. In this final section, discussion turns to an identification of an ethics of care that emphasizes embodiment by encouraging its intransigence, positioning nurses with patients in an in-between liminal location where mutual and singular responsibilities are acknowledged.

Nursing embodying care

It is the case that nursing people with burns requires a stance towards them that sustains awareness of differences; in bodies, power and ethical responsibilities (Gatens, 1996). In nursing, caring is seen as central to practice, acting ideologically to govern how nurses respond to the patient's situation (see Watson, 1988; Benner and Wrubel, 1988; Parse, 1995). However, increasingly nurses have recognized that clinging to such ideologies has led to care being imbued with a rarefied – one could say ethereal – aspect. Moreover, one of the deficiencies of this form of thinking about care is that often nurses using such dogma fail to consider the power relations inherent in them (Barnes and Rudge, 2005) unconsciously replicating the very positions they are wanting to avoid.

Bacchi and Beasley (2005) believe that 'care' has come 'to be shorthand for both a sensitivity to context and a willingness to consider the preservation of relationships as a moral priority' (2005: 177). Caring from this point of view has an oddly restricted concern about the effects of power relations in society, stemming as it does from a social psychological focus in the earlier work on moral development (cf Gilligan, 1982). Rather than taking such an approach, Bacchi and Beasley (2005) argue 'that intimate relationships are not necessarily straightforwardly replicable with strangers' (2005: 183). One can almost hear a collective sigh of relief from many nurses who find the elision of caring with 'loving' implicit in much of this previous nursing dogma, a trial (see Allen, 2004; Drummond, 2000, 2004). Moreover, this stance agrees with the view that care cannot be underpinned by a personalized moral or virtue script (Gordon and Nelson, 2006), but rather care requires to be operationalized as a deeply important social practice (Latimer, 2000). Care, Bacchi and Beasley (2005) assert, is a collective, not an individual, responsibility.

In following what Gordon and Nelson (2006) have termed a virtue script for care, nurses have entered a *cul-de-sac* that:

> effectively duplicated the master discourse and maintained the split between a secure sense of the transcendent self as moral agent and a more or less unruly body that must be subjected to its dictates. (Shildrick: 2005: 3).

In the chiasmatic relations evident in the practised eye of burns care, the embodied clinical knowledge of the nurses on the unit appears to be merely physical care based on the application of knowledge to govern the unruly body. It is that, but it is also clearly embodied care where nurses assume responsibility and accountability for what occurs with the patient's skin, with its wider implications for successful rehabilitation and a successful return to their former lives. As we see from their reflections on their failures as much as their successes (Diedrich, 2005), the position they take towards their patients embodies care as knowledgeable, ethical practice.

Recuperating care

The person who is burnt bears witness to the fragile nature of certainty. The scars of treatment attest them as different from others with an experience we would all want to *not* know. However, once known, the medical focus on covering the burn contains the treatment to a focus on regaining certainty. Rather, ethical care requires paying attention to what results from this rupture of the tapestry of certainty, that is, to the presence of abjection in the lives of people with burns (Kristeva, 1982). Living and working with the uncanny as it is represented by unknowness of the body in illness – a body that nevertheless is not entirely strange – rests on a failure of language in the face of pain and suffering (see Scarry, 1985; see also Kristeva, 1982). Illness transforms the surety of the binary structure, makes it porous and vulnerable (Diedrich, 2005: 145). Nurses and other health care workers disavow its presence in their lives too, many rendered inarticulate as they witness pain and suffering. As Lakoff and Johnson (1999) highlight we are required to acknowledge how incomplete our knowledge is and can be as well as recognise the limits of language to articulate such experiences.

Moreover, burns care takes place in a location where the binaries are leaky and porous as well as in an area of nursing considered anachronistic – in terms of length of stay, body work and its use of nursing expertise – and hence easily discounted. Because it is outside or marginalized, I am reluctant to leave behind an exploration of nursing care through nurse-patient interactions or to call such a focus irrelevant. To do so may well reduce many of the important differences in nursing. Clearly, ethical burns nursing care cannot be framed as a bioethical neon issue (see also Hacking, 2006), but is an issue of micro-ethical relevance. Exploring the everyday practices of nurses and patients for their bioethical components is possible because 'a postmodernist bioethics demands ... an openness to the risk of the unknown, a commitment to self-reflection, and a willingness to be unsettled [in an] enterprise of high responsibility (Shildrick, 2005: 17). It involves the risks of thinking beyond the boundaries of the familiar; using non-conventional forms of ethical analysis that 'can expose the interests and partialities at work in the medical setting' (Rothfield, 2005: 46). In exploring both the patients' and the nurses' pleasure in the success (or not) of technical care, I seek to destabilize its very taken-for-granted technical framing and instead locate such care as a clinically driven but nevertheless socio-ethical activity.

Final remarks

Margrit Shildrick (2005) suggests that it is more germane to our search for an ethics of the body to take the position afforded by postmodernism. What this offers for bodies both known and unknown is an approach to care open to riskiness, instability and provisionality. In such an exploration of the embodiment of burns care it is clear that one can challenge the conventional stance towards such care as merely technical. Care from such an ethical standpoint acknowledges the complex nature of the interactions among embodiment, social processes, and subjectivity (Bacchi and Beasley, 2005). What is more central to the ideas put forward is that it is important to refrain from privileging a single point of view about what counts as care. Nurses' bodies intermingle with patients' bodies in the outcomes of care after burn trauma and the mutual responsibilities for its success (or not) are clearly acknowledged. More importantly, in an open ack-nowledgement of the horror residing in such an experience lies the power of such care.

Notes

1 Surgery is used to remove mid to full thickness burnt skin known as debridement, and skin grafts are made by the removal of skin from a donor site (split skin thickness) to cover the area cleaned through the surgery. Other ways of covering are through growth of cloned skin cells or by cell slurries that are kept in place with a special dressing. Cell slurries and cloning techniques use the patient's skin cells. Cell slurries are skin cells in fluid suspension; cloned skin is grown in sheets that are placed on the surgically cleaned areas.

2 Graft care includes daily dressings as well as more frequent work after the first days to ensure that the split skin grafts adhere to the surgically cleaned area. Nurses undertake this work, learning to tell the signs that the skin is 'taking' and clearing out anything that will prevent this from occurring. This work requires knowledge of skin healing and grafting as well as adept dressing techniques on the part of the nurse.

3 Patients are considered critically ill for the first 36 hours until their fluid balance stabilizes and, if they have inhaled flames, their lungs, trachea (windpipe) and upper respiratory tract is no longer swollen. Infection and other causes of death do not occur in the first few days. The key functions

of skin, such as maintaining fluid balance and prevention of infection are considered the main issues.

4 Psychometric testing is used to tell how affected the patients are by the trauma or to exclude mental illness as a cause of the burn accident.

5 The trachea is the tube going from the top of the mouth to the lungs. This and the lungs can be burnt by flames when a person draws in their breath at the time of the accident or because they are surrounded by flames. Assisted ventilation is required until the swelling subsides in the trachea.

6 Contractures occur where skin cannot stretch over and around joints and these restrict movement. Release of contractures occurs surgically.

7 ICU is the acronym for intensive care unit, where patients are cared for if they require 24-hour monitoring and maintenance of vital activities such as breathing through artificial means of assisted ventilation or for critical injuries such as head injuries, burns or major trauma surgery.

8 Trimming a graft is necessary to ensure that the grafted skin fits, that the surgically cleaned or debrided area is covered properly by the new skin and there is no overlapping or area where skin and burn surface are not covered. The difference between this section and bruising or blood clots under the graft are distinctions learned by nurses to ensure that the graft takes onto the cleaned area and after 5 days the new skin develops its rudimentary blood supply ensuring the take of the graft that will with proper care now stay in place.

References

Adcock, R.J., Goldberg, M.L., Patterson, D.R. and Brown, P.B., (2000), Staff perceptions of emotional distress in patients with burn trauma, *Rehabilitation Psychology* 45(2): 179–192.

Allen, D., (2004), Re-reading nursing and re-writing practice: towards an empirically based reformulation of the nursing mandate, *Nursing Inquiry*, 11: 271–283.

Anzieu, D., (1989), *The Skin Ego* (trans. C. Turner), New Haven: Yale University Press.

Bacchi, C. and Beasley, C., (2005), Reproductive technology and the political limits of care. In M. Shildrick and R. Mykitiuk (eds), *Ethics of the Body: postconventional challenges*, Cambridge (MAS): MIT Press.

Barnes, L. and Rudge, T., (2005), Virtual reality or real virtuality: the space of flows and nursing practice, *Nursing Inquiry*, 12: 306–315.

Benner, P. and Wrubel, J., (1988), *The Primacy of Caring*, Menlo Park CALIF: Addison-Wesley.

Brennan, T., (1993), *History after Lacan*, London: Routledge.

Brych, S.B., Engrav, L.H., Rivara, F.P., Ptacek, J.T., Lezotte, D.C., Esselman, P.C., Kowalske, K.J. and Gibran, N.S., (2001), Time off work and return to work rates after burns: systematic review of the literature and a large two-center series, *Journal of Burn Care and Rehabilitation*, 22(6): 401–405.

Connor, S., (2004), *The Book of Skin*, London: Reaktion Books.

Diedrich, L., (2005), A bioethics of failure: antiheroic cancer narratives. In M. Shildrick and R. Mykitiuk (eds), *Ethics of the Body: postconventional challenges*, Cambridge (MAS): MIT Press.

Douglas, M., (1966), *Purity and Danger*, London: Routledge & Kegan Paul.

Drummond, J., (2000), Nietzsche for nurses: caring for the *Übermensch*. *Nursing Philosophy*, 1: 147–157.

Drummond, J., (2004), Nursing and the avant-garde. *International Journal of Nursing Studies*, 41: 525–533.

Duncan, D.J. and Driscoll, D.M., (1991), Burn wound management, *Critical Care Nursing Clinics of North America*, 3: 199–220.

Foucault, M., (1977), *Discipline and Punish*, London: Tavistock.

Gatens, M., (1996), *Imaginary Bodies: ethics, power, corporeality*, London: Routledge.

Gilligan, C., (1982), *In a Different Voice: psychological theory and women's development*, Cambridge, MASS: Harvard University Press.

Gordon, S. and Nelson, S., (2006), Moving beyond the virtue script in nursing. In S. Nelson and S. Gordon, *The Complexities of Care: nursing reconsidered*, Ithica NY: Cornell University Press.

Grosz, E., (1994), *The Volatile Body: towards a corporeal feminism*, Sydney: Allen & Unwin.

Hacking, I., (2006), The Cartesian body, *BioSocieties*, 1(1): 13–15.

Hicks, G., (2007), *One Unknown*, London: Rodale.

Holmes, D. and Gastaldo, D., (2002), Nursing as a means of governmentality, *Journal of Advanced Nursing*, 38(6): 557–565.

Jackson, M., (1983), Thinking through the body: an essay on understanding metaphor, *Social Analysis*, 14: 127–149.

Kirmayer, L.J., (1992), The body's insistence on meaning: metaphor as presentation and representation in illness experience, *Medical Anthropology Quarterly*, 6: 323–346.

Kristeva, J., (1982), *Powers of Horror: an essay on abjection*, New York: Columbia University Press.

Lakoff, G. and Johnson, M., (1999), *Philosophy in the Flesh: the embodied mind and its challenge to western thought*, New York: Basic Books.

Latimer, J., (2000), *The Conduct of Care: understanding nursing practice*, Oxford: Blackwell Science.

Madjar, I., (1997), The body in health and illness. In J. Lawler (ed.), *The Body in Nursing: a collection of views*, Melbourne: Churchill Livingstone.

Menzies, V., (2000), Depression and burn wounds, *Archives of Psychiatric Nursing*, XIV(4): 199–206.

Merleau-Ponty, M., (1968), *The Visible and the Invisible*, Evanston, ILL: Northwestern University Press.

Nagy, S., (1998), A comparison of the effects of patients' pain on nurses working in burns and neonatal intensive care units, *Journal of Advanced Nursing*, 27: 335–340.

Parse, R.R., (1995), *Illuminations: the human becoming theory in practice and research*, New York: National League for Nursing.

Patterson, D.R. and Jensen, M.P., (2003), Hypnosis and clinical pain, *Psychological Bulletin*, 129(4): 495–521.

Podolsky, D.M., (1987), *Skin as the Human Fabric*, Washington DC: US New Books.

Rothfield, P., (2005), Attending to difference: phenomenology and bioethics. In M. Shildrick and R. Mykitiuk (eds), *Ethics of the Body: postconventional challenges*, Cambridge (MAS): MIT Press.

Rudge, T., (1997), Nursing Wounds: a discourse analysis of interactions between nurses and patients during wound care in a burns unit, Unpublished PhD Thesis, LaTrobe University, Bundoora VIC.

Rudge, T., (1998), Skin as cover: the discursive effects of 'covering' metaphors on wound care practices, *Nursing Inquiry*, 5(4): 228–237.

Rudge, T., (1999), Situating wound management: technoscience, dressings and 'other' skins, *Nursing Inquiry*, 6: 167–177.

Rudge, T., (2003), Words are powerful tools: discourse analytic explanations of nursing practice In J. Latimer (ed.), *Advanced Qualitative Research for Nursing*, Oxford: Blackwell Publishing.

Scarry, E., (1985), *The Body in Pain: the making and the unmaking of the world*, New York: Oxford University Press.

Shildrick, M., (2002), *Embodying the Monster: encounters with the vulnerable self*, London: Sage.

Shildrick, M., (2005), Beyond the body of bioethics: challenging the conventions. In M. Shildrick and R. Mykitiuk (eds), *Ethics of the Body: postconventional challenges*, Cambridge (MAS): MIT Press.

Tulloch, J., (2006), *One Day in July: experiencing 7/7*, London: Little Brown.

Watson, J., (1988), *Nursing: human science and human care. A theory of nursing practice*, New York: National League for Nursing.

Weichman, S.A. and Patterson, D.R., (2004), Psychosocial aspects of burn injuries. *BMJ*, 329: 391–393 online http://www.bmj.com. [accessed 22 August 2007]

Williams, R., Doctor, J., Patterson, D. and Gibran, N., (2003), Health outcomes for burn survivors, *Rehabilitation Psychology*, 48(3): 189–194.

Yu, B-H. and Dimsdale, J.E., (1999), Posttraumatic Stress Disorder in patients with burn injuries, *Journal of Burn Care and Rehabilitation*, 20(5): 426–433.

Embodying loss and the puzzle of existence

Floris Tomasini

Introduction

This chapter examines the puzzle of bodily existence through the experience of loss in two, quite different, case studies. Whilst treating both case studies separately, the running theme of this chapter connects the two cases together by positing the idea that embodied loss is a form of ambivalent knowing, generating seemingly contradictory ideas and feelings about knowing and (un)knowing a body.

This ambivalent bodily knowing first of all manifests in our feelings; in our sensuous and embodied experience of loss. For example, amputees experience an uncanny knowing, where the felt presence of phantom limb experience contradicts the seen absence of the amputated limb. This felt ambivalence is a form of existential absence (a felt presence in a seen absence). Existential absence[1] (Sokolowski, 2000: 36–37) is also a phenomenon experienced by those grieving the death of a loved and is significantly 'complicated' if a body is harmed post-mortem.

Ambivalence of bodily knowing is also a feature of reason and explanation. In terms of saying what embodied knowing is (as opposed to simply describing what it is like), it may be argued that it is akin to a form of implicate ordering, where the mind *and* body, subject *and* object, individual *and* social, socially determined *and* individually free are not mutually exclusive concepts; each dyad implicating and involving the other.

The ambivalence of bodily knowing – knowing in terms of feelings *and* reasons – is explored at some length through two extended case studies. The first case study examines embodied loss in the context of rehabilitation clinic for amputees who are affected by the puzzling phenomenon of phantom limb experience (Tomasini, 2005a). The second case study examines embodied loss in the context of parental grief: losing a child whose dead body is perceived (by parents) to be harmed post-mortem through removal and retention of organs without consent. Whereas the first case study involves a phenomenological fieldwork in rehabilitation clinic, the second case study involves some analysis of parental oral evidence presented to Alder Hey Children's Public Inquiry[2] (Redfern, 2001).

The chapter is divided into three sections. The first section examines the puzzling phenomenon of having a felt absence where a limb used to exist before amputation (phantom limb). Knowing the phantom is *puzzling* in at least three senses. First knowing what the phantom is like is *puzzling* in terms of feeling; the ambiguous feeling of having phantom limb when the actual limb has been amputated. To be more precise it is knowingly uncanny from the perspective of an amputee, because it feels 'quasi-real'. Second, knowing what the phantom limb is, is *puzzling* in terms of time, since it is both psychically invested in the past (what the limb was like before) and the present (that there is still a 'quasi- present feeling of having a limb even though the diseased/traumatized limb has been amputated). Third, knowing the phantom is *puzzling* to reason and explanation: whilst it can be explained from a scientific third person perspective, this is not sufficient to understand what it is like from a first person perspective. In other words while mediational epistemologies may be *necessary to explain* what the phantom is, it is *insufficient* to account for phantom limb *experience* from the amputees' subjective experience of what the phantom is like. This is only possible through an embodied epistemology – partially accessible through the phenomenology of embodied loss (what it is like to lose a limb). Moreover, understanding the amputee experience and phantom limb cannot be reduced to a single disciplinary explanation. It is not reducible to biology, or psychology, philosophy or sociology, because it implicates all of these disciplinary perspectives in the context of the rehabilitation clinic.

The second section examines the puzzling phenomenon of post-mortem identity and harm. Knowing that the dead are subject to harm is deeply *puzzling*. Whilst it is not possible to do any intrinsic harm to the dead, harm can also be embodied in our relationship to dead loved ones. It is in this sense that post-mortem harm becomes intelligible. That is, it is possible to harm loved ones' expectations and beliefs of how their dead should be treated. This is reinforced through a phenomenological analysis where missing and losing someone (in death) can be understood as an existential absence, where death of a loved one for grieving survivors is not identical to non-existence. Grieving, it will be shown, can be 'complicated' if organs and organs systems are removed improperly without parental permission: the dead having a residual subjectivity for the living which can be harmed post-mortem. Post-mortem harm does not necessarily follow: if parental permission for organ removal is properly obtained from parents and relatives of the recently deceased, and put to some 'good' use in saving another life (through organ transplantation). In this sense, the normative evaluation as to what harm is, is as much socially constituted as phenomenologically mediated.

The third and final section is a conclusion that draws on some parallels between the two case studies through the cross-cutting theme of embodied loss and existential absence.

Understanding the experiences of amputees with a phantom limb

The first case study attends to two puzzling questions:

○ 'What is phantom limb experience *like*?'
○ 'How can phantom limb be explained?'

Phantom limb experience: a phenomenological and clinical study

To understand how phantom limb experience is evaluated within a socially specific setting, it is necessary to broaden the scope of what embodied experience is like for the amputee within the context of a rehabilitation clinic. What follows are a number of extracts from non-structured interviews and observations in the clinic, that have arisen out of a pilot phenomenological study (Tomasini, 2005a), that is now the subject of a larger ongoing research project funded by the AHRC (Thornton and Tomasini, 2008).

The felt presence of the phantom is highly ambiguous because it does not completely undermine the perceptual awareness of its absence, in that it feels 'shell like' and 'empty', often different in 'shape and position' to the limb as it had existed before its destruction. By contrast an amputee's healthy limb(s) exerts a certain 'weight' or 'gravity' and is not distorted in shape and/or position (Grosz, 1994: 41; Tomasini, 2005b: 1–15).

The embodied experience of the phantom limb is ambivalent and ambiguous. Most obviously, the amputee's experience of the phantom has two contradictory elements: its *felt* presence – the 'living' limb – and its *seen* absence – the organic limb's destruction (Grosz, 1994: 72). For example,

> I *know* [feel] I've got a foot I can stand on . . . even though me mind [reason] tells me I don't have a foot to stand on, I can walk [with the prosthesis] *Amputee 4* (Tomasini, 2005a: 23 – my brackets and emphasis)

Amputee 4 was making two related claims; the first involved the more straightforward claim that she trusted what she *felt* over and above what her eyes and reason – mind – told her. She was an experienced amputee and had become mindful of the fact that feeling her phantom inside the prosthesis could be practically beneficial in terms of using the prosthesis. This can be explained in neuro-physiological terms. Whilst proprioception (the bio-informational feedback mechanism that brings the body to awareness) can be deceptive when it feeds back a sensation of a limb that isn't actually there *without* a prosthesis, it *can* be a useful feedback mechanism with a prosthesis, because it does (with some amputees) help fill the prosthesis, thus locating where the prosthesis is in the activity of stepping, walking or balancing.

The felt presence of the phantom *partially* exists as a *Doppelgänger* ('double walker' from the German) of how the diseased or traumatized limb was before amputation: for example, one amputee described 'still feeling the screws in his phantom leg', mimicking the location and feeling of how the screws felt in his plated leg as it was before amputation (Tomasini, 2005a: 14). This presence in absence is psychically invested, not only in respect to what the limb felt like before amputation, but also in terms of how the amputee deals with it psychologically – the phantom acting as an uncomfortable reminder of the trauma experienced through disease, or accidental injury and loss. Whilst the phantom is partially psychically invested in the past its *active* presence in the here and now makes it *more* than a mere memory. It exists neither wholly in the past nor in the present. It can be said to be psychically invested in the past, both through how the limb felt before amputation and in an amputee's unresolved trauma around the particular circumstances of its loss. Phantom limb experience is also invested in the present, because it often acts like any other healthy limb in that it moves in a purposive way in response to the immediate demands of the environment. Like an actual leg/arm, the limb moves to step (foot) or lean (arm) on a surface. Unlike an actual leg, it often leads to accidents as the phantom steps or leans into thin air. For example:

> . . . I had an argument with my girlfriend and I just totally forgot that I didn't have a leg and just expected it to be there, but it wasn't there. I just went and fell, quite badly actually. That is how *real* it feels. *Amputee 5* (Tomasini, 2005a: 16).

Like the rest of the body, the phantom exhibits what Merleau-Ponty (1962) calls 'corporeal intentionality' – a mindedness that is embodied and constituted by its immediate and particular social environment. Of course, this proves to be a problem for recent amputees, who are not yet alert to the fact that they may be deceived by the senses of proprioception. In other words proprioception can be described as information about our bodily awareness that leads to bodily action eg information about pressure, temperature, friction and movement from receptors on the skin beneath the surface of the leg (see Bermudez *et al.*, 1998). In an objective sense this information is false and gives amputees a disordered sense of having a limb that extends beyond the stump. Whilst the *feeling* of the phantom is *real enough*, the phantom is *in the brain* – the homunculus (see Ramachandran and Blakeslee, 1999, for example). From this point of view the brain disorders where the amputee feels the phantom to be.

From a subjective point of view, what the phantom *is* objectively does not correlate what it feels *like*.

Phenomenologically the absence of the actual limb brings into stark relief the uncanny presence of the *Doppelgänger*. The un-canny feeling is deeply ambivalent and can be perceived as a taken for granted 'impairment effect' – a limitation on the physical activity of having an impairment (Thomas, 2007: 135–37).[3] Impairment effects have neutral, negative and positive valences for both the physical and the psycho-emotional aspects of the rehabilitation process. Clinicians have a neutral and/or relatively disinterested perspective on the value of the phantom in rehabilitation, partly as a strategy to assess amputee rehabilitation needs impartially and partly as a desire to avoid appearing somewhat helpless in dealing with the phenomenon that is difficult to treat (Tomasini, 2007a). By contrast, many amputees see the phantom negatively, as a hindrance to rehabilitation. This is especially true of young fit men who are keen to accept the reality of the stump, as the dexterity of it in relation to operating the prosthesis is critical in restoring the ability to walk, balance and run. In this way it is common for many amputees to avow the reality of stump over and above the phantom. For example:

> it is something that is *not there* . . . I don't know I just don't want it. You see *what is gone is gone.* Perhaps if the phantom were *useful* in some way it would be different. *Amputee 17* (Tomasini, 2005a: 15)

For many young and fit amputees without any significant complicating psychological trauma, impairment effects are interpreted as practical limitations on their physical activities, many having the expectation that their mastery of advanced prosthetic technologies is tantamount to successful rehabilitation (Tomasini, 2005b: 1–15).

The impairment effect of being an amputee with a phantom limb, whilst predominantly having a neutral or negative valence, is sometimes interpreted positively. Such amputees are usually experienced 'old timers' who have been coming to the rehabilitation clinic for a long time and have become *mindful* of the phantom in the prosthesis and how it maybe of benefit, for example, in terms of balance:

> Like I was climbing a ladder the other day . . . when I got to the top where the platform was I became more aware of where both legs were, because I could feel, if you like *inside* (the prosthesis) . . . It helped me find my balance. *Amputee 2* (Tomasini, 2005a: 23 – my emphasis)

The most common impairment effect of having phantom limb is that phantom limb sensation is often complicated by phantom limb pain. This can be severe and is very difficult to treat and for this reason is perceived by amputees and clinicians as being an unambiguous hindrance to rehabilitation and psycho-emotional well-being. Where phantom limb pain is not severe or significantly psychologically distressing it can act as an aid to rehabilitation, reminding the amputee not to be deceived by the phantom. For example:

> I see the phantom as positive . . . *The pain is warning me not to use it* [*arm*]. The phantom is saying there is nothing there . . . Quite often I think it is a good job that the pain is there or, I would have dropped that . . . *Amputee 4* (Tomasini, 2005a: 22 – my brackets and emphasis)

Some impairment effects invoke affective states that are purely psycho-emotional in nature. Again, these can be both negative and positive. In the case of the former, many amputees experience the phantom negatively because it represents a difficult reminder of a limb that they found difficult to come to terms with pre-amputation. For example:

> The trouble is that the phantom pain I had wasn't of a good leg it was of a bad leg . . . I woke up with this leg that was cold and I can't remember the leg as it was before the accident and so . . . I have *always had* a damaged leg [the paralysed leg that

the amputee had for one year before amputation] and I *still have* a damaged leg. [the phantom that mimics the leg as it was before amputation] *Amputee 7* (Tomasini, 2005a: 18 – my brackets and emphasis)

Conversely, some amputees see the phantom as a psycho-emotional boon, because it gives them a sense of bodily integrity, which can be comforting. For example:

the phantom is a way of feeling positive about yourself. There is a sense of *wholeness. Amputee 3* (Tomasini, 2005a: 26)

And:

The phantom is positive . . . Just for a moment I feel I've still got my leg . . . it just gives me a bit of *comfort. Amputee 15* (Tomasini, 2005a: 26 – my emphasis)

Importantly these amputees were not disturbed by the psychological impact of loss. They tended to be much older patients who had lost their limb(s) through disease rather than trauma, the phantom reminding them of better days when they were whole.

Discussion

'Almost everyone who has had a limb amputated will experience a phantom limb – the vivid impression that a limb is not only present, but in some cases, painful' (Ramachandran and Blakeslee, 1999: 45–46). In the case of phantom limb, the diseased or traumatised limb that the has to be surgically removed continues to induce sensation and/or pain in the location that the organic limb used to occupy.

The ambivalence of the phantom is a feature of both how the amputee experiences the phantom and how experts explain or account for the phenomenon.

In terms of the *experience* of embodied loss, it is an uncanny and ambivalent sensation: it is real (felt) *and* not real (not seen); invested in the past *and* an active surrogate limb in the present; experienced as a negative *and* a positive impairment effect.

In terms of explanation it has ontological and epistemological implications for how to theorize the body. In traditional psychological and physiological terms, the phantom experience is treated exclusively as a recollection (hence the phrase 'phantom' limb): a past experience simply reactivated in the present. However, to reiterate the phantom experience is not wholly invested in the memorial past, as it still responds, like the rest of the embodied subject, to social situations that arise in the here and now. There is the tenacity of the phantom to remain present and active, resisting a libidinal desire to mimic the limb as it once was before amputation.

The embodied experience of the phantom has significant ontological and epistemological implications. That is, in objective neuro-physiological terms the phantom can be said to be *in the brain*, activating neural pathways to give the subject the ambivalent sensation of the phantom (Ramachandran and Blakeslee, 1999; Gallagher, 2005). This has an effect on proprioception (see Bermudez *et al.*, 1998), where the body's feedback mechanism for becoming aware of itself becomes disordered, mis-locating the presence of a limb or body part where there is in fact none.

The problem with neuro-physiological third personal accounts is that while they are *necessary* to explain phantom limb they are not *sufficient* to understand the experience of it from a first-person point of view. This is because neuro-physiological accounts are mediational epistemologies of the sort that understand the outer world *solely* through explanations of inner processes. Unfortunately this leads to a number of epistemological lacunae. Most notably, it doesn't account for what embodied loss is like from an amputee perspective. Nor does it grasp the holistic inter-relationship of how we are embodied in an already meaningful and social environment.

Another way of theorizing the body is through the notion of an embodied epistemology, where the mental life of human beings is not a separate substance 'attached' to the body but rather an 'emergent structure' constituted by the organism (taken as whole) in interaction with its environment (see Merleau-Ponty, 1962). Mind or agency does not reside in the head but in the 'body-subject' in interaction with its environment. In doing so, body-subject acts as a third term that overcomes a number of classic dualities and dichotomies namely: mind/body, subject/object, determined/free and individual/social. The body subject is a more technical term for how we are embodied and deeply implicated in our environments.

Cartesian mind/body dualism is debunked by phantom limb. That is, if the mind and body were separate substances that mysteriously interact, then phantom limb would not be possible. Phantom limb also problematizes subject/object dualism. In other words, phantom limb, like the rest of 'body-subject,' is something real enough to be felt: it is primarily minded as a site of experience, *the subject* of experiences. It is also real enough to respond to its environment without thinking about it. In this way it is not like deliberately moving an object – the phantom as part of the body-subject has a corporeal intentionality that is pre-reflective and is part of what Merleau-Ponty calls the 'habit-body', which sediments skills appropriate to its social environment.[4]

If phantom limb problematizes mind/body and subject/object dualisms, it also resists hard biological determined/free will dualism. That is, as we have seen the impairment effect of phantom limb can have a positive as well as a negative valence in the rehabilitation process for amputees. Impairment effects have both physical and psycho-emotional dimensions, hindering and aiding what are perceived to be rehabilitation norms.

The phenomenological account implicates a final dualism that is underdeveloped in the empirical data but nevertheless warrants some speculative remarks. Another way of thinking about phantom limb experience in a broader social context is through theorizing the body from the 'outside-in', from assumptions, expectations and attitudes which clinicians have about amputees and how certain 'bodily styles' (Merleau-Ponty, 1962) either conform to rehabilitation norms or are in some way deviant from them. Bodily styles in rehabilitation are susceptible to 'body-power' (Foucault, 1979, 1980), where rehabilitation norms, assumptions and expectations pre-consciously effect and affect how the body is disciplined and monitored within the materialities of everyday rehabilitation practice. Moreover, amputees who self-discipline, in accordance with the predominant view of how good practice in rehabilitation is framed, can introject these clinical norms.

Having looked at the puzzle of embodied loss in respect to the loss of a limb and consequent phantom limb experience, I now turn to the equally puzzling experience of embodied loss through the death of a significant other.

Understanding post-mortem harm from the experience of grieving parents

The second case study addresses the puzzling question:

○ 'Is it possible to harm the dead?'

This question can be interpreted in two ways:

○ From the perspective of death as an intrinsic or Oxford Change (the physical death of a person)
○ From the perspective of death as a relational or Cambridge Change (the consequences of physical death on others)

Understanding death as two different kinds of change

Before we can understand whether or not the dead can be harmed, we need to be clear how to interpret death.

Death is most commonly perceived as a real or Oxford Change; an irreversible change in the *intrinsic* property of the body-subject from a vital living person infused with consciousness to a decaying corpse devoid of all conscious vitality. There are other changes that matter, however, as a *consequence* of real changes, that have an actual impact on survivors and their perceptions. These changes have been called Cambridge Changes (as opposed to Oxford or real changes) and can be illustrated by the changes that living relatives undergo as a consequence of experiencing the death of a loved one. Cambridge changes are not like Oxford or real changes in the intrinsic property of things; they do, however, happen as a relational consequence of a real change (Scarre, 2007). For example, if Harold and Maud are married and Harold dies, Harold undergoes a real change – he ceases to be a living man – while Maud undergoes a Cambridge change from being a wife to being a widow. Whilst this relational or Cambridge change is purely a formal change in the status of a relationship to the deceased, it does not preclude *further* Cambridge changes. That is, Maud is not only a widow, she is also likely to be a *grieving* widow as a consequence of the death of her beloved Harold. Death as a Cambridge change is a form of *embodied loss* that implicates a significant other into *what it is like* to grieve and experience the loss of a partner. Death as a Cambridge change also implicates Maud into having certain *beliefs* and *expectations* about how her beloved Harold should be treated now that he is dead. The beliefs and expectations that survivors have about how the dead should be treated may or may not be harmed.

Is it possible to harm the dead? Understanding death as intrinsic or Oxford Change

Epicurus is one of the first western philosophers to think of harm in relation to the dead. His question is: 'Is my death a form of harm to me?' He reminds us that:

> For all good and evil consist in sensation, but death is the deprivation of sensa-
> tion . . . So death, the most terrifying of ills, is nothing to us, since so long as we exist,
> death is not with us: but when death comes, then we do not exist. It does not then
> concern either the living or the dead, since for the former it is not, and the latter are
> no more. (Epicurus, 1926)

The *more* fundamental argument in Epicurus concerns the existence of a subject: all harm and/or benefit, in Epicurus' argument, requires an existent subject. So, discounting all speculative supernatural explanations on the continuing existence of the soul after death, there is no person that suffers the evil of death for Epicurus because the living are not *yet* dead and therefore *still exist*; and the dead cannot suffer because they *no longer exist*. So, death can never be bad for anyone. The force of the Epicurean argument lies in what Fred Feldman has called the 'Existence Condition' that nothing either good nor bad can happen to a subject *s* at time *t* unless *s* exists at *t* (Feldman, 1991).

One way of thinking about harming the dead is if one appeals to the post-humous interests[5] that survive death. One critically cogent response to this view has been delivered by Partridge (1981) who argues, quite rightly, that there is no person to affect and that events occurring after a person's death appear to occur too late either to harm or to benefit the person. As Partridge puts it:

> After death, no events can alter a moment of a person's life. Nothing remains to be
> affected . . . [W]e cannot alter the completed lives of the dead. (Partridge, 1981:
> 248–9)

While Partridge is right to say that one cannot alter a dead person's life experiences, his argument rests on a common sense view that one cannot harm a person *post-mortem* because a person's well-being cannot be affected by actions or events that occur after their death. However, this argument assumes a view of well-being and personhood of a particular kind – one that invokes the Oxford or intrinsic notion of death. That is, it rests on a mental states conception of well-being and since dead 'persons' have no mental states they cannot be harmed.

However, there is an alternative conception of personhood and well-being, where harm in relation to the dead maybe an issue. According to the philosopher George Pitcher (1985) there is a significant difference between describing a dead friend as she was at some stage of her life – what Pitcher refers to as the *ante*-mortem person – and describing that same friend as she is now in death, a *post*-mortem corpse – mouldering, perhaps, in a grave. It is Pitcher's contention that although both ante-mortem and post-mortem persons can be described after their death, only *ante*-mortem persons can be wronged and/or harmed. The reason it is possible to harm the *ante*-mortem person is because such a conception of personhood invokes a different sense of well-being altogether ie one that does not *restrict* wellbeing to either *having or not having* mental states at any one particular point in time. It is because one can understand well-being as anticipated desires and/or preferences that one can understand that the *ante*-mortem person has been harmed by events after his death.

Despite how logically compelling such analytical perspectives are, they are limiting because:

○ They *tend* to presuppose a particular view of death. For example by invoking the idea of ante-mortem harm, the existence condition on which intrinsic harm relies is upheld.

○ They un-necessarily restrict how harm to the dead is experienced in socially specific cases. For example, in the case of Alder Hey and Bristol Public Inquiries – that looked into the improper removal and retention of children's organs post-mortem – the bereaved parents of these children were clearly upset and distressed at what they understood as post-mortem harm.

Is it possible to harm the dead? revisited. Death as a relational or Cambridge Change – towards an understanding of the Alder Hey Inquiry and the idea of post-mortem harm

From a straightforward analytic perspective, death is identical with non-existence, since a non-existent person cannot be harmed, harm is unintelligible. This view involves an intrinsic notion of harming the dead and not a relational one. The relational view of harm – death as a Cambridge as opposed to an Oxford change – can be understood through the phenomenology of missing and grieving, where missing and grieving some one is an embodied perspective that involves the emotional entanglement of self with other. This is illustrated by the existential absence of missing someone, which can be extended to grief and 'complicated' grief (in the case of the removal of children's organs post-mortem, without properly informing their parents at Alder Hey).

Instead of thinking of the ante-mortem and post-mortem person in dichotomous terms, *either* in terms of having an existence and an identity (a living person) *or* in terms of not having an existence and identity (a dead body), it is also possible to appreciate the phenomenological experience of embodied loss from the perspective of grieving for a loved one. In this case personal identity is not identical to non-existence. To understand this I turn to Sartre and the phenomenology of loss and how this may manifest as an existential absence. I go on to extend this notion to the phenomenology of grief and post-mortem harm.

Sartre (2006: 34–35) provides a good example of what he means by existential absence, by describing the experience of his friend's absence in the café where they had prearranged to meet: 'when I enter this café to search for Pierre, there is formed a synthetic organisation of all objects in the café, on the ground of which Pierre is given as about to appear.' The significance of the café obtrudes – for example, the familiar table that two friends sit at together, the particular liquors and beers they drink all come to the forefront of consciousness in Pierre's absence. In Sartre's own words the café itself is 'a fullness of being', throwing the character of the place into stark relief. It is only so, however, with respect to one's *expectations and anticipation* of finding someone there with whom one is familiar; in Sartre's case, Pierre.

The distinction between existential and formal absence is significant for Sartre, because it emphasizes that non-existence does not simply arise through judgments made by consciousness *after* encountering the world, but that absence (Sartre's reformulation of non-existence or non-being) belongs to the very nature of the world as it is *for* consciousness. So, Pierre's absence is not merely a thought; his absence is an actual event at the café that characterizes the café as the place from which Pierre is absent. However, Pierre not being there, as Sartre may say, is my responsibility because it arises from defeated expectation: 'my expectation has caused the absence of Pierre to *happen* as a real event concerning this café.' Arguably, if one was nonplussed about whether he arrived or not, he might not be a significant object for consciousness. It is our *attachments* in our relationships to others that raise the spectre of dashed hopes and thwarted expectations, on which the possibility of existential absence depends. This can be contrasted to all sorts of others in a café whose presence is as irrelevant to me as the absence of a large numbers of people to whom I am indifferent. In other words, Sartre is making a distinction between formal and existential absences. The former is a logical fact, whilst the latter is an issue for a particular consciousness.

This phenomenological analysis of loss can be extended to more profound experiences of loss; for example, the death of a loved one can be experienced as existential absence in grief. This is evidenced by what people describe the earlier stages of the grieving process to be like; for example, the grieving often talk about their expectations of loved ones being there in the familiar everyday pattern of lives once shared. This does not mean that they do not logically understand that a loved one is, in *fact*, dead. While this fact *can* be denied immediately after death, it is frequently replaced by the experience of being *caught off guard for a moment, expecting* to see a loved one at home, say in their favourite chair, only for that expectation to be defeated by the realization that they are actually dead.

If expectations can be defeated in the experience of grief, it seems possible to suggest that they could also be 'harmed.' Moving back to the Alder Hey case, parents' expectations of how their dead loved ones 'should' have been treated (and were not) constitutes a form of harm to parent experiences.

For example, the fact that post-mortem identity is still an issue for the grieving is illustrated by the mother of Sam (18 months):

> The impression given by Alder Hey was that an individual's *identity* ends at post-mortem if not death. (Redfern, 2001: 412)

Moreover, one parent even talked about *protecting* the dead (in the present tense) underscoring the residual subjectivity (presence in absence) that the recently dead can have for a grieving parent. Not being able to have expressed this desire complicated her grief, causing her to feel guilt.

For example, from the mother of Alexandra (stillborn), oral testimony:

> The third and most compelling reason for her emotion as a parent is that she would have done anything to protect her child. That was what she was there to do even more so in death because it was the only thing she could do for her child at that stage . . . There was only one thing she could do and that was to *protect* her in death and she did not do it and she has to live with that. (Redfern, 2001: 408)

Post-mortem harm can also be understood in terms of bodily integrity. Many parents went through the distress of having to endure multiple funerals; body parts often being returned piecemeal for second and, even third burials.

For example, from the Alder Hey oral testimony of the parents of Philip (3months):

> They discovered that Philip's organs had been retained in December 1999. Initially, they were not told of the full extent of the retention, from brain to reproductive organs, and were shocked. A second burial took place in January 2000. It had always been their desire to bury their child intact. (Redfern, 2001: 394)

Finally, it is important to understand that the *locus* of harm is the post-mortem body, affecting how parents remember the person when they were still living. For example, from the mother of Kenneth (5 weeks) oral testimony:

> . . . the memory of her child has been ruined by living under the illusion that he was buried intact when in fact he was missing his heart. She cannot even look at pictures of him now because she just sees him in a different way. (Redfern, 2001: 396)

It might be tempting to conclude that harm follows if organs are removed post-mortem from the recently dead. However, this would be a mistaken conclusion. What characterized Alder Hey and Bristol scandals was that organs and organ systems were removed without the consent of parents, either through inadequate consent procedures (presumed consent) or worse, by deception. Moreover, organs and organ systems were, more often than not, stored for months and years without being put to good medical use. Parents felt that their children's bodies had been disrespected: their sons and daughters had been stripped of their organs for no good reason. Phenomenologically speaking, parents' *expectations* about how their dead children should have been treated, were harmed significantly, 'complicating' the grieving process.

This can be contrasted with those who give consent to donate organs of a dead loved one, with the *expectation* that the organ(s) in question will help save another person's life. Whilst it is not easy to categorize generationally (age range 19–95), socially (various), or in terms of religious belief (various/none), the reasons that people do give are altruistic, and quite fiercely antagonistic to any suggestion of financial or other reward (see Richardson, 2006). The phenomenological context in this case is significantly different, expectations being positive rather than negative: organ donation with consent may have some real altruistic pay off.

Having examined embodied loss in relation to posthumous harm of the recently dead (see Tomasini, 2008), I now turn to an examination of some cross-cutting ideas that, I believe, connect the two case studies.

Conclusions: examining some cross-cutting ideas between case studies

To conclude, it is helpful to highlight the ideas that underpin this analysis and cross-cut between case studies:

- Embodied loss creates a puzzle for existence.

Losing a limb or a loved one creates a problem for what we mean by loss. In both the phantom limb case and the loss of a significant other, what remains in experience is not *either* something *or* nothing. What 'exists' in our experience of loss in both these cases is an uncanny palpable absence.

- Embodied loss can be understood as existential absence. Existential absence has normative implications for how we experience loss.

Palpable absences originate in our embodied and existential experiences of loss. This can be understood in relational terms, with regard to what we are aware of missing. In the case of a limb, there is a residual presence of a limb that was. Having a phantom limb is usually an issue for amputees, in that it has both a negative and positive valence in respect to rehabilitation. In the case of the loss of a loved one, presence is residually invested in an emotional attachment to the corpse. From this perspective embodied harm post-mortem is intelligible, since parts of the body like the heart, eyes, face and hands, for example, *represent relationships with others* that are symbolically inscribed, ie they are implied within body parts. So, if body parts are missing, such as the heart, then harm has been done, because body parts still represent the memory of personal relationships to body parts strongly identified with when the person was still alive. In this sense personal identity is at stake (see Ricoeur, 1992; Dickenson and Widdershoven, 2001).

- Embodied loss is ambivalent in terms of knowing and feeling.

Phantom limb experience and post-mortem harm are ambivalent concepts. To reiterate, how phantom limb is experienced depends on how amputees perceive the phantom as either a hindrance or an aid to rehabilitation. This depends on their attitude to it, their personal circumstances and expectations of rehabilitation in relation to their life circumstances, the extent of psycho-emotional trauma around the accident and lost limb as well the attitudes of clinical staff that help shape rehabilitation norms. This is also true of posthumous harm. Posthumous harm is not a given; harvesting the organs from the recently dead can be harmful or altruistic to parents of dead children whose organs have been removed post-mortem. Interestingly, it is how parental expectations are respected, handled, and managed that counts. The removal of organs without proper post-mortem consent procedures led to accusations of post-mortem harm at Alder Hey and Bristol, whilst the introduction of sensitive requests and fully informed consent at other institutions after the wake of these scandals has led to similar practices being viewed more altruistically.

Phantom limb experience and post-mortem harm are ambivalent, because mind/body, object/subject do not neatly separate in our experience of what it is to lose a part of ourselves or another. At a more fundamental theoretical level, then, an embodied epistemology underpins our experience of embodied loss and why we should care about it. Embodiment and our embodied relations with others *is* minded and a site for experiences of loss and grief that matter as a consequence of loss.

Notes

1 Existential absence is an absence that obtrudes through our experience of the human condition and plays a central role in the understanding of phenomenology. There are different kinds of existential absences in relation to the human condition. This chapter explores two kinds of existential absence in relation to embodied loss.
2 This is referred to throughout in the main body of the text as the Alder Hey or the Alder Hey Public Inquiry. Abbreviation as reference is (Redfern, 2001). The Alder Hey Children's Inquiry looked into the removal, retention and storage of organs post-mortem. Events at Alder Hey were by no means unique; a similar inquiry was conducted at Bristol Royal infirmary around the same time. Moreover, a census by Liam Donaldson the Chief Medical Officer in 2001, noted that the practice was widespread and had been going on for over 30 years.
3 Some of these phenomenological views on the disabled body dovetail with recent work in disability studies, especially the work of Carol Thomas (2007), who is a pioneer in the disability studies literature, moving the debate on from a narrow focus on political equality to issues that reassess the importance of the disabled body in relation to impairment effects and psycho-emotional aspects of disablism.
4 See also Bourdieu's concept of 'hexis' (Bourdieu, 1992; Crossley, 2001)
5 Posthumous interests are interests that may continue beyond the point of one's death, eg one's good name.

References

Bermudez, J.L., Marcel, A. and Eilan, N., (Eds) (1998), *The Body and The Self*, Cambridge, Massachusetts: The M.I.T Press.

Bourdieu, P., (1992), *The Logic of Practice*, Cambridge: Polity.

Crossley, (2001), *The Social Body: habit, identity and desire*, London: Sage.

Dickenson, D. and Widdershoven G., (2001), Ethical Issues in Limb Transplants, *Bioethics*, 15: 110–124.

Epicurus, (1926), *The Extant Fragments*, C. Bailey (ed.), Oxford: Clarendon Press.

Feldman, F., (1991), Some Puzzles About the Evil of Death, *Philosophical Review*, 100: 205–227.

Foucault, M., (1979), *Discipline and Punish*, Hammondsworth: Penguin.

Foucault, M., (1980), *Power/Knowledge*, Brighton: Harvester.

Gallagher, S., (2005), *How the Body Shapes the Mind*, Oxford: Clarendon Press.

Grosz, E., (1994), *Volatile Bodies: toward a corporeal feminism*, Bloomingtom: Indiana University Press.

Mauss, M., (1979), *Sociology and Psychology*, London: Routledge Kegan Paul.

Merleau-Ponty, M., (1962), *The Phenomenology of Perception* (trans. C. Smith), London: Routledge Kegan Paul.

Merleau-Ponty, M., (1965), *The Structure of Behaviour*, (trans C. Smith.), Metheun.

Partridge, E., (1981), Posthumous Interests and Posthumous Respect, *Ethics*, 91: 2.

Pitcher, G., (1985), The Misfortunes of the Dead, *American Philosophical Quarterly*, 21.

Ramachandran and Blakeslee, (1999), *Phantoms in the Brain*, London: Harper Collins, Fourth Estate.

Redfern Report, (2001), *The Royal Liverpool Children's Public Inquiry*, London Stationery Office.

Richardson, R., (2006), Human dissection and organ donation: a historical and social background, *Mortality*, 2006: 11: 2: 152–153.

Ricoeur, P., (1992), *Oneself as Another* (trans. K. Blamey), Chicago/London: University of Chicago Press.

Sartre, J-P., (2006), *Being and Nothingness* (trans. H. Barnes), London: Methuen.

Scarre, G., (2007), *Death*, Acumen.

Sokolowski, R., (2000), *Introduction to Phenomenology*, New York: Cambridge University Press.

Thomas, C., (2007), *Sociologies of Disability and Illness*, China: Palgrave Mcmillan.

Thornton, T. and Tomasini, F., (2008), AHRC Report, *The Epistemological puzzle of Phantom Limb Experience*, forthcoming.

Tomasini, F., (2005a), *The Phantom Limb Report: exploring the experiences of amputees with phantom limb*. Lancaster: Lancaster University.

Tomasini, F., (2005b), *Phantom Limb Research Diary*, (unpublished).

Tomasini, F., (2008), Is Post-mortem harm possible? Understanding death, harm and grief, *Bioethics*, Oxford: Blackwell Publishing.

Notes on Contributors

Olga Belova (PhD) is a Lecturer in Management at Essex Business School, University of Essex. Her publications are in visual imagery, narratives, phenomenology of body and language, and ethics. She has been awarded British Academy Grants and is a Visiting Professor at Copenhagen Business School, Denmark. Also, she was recently a guest editor of the special issue on polyphony for Organization Studies and can be contacted by email at obelov@essex.ac.uk.

Steve Brown is Professor of Social and Organizational Psychology at the University of Leicester, UK and Visiting Professor at the Universiteit voor Humanistiek, Utrecht, NL. His research interests are around the mediation of social remembering across diverse settings. These include commemoration of the 2005 London Bombings; personal, familial and institutional recollection of childhood traumas and challenges; self-archiving in virtual social networking. He is author of *The Social psychology of Experience: Studies in Remembering and Forgetting* (with David Middleton, 2005, Sage Publications) and *Psychology without Foundations* (with Paul Stenner, 2009, Sage Publications).

John Cromby is Senior Lecturer in Psychology in the Department of Human Sciences, Loughborough University. Previously, he has worked in mental health, learning disability and drug addiction settings. He is interested in the way that social influence and the body come together to produce experience, and is exploring this interest with respect to such topics as emotion, 'paranoia' and 'depression'.

Simone Dennis lectures in anthropology at the Australian National University, where she teaches courses on the anthropology of food and eating, human-animal relationships, and other specialist courses. Her interests are characterized by phenomeological intersections with anthropology, especially in the areas of food and eating, drugs and alcohol, and music; anthropology of human-animal relationships; anthropology of migration, memory, forgetting and remembering, and movement, especially among Persian women in Australia, and human relationships to place and environment. She is the author of two books: *Police Beat*, which deals with intersections of power and music in Aus-

Editorial organisation © 2009 The Editorial Board of the Sociological Review. Published by Blackwell Publishing Ltd, 9600 Garsington Road, Oxford OX4 2DQ, UK and 350 Main Street, Malden, MA 02148, USA

tralian domestic contexts, and *Christmas Island: An Anthropological Study*, which is the first ethnographic monograph produced of the Indian Ocean territory.

Miguel Domènech is Senior Lecturer in Social Psychology at the Autonoma University, Barcelona, where he coordinates a Group for Social Studies in Science and Technology. His research interests cohere broadly in the field of science and technology studies (STS) with a special focus on the interaction between technoscience and power relationships. Publications include: López, D. & Domènech M., (2008), 'On inscriptions and ex-inscriptions: the production of immediacy in a home telecare service' *Environment and Planning D: Society and Space* 26(4) 663–675; Vayreda, A. and Domènech, M., (2007), *Psicología e Internet*, Barcelona: UOC; Vitores A. and Domènech, M. (2003), From Inhabiting to Haunting. New Ways of Social Control. In M. Hård, A. Lösch & D. Verdicchio (eds.), *Transforming Spaces. The Topological Turn in Technology Studies.*

Monica Greco is a Senior Lecturer in the Department of Sociology at Goldsmiths, University of London. She is the author of *Illness as a Work of Thought: A Foucauldian Perspective on Psychosomatics* (Routledge 1998) and of several articles on different aspects of medical rationality. She is co-editor of *The Body: A Reader* (with Mariam Fraser, Routledge, 2005) and of *The Emotions: A Social Science Reader* (with Paul Stenner, Routledge, 2008).

Dave Harper is Reader in Clinical Psychology at the University of East London (UEL). Before he moved to UEL, Dave worked as a clinical psychologist in the National Health Service mental health services in the North West of the UK for nine years. His research interests are in critical psychology and social constructionist approaches in mental health, particularly in relation to psychosis. He is a member of the editorial collective of *Asylum: The Magazine for Democratic Psychiatry*, and he is on the Editorial Boards of *Subjectivity, the Annual Review of Critical Psychology* and the *Journal of Community & Applied Social Psychology.*

Katherine Johnson is Principal Lecturer in Psychology at the University of Brighton, UK. Her research interests include interdisciplinary approaches to theorizing self, identity and embodiment; gender, sexuality and Transgender Studies; critical and community psychology; qualitative research methods. She has recently published articles in *Men and Masculinities* and the *Journal of Lesbian Studies*, and she is currently working on a photographic research project with a group of Lesbian, Gay, Bisexual and Transgender (LGBT) mental health service users.

Bernd Kraeftner was trained as a medical doctor and worked as filmmaker and author. He is the founder of the transdisciplinary working group XPERIMENT!. His research interest centres around scientific ideas at the messy intersection of the sciences, health care, politics, publics and the arts. He was principal investigator of various research projects funded by the Austrian Ministry of Science; the Wellcome Foundation, UK; the ZKM, Karlsruhe etc. He co-curated the science exhibition 'the true/false.inc', Vienna 2006. He is a lecturer at the Digital Arts class at the University for Applied Arts in Vienna.

Judith Kroell studied sociology and social anthropology at the University of Vienna. Since 1998 she has been part of the group XPERIMENT! and works and navigates between different (research-) worlds and activities. A lecturer at the Institute for Social Studies of Science at the University of Vienna, she was co-Curator of the science exhibition 'the true/false.inc.', Vienna 2006, and is co-initiator and current coordinator of the association 'Researchers without borders'.

Joanna Latimer is Reader in Social Science at Cardiff University and Visiting Professor, University for Humanistics, Utrecht. She has published widely in medical and cultural sociology, particularly in relation to power and participation. Joanna is chair of the Ageing, Science and Older people Network and co-convenor of the Culture, Imagination & Practice Research Group at Cardiff, and is currently working on a number of research projects that investigate the relation between science, medicine, culture and conceptions of personhood, including a new book *The Gene, the Clinic & the Family: diagnosing dysmorphology, reviving medical dominance.* Joanna is associate editor of *Gender, Work and Organization*, and a member of the editorial board of *The Sociological Review.*

Hugo Letiche is Humanitas & Research Professor of 'Meaning in Organization' at the University for Humanistics Utrecht, The Netherlands, where he is Director of the part-time PhD programme. He is member of the RUOS ethics & organization research institute at Bristol Business School. He has lectured and/ or visited amongst others at Lancaster University, Keele University, University of California at Berkeley, Durham University, University of the West of England, Sterling University, NMSU, Essex University. Organizational values and the ethics of care are his current research interests. ZonMW (Research Institution on Healthcare financed by the Dutch Ministry of Health) has funded his recent research. His book *Making Healthcare Care* came out in September 2008 (Charlotte NC: IAP). He has published in *Organization, Organization Studies, Emergence/E:CO (Emergence, Complexity & Organization), JOCM (Journal of Organizational Change Management), BSR (Business Society Review), Culture & Organizations, Tamara Journal of Critical Postmodern Organizational Science, RSDG (Revue Sciences de Gestions), Critical Perspectives on International Business, Consumption Markets & Culture.*

Daniel López is a researcher and assistant teacher in the Department of Psychology at the Universitat Oberta de Catalunya. His research work is currently focused on the consequences of ICT innovations in care and medical settings (telecare) both from an organizational point of view and from a subjective and intersubjective dimension. Selected Publications: López, D. and Domènech, M. (2008), 'On inscriptions and ex-inscriptions: the production of immediacy in a home telecare service', *Environment and Planning D: Society and Space* 26(4) 663–675; López, D. (2006); 'La Teleasistencia Domiciliaria como extitución. Análisis de las formas espaciales del cuidado.' Published in F.J. Tirado i M. Domènech (ed.), *Lo Social y lo Virtual. Nuevas formas de control y transformación social* (pp. 60–78), EdiUOC: Barcelona; López, D. (2005). 'Aplicación de la teoría del actor-red al análisis espacial de un servicio de teleasistencia domiciliaria', in *Revista de Antropología Iberoamericana*, 44.

Rolland Munro is Managing Editor of *The Sociological Review* and Professor of Organisation Theory at Keele University. He has published widely on culture, power and identity and is internationally regarded for bringing new theoretical insight to the study of organization with his ethnographies of management practice. Writings on accountability, affect, bodies, cars, class, ethics, knowledge, landscape, language, money, polyphony, reason, time, wit, and zero, among other topics, have kept him at the cutting edge of interdisciplinary collaborations and have culminated in two forthcoming books, *The Demanding Relation,* which explores our entanglement with technology and *Dividing Cultures,* which illuminates the everyday divisions through which culture works us.

Fiona K. O'Neill recently gained her transdisciplinary PhD *Uncanny Belongings: Bioethics and the Technologies of Fashioning Flesh*, from Lancaster University. Her current research considers somatechnics (human-technology relations) with regard to bodied and embodied experiences and bioethical issues across standard and innovative medicine; specifically facial technologies including transplantation, the 'belongingness' of prostheses and bioengineered technologies and treatment-enhancement debates. She is a problem-based-learning tutor in the School of Health and Medicine, Lancaster University; Member of the North West Research Ethics Committee and a freelance researcher / facilitator, presently engaging young people in bioethical issues.

Paula Reavey is Senior Lecturer in Psychology at London South Bank University, UK. Her research interests are around embodiment, social remembering and feminist theory. Recent work includes co–edited volumes: *Memory Matters: Understanding contexts for recollecting child sex abuse* (with Janice Haaken, Routledge, 2009) and *New Feminist Stories of Child Sexual Abuse: Sexual Script and Dangerous Dialogues*, (with Sam Warner, Routledge, 2003), as well as a number of articles on child sexual abuse, sexuality and embodiment, using discourse analysis, visual methods and memory work. She is Associate Editor of *The Psychology of Women Section Review*.

Trudy Rudge is Professor of Nursing at the Faculty of Nursing and Midwifery University of Sydney. She practised clinically in areas of burns care, plastic surgery, and community mental health before joining the ranks of nursing academe after a research appointment. She teaches and researches in the areas of embodiment and the social analysis of nursing practices. Currently she is researching the organization of nursing work, body shopping and intersections between technology and nursing care.

Michael Schillmeier teaches Sociology, Science and Technology Studies (STS), Disability Studies and Empirical Philosophy at the Department of Sociology at Ludwig-Maximilians University, Germany. He received his PhD from Lancaster University, UK. He writes mainly on the material dynamics of societal ordering and change, cosmo-political events, on bodies/senses and dis/ability, on the societal relevance of objects and the heterogeneity of the social.

Floris Tomasini is a lecturer in Philosophy of Mental Health in the Institute for Philosophy, Diversity and Mental Health at the University of Central Lancashire and a Visiting Research Fellow at the ESRC's Genomics Network, Lancaster University (CESAGen). He is interested in Continental approaches to the philosophy of mind, body and mental health. He often uses phenomenological approaches to investigate the challenge of psycho-emotional difference, writing about it from an embodied perspective, particularly on amputation, memory loss, grief, death, suicide and other subjects of this kind. His ambition is to understand existential challenges to what it is to be a human being, particularly through perspectives that challenge the 'natural attitude' of the human condition.

Dr Megan Warin is a social anthropologist at Durham University whose teaching and research interests coalesce around themes of embodiment, food, memory and migration. Her research into anorexia examines concepts of commensuality and relatedness; and her work on obesity with social epidemiologists in Australia bring class and gender to the fore of obesity studies. Her collaborative work with Simone Dennis investigates the phenomenological aspects of food, memory and trauma amongst the Persian diaspora in the UK and Australia. She is also investigating medical migration between Spain and the UK, examining how competing discourses of health care use, provision, and entitlement, metaphorically refer to wider issues concerning the permeability (or impermeability) of state borders, the endurance of national identities, and resulting difficulties in the construction of a European identity and citizenship.

Paul White is Research Associate within the Department of Primary Care & Public Health in the School of Medicine, Cardiff University. He completed an ethnography of visibility, otherness and disposal (différance) within intensive care as part of a Ph.D. in Sociology at the School of Social Sciences, Cardiff University. He is currently completing an investigation of the impact of incentivized patient service evaluations on General Practitioners in South Wales.

Index

Aalten, A. 7
Abellán, A. *et al.* 183
abstract thought 31
actor – network theories (ANT) 7, 8–9,
  15, 141–2; of autonomy 182, 190–2; of
  dementia 144–8; of remembering 142–
  4; and the 'thinness of objects' 145–6
adaptation abilities 31
Adcock, R.J. *et al.* 237, 240
affect 7, 9, 92; and attention 96–7; body
  as register of 13; and exchange 95–6;
  group and embodiment concepts 17
affiliations and belongings 8
Affolter, F. and Bischofberger, W. 167
Akrich, M. and Pasveer, B. 191
Alder Hey children's hospital 18–19, 249,
  258–61
Allen, D. 241
amputee patients 19, 250, 251–6, 261–2
Andrews, K. *et al.* 171
'angst'; actor-networks 150–57; concepts
  explained 151
animals, adaptation to novel
  influences 31
Ankori, G. 51–2
anthropological studies 37–8, 103; and
  diplomacy 177–8
Anzieu, D. 234
Arcadia (Stoppard) 92
Architects of Air installation
  (Nottingham) 17
Armstrong, D. 182
'art of life', and the art of persistence
  30–31
art of persistence 30–31
Ashworth, P. 69–73

'assemblages' traditions (bodies and
  'world-building') 2, 7–8, 10, 59
assessment tools, nursing care 161–2,
  163, 166–9
Atkinson, P. 130
Atkinson, P. and Silverman, D. 65
attunements 15
Australian migrants, ethnography of
  Persian women's groups 101–5
autonomy 16–17; frameworks for
  study 182; phenomenological
  concerns 189–93; and telecare
  services 183–93

Bacchi, C. and Beasley, C. 243, 245
Bahá'i peoples 101–5, 106
Balazic 68
Barnes, L. and Rudge, T. 243
Bashshur, R. *et al.* 181
Bateson, G. 177
Beard, B. and Sampson, T. 225
Becker, G. *et al.* 104, 109
Beck, F.T. 51
Beeman, W. 101
Befindlichkeit (attunement), and
  angst 149–53
Behrangi, Samad 108–10
'being' 68; and guilt 155
'being present' 16
'being there' (Dasein) 64
'being-in-the-world'; actor-network
  interpretations 150–53; and
  remembering 142–4, 147–8
belief and certitude 217–18
Benson, D. and Hughes, J.A. 121, 127,
  132

271